NORTHERN STEAMBOATS

TIMISKAMING, NIPISSING & ABITIBI

NORTHERN STEAMBOATS

TIMISKAMING, NIPISSING & ABITIBI

RICHARD TATLEY

The BOSTON MILLS PRESS

CANADIAN CATALOGUING IN PUBLICATION DATA

Tatley, Richard
Northern steamboats : Timiskaming, Nipissing and Abitibi

Includes bibliographical references and index.
ISBN 1-55046-165-6
1. Steamboats - Ontario, Northern - History.   2. Steam-navigation -
Ontario, Northern - History.   3. Inland water transportation - Ontario,
Northern - History.   I. Title.

VM627.O5T37 1996   386'.22436'0971314   C96-930705-5

First published in 1996 by
The Boston Mills Press
132 Main Street
Erin, Ontario, Canada
N0B 1T0
Tel 519 833-2407
Fax 519 833-2195

An affiliate of
Stoddart Publishing Company Ltd.
34 Lesmill Road
North York, Ontario, Canada
M3B 2T6

Design by Mary Firth
Printed in Canada

The publisher gratefully acknowledges the support of the Canada Council and
Ontario Arts Council in the development of writing and publishing in Canada.

PHOTO, TITLE PAGE: *Steamers at Haileybury Wharf, 1909. To the left is the* Blanche, *and behind her the* City of
Haileybury. *To the right is the* Silverland, *with the* Meteor *behind the wharf. The small steamer partly hidden by the*
Silverland *may be the mystery vessel* Mahigama *(see page 143).*   Courtesy Mr. Gilles Amesse, Ville-Marie

BOSTON MILLS PRESS books are available for bulk purchase for
sales promotions, premiums, fundraising, and seminars. For details, contact:
SPECIAL SALES DEPARTMENT, Stoddart Publishing Co. Limited, 34 Lesmill Road,
North York, Ontario, Canada M3B 2T6
Tel 416 445-3333   Fax 416 445-5967

CONTENTS

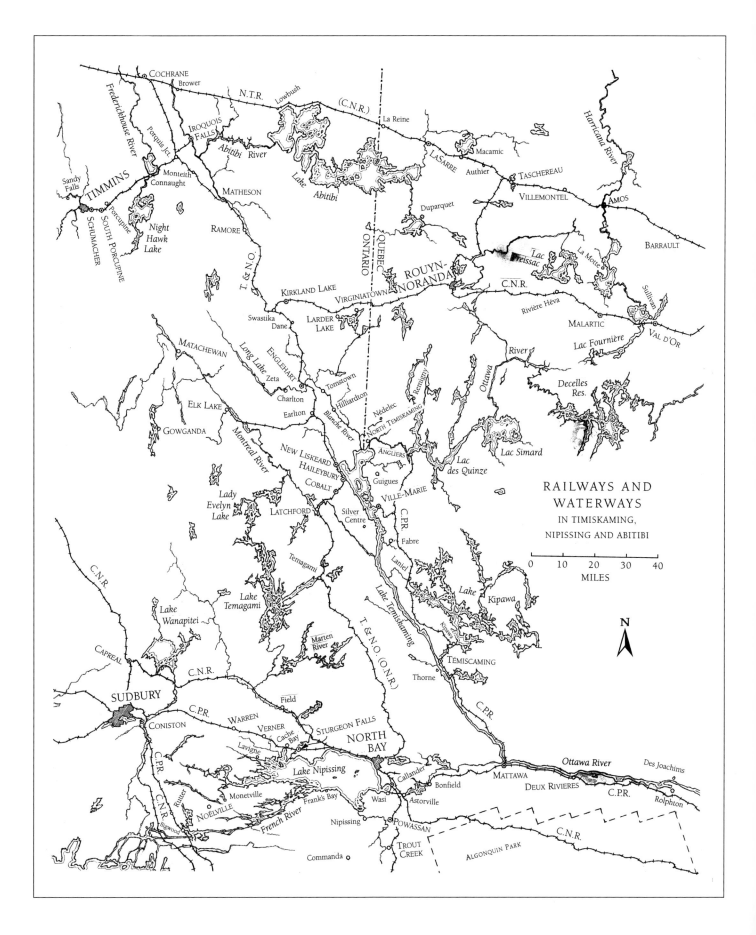

RAILWAYS AND
WATERWAYS
IN TIMISKAMING,
NIPISSING AND ABITIBI

0   10   20   30   40
MILES

N

INTRODUCTION

I n the rolling, hummocky forest ridges of Northern Ontario and Quebec there lies a region called Timiskaming on one side of the border, and Témiscamingue on the other. A vast, sprawling land it is, with pine, spruce and birch forests precariously subsisting on the thin soils overlying the granite ridges of the Canadian Shield, and spattered over with countless lakes and drained by wide rivers. Yet it is also a land of startling contrasts, for parts of it are level, open and fertile and boast farms as good as any in the south. Nothing surprises the modern motorist more than suddenly emerging from the vast forests of the Shield to find himself for the first time amid the fertile farms of the Wabi River valley. Surely, he thinks, he has lost his bearings and ended up back in the south!

The region takes its name from Lake Temiskaming, which forms part of the boundary between Ontario and Quebec. The lake itself is actually an enlargement of the Ottawa River, and extends about 90 miles from its source, the des Quinze River, to the Town of Témiscaming, where the Long Sault rapids begin. The name itself is derived from the Algonkian words "Temi-kami," which means "the place where the waters are deep and shallow." The description is apt. Lake Temiskaming lies in a long narrow fault line, which results in very deep waters in some places; yet it also has many shallow bays and expanses, especially around the north end. The lower end of the lake, which is more like a river, flows through typical Shield country, amid shorelines of hanging valleys sometimes forming immense cliffs some 400 feet high, rather like the Saguenay River. The upper end, above Opimica Narrows, lies amid softer rock, which has resulted in lower hills and some islands. Large rivers, including the Kipawa, Loutre and des Quinze Rivers in Quebec, and the Blanche, Wabi and Montreal Rivers in Ontario, all feed into Lake Temiskaming. Around the north end, the famous farms of the Clay Belts begin, forming the economic basis for the modern towns of Haileybury, New Liskeard, Notre-Dame-du-Nord and Ville-Marie.

The Clay Belts are an accidental by-product of geological prehistory. Around 8,000 years ago, as the ice sheets of the last glacial age receded, a vast meltwater lake, known as Lake Ojibway, formed across much of the region, and slowly grew larger as the ice continued to retreat. But for centuries there was no real exit. A glacial moraine lay across the upper Ottawa Valley, damming the lake. Finally, the waters of Lake Ojibway spilled over the "dam," sending vast torrents down the Ottawa Valley — but not before depositing thick layers of clay. The smaller Timiskaming Clay Belt forms a triangle at the north end of the lake; the larger Cochrane Clay Belt extends across the Abitibi region, west beyond Kapuskasing and east beyond Amos, Quebec. Both areas support hundreds of farms. Sawmills have become rather scarce, following the ruthless destruction of the original pineries during the past century, but the pulp and paper industry continues to flourish, notably at such centres as Iroquois Falls, Ontario, and Témiscaming, Quebec.

The region is also a major source of mineral wealth, and home to the immense gold mines of Timmins, the Porcupine country, Kirkland Lake and Rouyn-Noranda — to say nothing of the smaller but once-spectacular silver fields of Cobalt and Gowganda. And in some localities, where the scenery is wild and rugged enough to attract visitors without being too remote of access or too close to the mines and mills (as at Lake Temagami), the result has been a considerable tourist industry, luring hundreds of city-weary folk who want to hunt or fish or go boating, or simply sniff the pine-scented breezes and listen to the call of the loon from the verandah of a favourite summer cottage. All of these developments form themes in our story.

For this is a story about transportation history, and especially about one form of transportation: steamboating.

It is almost an axiom of history that steamboats have come and gone on all the naviga-ble waterways of Ontario where business beckoned. They have been used on the Great Lakes, the Ottawa River, the Rideau Waterway, the Kawartha Lakes, the Muskoka Lakes and else-where. But nowhere did they find greater variety of employment than in the North. In their unobtrusive way, steamboats served the lumber trade by towing logs and delivering provi-sions to the camps in scows. They served settlers by helping them reach their lands with their goods and chattels, and by taking hay and produce to the markets. They also added a little colour and relaxation to the hard, rough life of the pioneers by running excursion cruises. They assisted the railwaymen by bringing in timber, rails and supplies — and were often rewarded by being put out of business! They helped take prospectors and their gear out to the bush during the mining booms, and sometimes brought treasure back on their decks. They sustained the paper mills for decades by towing in millions of pulpwood logs. Occasionally they were used for commercial fishing. They also enabled tourists to reach their lodges and hunt camps, and cottagers to reach their summer homes on remote islands, at a time when the only alternative was a canoe. They provided lifelines to many remote, isolated commu-nities, some of which were once completely dependent on them. They pushed their way through many northern lakes and rivers, bucking logs, shoals, rocks, deadheads, ice and storms, often decades ahead of the railways and sometimes even before there were any roads. In most parts of Ontario, the tentacles of travel uncoiled in the following order: first canoes, then sailboats, then roads, then steamboats, then railways, then automobiles and finally air-craft. In Timiskaming the order was different: first canoes, then steamboats, *then* railways and (much later) roads.

Both Lake Temiskaming and Lake Nipissing have served as extensions of the Ottawa River, which — along with the St. Lawrence — has always been unparallelled as a natural highway leading deep into the heart of the continent. At the village of Mattawa, however, the route forks. Travellers, native or European, have always had the option of heading farther west, up the Mattawa River and across to Lake Nipissing (which, in turn, drains westward into Georgian Bay by way of the French River), or continuing farther north up the Ottawa River to Lake Temiskaming, beyond which lies the Arctic watershed and the many long rivers flow-ing into James Bay. As a result, it is possible to view Lake Temiskaming as a continuation of the Ottawa River (which it is), or as a north-south artery feeding more or less toward Toronto. Such has been the Ontario viewpoint, while Quebeckers have always viewed it as the umbil-ical cord connecting their communities with the ancestral homelands around Montreal and Quebec City. The lake steamers, which brought in all the early settlers and towed logs for the Ottawa Valley sawmills, reinforced that bond. It took the Temiskaming and Northern Ontario Railway — now the Ontario Northland — to counteract this pull and put Timiskaming into a direct line with Toronto. To some extent the Canadian Pacific Railway spur from Mattawa up the Quebec side of the lake to Ville-Marie and Angliers (built with the blessings of Ottawa and Montreal) helped to deflect this trend in Quebec, as the modern highways continue to do today. The railways' arrival, moreover, had the effect of turning the steamboat services into feeders to the railways or — where the routes parallelled — eliminating them altogeth-er, except for log towing, since land travel always enjoys primacy over water travel.

Regrettably, much of the Northern Ontario steamboat saga has been lost, probably for-ever. In most localities the last steamers (excepting a few tugs) ceased operating over 60 years ago, and few are the old-timers with memories long enough to recall the days when steam-boating was routine on the northern lakes. But interest seems to be reviving, as divers probe the depths for wrecks, museums devote more space to our marine heritage, and historians turn their typewriters and computers to a re-examination of this long-neglected side of our past. This book is meant to be modest contribution to the preservation of what remains of that lore. Let us begin with Lake Nipissing.

Steam tug Osprey *at Sturgeon Falls.* Courtesy Nipissing Archives, North Bay Area Museum

CHAPTER 1

STEAMBOATING

ON LAKE NIPISSING

(1881–1961)

Lake Nipissing, at the gateway to Northern Ontario, is one of the largest lakes in the province, about 50 miles long and 20 miles wide. It lies in a great natural trough resulting from an ancient geological fault stretching from Georgian Bay to the Ottawa River. The main section is rather shallow — often less than fifteen feet deep — and has very few islands and a fairly regular shoreline with extensive beaches. By contrast, the West Arm of the lake and the entrance to the French River sometimes reach depths of 75 feet, and are full of rocky little islands and spectacular scenery. The lake is 640 feet above sea level and its total area is about 300 square miles. That was large enough to impress Champlain, who, upon seeing it for the first time in 1615, wondered if it might be part of the great western sea. But his native guides laughed at the idea and replied that they called it "Nipisierinij" (or "Nipisingue"), meaning "little body of water." It has been so named ever since.

Lake Nipissing emerged about 9,000 years ago as the last glaciers retreated, but for a long time it was simply part of a much larger meltwater lake known today as Lake Algonquin, a giant precursor of the modern Lakes Huron and Michigan. As Lake Algonquin gradually drained away and the land rebounded after the weight of the ice was removed, Lake Nipissing was finally left as an inland remnant, draining into Georgian Bay by way of the French River. As such, it soon became part of a convenient Indian canoe route between Georgian Bay and the Ottawa River, despite its tendency to get rough during stormy weather. The height of land was traversed by a short portage from eastern Lake Nipissing to Trout Lake, where the modern city of North Bay now stands. Trout Lake, in turn, drains into the Mattawa River, which flows east to join the Ottawa River at the small town of Mattawa, about 40 miles east of North Bay.

Many famous figures from Canadian history — including Étienne Brulé, Champlain, Radisson and Groseilliers, La Vérendrye and Alexander Henry — all crossed Lake Nipissing during the 17th or 18th centuries, always from east to west or vice versa, and usually in pursuit of furs. Indeed, until ships became common during the latter part of the 19th century, the canoe route up the Ottawa River was greatly preferred to the stormy and more roundabout route through the Great Lakes. During the late 19th and early 20th centuries, surveys were actually conducted for a proposed Montreal–Georgian Bay ship canal, utilizing the Ottawa and French Rivers. By that time, however, the voyageurs in their giant freight canoes were a thing of the past, the Canadian Pacific Railway had already been built along the ancient corridor, and large steel ships were regularly crossing the Great Lakes, with the result that the Nipissing water traffic was reduced to a trickle. These factors, plus the absence of any really large centres of population and industry along the route, ultimately doomed the canal proposal and after 1907 the scheme was quietly dropped.

Given Lake Nipissing's position as part of an east-west water route extending half way across the continent, it comes as a bit of a surprise to find that, when the first boats other than canoes or sailboats appeared on the lake, the plan was to use them mainly for north-south commerce. Yet that is precisely what happened. Although the first European settlers in the area moved in along the old route from the Ottawa River around 1862, the main thrust of settlement soon came from the south. In 1850, the Province of Canada (which then comprised southern Ontario and Quebec), anxious to provide more land for

ABOVE LEFT: *Nipissing Village, from the South River Bridge.* Courtesy Nipissing Pioneer Museum

BELOW: *Steamer Sparrow, the first tug on Lake Nipissing. The vessel appears in her second version, circa 1910.* Courtesy Nipissing Archives, North Bay Area Museum

ABOVE RIGHT: *Steamer* Inter-Ocean. *A reconstruction sketch by the author, based on all available information.*

prospective settlers, persuaded the native Ojibwas to sell all their lands north of the Severn River, except for a few reserves, as far north as, and including, Lake Nipissing. But the lake was still so remote from the existing "front" settlements that very little happened there until the 1870s. True, a settler named James Chapman of Pembroke and his family took up land near the mouth of the South River as early as 1862, near the modern Chapman's Landing, and, by 1865, John Beatty of Eganville was founding the tiny village of Nipissingan, or Nipissing, about a mile upstream. A few hardy souls were also clearing a little land around Callander Bay, but otherwise about the only bastion of "civilization" in the area was a tiny Hudson's Bay Company post just below Sturgeon Falls, on the river of that name near the north side of the lake. For some time, James Chapman accepted the arduous task of bringing in the weekly mail from Mattawa.

Things began to change during the 1870s. By then, the Nipissing Road — one of several colonization roads built by the government at that time — was being blazed northwards through the bush from the head of Lake Rosseau, in the Muskoka District, to the South River, where it emerged at Nipissing village, a distance of 67 miles. By 1874, the road was considered fit for wheeled vehicles, and for years it was the only land route to the lake. Mail was soon arriving at Nipissingan twice a week by stage.

Population still remained sparse. Most of the local people were Ojibwas or of mixed ancestry, who did more hunting and fishing than farming. North Bay did not yet exist, Callander consisted of a few shanties and, in 1879, the first settlers crossed the lake to Sturgeon Falls. That same year, J. Daniel Cockburn, who had once built a trading post at Port Carling, arrived with his family to open a store at Nipissingan. At the time, the village was still the gateway to the region, and the largest centre. By 1881, it could boast two stores, two hotels, a blacksmith shop and a municipal hall. The village — or rather, Chapman's Landing, which was about a mile downstream — was also the transshipping point from the stages to small boats heading for Lake Nipissing. By 1880, too, Captain Wellington (Wesley) Green of Fergus had imported a sailboat called the *Louise*, which he used to take small groups of settlers and their chattels to Callander and the Sturgeon River, but the *Louise* soon proved unequal to the task. The stage was now set for the arrival of A. P. Cockburn.

Alexander Peter Cockburn (a cousin of Daniel) was one of those rare individuals destined to make an enormous impact on a sizeable portion of the Province of Ontario — in this case, Muskoka. Born in 1837 into a family of highly entrepreneurial Scottish immigrants, Alex Cockburn set himself up as a merchant, first at Kirkfield (1863), then at Orillia and later at Gravenhurst. He first toured the Muskoka District in 1865, and afterwards made it his life's work to promote and develop the region. In the course of his energetic career, he became the first voice of Muskoka in the Ontario legislature (1867) and the Dominion parliament (1872), as well as an active publicist, a tireless railway advocate, a zealous colonizer and the founder of Muskoka's first agricultural association. He was also one of the first to realize Muskoka's potential as a tourist haven and sportsman's paradise. Undoubtedly his greatest service to the North, however, was his steamboat line, which began modestly in 1866, when he launched the small steamer *Wenonah* on Lake Muskoka to carry freight, passengers and mail and to tow logs and scows amid a rustic pioneer setting. The enterprise proved very successful, and ultimately grew into the largest inland steamship company in Canada.

Understandably, A.P. Cockburn's activities around Lake Nipissing were limited, but even here he briefly made his mark. By the year 1880, the Canadian economy had largely recovered from the depression of 1873, the Conservatives under Sir John A. Macdonald were back in power in Ottawa, and transcontinental railway speculation was in the air once more. The Canada Central Railway, later to be merged with the Canadian Pacific Railway, was gradually extending its tracks up the Ottawa River towards Lake Nipissing. To Mr. Cockburn, watching from his vantage point in Parliament, all this came as a reminder of the Northern Railway's extension from Barrie to Gravenhurst in 1875, a development that brought great prosperity to his steamboat line. Once again, a railway from the cities was preparing to tap a major lake. It was generally expected that the Canada Central Railway would pass through

John Rudolphus Booth, Canada's greatest lumberman. To the left is his son C. Jackson Booth. They are inspecting some white pine from the company's Madawaska limits. From the Booth Family Collection, courtesy National Archives of Canada, PA 120161

Nipissing village and skirt the south side of Lake Nipissing, thus avoiding some of the marshy terrain north of the big lake. If so, there would be abundant scope for a steamship service acting as a feeder from Nipissingan to all other parts of the lake. Sawmills would surely be built, and the population would soar. Perhaps resort hotels would follow. The opportunity seemed too good to miss.

Cockburn discussed the prospects with some of his deskmates in the House of Commons, including Donald A. Smith, the future Lord Strathcona, and gradually the idea arose of forming a joint-stock company, which would take over and expand Mr. Cockburn's existing fleet and put a steamer on Lake Nipissing. Smith offered to invest $5,000 to $10,000 in such a venture. In September 1880, Cockburn trekked up to Nipissingan, where he no doubt met his cousin; the two apparently conducted a tour of the lake on Captain Green's sailboat. Both agreed that Sturgeon Falls was destined to become a town of considerable importance; Daniel was interested in opening a new store there. The pair purchased a lot beside the turning basin below the falls, now called Minnehaha Bay, and, by the following spring, J.D. Cockburn was clearing land there for a farm. Alex, meanwhile, completed his survey, taking notes and measurements, then returned south, convinced that his idea would float. He at once made plans for a new propeller steamship, to be about 100 feet in length with a five-foot six-inch wheel, and managed to get the machinery and boiler delivered to Rosseau before the winter freeze-up.

On January 10, 1881, Mr. Cockburn's new firm, called the Muskoka and Nipissing Navigation Company, received its charter. It was authorized to operate steamers, scows and other vessels on the Muskoka Lakes, the Magnetawan River in central Parry Sound and Lake Nipissing, and to issue up to 2,000 shares of stock valued at $50 each. A total of 1,280 shares were subscribed, of which Cockburn held 800, Smith 100 and Alexander Mackenzie (the former Prime Minister of Canada) 20. Mackenzie was elected president and Cockburn became the general manager.

Meanwhile, a gang of men was busy building the new steamer at Chapman's Landing. The parts were probably cut in advance at Gravenhurst and hauled up the Nipissing Road on sleighs. Presiding over the work was Captain Alfred Burritt of Thornbury, who had learned his sailing on Georgian Bay. Burritt was to be more than just captain of the steamer; he was to act as regional manager of the Nipissing branch of the new company, since A.P. Cockburn could devote very little time to it. Daniel Cockburn became the local agent.

The new steamer, called the *Inter-Ocean*, was launched, stern first, in April 1881. Regrettably, little is known of the vessel today beyond the registry records, and no photographs have been found. Fortunately, however, in 1969 this writer encountered an elderly resident of North Himsworth Township, who remembered the ship vividly from the days of his youth. All this allows us to affirm that the *Inter-Ocean* was a conventional wooden passenger and freight steamer, some 103.4 feet in length, with two full-length decks and a rather ample beam of 22.5 feet — a wise precaution on a shallow open lake. She was fully enclosed between decks, had a round stern, and registered 98.12 tons. Her superstructure consisted of little more than a wheelhouse, a small aft cabin, a rather short stack and a hurricane deck, but in case of stormy weather the upper deck could be enclosed with tarpaulins. She had a 15-hp high-pressure engine and a twelve-foot boiler mounted with the fire boxes facing aft. Her livery was white with black trim, a red bottom and a red-and-black stack.

Using Nipissingan as her home port, the *Inter-Ocean* soon began making regular trips to all parts of the lake, usually departing at 8:00 A.M. and arriving at Sturgeon Falls about 11:00. Averaging twelve miles per hour, she could reach the beaches of North Nipissing (North Bay) in about an hour and forty-five minutes, but this was initially considered a minor port of call. The main destinations were Callander and Sturgeon Falls.

As expected, the *Inter-Ocean* proved a great boon to the early settlers, who had previously been terribly isolated. No doubt she was a welcome sight to many a badly bruised traveller who had endured a bone-breaking trip on a stage or wagon up the meandering Nipissing Road — and to merchants eagerly awaiting fresh provisions. Nipissing village was

humming with activity. It now had a population of perhaps 300, while docks and sheds were built at Sturgeon Falls, Callander, North Nipissing and Chapman's Landing. Sturgeon Falls also received a post office (located in J.D. Cockburn's new store) just weeks after the steamer first blew her whistle at the foot of the cataract. The steamer also carried lumber, hay and package freight of all sorts, plus livestock, and apparently seldom had an accident, despite the fact that the lake was uncharted and the water levels continually fluctuated for lack of a control dam at the exit. On weekends, she was in great demand for excursions, especially to the French River; some patrons even trekked in for miles to take part. Business proved so good that within a few years the Muskoka and Nipissing Navigation Company decided to add a second steamer to the Nipissing Division, and accordingly purchased the *Sparrow*, a 50-foot screw tug then under construction at the mouth of the Duchesnay Creek, near North Bay. The *Sparrow* was a staunch little craft with an 8-hp high-pressure Doty engine and she was listed at 25.23 tons (later increased to 36.17). Under the command of Captain Green, who had just obtained his tug master's papers, she assumed most of the log towing and scowing of bulk cargoes on the lake. Captain Green would stay with the *Sparrow* for over a decade.

For the Muskoka and Nipissing Navigation Company, all had gone very well. Business was brisk and its boats were busy. The Ontario government undertook to help out by building a dredge in 1883 to remove some of the sandbars in the Sturgeon River and other spots.

Then the first blow fell. As the Canadian Pacific Railway (which had absorbed the Canada Central) approached Lake Nipissing in 1882, its promoters suddenly changed their plans. Instead of constructing their line south of the lake through Nipissingan, as expected, they decided to build along the north shore, past a shallow and exposed spot which, by a stretch of imagination, was now called a bay — North Bay, which then consisted of a few shacks built near the shores, mostly by the Canadian Pacific Railway crews. The new route also went straight through the hamlet of Sturgeon Falls. The reason for the change was to avoid some of the rough terrain west of Nipissingan, and the cost of an expensive bridge over the French River. Overnight, the village of Nipissingan saw its hopes of becoming a major centre dashed forever, while land speculators had a field day at North Bay and Sturgeon Falls. In an age that worshipped the iron horse, all the spoils and glory went to the place that possessed a railway. North Bay was a poor port — but a good site for sidings. It rapidly sprouted churches, stores, a school, three hotels and a jail (all built initially of logs) and, by 1890, had a population of 1,726.

The railway's decision was a bitter disappointment to the Muskoka and Nipissing Navigation Company, and apparently prompted Alexander Mackenzie to quit as President late in 1882. Needless to say, it did not improve the earnings of the *Inter-Ocean*, which was now largely supplanted. Ironically, the little steamer even made a contribution to her own obsolescence, in that she is said to have hauled stones from the Manitou Islands to help build a bridge for the Canadian Pacific Railway.

The coming of the railway in 1883 left little work for the Lake Nipissing steamers beyond the towing of logs. But here, too, things were changing. Several lumber companies arrived at this time, including that of John Rudolphus Booth, the famous Ottawa lumber king who reputedly became the richest man in Canada. Booth was eyeing the pineries of the Lake Nipissing basin and wondering how to add this huge territory to his already vast timber empire. He decided to build a jackladder at Wassi Falls, just south of Callander, to carry logs over the height of land to Lake Nosbonsing, which, in turn, drains into the Mattawa River. Soon discovering that this didn't work well, he built a short tram railway, about five or six miles in length, to cover the divide, and adapted the jackladder to dump the logs onto the flatcars. Late in 1883, Booth made overtures to the Muskoka and Nipissing Navigation Company, offering large towing contracts at good rates, provided that the company, in turn, would build a large new paddlewheel steamer for that purpose. Booth even offered to provide the machinery for such a vessel, but he was not interested in the *Inter-Ocean* or the *Sparrow*. Both, in his opinion, drew too much water for some of the shallow bays of Lake Nipissing, and besides, the *Inter-Ocean* was not a tug. A.P. Cockburn promptly went to Ottawa and came to an agreement

with Booth, subject to the ratification of his Board of Directors, but upon his return the Board repudiated the entire deal, despite the manager's protests. Why they did so is uncertain. Perhaps they had more or less given up on the Nipissing Division anyway. Booth, of course, simply proceeded to build a tug of his own at Gormanville, just west of North Bay. This was the *Booth*, a powerful light-draft sidewheeler with a 120-hp high-pressure engine made in Montreal. Registered at 194.23 tons, the *Booth* had a single deck, a round stern, and a length of 120 feet. The beam of her paddleboxes came to 37 feet. She was immediately put to work, endlessly towing huge booms of logs across Lake Nipissing and transporting men, horses and provisions to the lumber camps. She was a very slow craft with noisy, slow-moving machinery, but she was extremely reliable. By 1885, she was in regular service.

For the Muskoka and Nipissing Navigation Company, the arrival of the *Booth* was more bad news. During the seasons of 1884 and 1885, the *Inter-Ocean* continued to ply from the stranded port of Nipissingan (and to connect with trains at North Bay and Sturgeon Falls), but almost all the east-west traffic now went by rail and she earned little money. The final blow came in January 1886, when the Northern Extensions Railway, thrusting north from Gravenhurst to connect with the Canadian Pacific Railway, was finally declared open to Callander. The result was to shift the north-south transportation artery away from the Nipissing Road forever. Traffic on the Road declined so much that parts of it have reverted to the bush and are now impassable. All of the hamlets and embryo villages along the road (except Rosseau and Magnetawan) either languished or disappeared, while those in the path of the railway flourished. Nipissingan survived as a minor lumber village and service centre for the local farms, but it enjoyed no further growth and almost ceased to be a port; soon it was provisioned overland from Powassan. Callander, seemingly ruined when the Canadian Pacific Railway bypassed it, now enjoyed a vigorous comeback and became an important sawmill centre. But there no longer seemed to be any future for a passenger boat service, and the Muskoka and Nipissing Navigation Company gave it up. After a couple of not very successful attempts to retrieve its fortunes on Georgian Bay and the Magnetawan River, the company retreated back to the Muskoka Lakes where — under a revised name — it carried on for another 69 years. A revived version of the line still runs a steamship there to this day. [1]

In the spring of 1886, the *Inter-Ocean* and the *Sparrow* were put up for sale. The larger vessel was soon sold at a heavy loss to a pair of businessmen from the Collingwood area, who hoped to use her on Georgian Bay. Three local men agreed to sail her to the French River, but one look at Chaudière Falls revealed the hopelessness of trying to warp her downstream. The little ship was then dismantled. Every piece of metal in her construction was extracted, down to the last iron spike, while her timbers were piled up and burned. The *Sparrow* was on hand to bring back the fragments, and later they were incorporated into a new, smaller, *Inter-Ocean*

1   The R.M.S. *Segwun*, built in 1887.

on Lake Huron. Years later, Captain Burritt, having returned with his family to Thornbury, was to write to friends in Nipissing that occasionally he could hear the whistle of the old *Inter-Ocean* wafting over the waters of Georgian Bay like a ghost from the past. A pitiful, undeserved end for a staunch little pioneer steamship.

The *Sparrow* was luckier. On May 3, 1886, she too was sold, to the lumber firm of John B. Smith, which had followed the railway up to Callander. We shall encounter her again.

For several years, the only steamboats left on Lake Nipissing were lumber tugs, although occasionally they were known to take passengers on special picnic or sightseeing cruises on holidays such as Dominion Day. This was especially true of the *Booth* which otherwise kept plodding back and forth with her tows, usually under the command of Captain Sacred, who seems to have come from the Lake of Bays, or Captain John White of Wisa-Wasi. Naturally, she also accepted towing contracts from most of the lumber companies in the region.

The operations of the lumber firms are described in more detail in the next chapter. Here, we will merely observe that the industry was big business in Canada throughout the last century, often employing hundreds of men locally and frequently dominating the economies of pioneering regions. The Booth Company was much the largest, and eventually secured timber limits almost from coast to coast. At Wisa-Wasi Mr. Booth established a depot and a store for his employees (most of whom were French Canadians), along with his jackladder and tram railway. The railway used only a single small locomotive affectionately nicknamed "Betsy," which constantly faced east, running from a trestle at the end of the jackladder along the route of the modern road to Astorville on Lake Nosbonsing. It is said that surveyors for the Northern Extensions Railway were dumbfounded to discover another little track in the bush, crossing their own projected route to Callander. They demanded the right to build a crossing; Booth in turn demanded a "diamond" junction, giving him the option of shipping his logs south if he chose. He also insisted on a primary right of way for his logging trains. For a time, violence threatened to erupt between the employees of the two lines, but in the end Booth got his way. Until 1912, when the logging railway was shut down, the trains from Toronto were frequently obliged to wait.

On Lake Nosbonsing (which is about seven miles in length), the Booth Company built a simple little screw tug in 1884. She had a single deck, a square stern, and an 8-hp engine and was named after the lake. Registered at 18.67 tons, she was 56.6 feet in length and was used to tow as far as Callander Station (now Bonfield) on the Canadian Pacific Railway. Since Booth preferred to use the waterways rather than pay the Canadian Pacific's freight rates, it usually took about two years to move his logs all the way to Ottawa. Such long immersions left them devoid of pitch and easy to peel, but the waste was colossal; thousands of logs never reached the sawmills. The *Nosbonsing* lasted until about 1905, when she was broken up.

The Booth Company also used a swarm of small tugs on Lake Nipissing, mostly for sweeping up stray logs and "bagging" them inside boom timbers to be towed by the *Booth*. One of them was the *Zephyr*, a 27-foot screw vessel with an 8-hp engine. Built at Hamilton in 1886, the *Zephyr* registered only 1.90 tons, though she was evidently enlarged at a later date. She was imported to Lake Nipissing by Thomas Darling, the Booth Company superintendent at Wisa-Wasi, perhaps around 1890, and put to work towing and assembling tows, often under the command of his son, Captain Victor Darling. In later years, when houseboats became popular, she was sometimes engaged in towing those as well. Despite the occasional mishap — including a sinking at Lonely Island — the *Zephyr* lasted over half a century. Perhaps her iron frame had something to do with it.

Another, even smaller, steamer from this period was the *Spitfire*, which was likewise owned by Thomas Darling. Seemingly unregistered, the *Spitfire* was no more than an open boat, about 26 feet in length, with an upright engine and boiler. Nonetheless, she was big enough to collect logs, take small parties of passengers, and tow houseboats. Captain Green used her for a time in 1911, but her history is otherwise unrecorded.

A larger craft called the *Annie Laurie*, built at Sturgeon Falls in 1890, was for a time partly owned by the Booth Company. The *Annie Laurie* was 36.5 feet in length, registered 2.65

tons, and had the usual single deck and round stern common to most small steamers of the day. Screw driven, she was powered by an upright 4-hp engine. In 1900, she was sold to a pair of railway conductors from North Bay, who apparently used her as a pleasure boat. Then, around the fall of 1910, she was purchased by two men from Lavigne, a newly emerging farm village on the northwest side of the lake, and taken to Sturgeon Falls to haul a load of bricks, coal oil, nails and a barrel of molasses to Lavigne. But by then ice was forming on the lake, and she managed to proceed barely half a mile beyond the mouth of the Sturgeon River before a hole was sliced through her bow. The four men on board took to a canoe they were carrying, but the *Annie Laurie* went to the bottom and became a total loss.

The Booth Company was not without its troubles on Lake Nipissing. Sometime in 1898 it lost the steamer *Booth*, seemingly in a fire at Wisa-Wasi. But the vessel was well insured, and Thomas Darling was ordered to build a new tug to replace her. The second *Booth* was 140 feet in length by 39 in beam and registered 218.33 tons, which made her the largest steamer ever to ply the lake. Her engines, predictably, came from the original boat. The *Booth* (II) was launched at Wisa-Wasi in 1899, and plied for nine seasons.

Little is known about the big tug's activities in detail, although one incident is still remembered around Sturgeon Falls, where the *Booth* collected most of her tows. It seems that the steamer, then commanded by Captain Christopher Ricker of Wisa-Wasi, once picked up a tow at the mouth of the Sturgeon River. A light breeze was blowing, sufficient to keep the towline taut. It was late at night and, very gently, the vessel's bow grounded on a flat rock about four feet beneath the surface, without anyone noticing. The paddlewheels churned slowly away all night, but the next morning the crew were chagrined to find that they hadn't moved more than half a mile from where they had started! From that day henceforth, the rock was known as "Ricker Rock."

The *Booth* (II) had an even shorter career than her predecessor. On January 7, 1908, while in winter quarters on the ways at Wisa-Wasi, the big tug took fire and was completely destroyed. This time, there was no rebuild. Instead, she was replaced in part by a handsome little wooden screw tug called the *King Edward* which had been built at Trenton the previous year. The *King Edward* was 50.5 feet in length, registered 16.28 tons, and was powered by a 2.15-hp high-pressure Polson engine. Like most tugs, she had a single deck and a round stern. Booth bought her in February 1908, and assigned her miscellaneous duties, including light tows around the French River. Usually commanded by Captain Darling, she occasionally took small parties of passengers and is also said to have delivered the beams for the gates of the control dam at Chaudière Falls from Callander around 1909. By 1910, however, she had been transferred to Lake Nosbonsing, perhaps to replace the tug on those waters. Three years later, she was no longer running, and was soon afterwards taken north by rail to Timiskaming, where we shall find her plying again at Charlton on Long Lake.

Several more lumber companies established themselves around Lake Nipissing during this period, mostly at Sturgeon Falls and Callander, both of which had railways by 1886. Sturgeon Falls, commanding excellent water power plus the vast hinterland of the Sturgeon River basin, was the preferred site for sawmills, but it had only limited space for lumber yards. Callander had little water power, but a fine harbour, capable of holding three or four booms of logs at a time. As a result, the main towing route on the lake was from Sturgeon Falls to Callander. By 1899, Sturgeon Falls had three churches, five hotels, a pulp mill, two planing mills, several saw and shingle mills, and a population of about 1,500. Callander was about half as big, with two hotels, a planing mill, a shingle mill and two or more sawmills. North Bay had a poor harbour and no water power, and consequently had very few mills, although some logs were towed in from the South River. Most of the town's 2,500 inhabitants worked directly or indirectly for the Canadian Pacific Railway, which selected the place as a division point and built a roundhouse big enough for sixteen locomotives. In 1891, North Bay was incorporated as a town, to be followed by Sturgeon Falls in 1895. That year, too, North Bay, after a very close vote, beat out both Mattawa and Sturgeon Falls to become

the district seat for Nipissing, partly with the support of the new mining town of Sudbury, about 80 miles west.

Lumbering was still the main industry in the region, however. Although a little spruce and hemlock was shipped out by rail, all of the lumbermen concentrated on pine; hardwoods tended to sink before they could be floated to the mills. The leading firms included J.R. Booth, J.B. Klock, the John B. Smith Company, the McBurney and Payette Companies of Callander, George Gordon of Cache Bay, and the Cockburn Company of Sturgeon Falls. Most of them never used tugs, because they could rely on the Booth Company to tow for them.

The John B. Smith Company was one exception. This famous firm arrived early in the 1880s and opened a sawmill at Frank's Bay on the south side of the lake. It cut mostly long timbers, which were hauled across the ice using horse teams, for export on Canadian Pacific Railway flatcars at Sturgeon Falls. In 1888, the company closed its mill at Frank's Bay and built a large new one at Callander. Despite a serious fire in the fall of 1895, the enterprise flourished and, indeed, closed its mill only in 1968 — the longest-lived of any lumber company around Lake Nipissing.

We have already noted how the firm bought the *Sparrow* from the retreating Muskoka and Nipissing Navigation Company in 1886 for the sum of $2,500. The vessel was drydocked and refitted at Callander, then assigned to Captain Wellington Green. Assisting him was Albert McKenney of North Bay, previously a deckhand on the *Inter-Ocean* and soon to be a captain himself. Other masters included Captain Darling and sometimes Captain Burritt.

Next to the *Booth*, the *Sparrow* was probably the most powerful tug ever used on Lake Nipissing. She had a high-pressure engine and a propeller four feet in diameter, which meant

that, coupled with her six-foot draft, she could tow two boom pockets containing up to 48,000 logs at a time — about twice as many as most other tugs. (Such a tow might easily be half a mile wide.) One time she was ordered to pick up a pocket of 60,000 logs near Frank's Bay; this had to be broken up into smaller ones, so the sturdy little tug pushed right into the pocket to separate them.

She also towed scows, which might be loaded with groceries such as potatoes, turnips and barrels of flour, lard, butter and salt pork for the lumber camps and depots, along with tools, hardware, machinery, tobacco and building supplies. There might also be horses, hay and sleighs needed for winter work in the bush. Occasionally, even a small logging locomotive might be loaded onto a scow to be towed by the *Sparrow*. And, of course, she took passengers, up to 40 at a time. Most were loggers bound for the camps around Frank's Bay, but sometimes she would take parties of hunters in the fall, or the odd traveller needing a lift into town. Occasionally, she even ran excursion cruises, usually on Sundays or holidays.

Long commanded by Captain Green — a powerful, rugged giant of a man, accustomed to doing almost everything by himself — the *Sparrow* was busily occupied for 45 years. It was not until 1906 that the John B. Smith Company provided a running mate for her. In the spring of 1903, she received a new boiler, and sometime before 1910, she was completely overhauled and lengthened to 56.4 feet. Her beam was likewise increased by two feet (to 13.9). By that time, she burned coal rather than wood, and sometimes delivered it by the scowload to various boiler-powered mills around the lake.

Navigation was often imperilled by rocks and stray logs, but storms constituted the worst menace, especially at night. Experienced mariners could usually read the symptoms of an impending blow; a dead swell, for example, might offer a half-hour's warning. The usual response was to seek shelter behind some islands. One especially favoured place was a completely sheltered cove off Sandy Island near the source of the French River, a spot the boatmen fondly called the "Sparrow's Nest." Another was Satchell's Bay, on the south side of the French River channel, about seven miles farther in; the bay was safe and commodious, but the exits were narrow, and any logs gathered within had to be shepherded out to be "bagged" with boom timbers. Sometimes a tow had to be abandoned in stormy weather. If the boatmen were lucky, the boom timbers would hold together until the tow could be retrieved; if not, they might break up and scatter the logs for miles. This always meant extensive work for the sweep gangs who had to gather them up again. Sometimes wave action might pound the logs up against the rocks, rendering them useless. Captain Green would later recall gales that left an inch of rainwater inside the *Sparrow*'s wheelhouse, since it often became necessary to open the doors and windows to see anything. Autumns were worse than summers, in that the days were shorter and the weather colder. Sometimes the *Sparrow* would finish the season in a snowstorm, perhaps bucking ice in order to reach port.

Another company that used a tug on Lake Nipissing was that of John Fraser of Powassan, which was active for a time on the South River. Around 1887, the Fraser firm built a sawmill at the mouth of the river, near Nipissing village, and in its vicinity fitted out a large sturdy sidewheel steamer. The steamer, known as the *John Fraser* (or sometimes, erroneously, the "John B. Fraser"), was used to tow lumber and squared timber across the lake to North Bay, and doubtless to provision the camps. She was an impressive, well-equipped vessel, some 102.5 feet in length by 28.8 in beam around the paddlewheels. She registered 99.52 tons, and had a horizontal high-pressure engine, an auxiliary hoist, two anchors, three decks, a round stern, and a double hull with oak ribs about eighteen inches thick. She also carried two lifeboats. If any vessel on the lake was safe, it was surely the *John Fraser!*

Mr. Fraser kept the tug for only a few years. He sold her in 1892 to John Irvin Davidson and John Dunlop Hay, a pair of Toronto wholesale grocers who had become interested in lumbering. Around 1885, they built the first sawmill at Cache Bay, about four miles west of Sturgeon Falls, and bought extensive timber limits near the entrance of the West Arm. They also set up six camps and put the steamer to work towing logs to Cache Bay and running scowloads of provisions from Callander. A cable tug called the *Turtle* (27.33 tons) was also

Steamer John Fraser *(burned November 7, 1893). Note the paddle box over the vessel's name.*

built in 1893 to bring the logs into Cache Bay, which was too shallow for conventional tugs.

The *John Fraser* might have plied without stirring a ripple as far as the historical record is concerned, had it not been for the voyage of Tuesday, November 7, 1893, which turned her name into a synonym for the worst disaster in the history of Lake Nipissing.

It was a bright, clear, mild autumn morning as the *John Fraser* set off from Callander around 8:00 for the camps at the west end of the lake. In addition to her six-man crew, she was carrying at least fourteen passengers, all shantymen bound for the camps, although the cook would afterwards testify that he counted 24 men on board. She also had a cargo of oats, sugar, dried apples and other supplies, most of which were loaded into a scow towed astern.

For several hours, the *John Fraser* chugged leisurely along into the open lake. Everyone was in good spirits. About a mile ahead lay the Goose Islands. Shortly after 11:00 A.M., the cook was ready to serve lunch and sounded the dinner bell.

Just then the engineer, William Storey of Cache Bay, noticed smoke coming from above the boiler, near the stack. He at once ordered the fireman, John Adams of Toronto, to investigate. Adams opened the manhole above the boiler — a fatal mistake. Instantly a blast of flames belched out, forcing Adams back. The engineer rushed for a pail of water, while Adams started the auxiliary pony engine and tried to couple up the fire hose. But within moments the midship was an inferno and the hose had to be abandoned.

Adams dashed to the upper deck, just as the captain, William Carr of Cache Bay, rang the bell to stop engines and go into reverse. But the blazing boat kept churning on. The engineer, who was never seen again, apparently met his death trying to stop the engines.

All was pandemonium on board. Some of the men panicked. There was no chance to grab the life preservers, which were stored over the engine room and were already feeding the flames. Only Captain Carr remained calm, ordering the hands to lower the boats, but not to rush. Adams ran over to the starboard yawl, but he couldn't handle it alone, and meanwhile the flames broke through the deck beneath his feet. Rushing around to the port side, he found the other boat in the water. Several of the men scrambled in, and Adams threw in his coat and bundle and jumped for the stern. But the paddlewheels were still revolving mindlessly, and the blades caught the boat and pushed it under water, spilling all the occupants into the drink. Adams was sucked under and received a kick in the face from someone's boot. Surfacing, he found the water filled with struggling, screaming men. Swimming desperately, he managed to grab the towline and haul himself over to the scow. Four men who had already reached the scow helped pull him aboard, and Adams used his knife to cut the line.

The burning steamer, now some distance ahead, chugged along on a curved course, swinging to the north, then stopped. As she idled, the flames engulfed her from stem to stern, forcing the remaining men into the freezing waters. Captain Carr, the mate, Alfred Barbeau of Roclyn, and a deckhand hung on to the anchor at the bow, but one by one they were forced to let go. The doomed vessel burned almost to the waterline, then sank, leaving the top of the stack still protruding from the water. Having no oars or any other means of propulsion, there was nothing that the men on the scow could do except rescue two more men who were within reach. Of the entire crew, only Adams and Edward Majore, the cook, survived. It was only thanks to the scow that they did.

Although far out in the lake, the fire did not go unnoticed, and Captain Burritt, who was then at Frank's Bay about six miles away, at once set out in a sailboat, along with an Ojibwa named Peter Commanda. The winds were so light, however, that it took an hour and a half for them to reach the scow, which was lying almost motionless in the water. The seven chilled and exhausted survivors were picked up, and Captain Burritt circled around the wreck site, searching vainly for further signs of life. Then he made for Frank's Bay, where the men were taken care of. The following morning, the *Sparrow* arrived, and took them over to Sturgeon Falls.

The *John Fraser* disaster made headlines all over Ontario, and for weeks afterwards cast a pall of gloom over all the Lake Nipissing communities. Over the following winter, Captain Green recovered the bodies of several of the victims by dog team, near the Goose Islands.

Then, gradually, the tragedy faded from memory. The following year, the vessel's owners, Davidson and Hay, tried replacing her with a small screw tug called the *Ladas* (37.04 tons), a single-decked, 73-foot vessel with a 20.93-hp steeple-compound engine. But soon afterwards they suffered another loss, when a hundred of their horses vanished after being turned loose to forage near a small lake (perhaps amid quicksand), and the luckless pair gave up. Their mill was sold to the Gordon Lumber Company, which was controlled by Senator George Gordon of Pembroke, while the graceful *Ladas* eventually went to the Victoria Harbour Lumber Company, which may have used her to tow logs to Chaudière Falls. By 1905, however, the vessel had sunk near the government wharf at Sturgeon Falls and was apparently never raised. As for the *John Fraser,* she was more or less forgotten — until August 1972, when a team of divers from North Bay, after a careful study of the surviving records and an intensive search, announced that they had found the wreck in about 40 feet of cold, dark water. Since then, the vessel's water pump, anchors, rudder and steering wheel have been raised, and are now in the possession of the North Bay Area Museum.

From 1900 to 1965, the Gordon Company mill dominated the scene at Cache Bay, which soon grew into a village of 600 souls and one or two stores. It was always exclusively a lumber town, and once boasted three mills, including those of the Cockburn and Strong Lumber Companies. The Gordon Company used at least one small screw steamer called the *Dorothy* (7.73 tons), a 48-foot launch with one deck, a compound engine and a spoon stern. She was built in 1903 by Mathew Craig McCaw, a cheerful Scot who had recently arrived from Huntsville, but her later history is unknown. Given the shallowness of the stumpy bay, however, the company chose to build mostly alligator tugs, which have a very shallow draft.

Alligators — more correctly called warp tugs — are described in some detail in the next chapter. Here we can say that they were basically scows, usually equipped with steam-driven paddlewheels and long steel cables. They did their towing by anchoring themselves to the bottom and winching in their cables, which were attached to the tows. They were invented around 1889, and indeed, one foundry firm, that of West and Peachey in Simcoe, Ontario, long made a specialty of building these ungainly boats for lumber companies all over Canada and abroad. Many were used on Lake Nipissing and other shallow lakes in Northern Ontario. They were squat, ugly and slow, but they were also cheap, powerful and effective. And they could be portaged easily from one lake to another.

Probably the first alligator to appear on Lake Nipissing was the aforementioned *Turtle,* a 48-foot barge powered by an upright single-cylinder Doty steam engine, generating 15 hp Unlike most warp tugs, the *Turtle* was a screw vessel. She was usually assigned to pick up tows from the *John Fraser* or the *Ladas* and bring them into Cache Bay, although she was probably used elsewhere as well. Sold off in 1896, the *Turtle* seems to have operated until 1901. She bequeathed her name to a second *Turtle* (33 tons), which was built at Cache Bay for the Gordon Company in 1902. The *Turtle* (II) was a sidewheeler, some 49 feet in length, with a 1.66-hp engine. She served until sometime in the 1920s, usually under the command of John Ebert or Arthur Nesbitt of Cache Bay.

From a logbook kept by Captain Ebert come a few details of the *Turtle's* plodding routine. To quote him:

S.S. *Turtle* — Tow for Strong Lumber Co.

May 6th, 1912. Took the tow from the *Seagull* [a John B. Smith Company tug] and pulled for three hours. Held the tow all night in heavy wind. Wind lulled at four in the morning of the 7th. A heavy wind rose. Held the tow for 14 hours. There was a lull in the morning of the 8th. Pulled up to two-mile point. A gale of wind rose and dragged us back to Garden Island with the tow.

Left Garden Island at 8 o'clock in the evening of the 8th and towed all night. We snubbed the tow at the pier of Cache Bay at 10 o'clock in the morning of the 9th.

ABOVE:

Steam tug J.C. Else.   Courtesy Nipissing Archives,
North Bay Area Museum

BELOW LEFT:

Steamer Spitfire.   Courtesy Nipissing Archives,
North Bay Area Museum

BELOW RIGHT:

Lumber yards at Callander, facing north.
Courtesy North Himsworth Museum, Callander

Thus, three days were required to winch a tow from the mouth of the Sturgeon River to Cache Bay!

The workload for the Cache Bay sawmills must have been heavy, since we hear of a West and Peachey warp tug called the *Temagami* being used there, starting in 1906. The *Temagami* was a standard-sized 37-foot model and was still running in 1914. In 1908, the Gordon Company engaged a Sturgeon Falls mechanic and boatbuilder named Fred E. Clark to build another alligator. This was the *Veuve* (14.11 tons), a 38-foot craft with a recycled engine and boiler. Named after a local stream, this tug seems to have lasted only until 1918, when she was dismantled and replaced by another warp tug called the *Whitney* (12.73 tons). The *Whitney* was 48 feet in length with an upright 1904 Doty engine which gave her speeds of five miles per hour when not under tow! Usually commanded by Captain Jack Nesbitt, a son of Arthur, she ran for 20 years — about average for a wooden alligator. Finally broken up in 1937, she, in turn, was replaced by the *Whitney II*, a slightly larger craft, some 49.6 feet in length. The *Whitney II* served until 1955, when she was dismantled and replaced by a more modern steel-hulled diesel winch boat obtained from Owen Sound. This vessel became the *Whitney III*. She plied right up until 1965, when the Gordon Company ran out of suitable timber and had to shut down its mill at Cache Bay. The *Whitney III* then went to the Ottawa River.

This by no means completes the list. In 1895, the Booth Company ordered an alligator called the *Lorne Hall* (8.86 tons) from West and Peachey. This craft was assembled at Cook's Mills, just north of North Bay, and may have been used on some of the lakes north of Lake Nipissing. She was 37 feet in length and had a 20-hp engine, but little more is known of her. In 1909, the company purchased a much larger 'gator, built by Fred Clark at Sturgeon Falls two years earlier. This boat was to have been called the *Monarch*, but the name was not allowed, and in 1909 Booth chose to call it the *Wisawasa*. The *Wisawasa* was 60 feet in length, registered 45.62 tons, and was powered by a 75-hp compound Bertram engine, giving her speeds of ten miles per hour. She was used for sweeping operations around Sturgeon Falls, and to take tows out to the *King Edward*, which could not navigate in the shallow bays. She operated until 1920, and was then dismantled and sunk near Wassi Falls.

A few more can be added. In 1904, Fred Clark also built a 29-foot craft called the *Mollie* (7.52 tons, soon renamed the *Gooding*) for his own use, but sold her to the Abitibi Power and Paper Company in 1920. In 1910, the *Mattawapika* was built at Callander, but soon afterwards moved to the Montreal River in the Timiskaming region. She is said to have been 42 feet in length and powered by a four-cycle gasoline engine. A large 'gator called the *Nighthawk* was used around Cache Bay in the 1930s, and old-timers have vaguely recalled two more, respectively called the *Grasshopper* and the *Mafeking*. Finally, we must document the *Woodchuck* (18.18 tons), which was built at Simcoe in 1926 for the Driving and Boom Company of North Bay, an umbrella group of lumber companies once busy on the upper Sturgeon River. The *Woodchuck* was 54.3 feet in length by 10.5 in beam, and powered by a twin high-pressure reciprocating engine, giving her speeds of seven miles per hour. She spent eighteen years plying Cedar and Island Lakes on the Temagami River, south of Lake Temagami, until her hull gave out and she was replaced by a more modern 40-foot steel alligator called the *Skimmer*. But the *Woodchuck*'s days were not yet over. The Driving and Boom Company sold her to the John B. Smith Company, which required a new shallow-draft tug to tow booms out from the Sturgeon River and into Callander, replacing a gas boat. Unable to obtain a more modern craft in wartime, the Smith Company had the old tug's machinery and superstructure floated down the Sturgeon River on rafts and installed in a new 30-foot hull in 1944. Now a coal burner, she was assigned first to Captain Darling and later to Captain Michael Joseph ("Mac") Masson of Callander. The *Woodchuck* continued to serve until 1955, when her second hull rotted out and she had to be scrapped at Sturgeon Falls in 1956. This made her the last wooden steam alligator on Lake Nipissing.

Predictably, there were also several private tugs on Lake Nipissing, owned by free-lance captains ready to tow or scow provisions (and sometimes take passengers) wherever they could get a contract. One of these boats was the *Callander* (1.09 tons), a vessel with a rather convoluted history. She was a small propeller steamer, built at North Bay in 1892 and owned initially by a farmer from Fairbank, north of Toronto. The registry gives her a length of only 20 feet and no decks. Yet she must have been rebuilt and drastically enlarged; photographs show a vessel about 65 feet in length, with three decks (one full-length), and a disjointed window-sill line on the main deck — as if the two ends had been built by two different contractors.

When did this occur? In her register the *Callander* is also called the *Hazel B.*, which, according to a second register, was built (or rebuilt) at North Bay in 1904 by Captain John A. McCaw, with the backing of William R. Boucher, a North Bay locomotive engineer, and Thomas Wallace, a local merchant. Named after Boucher's daughter, the *Hazel B.* was 65 feet in length, had two decks and a spoon stern, and registered 22.17 tons. She had a 2.70-hp upright high-pressure engine, and was licensed to take up to 40 passengers and freight, with the help of a scow called the *Windsor*.

The *Hazel B.* was often seen puttering around Lake Nipissing from her wharf at North Bay, and seemingly took a great many tourists and sportsmen to the French River and the West Arm. But it would appear that the venture was not very profitable. The vessel had to be mortgaged in the spring of 1907, and around the same time Boucher sold out his share. In 1912, she was apparently sold to Thomas Darling, who was still running the Booth Company's affairs at Callander. Darling evidently revived the vessel's old name; his 1912 diary contains several references to the *Callander*, which he assigned to a Captain Joseph Amour. She is mentioned as taking a Y.M.C.A. party to the French River on July 14th, scowing a load of oats and hay to a logging camp on August 1st, carrying 40 passengers and their baggage for a holiday on a houseboat at the French River on August 27th, breaking a propeller on the Sturgeon River on August 30th, and grounding on a rock off Lonely Island on her way to the South River on November 11th. The *Sparrow* came to her rescue and pulled her off.

In the spring of 1915, the *Hazel B.* (as she was again called) was massively rebuilt by the new firm of Armstrong Towing, with which Darling had become associated. She was then sold to Captain William Thomas Windsor of Callander, another free-lance skipper, who had previously run the little steamer *Albino* (8 tons gross)[2] on Lake Nipissing. Windsor seems to have used both vessels to scow lumber and tanbark from Nipissing village to Callander, plus sundry other jobs, including charter cruises. By 1920, however, the *Hazel B.* was listed as "not in commission," and soon afterwards she was stripped and left to rot away in the river at Sturgeon Falls. Her propeller was retrieved by divers in 1981 and given to the museum at Callander.

Another private tug, known today only from the register, was the *Shoofly* (8.32 tons), said to have been built at Sundridge in 1893. The *Shoofly* is described as an all-purpose boat, 35.8 feet in length, with one deck, a round stern and an 8-hp engine. By 1896, she was owned by Thomas Kingston, a Callander lumberman, who in turn sold her to James Alexander Stellar of Sturgeon Falls in 1899. Later she went to Elk Lake, on the Montreal River, where she was reported dismantled by 1921.

Better known is the *West Arm*, a little tramp steamer built at Sturgeon Falls in 1901 by Joseph Deschene (or Deschesne), a local mechanic who evidently leased her from the owner, Henry Quesnel, also of Sturgeon Falls. The *West Arm* was 55 feet in length, with two decks, a spoon stern, a bowsprit and an upright Petrie engine, and registered 23.95 tons. The Deschene family used her to sweep up stray logs after storms and deliver them to the mills, and to scow cattle, hay and tanbark. Sometimes they lived on the boat, and it is said they always hid the vessel when the steamship inspectors were in the neighborhood!

The *West Arm* had but a short life. One bright, windy day around 1906, she was steaming from Nipissing to Callander with a scowload of tanbark in tow. As she made for a passage south of Lonely Island another steamer was spotted from the northwest on the same course; she proved to be the *Sparrow* under Captain Green. The two vessels began to race for the channel, but the unencumbered *Sparrow* easily made it through first. Captain Deschene then made a

---

2   All tonnages given in this book are register tonnages unless otherwise specified.

fatal error: he tried to take a shortcut by running between some rocks — and piled his vessel up high on a shoal. The scow then slammed into the stern, and the damaged steamer began to fill. The family hastily abandoned ship and took to the scow, which was soon washed ashore. By the following day, the tug had slipped off the rocks into about 20 feet of water, and quickly settled into the mud. She was never raised, and became a total loss. The ever-active Mr. Deschene remained on the lake, sometimes acting as engineer on other steamers.

One more tug was the *Dalton K.* (12 tons), which was built by Captain McCaw at Sturgeon Falls in 1915. She was named for Dalton Kirkup, whose father owned a hotel in Sturgeon Falls and a part-ownership of the boat; the other owners were W.J. Devlin, a North Bay foundry-man, and Charles Williams, a dredge captain from the Picton region, who acted as master of the vessel. The *Dalton K.* was 46.6 feet in length and had a second-hand Polson engine and boiler, good for 33.3 hp and a speed of six knots.

Although Captain Williams often served on dredge tenders, he apparently never used the *Dalton K.* that way. Her usual business was scowing huge barges loaded with logs to the Spanish River Pulp and Paper Company mill at Sturgeon Falls and returning the scows to the lumber camps laden with horses, hay and oats, and groceries for the loggers. Around 1920, Captain Williams formed a partnership with Harry Crouchman of Sturgeon Falls, and together they bought and exploited a timber limit near Frank's Bay. In the fall they also accepted charters to take parties of hunters from Sturgeon Falls to Campbell's Bay and other sites around the French River; this entailed stocking the tug with food and allowing the hunters to use it as a base of operations.

Late in 1921, however, the pair had bad luck. The steamer sank in shallow water about 200 yards off Johnson's Point, on the south side of the lake, during a hunt, causing considerable excitement. (Perhaps the oakum had come out of her seams.) The hunt was terminated and the vessel was allowed to freeze in the ice. A watch was put on her over the winter, and later a team of men arrived to cut the ice and get her back on an even keel. She was beached and repaired in the spring, but, in the meantime, Captain Williams had a falling-out with Crouchman and the partnership was dissolved. Williams remained in charge of the *Dalton K.*, but there was still a mortgage on her when she was sold to Captain Britton in 1926. Britton promptly resold her to the Lumber and Ties Company of Montreal, which used her for a few more years. Around 1928, however, she was beached and left to fall apart; ten years later only the engine and boiler remained.

Steamboats were used for other purposes besides towing, scowing and taking passengers. Lake Nipissing once abounded with game fish, including pike, pickerel, whitefish, muskellunge and sturgeon, which had been netted and speared by the native people from time immemorial. The early settlers also gladly supplemented their diet with fish but, as usual, the white men soon began to overdo it. Fish, like trees, were deemed to be an inexhaustible resource, and indeed there was once some excuse for thinking so. Ontario government records indicate that about 193 tons of fish were taken from Lake Nipissing between 1885 and 1907. Much of this was cleaned, packed in ice, crated and shipped to distant markets by rail. Some Nipissing caviar is said to have reached the plate of the All-Highest of Germany, Kaiser Wilhelm II himself. The onslaught was more than the native stocks could sustain and, by 1908, the catch was down so much that commercial fishing was banned until 1917.

The first fisherman to use a steam tug on Lake Nipissing was apparently Captain W.T. Windsor of Callander, who began his career by purchasing the *Dauntless* (5.40 tons), a small 44.6-foot craft with a 1.4-hp engine. Built at Gravenhurst in 1884, the *Dauntless* had been used for both towing and fishing on Lake Muskoka. Windsor did the same at Callander, working in partnership with Captain Green, who commanded the vessel until Windsor secured his own ticket. Their families lived in a houseboat towed by the tug.

The *Dauntless* foundered on October 4, 1895, apparently with no loss of life, but she was soon back in service. Then, in 1900, Captain Windsor took charge of a passenger steamer, and sold the tug to the Empire Fish Company of Buffalo, New York, represented by a fisherman

ABOVE:

Steam tug
Dalton K. *The*
vessel has been
chartered for a
deer hunt.

Courtesy Mr. Herbert
Knapp

BELOW:

Steamer Callander
(ex-Hazel B). *The*
vessel is docked at
Callander. Note
the rebuilt stern.

Courtesy North
Himsworth Museum,
Callander

from Dunnville. After 1903, the vessel fades from the record.

That same year, another fishing tug was built at Sturgeon Falls for Walter Adam Cockburn and his younger brother, Hamilton. The pair were sons of J.D. Cockburn, who (as noted earlier) pioneered at the Falls around 1881. Their tug was named the *Catharine C.* in honour of their mother; it is interesting to find different branches of the same family engaged in steamboating at this time! The *Catharine C.* was 48 feet in length, with one deck and a round stern, registered 15.70 tons and had a vertical high-pressure engine. She was used for fishing and freighting only until the fall of 1906, when the Cockburns sold her to the Ministry of Public Works to serve as a dredge tender. Captain Williams then took charge.

A third fishing tug was the *Osprey* (6 tons gross), which was built at Port Robinson, on the Welland Canal, in 1895. She was 32 feet in length and seems to have been imported to Lake Nipissing around 1902 by Captain Daniel Lang of Elgin. As catches diminished, Captain Lang apparently shifted north to Haileybury, and resumed his fishing on Lake Temiskaming. The *Osprey* seems to have gone to the Clark family of Sturgeon Falls, who were developing their own small fleet of passenger steamers. Now licensed for ten people, the *Osprey* apparently served as a reserve boat, sometimes escorting the big steamer *Northern Belle* on her runs. She is last mentioned in 1914, at which time her certificate was not renewed.

By this time, commercial navigation on Lake Nipissing had become so important that the government decided to resume dredging operations. In 1900, the Public Works Department built a large dipper dredge called the *Mattawa*, which was put to work deepening the waters at Cache Bay, the Sturgeon River and even the South River. The *King Edward* may have been her part-time escort, but in 1906 the *Catharine C.* took over.

During the season of 1913, the *Catharine C.* fell victim to fire near Sturgeon Falls, apparently following an accident with a gas boat. She was totally destroyed. The department replaced her with the *Maggie K.* (12.55 tons), a wooden screw tug built at Buckingham, Quebec, in 1912. The *Maggie K.* was 48.2 feet in length, with a 4.8-hp vertical high-pressure engine. She, too, was assigned to Captain Williams, but not for long. The dredge remained in use only until 1915, and by then Williams was arranging to build the *Dalton K.* Little more is heard of the *Maggie K.*, although she was still owned by the government as late as 1920. Eventually, she went to Captain John A. Clark of Sturgeon Falls and may even have outlasted him. By 1937, however, she had been broken up to extract her machinery.

A few more tugs demand their due. In 1906, the John B. Smith Company decided on a large new boat to assist the *Sparrow*, and built the *Sea Gull* at Callander. The *Sea Gull* was a fine vessel: 82.6 feet in length by 18.7 in beam, with a white oak hull and a fore-and-aft compound Polson engine. She registered 73.48 tons, and was licensed to carry 40 passengers. Various officers commanded her, including Captains Green, Darling, Ricker, Edward Muir of Gamebridge, and Stewart Hicks of Creemore.

An incident involving the *Sea Gull* is still remembered. One time, around 1910, the big tug, then under Captain Ricker, was returning from the Manitou Islands when the engines malfunctioned. Her whistle toots soon attracted the little *Zephyr*, which came out to provide a tow, but the towline was short. Meanwhile, the *Sparrow*, with Captain "Wes" Green at the wheel, also appeared, but then the *Zephyr* crossed her path! Captain Green at once rang for "slow astern," but it was too late. The *Sparrow* missed the *Zephyr*, but struck the towline. The *Zephyr* immediately jerked over, sending some of her crew dashing to the lifeboat in a panic. Luckily, the towline snapped in two; otherwise, the little tug would have capsized. Instead, she rebounded at once, and the crisis was averted.

Steamer Hazel B.

Courtesy Mr. Gordon Restoule

ABOVE:
Fishing tug Dauntless, *with a houseboat.* Courtesy Mr. Alex Dufresne

BELOW LEFT:
Crew of the tug Sea Gull. Courtesy Capt. "Mac" Masson

BELOW RIGHT:
Steam tug Screamer. *Under construction at Callander.* Courtesy Sturgeon Falls Public Library

Perhaps deciding that two tugs were unnecessary, the John B. Smith Company sold the *Sea Gull* to the Temagami Lumber Company of Orillia in the spring of 1908. Three years later, she went to the Armstrong Towing Company, an offshoot of the Canadian Timber Company of Callander. The Armstrong Towing Company made a policy of towing wherever it could get a contract.

The John B. Smith Company, meanwhile, carried on with the old reliable *Sparrow* until 1922, when it again decided on another tug. The result was the *Screamer*, a 71-foot coal burner built at Callander of British Columbia fir. She had one deck (initially), a round stern, a 170-hp engine that was almost too big for her, and some decidedly boxy cabins. One of her captains, Donald Green of Callander (son of Wes), surmised that she was called the *Screamer* because she was a scream to look at, but apparently the name was an indirect reference to gulls.

The *Screamer* entered service with a double crew, including two captains, two engineers and two firemen working alternate six-hour shifts, two logmen (on duty whenever necessary) and a cook — for the reason that a run from Sturgeon Falls to Callander under tow sometimes took 41 hours. (In good weather it might take only 36 hours, but when a storm hit, it could require three days.) She was intended to replace the *Sparrow*, which was now 40 years old, but her engines and boiler took up so much space that she could not carry more than fourteen tons of coal, which was not enough for extended trips. Not infrequently she would run short, and the captain would have to send some of the crew ahead to Callander in a yawl to request more. Consequently, the *Sparrow* was kept on standby service, running extra coal out to the *Screamer* when needed; they usually met near the Manitou Islands. Thus reprieved, the old tug survived until 1927, when she finally went to the scrapyard.

The *Screamer* soon displayed another unsettling trait: a tendency to roll over, especially when towing. After a number of close calls during her maiden season, she was drydocked over the winter while false sides were added to her hull, widening it by six feet. She was also given a second deck and her sides were enclosed between decks. Finally, the boiler was turned around, with the firebox now facing away from the engine. These improvements made her less top heavy.

The *Screamer* was initially commanded by a Captain King of Toronto, with Captain Ricker as his second-in-command; later, Captain Ricker took full charge. In one season he took 22 tows. Once the tug was gone from Callander for eight days on account of bad weather, and had to take shelter behind the Manitou Islands. Another time Captain Ricker, with several log pockets in tow, faced a serious blow and again took refuge behind the Manitou Islands for the night. To avoid risk to his vessel, he cast off all the pockets but one — and lost a boat in the process. As a result, the sweep gangs took two weeks with pointer boats and bulldozers, gathering up several thousand logs that were strewn for miles along the south shore of the lake. On a third occasion, the *Screamer* encountered a storm around Long Point. Captain Ricker, running short of fuel, abandoned the tow and ran over to Callander for more coal. The next day, he set out again and retrieved the tow — still intact — at the mouth of the La Vase Creek. No logs were lost that trip!

Chris Ricker also had a humiliating mishap shortly after assuming command of the *Screamer*, though it was hardly his fault. He was bringing her into Callander Bay one dark night, relying on the lighthouses to find his way in. The lights were supposed to be aligned in straight rows, but they were not, and Ricker, not knowing this, ran his vessel right into a marsh. From that time onward, he resolved to use only his compass for navigating by night.

Captain Donald Green became Ricker's second-in-command, and eventually succeeded him in 1935. At the end of his shift (6:00 P.M.) one warm August evening in 1931, Green handed over the wheel to a young deckhand and instructed him to steer for the flashing light at Gull Rock. The deckhand, tired after a party at Sturgeon Falls the previous night, found three hours of steering at a speed of one mile per hour (the vessel being under tow) a little too much. He fell asleep at his post and awoke nearly three hours later, to find the Gull Rock light right below the bow! Instinctively, he swerved to port to avoid the rock. The manœuvre worked, but it caused the cable to slide over, pulling the tug part way over, too. As a result, water gushed in through some of the open portholes, causing near panic among the rudely awakened crew. But Captain Green dashed into the wheelhouse, took over, and signalled the engineer to reverse engines. The tug then righted herself, with no worse damage than a tangled cable — and some bruising to the young deckhand's ego. Captain Green, however, never even mentioned the incident again.

The *Screamer* lasted until 1939, but by then some of her timbers were badly rotted, perhaps because water was getting trapped between the two layers of her hull. As a result, the vessel was allowed to sink at her dock at Callander over the winter. She was refloated in the spring, but only to extract her engines. The hulk, minus her wheelhouse, was towed over to Smith Island at the entrance of Callander Bay and there it was soaked in gasoline and set on fire. The wreck was rediscovered in 1981.

The John B. Smith Company would use one more tug during its long history around Lake Nipissing, but for now we must return to the Armstrong Towing Company, which we left in possession of the *Sea Gull*. In 1924, the firm acquired a second vessel, the fine steel tug *J.C. Else*, which had been built some nine years earlier at Midland for the Georgian Bay Lumber Company of Waubaushene. The *J.C. Else* had a nice sheer, rode well in the water, and was powered by a single-cylinder high-pressure engine. Commanded usually by Captain Napoleon (Poley) Grozelle, she was commonly used for sweeps, but would sometimes also take passengers on autumn hunting trips. Unluckily, by the 1930s the Depression struck, and the vessel was often tied up for lack of work. In 1941, she went to Johnny Larochelle, a Callander lumberman, who moved her to Turtle (Mud) Lake, near Trout Lake, where he had a mill. In 1947, however, the *J.C. Else* was dismantled.

The old *Sea Gull* did not last that long. By 1929, her hull was rotten, and the Armstrong Towing Company decided to build a new *Sea Gull* to replace her. The *Sea Gull* (II) was slightly smaller than the original, having a length of just 79.5 feet and a register tonnage of 63.76. She inherited her predecessor's engine, boiler and superstructure cabins, and looked almost exactly like her, except that she carried her lifeboats on the bridge instead of on the afterdeck. Another important difference was her frame, which was built of steel. The *Sea Gull* (II) was launched at Callander in 1930, and proved the last steamboat ever to appear on Lake Nipissing, except for the alligator *Woodchuck*. The hulk of the old tug was meanwhile burned and scuttled in Callander Bay.

The new *Sea Gull* was used primarily to tow for the John B. Smith Company, though never more than three pockets at a time (which amounted to about 15,000 logs). Most towing was done in the spring or fall, from the Sturgeon River to Callander Bay, where a gas boat (and later the *Woodchuck*) took over. The *Sea Gull* sailed with the usual double crew, all of whom slept on board, except when the vessel was in port. The captain had a cubicle and washroom in the upper-deck cabin, while the cook (who was often a woman) had a tiny compartment to herself next to the galley. The other hands slept in the hold. There was a small cozy dining room behind the engine room, and a wood stove in the galley; here the cook would prepare coffee, tea and muffins first thing in the morning. Oil lamps were used for lighting, since the *Sea Gull* had no generator, but she was equipped with radio, mainly to report bad weather. Storms were frequent, and it was not uncommon for some of the hands to get seasick, but very seldom did a tow have to be abandoned. One time, around 1954, a blow kept the vessel bobbing about four days behind the Manitou Islands and a police boat had to be despatched from Callander with extra food. In general, though, the crew's morale was good; the John B. Smith Company, which bought the tug in 1940, treated its employees fairly well.

Captain Victor Darling usually ran the *Sea Gull* until 1954, with George Jenkins of New Westminster, B.C., as engineer. In 1947, "Mac" Masson of Callander, who was then 25 and had been working at various jobs, signed up as a deckhand and logman aboard the *Sea Gull*. Almost at once he was outraged to discover that only officers were allowed sheets and pillowcases for their bunks; the rest of the hands were considered so dirty (on account of their jobs) that bed linen was wasted on them. When Captain Darling explained that this was simply the way things were done, Masson, refusing to "live like a pig," complained to the manager, who authorized him to order fresh sheets for all the hands. Captain Darling was not pleased to find that the feisty little deckhand had gone behind his back, and over the next seven years the two had many a row.

One night near the season's end, Masson was setting out the lanterns on the booms when Captain Darling shifted the searchlight away from him. In the dark, Masson fell flat on his face and was slightly hurt. He had long been urging that the logmen should be supplied with battery-powered lights strapped to their heads at night, as miners were, but Darling was too set in his ways to consider such a change. Masson, in a rage, resigned as soon as he went ashore, but the manager, Harold Bush, after hearing him out, urged him to stay, and agreed that such lights should be procured. On another occasion, Masson, who wanted to obtain his own ticket, asked Darling to acknowledge and credit his time at the wheel; Darling refused, on the grounds that Masson hadn't been hired for that! Again, Masson went to the manager, who confirmed the time spent as part of his qualifications for a certificate. In total, Masson was fired three times by Captain Darling and resigned three more times, but he was always re-engaged at once; evidently Mr. Bush had a high opinion of him. In 1954, Masson obtained his own master's certificate, and the following year he replaced Darling on the *Sea Gull*. At long last, he had found his niche. He loved his vessel intensely, and remained with her to the end. Bothered by the fact that Jenkins had been running the engine room in a slipshod way, Captain Masson engaged Arthur Kelly, originally of Kipawa, Quebec, to take over as engineer. Kelly at once spruced up the engine, steamed out the grimy stokehold, repaired the loose gates on the boiler firebox and the crumbling boiler insulation, and reactivated the hot-well pump for recycling spent steam into the boiler (which Jenkins hadn't bothered to use). Masson also demanded — and got — good coal for the boiler, instead of inferior stuff full of sand. The result was that the *Sea Gull* ran far more efficiently on much less coal, and the firemen had a much easier task of keeping the steam up. As mate, Captain Masson lured back the semi-retired Captain Donald Green, formerly master of the *Screamer*. Green was senior to Masson, but he was no longer interested in supreme command. Thus the *Sea Gull* entered her final years.

Occasionally Captain Green did find himself in charge of the *Sea Gull*. One such time, around 1956, while the vessel was on her way to Callander with Marcel Masson (a brother of "Mac") at the wheel, a storm blew up from the southeast, around 9:00 P.M. In the midst of it the tug grounded on a rock northwest of the Waltonian Inn on the south side of the lake. Marcel got very excited and forgot to signal to shut off the engines, but Captain Green at once hurried to the wheelhouse and gave the order. The steamer was not damaged, but she was caught fast on the rocks, and Green dared not try to back her off, for fear of hitting another rock and shattering the propeller. Instead, he radioed for help. The tug remained stranded all night, but the next day the *Woodchuck* arrived and pulled her off. That was the last time Donald Green took charge of the *Sea Gull*, and soon afterwards he retired.

We shall have more to say about the *Sea Gull* when we are discussing the passenger ships, but first we must briefly acknowledge three more tugs: the *Helen R.* (7.13 tons), a 40-foot screw steamer built at North Bay in 1915 for Thomas Reynolds (the railway conductor who had previously owned the *Annie Laurie*), and subsequently sold to the Gordon Company in 1920; the *May Flower*, a 35-foot craft of unknown registry, said to have been used for sweeping logs early in the 20th century; and the *Ganton D.*, a 56-foot craft built by David Ganton Dobson of the Georgian Bay Shipbuilding and Wrecking Company of Midland in 1924. In 1930, the *Ganton D.* was busy towing logs for the Payette Lumber Company of Callander, but the following winter, while frozen in the ice, the vessel took fire one night and burned to the waterline. Most of the machinery was later sold for scrap, and, in 1978, numerous relics were retrieved and turned into an exhibit at the North Bay Museum. We might add that, in 1898, the Victoria Lumber Company put a 66-foot passenger tug called the *Verva* (37.09 tons) on Lake Wanapitei, northeast of Sudbury; this vessel changed hands in 1925 and burned in 1930.

In 1902, the Tadenac Club of Toronto imported a 40-foot tug called the *Tadenac* (9 tons gross) from Collingwood to Trout Lake, and ran her until about 1914. And finally, in 1904, a little screw tug called the *Torpedo* (5.58 tons) was moved from Toronto to the French River to tow for the George Bruce Lumber Company. The *Torpedo* was 34.4 feet in length, had one deck, and was used until about 1915.

Log towing and steamboating in general, fell into decline on Lake Nipissing during the Depression, but towing and fishing were not the only activities on the lake. For a time, there was actually a revival of the passenger business.

We have seen how the Nipissing passenger steamers were ruined by the two railways as of 1886, and for years afterwards only tugs were available for travellers or excursionists. Yet gradually tourists and sportsmen were attracted to the region, perhaps as a sort of overflow from Muskoka and, meanwhile, a few local people were rich enough to afford a yacht.

One of them was John M. Ferguson, a lumber dealer and real estate speculator who is usually credited with being the founder of North Bay. Ferguson, who later served as mayor (1919–1922), had had the good fortune to be a cousin of Sandy McIntyre of the Canadian Pacific Railway, a connection that apparently inspired him to buy much of the site of North Bay just after the railway arrived. He afterwards made a fortune by selling lots to new arrivals. In 1894, in his wife's name, he bought a very elegant steam yacht called the *Camilla* (26.50 tons), which had been built at Roach's Point on Lake Simcoe four years earlier. The *Camilla* was a deluxe vessel, with fine furnishings and drapes in her cabins. She had a clipper bow and a fantail stern, and the windows of her superstructure and wheelhouse were set at a rakish angle. She was powered by a 75-hp Polson compound engine, and bore a considerable resemblance to the famous Muskoka steam yacht *Naiad*, which was the same length (68 feet) and was built by the Polson Iron Works the same year.

The *Camilla* evidently arrived at North Bay in 1893; the Toronto *Globe* speaks of her as taking J.I. Davidson, of Davidson and Hay, to view the remains of the steamer *John Fraser* the day after the fire. For a time, she was entrusted to Captain Burritt. But in 1897 the Fergusons sold her to a contractor from Copper Cliff, near Sudbury, and, in 1905, she was taken to Little Current on Manitoulin Island. Two years later, she was resold to a fisherman from Killarney, who remodelled her and changed her name to the *Russell Rogue*. In 1931, she burned at Gore Bay.

Perhaps the first actual passenger steamer on the lake following the demise of the *Inter-Ocean* was the *Olive*, which was built at North Bay in 1895. Owned by a syndicate of North Bay businessmen, the *Olive* was 25.6 feet in length, registered 1.11 tons and had a round stern and no decks. She is said to have taken passengers and freight, but nothing is known of her history — except that she foundered around the winter of 1917-18 and was never raised.

Another steamer of this ilk was the *Queen*, an odd-looking little vessel of 12.49 tons. She was built at North Bay in 1899 by Captain McCaw, then newly arrived from Huntsville, and was used to take small parties of passengers and haul provisions in a scow. On October 25, 1899, the little 50.2-foot craft grounded near the Goose Islands, broke her crankshaft and had to be towed into Callander by the *Sparrow*.

In 1904, Captain McCaw left to build and run the *Hazel B*. Perhaps at the same time the *Queen*'s owners decided to move her to Trout Lake. She was operating there in 1910, but in 1919 Captain Windsor would advise the registry office that the *Queen* had been dismantled and left to go to pieces on Trout Lake some years before.

One of the first local men to begin catering seriously to tourists was William Kervin, who came to Callander from Simcoe in 1890. As parties of sportsmen and fishermen started trickling in during the nineties, the energetic Mr. Kervin began arranging fishing trips for them. Soon he also developed camping facilities near Callander. Realizing that better accommodations were needed, around 1900 Kervin built a houseboat on a timber raft for patrons to rent, and would arrange for some local tug to tow it wherever desired; favourite destinations were the West Arm and the French River. This was only the beginning, and soon the busy boat owner had a whole fleet of houseboats, including the *Hiawatha* (built in 1906), the *Shamrock*

ABOVE:

Steam tug Sea Gull *(II)*.
Courtesy Capt. "Mac" Masson

MIDDLE LEFT:

Steam yacht Camilla.   Courtesy
North Himsworth Museum, Callander

MIDDLE RIGHT:

*Captain Michael Joseph
Masson*.   Courtesy Capt. "Mac"
Masson

CANADA   No. 20015

By the Honourable the Minister of Transport for the Dominion of Canada

Certificate of Competency

— AS —

MASTER

of a ——— Tug·Boat ——— in the Minor Waters

To *Michael Joseph Masson*

WHEREAS it has been reported to me that you have been found duly qualified to fulfil
the duties of Master of a ——— Tug·Boat ———
in the Minor Waters,

I do hereby in pursuance of the Canada Shipping Act, 1934, grant you this Certificate
of Competency.

GIVEN under the SEAL of THE MINISTER of TRANSPORT at OTTAWA,

this ——— twelfth ——— day of ——— May ——— , 19 54

Registered
1696   for Deputy Minister of Transport   for Minister of Transport

ABOVE:

Steamers Northern Belle *and* Osprey. *The* Belle *is in her original version, taking an excursion.*

MIDDLE:

Solid Comfort Camp, French River. Courtesy Mr. Roland Bergeron

BELOW:

Houseboat Wasa Lily, *at Callander.*

(1908), and the *Chrysler* and the *Blue Bell* (built around 1910). The houseboats were usually two-storey structures mounted on scows, and equipped with cabins and cookstoves. Generally, they tended to get more elaborate as time went by, until they boasted almost all the comforts of home. Kervin also built or acquired punts, canoes, cottages and motor launches for his customers. Around 1908, for obvious reasons, he led the fight to have net fishing banned on Lake Nipissing.

Inspired by Kervin's success, a few other entrepreneurs, including Thomas Darling of Callander and the Hendrie brothers of Hamilton, also built their own houseboats. Darling's craft was the *Wasa Lily*, which had a canopy over its upper deck to provide shelter from the sun or rain. She was often taken to Darling's Island or other destinations in the tow of the *Zephyr* or the *Spitfire*. Eventually, there were at least eight houseboats on the lake, a few of which were actually converted alligators.

Predictably, the growth of tourism also led to the construction of summer hotels. Early in the twentieth century, the Manitou Summer Hotel was built on the Manitou Islands by a group from North Bay, who (naturally) built a large motor launch as a water taxi, but this venture was not a success: the Manitou Hotel was far too remote and exposed to be popular, especially in the days before motorboats became common, and it was soon closed and demolished. Other hotels, such as the Lighthouse Beach Hotel near Callander, the Waltonian Inn on the south side of the lake, and Tomahawk Lodge (now Chaudière Lodge) on the French River, were more successful. Camps likewise proliferated. The Solid Comfort Camp on the French River was one of the first. The Canadian Pacific Railway opened a bungalow camp around 1924, while North Bay created its own tourist camp at Lakeside Park.

With the tourist industry expanding rapidly, there seemed to be ample opportunity for boat services, especially to the West Arm and the French River, where roads and railways were almost non-existent. The most persistent believer in the Lake Nipissing passenger business was Captain John Ashley Clark.

Captain Clark was the fourth son of John Clark, whose family had forsaken the Maritimes for Simcoe County, where they raised six sons and one daughter. Ashley himself was born in Medonte Township in 1865. During the late 1870s, the Clarks moved up the Nipissing Road, where they established a halfway house and a sawmill around Mecunoma (the "Bummer's Roost"). Then, around 1880, the three older boys trekked farther up the road to scout out the prospects of Sturgeon Falls. Favourably impressed, they returned and persuaded the rest to follow. Taking a sailboat across the lake, they settled on the east side of the river, where they cleared some land and fished. Soon they also built a steam sawmill on Sandy Island, across the lake from Sturgeon Falls, and cut up stray logs. From there they graduated to building punts and rowboats. In time, they also built steamers. Ashley's older brother, Fred Ellsworth Clark, was the family engineer, whose mechanical skills proved invaluable to the enterprise.

The Clarks' first steamer was the *Empress* (27.61 tons), built at Sturgeon Falls (or the island) in 1891. She was 60 feet in length, with one deck and a spoon stern, and is usually described as a tug. For power she had an upright 3.1-hp engine, although she may have been given a large new Bertram compound in 1895. In 1893, the *Empress* is described as being in the towing and fuel business. A widow from Sturgeon Falls seems to have put up some of the money to build her, but by 1904 Captain Clark had become sole owner. In 1896 he also built a 66.5-foot barge called the *Chaudière*, which was probably taken in tow of the *Empress*. The *Chaudière* later became another houseboat.

Late in 1905, the *Empress* was "sold" to the French River and Nipissing Navigation Company, of which Captain Clark was the president. The new firm planned to take settlers and their possessions to remote parts of the lake, like the rising village of Lavigne and to scow provisions and run charters and excursions for the benefit of tourists and local citizens. Nothing more is heard of the *Empress*, and it seems likely that she was dismantled immediately afterwards. Her machinery is said to have been installed in a new passenger steamer the Clarks were then building at Sturgeon Falls.

The new ship was the *Northern Belle*, which for 20 years was undoubtedly the queen of Lake Nipissing. She was an attractive double-decked vessel, with a galley and a dining room on the main deck. With a length of 104 feet and a beam of 21.6, she registered 168.59 tons, which made her the largest steamer ever to sail on the lake, next to the two Booth tugs. She drew three and a half feet of water at the bow and six and a half at the stern. Her compound Bertram engine could deliver 30 net hp, and the inspectors pronounced her one of the best-built boats on the inland waters.

The *Northern Belle* was licensed for 300 passengers, although at first she was primarily a freighter. Once she took one carload of groceries, two carloads of oats, a ton of flour and fourteen tons of hay. Fred Clark briefly acted as engineer, until he left the partnership around 1908 to build and maintain boats at Cache Bay. His place was then taken by his brother William. The steamer, based at Sturgeon Falls, ran picnics to Sandy Island, plus charters to the French River and occasionally did a little towing — apparently she had no fixed schedule. Captain Clark was a very cautious navigator and, with reason, he disliked the West Arm, which is full of rocks and shoals. In 1907, the family built a third steamer, a little 46.8-ton screw tug called the *Ivy Clark* (19.51 tons), which was named for a daughter of the owner, Charles William Clark, Ashley's eldest brother. The *Ivy Clark* plied until 1919, when her owner died. She was afterwards sold to the Marathon Lumber Company of Bigwood, on the lower French River, where she continued to tow logs and scows for another four years. Around 1924, she was dismantled as unfit for further service.

Few competitors faced the *Northern Belle* on Lake Nipissing, and none remained in service very long. Captain McCaw briefly tried it with the *Hazel B.*, and in 1900 Captain William Windsor of Callander, who formerly ran the *Dauntless*, also went into the passenger business by importing the steamer *Van Woodland* from Orillia.

The *Van Woodland* was then a new passenger launch, some 75 feet in length, and intended for the tourist trade on Lake Couchiching. Her rather peculiar name was derived from her owners, T. Vanderlip of Buffalo and Thomas Wood of Orillia. After one not very successful season, the 24.07-ton vessel was sold to Captain Windsor and taken to Callander. Windsor put her to work taking supplies to the French River and running charter excursions, sometimes by moonlight. She also hosted a team of surveyors who were then laying out the route of the proposed ship canal on the French River. The vessel could steam from Callander to North Bay in about 45 minutes. She would greet any other steamer with a long blast on the whistle, followed by two short ones, but such encounters were rare.

Thanks to the late Mr. Bill Johnston of Callander, a few incidents in the *Van Woodland*'s brief career are still known. In 1902, Johnston was hired to run the engines and "wood-up" the firebox on the steamer; he and Captain Windsor were the entire crew. (He was paid $2 per day, plus board.) One weekend, the vessel was chartered to take a couple of families fishing at the French River. It proved a singularly unlucky trip. They left Callander around 11:00 A.M., but the propeller soon became ensnarled with bark and other debris. It took hours to untangle it. The wind began blowing and Captain Windsor, finding his passengers unwilling to cancel the outing, cautiously took refuge near an island at the mouth of Callander Bay, where they spent the entire night. (The passengers had brought their own sleeping bags.) The following day, they reached the French River, but late in the day another windstorm came up and the steamer took refuge amid the islands in South Bay, where they spent a second night. By then, food was running short, and Johnston was sent in a small boat to Nipissing village to fetch more. It was dark by the time he returned, and meanwhile the passengers had left for Nipissing, where they arranged a ride back to Callander, leaving Captain Windsor alone on the boat. He was not in a very good humour. Late that night, he asked for a "mickey," but there wasn't even any liquor left! Not until late the next day did the *Van Woodland* return to Callander.

Another time, the big launch was returning to Callander late at night, and Johnston tried using a pike pole to fend the bow off the dock. The whistle erupted with long, continuous blasts! Captain Windsor shouted at him, "What're you trying to do?" It turned out that the other end of the pole was caught in the whistle cord.

Johnston returned for the 1903 season, to find that the steamer had been converted to coal firing. There were more adventures that year. In late June, the vessel grounded on a rock near Moose Bay and had to be rescued by the *Sparrow*. Johnston soon became discouraged by the irregular work hours (once, he had to spend most of the night helping the captain fend the vessel off the dock during rough weather), plus periodic intervals when there was no work — to say nothing of bedbugs! — and part way through the season, he quit. Bill Johnston never returned to the boats again.

At the end of the 1906 season, Captain Windsor sold the *Van Woodland* to the Clarks. But he was not yet ready to abandon steamboating, and sometime afterwards he acquired the small steamer *Albino*, of which little is known, except that she was about 40 feet in length and licensed for ten passengers in 1910. Later, he sold the *Albino* and bought the *Hazel B.*, which, as we have seen, lasted until about 1920. Later still, he commanded a supply boat from Sturgeon Falls. In 1923, Captain Windsor retired, and passed on in 1927, at the age of 78.

The Clarks, meanwhile, gave the *Van Woodland* a complete rebuild, and when they were finished she was unrecognizable. What emerged from the yards was an attractive little double-decker, with an additional hurricane deck, and in 1907 she was officially renamed the *Highland Belle*. The *Highland Belle* was still 75 feet in length, but she had been widened to 16.8 feet and now grossed 50 tons. She was licensed for 40 passengers and was initially commanded by Captain Wellington Green. Her career is poorly documented, but we know that she plied regularly from Sturgeon Falls to all parts of the lake. On August 14, 1911, Captain Green told his logbook that he had pulled the *Highland Belle* off a rock in the Little French River (probably using the *Sparrow*). On another occasion, the *Belle* ran aground near Lonely Island, at a time when the captain was having dinner and a subordinate was at the wheel. Again, the *Sparrow*, then en route to Frank's Bay, arrived and pulled her off without difficulty. And on November 20, 1911 (when the waters were probably low), the *Highland Belle* got stuck on the bottom at the railway wharf at Callander and again had to be rescued. Apparently, she was trapped by ice in Callander Bay that same winter; on April 29th, Thomas Darling noted that the ice was still too thick to allow her and the *Sparrow* to leave.

About this time, a great many settlers were taking up land around the west end of Lake Nipissing, south of Verner on the Canadian Pacific Railway. Many of them were French Canadians from Michigan, who were lured in by Père (Father) Charles Alfred Paradis, a former Oblate missionary who had earlier played a great part in promoting settlement in Témiscamingue, Quebec, of which more in the next chapter. By the 1890s, there were several tiny hamlets established on both sides of Lake Nipissing's North West Bay. A bridge was built across the bay in 1908, and a church followed in 1914. In that year, a post office, called Lavigne after the parish priest, was opened. Accessible by boat from Sturgeon Falls, Lavigne soon emerged as an attractive little village, complete with a sawmill, general store, blacksmith shop, and, later, a cheese factory.

In 1895, meanwhile, Cyrille Monette, originally of Longueil, Quebec, arrived from Sturgeon Falls and began developing a settlement south of Lavigne at Shanty Lake, about four miles from the end of the West Arm. Originally called Martland, it was soon renamed Monetville in his honour. Amongst his other services to the region, Monette ran a sailboat from the West Arm to Sturgeon Falls (a distance of 28 miles) to bring in supplies and settlers, and arranged to have several new townships surveyed. Before long Monetville sprouted a school, hotel, post office and store, and in 1909, Monette persuaded the government to grant money to blast two short channels to link Shanty Lake with the West Arm. Thus Shanty Lake became Shanty Bay, an extension of the West Arm. The channels were opened in 1914, and led to the establishment of a sawmill at Monetville. Nonetheless it came as a bitter blow to Cyrille Monette when, in 1914, the regional church was built west of his settlement at the upstart village of Cosby (now Noëlville), which meant that Noëlville soon became the commercial centre for the region.

As early as 1906, steamers were plying from Sturgeon Falls to the government dock north of Monetville, and also to Lavigne. (In winter supplies had to be cadged overland from Verner or Rutter station on the Canadian Pacific Railway using sleighs.) The *Highland Belle* was sometimes known to ply three times a week to the new settlements, but she was not permitted to monopolize this route. That same year, two Sturgeon Falls residents, Henry Elwood McKee, a lawyer, and Captain Charles Britton, a self-taught building contractor and boatman, formed a partnership and founded the Nipissing Navigation Company to take freight and passengers to and from the West Arm and the French River — in other words, to compete with the Clarks. To accomplish this, they, like Captain Windsor, imported a large steam launch from Lake Simcoe. This vessel was the *Elgin L. Lewis* (30.40 tons), which had been built at Orillia in 1904 and used for a year for excursion cruises. The *Elgin L. Lewis* was a top-heavy craft, some 70 feet in length by a mere 12.3 feet in beam, and quickly displayed an alarming tendency to roll, especially in rough weather. This spoiled her reputation, and she was soon shipped off to Lake Nipissing. Here she was put to work freighting cheese, vegetables and blueberries from Lavigne and Monetville, and sometimes towing logs. She was also licensed to take 40 passengers. On May 8, 1914, she brought the family of Michael Purcell from Sturgeon Falls to Monetville, through the newly opened channels, towing a scowload of furniture, livestock, poultry and all their personal effects. The trip took from noon to sunset.

The *Elgin L. Lewis* plied for several years, and was sometimes known to race the *Sparrow* to the French River. (She usually won!) But she was not a popular boat. She continued to roll in rough weather or when towing, and in fact had at least four different captains in ten years, including Albert McKenney, Dan May of Huntsville, and (in 1914) Charles Williams. After just two seasons, the boat went to the Traders' Bank (now part of the Royal), probably because of unpaid debts. Then, in March 1910, she was sold to Captain Clark's line, which now owned both the *Belle*s, a houseboat called the *Dundonald* (63.90 tons) and perhaps the little *Osprey*.

The French River and Nipissing Navigation Company did not long outlast its rival. It enjoyed the support of many shareholders, including Sir John and William Hendrie of Hamilton, who liked to spend their holidays around Sturgeon Falls, and who often engaged the company to tow their houseboats to the French River. But the firm was apparently disappointed in the local patronage, and besides that, many excursions were spoiled by bad weather. In 1913, there were rumours afoot that the *Northern Belle* was unsafe. Inspectors arrived unexpectedly from Ottawa to examine her, and concluded that she was not only staunch and seaworthy, but could also carry another deck! But by the fall of 1914, perhaps disheartened by the outbreak of the First World War and the disruption this must have caused, Captain Clark decided to call it quits, although he continued to run a few small steamers as late as 1930. His company did not surrender its charter until 1923.

No doubt getting wind of Clark's decision, a syndicate including many of the shareholders of the old company promptly formed a new one, which they called the Lake Nipissing Shipping and Transportation Company. This firm, which received its charter on August 21, 1914, was headed by Frank E. MacDonald of Newcastle. By September, it had purchased the *Elgin L. Lewis*, the *Dundonald* and the two *Belle*s, and promptly shifted their home base from Sturgeon Falls to North Bay. Apparently, they also gave the *Northern Belle* a hurricane deck and moved her pilothouse up to the third deck — which made her far more impressive than before. A new lounge cabin, and perhaps a few staterooms, were also added to the second deck. Now commanded by the tall, genial Captain Albert McKenney, who had been working on the Nipissing boats since 1884, the *Northern Belle* was licensed to carry an extra 50 passengers. She became an institution on Lake Nipissing, and the pride and despair of her owners.

The new company stepped into the shoes of the old, and earnestly tried to make a success of steamboating. It also bought Great Manitou Island and used it as a picnic ground. But the war was on, the season was essentially confined to the summer months, and most of the patronage came from American tourists. The lodges and fishing camps on the French River were largely dependent on the boats, but their patrons were too few. Moonlight cruises with

ABOVE:
Steamers Northern Belle, Highland Belle *and* Elgin L. Lewis. *The three vessels are docked at Sturgeon Falls, circa 1910.* Courtesy Mrs. Rita Moon

BELOW:
Steamer Elgin L. Lewis *at Monetville, circa 1912.* Courtesy North Himsworth Museum, Callander

music and dancing were tried in an effort to attract the local people, but few came; the service was unappreciated.

After just a few seasons, the *Highland Belle* was withdrawn from service, and soon went the way of all boats. In or around 1917, the *Elgin L. Lewis* was also dismantled. In the spring of 1916, the *Northern Belle* was sold to yet another new firm calling itself the North Bay and French River Navigation Company, which was basically the old concern trying again under a different name. It managed to stagger on for another seven years, but always at a loss. In 1919, during the off-season, a vandal raided the ship one night, smashed most of the dishes and ruined the compass. More stringent security measures were adopted to avoid a repeat of the incident.

During the 1920s, we hear more about the *Northern Belle*, thanks to the files of the North Bay *Nugget*. On September 30, 1921, a violent storm lashed spray over the top decks of the steamer, which fortunately was lying at her dock at the time. Pieces of debris were later found embedded in her railings. Another time, Captain McKenney reported seeing a waterspout on the lake, which sucked up some of the coal smoke from the ship. Fortunately, the spout was about half a mile astern. In July of 1922, the steamer was immobilized for a couple of days with engine trouble, but on the 27th she was able to take about 65 tourists to the Solid Comfort Fishing Club camp on the French River. That same season, she towed the houseboat *Sunbeam* over to the French for a camping trip, and late in August she was busy bringing campers and cottagers back from the river. After Labour Day, the only remaining cottagers were those who had their own private motorboats. In September, she was busy scowing cords of hardwood into town, and on the 15th she hosted members of the Toronto Board of Trade on a tour around the river.

Despite all this activity, the North Bay Navigation Company, like its predecessors, declared bankruptcy in 1923. Still another syndicate was formed, now calling itself the Northern Navigation Company, to give it another try. One of its shareholders, F.A. York, was appointed president. This proved the final effort. The new firm, which owned a half interest in the marine railway at Callander, spent $4,000 in replanking about 75 percent of the steamer's hull, plus other repairs, partly to counter further rumours that she was not safe. Not until August 9th was she relaunched. Several hundred people were on hand to watch, including all the directors, but when the shoring blocks were removed, the *Northern Belle* just sat on the ways. Horses were tried, but failed to move her. The *Sea Gull* then came over with blocks, and tackle, but to no avail. Then the *Screamer* joined in, and finally, around 3:30 in the afternoon, the *Northern Belle* slid into her proper element, amid the cheers of the crowd.

The *Northern Belle* re-entered service a few days later, sailing from North Bay to the Solid Comfort Camp on Wednesdays and Saturdays and to Chaudière Falls (a 40-mile trip) on Sundays, Mondays and Thursdays. The other days were set aside for charters. On August 12th, she encountered a violent thunderstorm while returning from the French River, causing passengers to scurry for cover. Many became seasick and clung miserably to the railings amid huge waves. The gale turned into a hailstorm as it moved inland, dropping ice pellets as big as golf balls. Amidst it all, a fire started in the ship's galley where the supper was under way, but it was promptly put out. The officers rode out the storm without difficulty, and by the time she returned to dock, the lake was calm again. Indeed, only once did Captain McKenney ever have to "lie in" because of a blow, in late August 1922, when the *Northern Belle* sought refuge overnight at Lech's Bay.

As usual, the 1923 season was not a good one for the *Northern Belle*, although she reputedly paid for her operating expenses for the first time ever! In part, the weather was to blame for her troubles. The seasons of 1923 and 1924 were largely chilly and cool, and repeatedly we read of picnics and excursions being postponed or attracting few patrons for exactly that reason. Nineteen twenty-five was her best year, and entailed outings by the North Bay Board of Trade, the Bell Telephone Company staffs, and various schools, including those at Sturgeon Falls, but even so, the *Belle* could never seem to earn a profit. Tourists and cottagers from the cities to the south were simply too few in number, and most of the local people weren't interested. Finally, in the spring of 1926, the Northern Navigation Company announced that it would not be running the *Northern Belle* that year; the costs were just too great. Instead, it would obtain a smaller vessel, with a capacity of 40 passengers, to service the camps and cottages. There was talk of moving the ship to other waters, but as it happened her time had already run out.

Before sunrise on the morning of Monday, June 26, 1926, some workmen at the Canadian Pacific Railway shops near the North Bay waterfront noticed a fire on the *Northern Belle* as she lay at the government wharf. They immediately called the fire department, but the nearest hydrants were too far away. Then the Ontario forestry service was summoned, along with two gas pumps, but by then it was too late. A crackling inferno, fanned by an off-shore wind, was devouring the steamer. To save the wharf, the forestry launch towed her away and beached her in shallow water. Two small explosions tore at the dying ship, which burned down to the waterline and then sank. The loss was reckoned at $12,800, though the boat was fairly well insured. A cigarette butt tossed by a passing tramp was suspected of causing the blaze, but perhaps the truth was that she simply gave up and committed suicide. One feels that she deserved a better fate.

True to its promise, the Northern Navigation Company imported a new steam cruiser, at almost the same moment that the *Northern Belle* met her end. This was the *Lotus* (17.68 tons), a 52-foot craft built at Detroit in 1906 and used hitherto as a rich man's yacht around Beaumaris on Lake Muskoka. She was a fairly speedy coal burner, with a triple-expansion 10.2-hp engine. Her design was intermediate between a traditional steam yacht and a more modern cabin cruiser, with mahogany cabins and a square stern. On her arrival at Callander she seems to have been fitted out with a wheelhouse and two lifeboats. Perhaps she was also lengthened (to 68 feet) at the same time. By July 13th, she was in service, taking supplies and some passengers to the French River, with Captain McKenney at the wheel. A week later the Northern Navigation Company began advertising that the steamer *Lotus* would leave North Bay for Tomahawk Lodge and Chaudière Falls five days a week at 9:30 A.M., returning at 8:00 P.M. On Saturdays she would depart at 1:30, and on Sundays at 10:30.

The *Lotus* sank at her moorings on the night of September 25th, after season's end; only her lines kept her stern afloat. The following year (1927), she was renamed the *Miami Beach*, but she was still plagued with accidents. One time she struck a rock near the French River, and Captain McKenney had to run her ashore in shallow water. The passengers were soon picked up, and later the launch was salvaged by an alligator and two scows — fish were found inside! Worse followed around 1931, when her boiler exploded, apparently with no loss of life. She was then re-engined and fitted out with a 45-hp Fairbanks-Morse diesel. So equipped, she continued to ply until 1940, when fire claimed her.

On the West Arm, meanwhile, a supply boat service was established in 1918 by the firm of Michaud and Levesque, owners of the largest store in Sturgeon Falls. This move followed the disappearance of the Clark and Britton boat lines a few years earlier. The steamer used was the *Queen of Temagami* (24.70 tons), which, as her name implies, was built on Lake Temagami in 1909. Her original activities are described in Chapter 5. Here we need only say that she was a 71.5-foot screw vessel with a steel frame and a powerful triple-expansion engine and was licensed for 40 passengers. The vessel, entrusted to Captain Bill Windsor, probably entered service in 1919 (mainly as a freighter), despite the fact that the Michaud and Levesque store was gutted by fire that year. For five seasons, she was the only direct link with Lavigne, Monetville and Noëlville. It is said that cables had to be used regularly to help the *Queen of Temagami* get through the newly blasted channel running into Monetville.

The business seems to have prospered. By 1921, the firm had rebuilt its store into the largest in Northern Ontario, and the local economy was booming. But in October 1922, a macadamized gravel road was opened from Verner, about ten miles west of Sturgeon Falls, to Noëlville, thus breaking the isolation of the West Arm settlements, and hence it is not surprising that the *Queen of Temagami* was sold off the following September. She went to the

Upper Ottawa Improvement Company, whose business was exclusively towing logs, and became a provision boat on Lake Temiskaming. We shall find her there in Chapter 6.

Very few people around Lake Nipissing seem to have owned a private steamboat, but Dr. W.C. Pedlar was an exception. He was a self-reliant physician, credited with bringing several hundred babies into the world. In 1923, he purchased a large steam launch called the *Canna* (6.73 tons) from Brockville, and used her to commute to his island at the mouth of the Sturgeon River, where he kept a garden. Built in 1915, the *Canna* was 39 feet in length, and in "Doc" Pedlar's day had a cabin amidships. She remained in service at least until 1937, but was out of commission by 1946.

The Clark steamboat service, meanwhile, persisted into the 1920s. Sometime after 1917, Captain John Clark built another 50-foot tug called the *Elgin Lewis* (II), which probably inherited the engines of her namesake. He used her as he had the others: towing, scowing, and taking passengers. She ran the occasional picnic to Sandy Island, as of old, and sometimes towed the Hendrie houseboats from Sturgeon Falls. In May of 1924, however, Clark sold the *Elgin Lewis* to Herbert Baker (also known as Herman Mutchenbaker), of the Marathon Lumber Company, for $3,700. The vessel was then taken to Bigwood on a Canadian Pacific Railway flatcar, where she replaced the *Ivy Clark*. She lasted until April 13, 1937, when fire claimed her at her dock. That same year, Mr. Baker ceased to operate the Bigwood mill, which was leased to other parties.

Captain John Ashley Clark did not live that long. He retired after selling the *Elgin Lewis* (II) and passed away on July 26, 1931, at Sturgeon Falls, having spent at least 34 years on the lake.

Steamers continued to ply from Sturgeon Falls, thanks to Captain Britton and Henry McKee. During the 1920s, they purchased the attractive little steamer *Modello* (29.47 tons), which had been built at Kingston in 1915 and used briefly on Lake Simcoe. Named after Maude and Ella, two daughters of the president of the short-lived Lake Simcoe Navigation Company, the *Modello* was shipped north by rail and began plying from Sturgeon Falls to the French River and elsewhere, taking freight, passengers and mail. No meals were provided, and patrons would usually bring their own lunches. Sometimes she also towed pulpwood logs into Sturgeon Falls. Around 1928, Captain Britton also built the Memquisit ("hidden bay") Lodge on the French River, and usually once a week the steamer would call, bringing fresh provisions and perhaps up to 35 new guests, who would commonly stay about two weeks. The *Modello* was 66.4 feet in length by 12.2 in beam, and had two decks and an elliptic stern. Her fore-and-aft compound engine and boiler came from the old Kawartha steamer *North Star* (1895), and gave her a speed of ten knots. She had no regular captain, but Charles Williams once took charge, and later Stewart Hicks and sometimes Captain Britton himself.

Always a tireless worker, Captain Britton eventually injured his hip, and when his health began to fail, he was obliged to sell the *Modello* in 1941 to the Nipissing Navigation Company (probably a continuation of his own firm), which seems to have replaced the North Bay and French River line at about that time. The steamer's home port was now shifted to North Bay, where she became the successor to the *Miami Beach*, which had just burned. Probably in the name of economy and efficiency, the new owners also replaced the *Modello*'s engines with a new 125-hp Cummins diesel at the same time. Now commanded by Captain William J. Rowe of North Bay, who had succeeded McKenney on the *Miami Beach* after the latter's death in 1936, the *Modello* became the provision boat for the French River camps and lodges that were as yet unserviced by roads.

By this time, steamboats had almost disappeared on Lake Nipissing, killed off by the Depression, the decline in lumbering, the advent of new roads and their attendant trucks and automobiles, and the competition of private motor launches. Some of these were purchased by the Ojibwas who had made money selling timber. The little tug *Zephyr* perished by fire in 1938, after over half a century of service, while the dieselizing of the *Modello* in 1941 left only the tug *Sea Gull (II)* and the alligator *Woodchuck* still running under steam.

ABOVE:

Steamer Northern Belle *on Lake Nipissing.* Courtesy Nipissing Archives, North Bay Area Museum

BELOW LEFT:

Steamer Queen of Temagami *at Sturgeon Falls. The vessel appears with two scows and an unidentified steamer at left.* Courtesy Sturgeon Falls Police Department

BELOW MIDDLE:

Steamer Modello, *near the French River.* Courtesy Mrs. Shirley Muir Speers

BELOW RIGHT:

Diesel launch Miami Beach *(ex-steamer* Lotus). Courtesy Mr. Gordon Restoule

Meanwhile, a most unexpected event occurred at the tiny village of Corbeil, near Callander, in the spring of 1934, right in the midst of the Great Depression — an event that would accidentally bestow a little welcome prosperity on the local scene. On May 28th of that year, five baby girls were born at the humble home of Oliva and Elzire Dionne, and, more amazing still, all five survived — for the first time in medical history. The news spread like wildfire, all over Canada and the United States, and for years afterwards thousands of motorists braved the dusty winding road to Callander to catch a glimpse of the five little tots at play. The Dionne quintuplets became the largest tourist attraction in Canada, and a $500,000,000 asset to the Province of Ontario, which chose to make them wards of the state to protect them from exploitation. The country doctor who delivered them found himself a celebrity. Hollywood even made movies about it. The onslaught certainly woke up the depressed little village of Callander, which had been especially hard hit by fires that destroyed almost all its mills and (in 1931) much of the business section as well.

One beneficiary of the whole situation was the Armstrong Towing Company, which had been operating at a loss at the time; its tug, the *Sea Gull*, was idle in 1933. The firm suddenly announced that the *Sea Gull* would take passengers on sightseeing cruises from Callander to Keystone Camp and Lunge Lodge, with flagstops at Lighthouse Island, Manitou Island and Frank's Bay (and sometimes at Tomahawk Lodge and the Akron Club), leaving at 10:30 A.M. daily — for the fare of $2. These were one-day trips, with light refreshments offered, and sometimes there was a stop at Chaudière Falls, where patrons could admire the scenic vistas from the top of the dam. (They were also assured that they could see the "quints" the same day!) Whenever the vessel was crowded with over 100 people, the owners would engage a friendly exiled aristocratic Englishman, Sir Henry Jervis of Callander, who happened to have the necessary certificate, to act as honorary captain — while Captain Darling did the actual work! In 1940, however, the John B. Smith Company bought the *Sea Gull* to replace the *Screamer* and the vessel became a towboat once again.

At the end of the war, the Ontario Northland Transportation Commission, which had been assigned the task of servicing the French River area and Lake Temagami by boat (in addition to running the Ontario Northland Railway), bought out the Nipissing Navigation Company and all its assets. Included was the *Modello* which ran for one more season before being shipped to Lake Temagami, where we shall find her again in Chapter 5.

Her successor was the 98.7-foot motor vessel, *Chief Commanda*, which was built at Trenton and assembled at Callander in 1946. Steel hulled, with two decks and a round stern, the *Chief Commanda* had two eight-cylinder diesel engines, carried 210 passengers, and took a crew of ten. She plied faithfully from North Bay wharf to the French River resorts until 1975, first under Captain Darling, then under the gentlemanly Captain William Rowe of North Bay until his sudden death in August 1961, and finally under his son, Captain Lorne Rowe. The "Chief" was retired in 1975 and handed over to the Dokis native band, who have a reserve on the French River, for use as a museum and restaurant. Not much came of this idea, however, and in 1992, the *Chief Commanda* was brought back to North Bay, beached in a concrete pad, and converted into a summertime restaurant near the city marina. She has been serving in that capacity ever since.

Her place has been taken by the *Chief Commanda II*, an aluminum double-hulled catamaran-type cruiser powered by four turbo-charged engines made in Gothenburg, Sweden, in 1975. She is 98 feet in length and can cruise very smoothly at about 15 miles per hour. Just lately, however, the Ontario Northland has announced that it might not run the *Chief Commanda II* any more; it loses too much money, and most of the lodges now have their own boats. (She ran again in 1995, thanks to the North Bay City Council, which was unwilling to lose one of its prime tourist attractions.)

The steamers, of course, are long gone. The last to go was the *Sea Gull*. The big tug was idle in 1954, and before the end she was unwisely shortened at the stern, with the result that her huge propeller was too close to the surface, and the crew had to ballast her with pig iron. Despite this indignity, she gave good service up until 1961. But then the John B. Smith

ABOVE:

Steam tug Sea Gull, *on the ways at Callander.* Courtesy Capt. "Mac" Masson

BELOW:

Tug Sea Gull, *being replanked at Callander.* Courtesy Capt. "Mac" Masson

Company decided to replace her with a diesel tug called the *Siskin* until the late 1960s, when it proved cheaper to bring logs in by truck than by boat. (In 1968, the firm shut down its mill at Callander and withdrew to Toronto to enter the wholesale lumber business.)

In 1961, the company offered the *Sea Gull* to the City of North Bay as a museum piece, and suggested that she might make an excellent passenger excursion ship. But the City Council, indifferent to its heritage, refused to take her. The famous tug was then taken back to Callander for the last time and cut up with chain saws. Her machinery still exists (in private hands) but the timbers were burned. To many an onlooker, it seemed a crime; she was still in perfect condition. On that melancholy note ended the steamboat era on Lake Nipissing, after a duration of 80 years.

Today, there is little to remind us of the Nipissing steamers. Here and there, abandoned in the bush, one can still find the rusting, mouldering remains of an alligator, or the skeletal timbers of some wreck in the shallows or depths of the lake. A number of modest photographs and a few relics still remain in private hands or at some local repository: the North Bay Area Museum now owns the rudder from the *John Fraser* and the propeller shaft from the *Northern Belle*. And in October 1994, as a gesture of atonement, a panel mounted with several brass plaques was officially unveiled at a park in Callander, honouring the vanished *Sea Gull*. The guest of honour at the ceremony was, fittingly, Michael Joseph Masson, now the last of the Nipissing steamboat captains. The boats are gone and their whistles are silent — but they are not entirely forgotten.

Motor vessel Chief Commanda *(II), preparing for another cruise.*
Courtesy Nipissing Archives, North Bay Area Museum

~~~~~~

From this point on, we shall focus on the regions north of Lake Nipissing. Let us begin with the timber trade around Lake Temiskaming.

53

Squaring timber near the Jocko River, Nipissing District, circa 1912. Photo by W.D. Watt, from the Booth Family Collection, courtesy National Archives of Canada, PA 121799

CHAPTER 2

STEAMBOATS
AND LUMBERING

During the 19th century, the lumber trade was big business in Canada. It was, in fact, the only type of enterprise that transcended the local scene in pre-industrial times, often spreading its operations over hundreds of square miles of bush. Like the fur trade before it, the timber trade created camps and depots deep in the forests, always following the natural waterways, which alone could provide the means of floating out logs and freighting in supplies. Unlike the fur trade, however, lumbering came to employ hundreds of men and animals, and often dominated the local economy with its immense demands for hay, foodstuffs and labour. Entire regions of the country were to depend on the lumber trade.

The first Canadian sawmills did their cutting for a very limited local market, but, as it happened, an outside market was artificially created as early as 1806. At that time the French Emperor Napoleon was almost at the height of his power, with only Great Britain still able to defy him, shielded as she was by the English Channel and her invincible navy. Unable to strike directly at his insular adversaries, Napoleon retaliated with his Berlin Decrees, which aimed at closing every port in Europe to British trade. This meant — among other things — that Britain could no longer obtain Russian or Swedish timber and hemp for her all-important fleet. As a result, the British turned to Canada for the necessary timber, promising Canadian lumbermen preferred access to the British market even after the Napoleonic wars came to an end. Many Canadians responded to the opportunity, though the risks and difficulties were immense: the organizational problems were stupendous, prices fluctuated widely, and the lumber mechants never got paid until the timber was cut, hauled to the lakes and rivers, floated to the nearest seaports, loaded aboard sailing ships, and finally delivered to the United Kingdom. As early as 1809, Philemon Wright, the founder of Hull, Quebec, was demonstrating the practicality of floating huge timber rafts down the Ottawa River to Montreal, and on to Quebec City.

At that time, the British demand was entirely for square timber, not sawn lumber, mainly because "sticks" of squared timber could be packed away neatly inside the hull of a sailing ship without shifting. Squaring the timber was always done in the bush where the trees were felled, and soon many French-Canadian axemen were expert at it. The trade was exceedingly wasteful, since much of the wood in every tree was whittled away into chips, and besides, the British were extremely choosy about what they would buy. No knots or flaws were tolerated and many a noble pine was cut down and left to rot in the bush because of some slight defect. Not that anyone particularly cared; in those days everyone took for granted that the forests were limitless and would last forever.

Until the mid-19th century, most Canadian timber exports went to Britain, but then a new market opened up south of the border. The Americans, pushing steadily into the regions south of the Great Lakes, were rapidly depleting the pine forests of Ohio and Michigan in an effort to satisfy the voracious demands of their cities for lumber and firewood. As American timber began to run short, attention shifted north of the Great Lakes towards Canada West (now Ontario). Aided, no doubt, by the Reciprocity Treaty of 1854 (which remained in effect until 1866), American lumbermen pushed inland, mostly from Georgian Bay, opening camps and mills and floating their wood across Lake Huron, until the extension of the railways into the Canadian Shield gave them the option of exporting by way of Toronto. Unlike the British, the Americans wanted sawn lumber, not squared timber, and they were prepared to accept whatever they could get, even if some of it was less than perfect. However, few American firms were active in Timiskaming, which forms part of the upper Ottawa River watershed, and which was accordingly exploited mostly from the lower Ottawa Valley, notably by such famous old firms as the Gillies Brothers of Braeside, the McLachlin Brothers of Arnprior, E.B. Eddy of Hull, and the J.R. Booth Company of Ottawa. One result of all this was the persistence of the square-timber trade in this region until around the turn of the century, well after it had petered out in most other parts of the country.

The first lumbermen to begin cutting square timber around Lake Temiskaming were the McConnell brothers of Aylmer, who set up a few camps opposite Point Opimica, on the Ontario side, as early as 1836. Four years later, the Hudson's Bay Company began cutting near Fort Temiskaming and Opimica. But these operations were premature. There were no railways in the Ottawa Valley at that time (or anywhere else in Ontario), and few settlements west of Arnprior. The only steamboats on the river above Bytown (Ottawa) were the *Lady Colborne*, a sidewheeler which plied from Aylmer to Fitzroy Harbour from 1833 until the 1840s, and the slightly smaller *George Buchanan*, which offered a somewhat erratic service from Arnprior to the Chenaux, or Snows, Rapids north of Renfrew three times a week, from 1836 until 1847. Beyond this point, organized transport facilities simply did not exist. Because of these problems (and low prices), logging was suspended in Timiskaming in 1843.

It was not until 1860 that another concerted effort was made to cut timber in Timiskaming. By that time, the pineries of the lower Ottawa Valley were thinned out, and the headwaters of the river beckoned again. In that year, Richard McConnell and his brothers tried again and engaged two French Canadians, J.B. Jolicœur and Joseph Bonin of Beauharnois, to open up three bush camps near Pointe à la Barbe. In 1862, Édouard Piché, financed by Thomas Murray, the presiding genius of the rising town of Pembroke, began cutting in the Township of Guigues, around the northeast side of Lake Temiskaming on the Quebec side. By the time the Oblate missionaries arrived in 1863, they found five camps in operation. By 1866, the McLarens of Ottawa were at work on the Ontario side, and about that time a squatter named Humphrey built a depot about five miles south of Wabi Bay, at what later became the Town of Haileybury. He afterwards put up another at the future site of Laniel, Quebec, where the Kipawa River begins its exit from Lake Kipawa. Provisioning the depots must have been done by canoe or sailboat, since nothing else was available on Lake Temiskaming.

It appears that the first man actually to build a sawmill on Lake Temiskaming was a French Canadian named Olivier Latour of Hull, whose brother Camille was busy teaming in freight and passengers along the Ottawa River from Deux Rivières to Mattawa as early as 1863. Olivier Latour seems to have started out in business by buying furs and selling provisions to the Nishnabis on Lake Kipawa, where he established a depot at the site of the modern Kipawa village. The most profitable item was hard liquor, and Latour was clever enough to get around legal prohibitions by setting up his store on a barge moored offshore. (Since his premises were not on dry land, the usual restrictions did not apply.) In 1873, he engaged one Frederick Watt of Pembroke to erect a sawmill on Latour's Creek, about four miles south of the mouth of the Kipawa River. It was a water-powered mill, with a dam to assure the necessary power. Slab piles from the mill were still obvious as late as the 1930s. At this site, Latour could exploit the pineries, not only around Lake Temiskaming, but also from the basin of Lake Kipawa, where he purchased a number of berths, or limits. In time, he had most of the local settlers (who were very few in number) engaged in cutting for him, while he himself no doubt accepted "jobbing" contracts to supply logs and lumber to the larger lumber companies.

We must presume that business was very slow at first, since there were few local customers for lumber, and — worse — the markets abroad were paralyzed during the 1870s by a catastrophic depression. But by 1878, the depression had lifted, the number of settlers was growing, and Mr. Latour was able to open a second mill ten miles upstream from Mattawa.

Things looked so promising that, in 1884, one Allan Grant felt encouraged to build a mill at North Temiskaming (now Notre-Dame-du-Nord), at the head of the lake.

It was under these circumstances that Olivier Latour decided on yet another pioneering venture. In the summer of 1882, he placed the first steamboat on the waters of Lake Temiskaming.

The steamer was the *Mattawan*, a 50-foot screw vessel built in 1876. Registered at 15.25 tons, the *Mattawan* had a single full-length deck, a hurricane deck surmounting the cabins, a square stern, and a 15-hp upright high-pressure engine. She was probably built expressly for her owner, Captain Bernard I. Mulligan of Mattawa, whose family had been very active on the Ottawa River boats. (One of his relatives, Captain David Mulligan, for a time command-ed the steamer *Emerald* on Lake Deschênes for the Union Forwarding and Railway Company, which by 1868 had gained a near-monopoly of shipping on the great river.) Bernard himself probably entered the service of the Union Forwarding and Railway Company by taking com-mand of the little steamer *Kippawa* on the upper Ottawa River, between Tait's Landing, near Des Joachims ("Da Swisha," as the English mispronounced it), and Rocher Capitaine in 1871. (Another steamer, the *Deux Rivières*, provided a further link to Deux Rivières by 1872.) In 1876, probably with the blessings of the Union Forwarding and Railway Company, Captain Mulligan bought the *Mattawan*, then newly built at Portsmouth (now a suburb of Kingston), and brought her up to the Ottawa River, presumably by way of the Rideau Waterway. Here she was put to work, running from the rapids at Deux Rivières to Mattawa, a route of about 22 miles. (In winter the traffic was handled by sleighs.) Mattawa was then only a tiny village, with barely a few dozen inhabitants, many of whom worked at the local Hudson's Bay Company post, but no doubt they all welcomed the arrival of the steamer.

For six seasons, the *Mattawan* plied back and forth, delivering mail, taking groups of up to 60 passengers (mostly lumberjacks heading for the camps around the Mattawa and L'Amable du Fond Rivers, Lake Nosbonsing and Antoine Creek), scowing hay, lumber and foodstuffs and, no doubt, towing logs downstream. But already change was in the air. During the 1870s, the Canada Central Railway, soon to become part of the Canadian Pacific, was gradually extending its tracks up the Ottawa River. By 1879, it had completed the ruin of the Union Forwarding and Railway Company, which soon went out of business, except for tow-ing logs. By 1880, it was also encroaching on the *Matttawan*'s route, and the following year, the rails actually reached Mattawa village. The steamer, now redundant, was taken out of ser-vice, and this gave Olivier Latour his chance. He formally purchased her in July of 1882, but even before then he had the engines and machinery removed at Mattawa, and, in the spring, engaged a crew of twenty men to move her up the river to Lake Temiskaming.

It was not an easy task. In 1882, Père Charles Alfred Paradis, an Oblate missionary from France, who was soon to become an avid proponent of settlement in Témiscamingue, hap-pened to be passing that way on an exploration trip and, according to his diaries, he and his companions agreed to help move the *Mattawan* upriver in return for transportation on Lake Temiskaming. He soon had cause to regret the offer. The *Mattawan* had to be rowed up the stretches of calm water and winched up the various rapids. All went well until they reached the Long Sault, a turbulent stretch extending about seven miles downstream from the lake. It took six days to haul her up. At one point the cable broke, and the vessel was swept back down the chutes a considerable distance before she caught on some rocks. The same thing happened again near the crest of the rapids, and this time the craft was swamped and the keel and rudder damaged. It seemed to Paradis that the passengers were transporting the boat and not the other way around! Only on May 24, 1882, did the *Mattawan* finally reach Lake Temiskaming, and then it took another two weeks to effect repairs and install the machinery. Père Paradis decided not to wait, and continued on his way by canoe.

The *Mattawan* first arrived at the St. Claude Mission, opposite Fort Temiskaming, on June 4th, probably still under the command of Captain Mulligan, although the following year he went up to Lake Kipawa to run another of Latour's tugs. His place was then taken by Captain Joseph Octave Blondin, another veteran boatman who had previously commanded the

ABOVE:

Square timber rafts on the Ottawa River.
Courtesy National Archives of Canada, PA 43248

MIDDLE:

Steamer Mattawan. *A reconstruction sketch by the author.*

BELOW:

Steamer R. Hurdman, *on Lake Kipawa.*
Courtesy Muskoka Steamship & Historical Society

R. TATLEY

steamer *Pembroke* on the lower Ottawa River, between Pembroke and Des Joachims. The *Mattawan* was soon busy hauling freight and towing logs on most parts of Lake Temiskaming. We may conjecture that she largely replaced the big freight canoes hitherto used by the Hudson's Bay Company. Of course, she also took small groups of passengers, who were usually either lumberjacks or priests. In 1885, we find her bringing Monsignor Lorrain of the Oblate mission and his party up to the Quinze rapids on their pastoral visit to Témiscamingue, Lake Abitibi, the Moose River and Fort Albany (thus saving the good fathers 70 miles of paddling!). The missionaries were full of praise for Mr. Latour, who could not seem to do enough to help them. Again, in the spring of 1886, the steamer, now under Captain Charles Morin, brought several parties of settlers to the Mission, where they were received by the priests until they were assigned their lands, and on August 24th she and the tug *Argo* hosted a colonization excursion to the Mission. The *Argo* took the dignitaries from the Baie-des-Pères (Ville-Marie) to and from the Wright Mine and the Île du Chef (Chief's Island), while the *Mattawan* ran them up from the Mission to the Blanche River and the Rivière des Quinze and back the following day. (The day after, she also took them back to the Long Sault.)

The *Mattawan* was not Latour's only steamboat. As early as 1882, the busy lumberman had another vessel under way, but the scene of the next portion of our story belongs on Lake Kipawa.

STEAM TUGS ON LAKE KIPAWA

Lake Kipawa, in Témiscamingue County, Quebec, is very closely linked with Lake Temiskaming, both historically and geographically. The name — also spelled Kippewa — comes from a Nishnabi phrase meaning "a narrow passage between rocks," a good description in that the lake, which totals 95 square miles, consists of several very long narrow arms which give it an overall length of 40 miles and about 600 miles of shoreline. In several places Lake Kipawa extends to within five miles of the southeast end of Lake Temiskaming, yet it is at least 300 feet higher, with the result that the Kipawa River, which connects the two, is extremely swift flowing and turbulent. The waters of Lake Kipawa used to fluctuate considerably every season, but since 1923 a hydro dam at the tiny village of Laniel has kept them fairly constant.

Until the 1870s, Lake Kipawa lay amid its rolling granite shorelines and tranquil forests, undisturbed except by small parties of Nishnabis, who knew it as an excellent region for moose and speckled trout, and by the occasional fur trader from Fort Temiskaming. Then came the Europeans, bringing "progress" and the timber trade, though for a time the rapids on the Kipawa River discouraged them from trying to float out logs. At first only Olivier Latour thought it worthwhile to put a tug on the lake.

The boat, which was probably built right on the shores of Lake Kipawa, was called the *J.O.B.*, very likely in honour of Joseph Oliver Benjamin Latour, an Ottawa shipbuilder who would later construct several other tugs for Olivier. Listed at 25.88 tons, the *J.O.B.* was a 76-foot screw vessel with a single deck, a round stern and a 30-hp engine. Her duties must have entailed moving men, horses and provisions to the camps all around Lake Kipawa, in addition to towing logs to the river. Again and again, she must have bumped her way along amid loose floating logs and gone aground on some undetected rock or shoal, but no record of her adventures has survived. Until 1889, she seems to have had the lake all to herself, but after 1892 she disappears from the record.

Meanwhile, other lumber firms were sizing up the potential of the Kipawa watershed and setting up their own camps, but the problems of the river rapids still remained. However, it was noted that Lake Kipawa was occasionally drained by another exit. Sometimes its waters rose so high that they would spill over into tiny Tee Lake and Lac aux Brochets (Pike Lake) and then race down the Gordon Creek into Lake Temiskaming, about 25 miles south of the Kipawa River mouth and just above the Long Sault rapids. If the Gordon Creek route could be made continuous and reliable, logs could be fed safely into Lake Temiskaming and the towing routes shortened by at least 50 miles. Would it be worth the cost? Around 1888, all the lumber companies working around Lake Kipawa agreed to form a consortium called the Gordon Creek Improvement Company to make the necessary adaptations. These included blasting, dredging and excavating channels to create what was essentially an artificial river, as well as building dams to control the waters and erecting a timber slide downstream from Lac aux Brochets. The work continued for most of a year, but finally all was ready — or so it seemed!

When the big day arrived for testing the system, a considerable number of people gathered from miles around to watch. Among them was C.C. Farr, the founder of the town of Haileybury. As Farr later recounted, after a few short speeches, the dam at Lumsden's Mills (at the foot of Lac aux Brochets) was opened and the waters rushed down the timber slide with a roar. Suddenly, a jet of water shot 50 feet into the air, as most of the great wooden structure teetered and collapsed with a resounding crash. The raging torrent, now unconfined, rushed through the channel, rolling and heaving boulders like beach balls. The banks caved in and the swirling waters quickly gouged out a new channel. It took some time before the dam sluice could be closed again, and meanwhile most of the timber slide was a wreck, with parts of it left high and dry. The lumber barons were not very pleased, but they promptly ordered their crews to start all over again. The second time round the system worked, and soon almost all the Kipawa lumbermen were using it.

Apparently the success of the timber slide led to a new rush of logging on the lake. This was reflected in the large number of tugs built for the Kipawa service, starting in 1889. All were owned initially by Olivier Latour. One was the *John Loughrin*, a large double-decked paddlewheeler listed at 79.93 tons and powered by a 40-hp high-pressure engine recycled from an earlier vessel. With a length of 97.5 feet, a beam of 22.4 feet and an elliptical stern, the *John Loughrin* was named as a compliment to the energetic Mayor of Mattawa, who would soon go on to become the Liberal M.P. for Nipissing. That same year (1889), Latour also engaged his namesake J.O.B. Latour, to build a second, smaller, tug called the *D.A. Martin*, which, like the *John Loughrin*, was built at Lake Kipawa. The *D.A. Martin* was a screw steamer, 66.5 feet in length, single decked, and powered by a tandem compound engine generating 30 hp. There were now three tugs on the lake.

These arrangements did not last long. Apparently the *John Loughrin* was not very successful as a tug. Perhaps her machinery failed, or her paddlewheels proved unsuitable for log towing on a lake with many narrow channels. Whatever the reason, she was stripped down and converted into a barge in the fall of 1890, and relisted at 35.92 tons.

By about 1892, the *J.O.B.* was getting worn out, and her owner was making ambitious plan to upgrade his fleet. In 1893, the *D.A. Martin* was rebuilt, and enlarged to 84 feet in length and 56.97 register tons. Meanwhile Mr. Latour was busy ordering yet another tug — his fourth — on Lake Kipawa.

This vessel was the *R. Hurdman*, the second largest steamer ever to ply on the lake. She, too, was built by J.O.B. Latour in 1893, at what was later called Kipawa village. Named for a prominent Ottawa lumberman with extensive interests of his own on Lake Kipawa, the *R. Hurdman* was a 68.12-ton screw tug with a 45-hp fore-and-aft compound engine. She had two decks, an elliptical stern, a length of 103 feet and a beam of 19.7 feet. According to the register, Olivier Latour owned the big tug until the spring of 1894, when he sold her — along with the *John Loughrin* — to J.O.B. Latour, who took a mortgage on her to Olivier shortly afterwards. All these convoluted transactions may have been a mere formality; perhaps Olivier found himself in financial difficulties arising from the stock market panic of 1893, and the depression that followed. Whatever his reason for selling, he repossessed the *R.Hurdman* in 1900.

There was now intensive competition amongst the lumbermen on Lake Kipawa, as rival firms vied for timber berths. By 1910, all the available limits had been taken up by such big name firms as McLachlin brothers, John R. Booth, and the Hawkesbury Lumber Company, along with smaller concerns such as Shepard and Morse, W.C. Edwards of

Ottawa, and others. The Booth Company, which had previously been logging out the regions of Lake Nipissing and much of Parry Sound, also bought up limits along the Montreal River in Ontario, and in Harris Township, north of Lake Temiskaming, while the E.B. Eddy Company concentrated mostly on the Montreal River. The Gillies Company of Braeside was most active farther north, on Lac des Quinze and the Gillies Depot area, near Cobalt, the crews never suspecting that a much richer treasure lay right beneath their feet! The Colonial Lumber Company of Pembroke, by contrast, operated solely around Lake Kipawa. Several firms established a depot at what is now Kipawa village, not far from South Témiscaming.

As a rule, the various companies tended to follow their own routes and waterways as they fed their logs downstream towards Lake Temiskaming. The Booth Company, for example, opened additional depots at Saseginaga and Grassy Lakes, while the McLachlins built their own at Red Pine, Brennan and Wolf Lakes. Their logs were fed down the upper Kipawa River to Red Pine Chute, and then towed across Lake Kipawa. For a time, some companies engaged Olivier Latour's tugs to tow their logs, but inevitably several began to bring in their own. Some of them were conventional steam vessels, usually screw driven, but occasionally paddlewheel. Others were "alligators."

The alligator, or warping tug, was a peculiarly Canadian craft, which towed log booms by winching them along. The boats developed from rafts that had once been fitted out with a winch and cable to move booms across still waters where there

Alexander Lumsden in 1870. Courtesy Miss Jean Stewart

were no tugs available to do the job. At that time, the procedure was to attach the cable to the tow, paddle or pole the raft forward, letting the cable unroll while doing so, then anchor the raft and winch in the tow — using human muscle power. The operation would then be repeated as often as necessary to get the logs across the lake. For the men involved in the endless treadmill action, it was slow, monotonous, gruelling work, especially in cold or wet weather.

The first major improvement in the procedure was the substitution of horses to power the winches. The second innovation was replacing the horses with steam engines, starting around 1892. The result was the invention of the alligator.

Typically, the alligator was a squat, ugly scow, with a cabin to house the engine and boiler, and a boxy wheelhouse on top of the cabin. There might also be a cookstove on board, and bunks for one or more of the crew. Most of these ungainly tugs were paddlewheelers, with two sets of gears, so that the engine could alternate between driving the paddlewheels and powering the winch (the two were never used at the same time). Thus, a true alligator always towed by warping or winching the tow along. It would anchor ahead of the tow, then run back, playing out its cable to its full length (which might be anything from half to a full mile), then secure the tow and turn on the winch, which then hauled both the tow and the tug forward. (This ensured that the anchor would catch on the bottom.) Occasionally, the tug might be anchored to a tree or a rock, and by the same procedure it could even winch itself

ABOVE:

Hunter's Point, Lake Kipawa.

Courtesy Mr. Gilles Amesse

BELOW LEFT:

Scene at Kipawa Village. Courtesy

Mr. Leonard Cunningham

BELOW RIGHT:

Steamer Clyde. *A reconstruction*

sketch by the author, based on a

photo in the Toronto Globe,

September 19, 1895.

ashore and portage from one lake to another. Skids were attached to the bottom to protect it, and if the boat were proceeding uphill, rollers might be placed underneath it. Alligators were exceedingly slow, but they could often handle two or even three booms at a time (more than most conventional tugs), and they were largely oblivious to wind or wave. Moreover, they were cheap, easy to build, and easy to transport on a railway flatcar.

It is not certain when or where the first alligators were built, but once their utility was demonstrated they proliferated rapidly, especially on small, remote lakes where it was difficult to import a conventional tug. At least seven are known to have plied the Kipawa watershed, and six more on Lake Temiskaming. A number of firms and foundries made a specialty of building the new boats, most notably the West and Peachey Company of Simcoe, Ontario, which was once even exporting them to other countries. Most of the alligators used in Northern Ontario after 1892 were built by West and Peachey.

Given the tendency to move the warp tugs from lake to lake, it is often difficult to determine where they were used. For example, the record shows that the McLachlin Brothers, Claude and Hugh, bought a West and Peachey alligator called the *Bonnechère* in 1893. This boat, a 35-foot, 5.52-ton model with a 20-hp engine, was in service on Lake Kipawa by 1910, but almost certainly it spent its earliest years around the Bonnechère River, a tributary of the Ottawa River, where the McLachlins had extensive limits. Similarly, William H. Hurdman of Ottawa bought a larger tug from the Simcoe firm in 1894 and named it the *C.E. Read*. This craft had been moved to Lake Kipawa by 1906, sometimes to work in conjunction with a 40.5-foot barge called the *Julio*. The *C.E. Read* was 43 feet in length and registered 7.92 tons. It would appear, however, that the first alligator to be used north of Mattawa was the *Otter*, which was built at Kipawa village in 1895, just around the time that the Canadian Pacific Railway was extending a branch towards the lake. Registered at 11.97 tons, the *Otter* was 48.2 feet in length by 16 in beam and drew 3.6 feet of water. She was powered by an upright 20-hp engine, and seems to have served both on the Kipawa watershed and on the Ottawa River down as far as Des Joachims. In September of 1895, the Mattawa *Sentinelle* noted the stir caused in the village by the strange new craft that could actually creep across land by herself! She was then at work helping to lay a crib for the railway bridge across the Ottawa River. In 1916, the *Otter* was dismantled and rebuilt on Lake Kipawa, where she spent her last years. In 1899, the McLachlins had a 50.2-foot alligator called the *North River* (10.79 tons) built at Kipawa, using a second-hand 20-hp West and Peachey engine. Named for a tributary of Lake Kipawa, the *North River* was used not only for warping logs but also for helping to provision the McLachlin camps. She is last mentioned in 1907, though she was probably in service long after that.

The coming of the lumbermen also spelled opportunity for a number of middlemen who sought a livelihood forwarding for them. On Lake Kipawa, the first to do this was Patrick Kelly, a native of Ballan, Ireland. Emigrating to Canada in 1880, at the age of sixteen, Kelly began working for the E.B. Eddy Company at Renfrew, then followed the lumbermen to Mattawa. In 1883, he was sent to Lake Kipawa to open a "farm" where horses could be pastured. He also built a small sawmill, then a wharf and tramway at Turtle Portage. As lumbering proceeded, he began carrying the mail as well, a job that entailed rowing across the lake in the warm seasons and sleighing with horses in the winters. By a combination of hard work and frugality, he managed to save enough to have a small steamboat built at Carleton Place in 1889 and transported to Lake Kipawa. The vessel, powered by an upright 5-hp engine, was 25.4 feet in length, registered 1.57 tons, and had one deck and a square stern. Kelly called her the *Sarah Agnes* as a compliment to his wife.

Sustained by a government contract, the *Sarah Agnes* ran for six years, taking groups of lumberjacks to their camps, scowing horses and hay, and sometimes towing logs to the sawmill. Kelly himself took the wheel; henceforth he was "Captain" Kelly. In time, he was assisted by his three young sons, Arthur, Harold and Regis, all of whom became engineers and captains on various boats.

In 1897, Kelly sold the *Sarah Agnes* to Isaac Hunter, a trader who had established himself at Hunter's Point on Lake Kipawa, and meanwhile (1896) bought a larger steamboat for the transport business. The was the *Charlotte*, a 37-foot screw vessel, registered at 9.42 tons. She was an attractive little vessel with a single deck and a round stern. Built at Quebec City in 1880, she had been used by a local contractor for five years before going to a merchant in Beauce County. That same year (1886) she was again sold, to the Lake Témiscamingue Colonization Railway, which was then being developed to ease the problems of transporting settlers up to Lake Temiskaming — of which more in the next chapter. The completion of a Canadian Pacific Railway spur from Mattawa direct to Kipawa in 1895, however, put her out of a job, and, after a season's idleness, she was acquired by Patrick Kelly. The vessel was now seventeen years old and past her prime, but the Irish forwarder got good service out of her for five more years.

By 1900, however, the *Charlotte* was wearing out, and Kelly arranged to have a ship-builder from Hull build him a larger vessel at Kipawa in 1901. This boat, the *Alice*, was twice the size of the *Charlotte*, having a length of 62 feet and a register tonnage of 18.95. She was a conventional screw tug, with the usual single deck, round stern, deckhouse and wheel-house, and was licensed to carry 37 passengers. She also inherited the *Charlotte*'s 10-hp engine.

Captain Kelly ran the *Alice* for several years, but he evidently became dissatisfied with her speed and power. Around 1907, he installed a new 16-hp compound engine and a 165-lb. boiler to improve her performance. But, in 1910, he fell ill, was hospitalized at Ville-Marie and finally died at Montreal on November 26th, while still just 46 years of age. His widow, Sarah, continued to run the store at Kipawa village, assisted by her youngest son, Regis, but the tug was sold to an Ottawa lumberman named John Deberry Fraser. No sooner was the transaction completed than the steamer was gutted by fire, but Fraser managed to rebuild her by 1913, even larger than before, to a new length of 70.8 feet and 34.02 tons. He kept the *Alice* until the spring of 1916, when he sold her to the Booth Company for $8,000. The *Alice* continued to serve until the early 1920s; much later her owners would report that she was destroyed in a second fire at North River. Her boiler was later raised and sold for scrap.

Even before Patrick Kelly retired from the boating scene, another entrepreneur was preparing to enter the forwarding business on Lake Kipawa. This was John Cunningham, who was born around Billings Bridge (now part of Ottawa) in 1874. Orphaned suddenly while in his teens, Cunningham headed west up the Ottawa River, taking odd jobs here and there, until he was hired to run the Ottawa House hotel at Mattawa. Here he met and married Sarah McMeekin, the daughter of a local clerk, both of whom would later become his assistants.

By around 1904, having saved a fair sum of money, Cunningham followed the McLachlins north to the Kipawa country. Here he built a new hotel at Kipawa village, cater-ing mostly to the lumbermen. Aided by his wife, a cook and two girls, he was soon feeding up to 500 men at a single sitting. The lumbermen were usually well behaved and well looked after by their foremen.

Mr. Cunningham was not content to be a mere hotel-keeper for long. Opportunity beck-oned farther afield as the lumber companies pushed deeper and deeper inland, and around 1908 he settled at Red Pine Chutes, soon to be renamed Gaudette, on McLachlin Lake, about 40 miles from Kipawa, and opened another boarding house for the loggers. The next logical step was forwarding food and supplies — which, in turn, required rowboats, punts and scows, and a steamer to tow them. Hence, Mr. Cunningham had the *Orvil* built at far-away Carleton Place and shipped to Lake Kipawa by rail in the spring of 1909.

Named after one of his sons, the *Orvil* was a large steam launch, registered at 5.04 tons. With a single deck, an upright single-acting six-hp engine and an upright steel boiler, the ves-sel was 34.6 feet long and licensed for ten passengers. Soon she was busy ferrying to all parts of the lake, with Cunningham himself usually at the wheel. A post office was opened at Gaudette. The steamer also carried the mail, and a tramway was built past the rapids to move provisions on the upper Kipawa River to Wolf Lake. Any horses or cattle bound for destina-tions beyond Gaudette had to be driven overland on makeshift tote roads, or over the ice in winter; otherwise everything was transported by boat. Cunningham also set up a number of sleeping camps for the lumbermen. J.R. Booth, Shepard and Morse, the Colonial Lumber Company and of course, McLachlin Brothers, all made use of his services, as did occasional groups of fishermen and moose hunters lured in by the Canadian Pacific Railway, which was anxious to increase business on its spur to Kipawa. As early as 1905, the rising village of Kipawa had a hotel, two stores, a station built partly over the water, and several storehouses. Visitors were assured that some of the local steamers such as the *R. Hurdman* or the *Clyde* (imported from Lake Temiskaming sometime around 1903) would take passengers around the lake.

Within just a few years Captain Cunningham's business grew so much that he decided he needed a larger vessel. Accordingly, around 1912, he imported a 67-foot steamer called the *City of Haileybury* from Lake Temiskaming and sold the *Orvil* to Albert Jones, who had just opened a tourist camp at Hunter's Point on Lake Kipawa. Jones converted the craft into a gas boat and used her as a water taxi and freighter for several more years. By 1920, however, the *Orvil* was no longer listed and was later reported scrapped.

We shall have more to say about the Cunningham steamers in Chapter 4, but for the moment we must briefly acknowledge the existence of a few more tugs once used on Lake Kipawa. One of them was the *Colonial*, a 52-foot screw vessel registered at 25.38 tons. She was built at Kipawa in 1906 for the newly formed Colonial Lumber Company; her builder, Napoleon Tessier of Hull, had previously built the *Alice*. The *Colonial* had one deck, a round stern, and a 9.6-hp steeple compound engine. She was commanded by Captain Isaac Hunter, for whom Hunter's Point was probably named, and was licensed for 25 (later 15) passengers.

The *Colonial* was dismantled in 1920 and her machinery installed in a second tug of the same name in 1922. The new *Colonial* was similar to the original, but larger, with a length of 62.8 feet and a tonnage registered at 33.54. Of her operations no details are known, though it is likely that she was included among the assets when her parent company sold out to the Consolidated Paper Company of Montreal in 1923. At some later date, the steamer apparently burned while docked at Sunnyside Depot on Lake Kipawa.

Even less is known about a tug called the *Burmah*, which is mentioned only in the inspection reports of 1910, wherein she is described as a paddlewheeler grossing 45 tons and certified for 40 passengers. Her owners and disposition are unknown. In 1909, McLachlin Brothers had another alligator, called the *Burwash*, built at Kipawa. This craft, like the *Burmah*, grossed nearly 45 tons and registered 23.05. (It is possible that the two tugs were identical, yet both are included in the same 1910 inspection list.) The *Burwash* was 70 feet in length, had an 18-hp high-pressure engine, and could go nine miles per hour when not towing. Unlike most towboats of her time, she had a steel-framed hull, which may explain why she was still operating as late as the 1920s, after the *Bonnechère* and the *North River* had been dismantled. Another warp tug, the *Muskrat*, which did long service on Lake Temiskaming for the Upper Ottawa Improvement Company, is reported to have served briefly in Lake Kipawa around 1913.

Only a few more tugs on the lake require mention here, and all of them spent parts of their lives elsewhere. One, the *Emma Mac*, was a 36.15-ton screw steamer, built by Napoleon Tessier at Kipawa in 1910 for John Lumsden, and perhaps named for the wife of one of the McLaren brothers. The *Emma Mac* was 81 feet in length overall, had two decks and a fantail stern, and was powered by a second-hand fore-and-aft compound engine delivering 24 hp and speeds of ten miles per hour. She served for several years on Lake Kipawa, under Captain Napoleon Osborne, but by 1919 she had been removed to Lake Temiskaming. In that year, she was rebuilt at Témiscaming, Quebec, and spent her last years towing for the Riordon Pulp and Paper Company.

Another tug, the *C.J. Booth*, was a veteran from the Montreal River service before she was brought to Lake Kipawa. The *C.J. Booth* was a flat-bottomed steel-hulled paddlewheeler, in much the same class as the *Burwash*. Named for a son of J.R. Booth, the *C.J. Booth* was built at Latchford in 1907 and spent the next seven seasons hauling men, horses and supplies up the Montreal River during the Gowganda silver rush — of which more in Chapter 4. Then,

after a year's idleness, she was pulled ashore at Latchford and dismantled for shipment by rail, some of her rivets being cut out in the process. She arrived at Kipawa in pieces, was reassembled and put to work.

A few incidents in the *C.J. Booth*'s career are still remembered. On one occasion during the mid-1920s, the tug was out towing on Sunnyside Lake, a portion of Lake Kipawa, when the gears connected with her cable drum started spreading, making it impossible to winch in the tow. Fortunately, the Cunningham steamer *Silverland* (imported in 1923) was in the vicinity. She came, secured the tow and moved it to the shelter of a bay, while the *C.J. Booth* chugged off to Kipawa for repairs. Afterwards she returned for the tow.

On another occasion, the *C.J. Booth*, then commanded by a quiet, confident Nishnabi named Barney Jawbone, was anchored early one evening at a sheltered spot, waiting for the wind to change. Besides her tow, she had a big scow alongside that was used as a floating cookhouse and dormitory for the deckhands and boom men. The crew were arguing and playing cards after supper, when an anguished cry was heard from the galley. The elderly cook had lost his false teeth over the side while dumping dishwater, and stood there cursing his luck. The only hope seemed to be in summoning Barney, who, though illiterate, knew how to hunt, trap, live off the bush and drive logs with equal ease. Barney emerged from his cabin, stripped, dived in, floated like a beaver, then dived again at the spot indicated, disappearing from view for about two minutes, then reappeared with the missing teeth cupped in his hand.

The *C.J. Booth* apparently remained on Lake Kipawa as late as the early 1940s, until the Booth Company — having left the region for Algonquin Park for about fifteen years — returned to harvest a second crop of timber from its Kipawa limits. This time, the company imported a twin-diesel steel-hulled tug called the *J.G. Fleck* to tow on the lake. About the same time, the aging *C.J. Booth*, having been removed to Lake Temiskaming, was stripped of her machinery and converted into the "Red Scow" for the Upper Ottawa Improvement Company. Her last years were spent carrying stone for piers in the lake. As for the *J.G. Fleck*, she remained on Lake Kipawa until the 1970s, when she was removed and taken back to Lake Temiskaming, and, more recently, down the Ottawa River to the Pembroke region. By then, trucks were taking over the work of hauling timber. She was the last of the towboats on Lake Kipawa.

TUGS ON LAKE TEMISKAMING

While tugs were proliferating rapidly on Lake Kipawa after 1882, the same was also true on Lake Temiskaming, though many a tug was to migrate from one lake to the other.

As on Lake Kipawa, all the early steamers on Lake Temiskaming were built by various lumber companies. We have already noted how Olivier Latour imported the propeller *Mattawan* to the big lake in 1882. But Latour seems to have phased out his activities not long afterwards: in 1885, for example, he sold his mill at Les Érables to a Mr. Lewis, and two years later, his original mill near the mouth of the Kipawa River went to E.B. Eddy. Hence, it is not surprising that Latour also sold the *Mattawan* in November of 1886 to the Lake Témiscamingue Colonization Railway Company, which was then completing an organized transport service from Mattawa north to facilitate settlement. The railway, however, built as few tracks as possible, preferring instead to operate steamboats on the navigable portions of the upper Ottawa River; this method was much cheaper. The *Mattawan* was taken back downstream to her old waters, this time to ply from Mattawa village up to the La Cave rapids — a distance of two miles! Her master at this time was usually Captain G.L. Lamothe, or sometimes Captain John Belanger. After 1895, however, she was again rendered redundant, when the Canadian Pacific Railway built its own spur direct to the south end of Lake Temiskaming. In February 1897, the railway bought the steamer, presumably with the idea of putting her to work somewhere else, but if so, nothing came of it — because the vessel burned soon afterwards while beached in winter quarters, just north of Explorers' Point, Mattawa.

Although the *Mattawan* was evidently the first steamboat to ply Lake Temiskaming, she did not monopolize the big lake for long. Another vessel joined her there within just a few weeks. This was the *Argo*, a large double-decked walking-beam sidewheel tug built at Témiscaming in 1882. Registered at 96.10 tons, she was more than five times as big as the *Mattawan*, with a length of 125 feet and a beam of 39.4. She also had a round stern and a rather shrill whistle. Owned by a consortium called the Témiscamingue Steamboat Company of Ottawa, she was intended to tow rafts, scows and log booms, and to carry men, horses and provisions on her spacious decks, notably for the Booth Company. The horses were usually just pushed overboard when they arrived at their destinations. Once one of them caught its fetlock while disembarking, and landed in the drink upside down, but it managed to swim ashore without any further trouble! The *Argo* was usually commanded by Captain William H. Reamsbottom of Mattawa, a short chunky man who would later move to Haileybury. In one instance, when a huge six-and-a-half-foot wrestler started picking a fight aboard his vessel, Billy took on the ruffian and laid him flat on the deck.

It would appear that the Témiscamingue Steamboat Company failed to make money, because, in the spring of 1883, the *Argo* was mortgaged to a pair of Ottawa lumber merchants for $6,409.95. Two years later, with the mortgage still intact, the vessel was sold into other hands.

Only a few years later, yet another steamer was put into service by Gillies Brothers. This well-known firm first started cutting in Lanark County in 1842, and worked its way steadily up the Ottawa River, until in 1887 it purchased 465 square miles of timber limits in Témiscamingue, Quebec. That same season, the company imported a tug called the *Anna Marie* to Lake Temiskaming. Little is known of this vessel today, except that she met with disaster that same year. In November, while apparently still in operation, she was caught in the ice. She could move neither forward nor back, and soon her sides were scoured and gouged so badly that she sank in shallow water, leaving about eighteen inches of her funnel above the surface — and soon the ice took that as well! (The scene of this incident is not known, but was probably near the south end of the lake.)

Undaunted by the loss, the company had built a new steamer at Baie-des-Pères (Ville-Marie) by the spring of 1888, and named her the *Clyde* after the firm's original operations on the Clyde River, in Lanark. The *Clyde* was a handsome, double-decked, 61.5-foot screw steamer with a round stern and was registered at 26.20 tons. Unlike most of the local boats, she had a 17-hp condensing engine, which allowed her to run very quietly. Her draft was very shallow, which made her a poor towboat, but she could handle scows quite well and could proceed easily past the snyes, or shallows, at Chief's Island or Wabi Bay. Moreover, she was licensed to carry 45 passengers, most of whom were lumbermen heading for the company limits around the des Quinze River, but sometimes she also took parties of settlers and their chattels. The *Clyde* is said to have been the first steamer to ascend the Blanche River, at the north end of Lake Temiskaming, as far as the future site of Tomstown, and hence it was probably she that brought in the Irish settlers who first settled on the river. In August 1890, she also took the Bateson family of Haliburton to their new home at Dawson Point, opposite New Liskeard. The fare from Mattawa to Haileybury was then $4.50, plus another 85 cents per hundredweight of freight. Usually — though not always — the vessel was entrusted to Captain Blondin, formerly master of the *Mattawan* who worked at the Gillies depots over the winters. Years later, C.C. Farr would recall a time in June 1893, when the *Clyde*, then under Eric McConnell, stopped offshore at his beach while Mr. Farr and his neighbours were engaged at a logging bee. The skipper urged Farr to take the boat to the foot of the lake and vote in the provincial election (preferably for the Liberals!), but C.C. declined, feeling that he then knew far too little about politics. As it happened, John Loughrin of Mattawa easily carried the seat of Nipissing without any help from Haileybury.

By the mid-1880s, then, there were still only a handful of steamers on Lake Temiskaming, all of which were tugs and workboats — with the possible exception of a little-known small steamer called the *Étoile du Nord* ("North Star"), which is said to have entered service around Ville-Marie in 1888. (Another small tug called the *Jean-Baptiste* was built in 1889 by François-Xavier Coursol, who had previously opened the first saw and grist mills at Ville-Marie). But dramatic changes were already on the horizon, as one especially dynamic lumberman started to make his mark on the local scene. That man was Alexander Lumsden.

Alex Lumsden was born on October 4, 1844. His father, John Lumsden, had emigrated from Belhelvie, near Aberdeen, Scotland, in 1833, at the age of nineteen, to work for Thomas McKay, the well-known contractor and businessman who was then building Rideau Hall and founding the village of New Edinburgh, now part of Ottawa. Around 1839, Lumsden married Elizabeth Sharp of Bytown (Ottawa), by whom he had four children. It was probably at New Edinburgh that Alexander, the second child and only son, was born. Nothing is known of his childhood except that he attended the local schools, but it seems that the stern Calvinistic creed of his Presbyterian forebears helped to instill habits of strict honesty, clean living and sturdy self-reliance that were to stand him in good stead over the years to come.

While still in his teens, Alex Lumsden left school to work as a labourer at the McLaren gristmill. Later he became a mill hand at the McLaren sawmill and soon learned all the skills of the sawyer's trade. He also worked periodically as a shantyman on the Ottawa River log drives. Eventually, he was promoted to foreman of the mill, and as his ambition and resolve became manifest, he was named a salesman for the firm. By this time, Alex Lumsden knew the lumber business inside out, and soon he felt ready to strike out on his own.

His first independent venture was a partnership with Samuel Bingham (afterwards Mayor of Ottawa) to run log drives down both the Gatineau and Ottawa Rivers. This probably meant accepting contracts to supply logs to some of the established lumbermen. Very likely it was Bingham who supplied the capital, and Lumsden the practical experience and hard work of setting up depots and camps, hiring and directing the men, and generally supervising operations. Be that as it may, the pair eventually dissolved their partnership — amicably, since they remained friends — and divided the workloads, with Lumsden taking on the Ottawa River drives alone and leaving the Gatineau River to Bingham. This, of course, took him farther and farther up the great river, as old limits gave out and new ones were tapped. By the 1880s, he was operating as far west as Mattawa and beyond, and in time he also secured a contract from the Upper Ottawa Improvement Company, whose business was almost exclusively towing logs.

By now Alex Lumsden was one of the leading logging contractors on the Ottawa River. To his colleagues in the trade he seemed the essence of the self-made Scottish business entrepreneur, combining honest reliability with rugged initiative, an eye for opportunity and detail, and tireless energy. To his employees he was a strict boss, but a reasonable one, who never forgot how it felt to be a humble working man of modest means. It is said that he sometimes paid for the funerals of men drowned on the log drives, and often supported their widows and orphans until they could look after themselves, although Mr. Lumsden was not the sort of man to parade his charities in public. To his wife and family — he had married a Scottish-born lady named Margaret Duncan around 1870 — he was a kind and affectionate husband and father, albeit frequently an absent one. To his neighbours in New Edinburgh, where he made his home, he was a quiet-living man and a generous benefactor to his church, St. Paul's Presbyterian, which he helped to found. To his friends, despite his casual attire, he was a true gentleman, whose rather stern and reserved demeanour masked a gentle personality and a spirit sensitive to the beauties of Nature — an odd trait in a lumberman, perhaps! Although devoted to his work, he was not a philistine; he seems to have enjoyed reading whenever he had the time, and to have developed a ready wit, often spicing his words with poetry, some of which was his own. Altogether, a truly remarkable man.

His business career was now running at full throttle. Having accepted so many towing and provisioning jobs, it was natural for Alex Lumsden to begin purchasing some timber berths of his own. Most of them were around Lake Kipawa and the North River, though he later picked up a two-thirds share on a limit on the Montreal River. Around 1884, he opened a camp near the south end of Lake Temiskaming, and in 1888 he erected his own sawmill at Lac aux Brochets on the Gordon Creek exit from Lake Kipawa, which waterway he helped to create. This gave rise to a small village known as Lumsden's Mills, which is now on the outskirts of the modern town of Témiscaming. It would appear, however, that until the railway arrived at South Témiscaming in 1895, Lumsden continued to export most of his logs down the Ottawa River as far as Des Joachims, where they could be boomed and towed downstream by the tugs of the Upper Ottawa Improvement Company, which had absorbed the old Union Forwarding Company fleet in 1886.

It was almost inevitable that Alex Lumsden would become a steamboat owner himself; indeed, his name soon became synonymous with steamboating on Lake Temiskaming. His first acquisition was the *Argo*, which he purchased from Isaac Smith of Ottawa in June of 1885. This meant securing a mortgage of $6,000, but business was so good that he was able to pay it off in just two years. The *Argo* continued to give good service for another seventeen years, but by the 1890s she was also being used periodically to take passengers.

In the fall of 1887, Mr. Lumsden purchased a small screw steamer called the *Toneata* (9.53 tons), which had been built at Kingston two years earlier. The *Toneata* was apparently a yacht, with one deck, a 48-foot keel, a round stern and a 12-hp engine, but it is not clear how or even where she was used, since the vessel is known today only from the register. However, the fact that she was sold to the Lake Témiscamingue Colonization Railway Company in 1893, indicates that she served on Lake Temiskaming or immediately below it. (The *Toneata* was reported dismantled in the spring of 1902.) In 1888, Mr. Lumsden decided to go into the passenger business in a serious way, but that part of the story we reserve to the next chapter.

Meanwhile, his fleet of tugs was growing steadily, until he almost monopolized the towing fleet on Lake Temiskaming. In 1889, he had another single-decked screw steamer built at Opemicon (or Opemican) Depot, about fourteen miles north of South Témiscaming and a mile south of Opimica Narrows, where both the Lumsden and Booth Companies had outposts. Opemicon Depot became the shipyard centre for the Lumsden steamers, largely because the sandy bay there is fairly sheltered and because the current in the lake keeps the winter ice from becoming very thick. Lumsden equipped his new base with a blacksmith shop, a carpenter's shop, a machine shop, an office, bunkhouses, storage sheds, a marine railway, and of course docks for his boats. The site was initially very isolated, though, and some of the employees established their own vegetable gardens.

His new steamer was 61.6 feet in length, registered 44.15 tons, and was powered by a 14-hp high-pressure engine. She was called the *Dora*, almost certainly after Mr. Lumsden's younger daughter, who occasionally took cruises on the boat. The *Dora* was essentially a towboat, commanded for many years by the amiable Captain James Warner of Témiscaming, although she is remembered today primarily as a dredge tender. It would appear that Alex Lumsden himself sometimes used her in that capacity, clearing channels around Ville-Marie and the mouth of the Wabi River before government dredges were introduced. But she also had other duties; by 1894, the vessel was licensed for 40 passengers, and in other years she is listed as a tug. In April 1904, Lumsden sold her to the Ministry of Public Works, which remodelled her cabins and used her to tow big dredges like the *Dredge Queen* which was first put to work at New Liskeard in 1900, using a windlass for scooping up clay and sediments from the bottom. This was vitally important work in the days before control dams. The *Dora* seems to have remained in service until about 1919, sometimes under Captain Goulet of Témiscaming, but after that she apparently went to pieces.

In 1893, Alex Lumsden bought his first alligator tug from the West and Peachey Company. This was the *Beaver*, a small 36-foot model with a 30-hp engine and registered at 6.37 tons. She was the first of three towboats of that name on Lake Temiskaming, and seems to have been the first warping tug to appear there. Lumsden must have been pleased by her performance, because two years later he bought the larger tug *Otter* (mentioned earlier) from the Simcoe firm to do his towing on Lake Kipawa.

The *Beaver* evidently ran only until 1898, when she seems to have burned. Lumsden immediately had a second, larger *Beaver* built at Témiscaming by the energetic Joseph Arthur Larochelle of Mattawa. The *Beaver* (II) was 47.4 feet in length, registered 7.54 tons, and inherited her predecessor's engine. Lumsden used this craft until the spring of 1903, when he sold her to the Upper Ottawa Improvement Company, which was then moving to extend its operations to Lake Temiskaming. Three years later, on September 2, 1906, the second *Beaver* likewise burned, apparently at Témiscaming, and became a total loss. In the meantime, Lumsden had acquired yet another alligator, the *Mink* (8.78 tons), from West and Peachey in 1896. This tug was included in the 1903 sale to the Upper Ottawa Improvement Company, but unlike the *Beaver*, the *Mink* carried on for many more years, and was, in fact, enlarged in 1912. Later still, she was converted to screw propulsion. She remained in service, sometimes on Lake Deschenes on the lower Ottawa River, until October 31, 1945, when she went down in a storm that came up so suddenly that the crew didn't even have time to cast off their tow. Somehow all the men escaped drowning.

Thus, before the turn of the century, Alexander Lumsden had built or purchased nine steamers, seven of which were tugs. In the spring of 1899, he went even further and purchased the steamer *Clyde* from Gillies Brothers. This move gave him almost complete control of navigation on Lake Temiskaming, and the following year he acquired yet another passenger steamer. Then, in April 1900, he also purchased Olivier Latour's entire fleet of tugs on Lake Kipawa: the *D.A. Martin*, the *John Loughrin* and the *R. Hurdman*. Perhaps included in the deal were Latour's depot on the lake, plus the tramway at Turtle Portage. Aside from the Kelly and McLachlin interests, the Lumsden boats were now doing most of the towing and transporting on Lake Kipawa.

Lumsden was now one of the leading lumbermen and forwarders on the upper Ottawa River. In 1895, the Canadian Pacific Railway completed a spur to what soon became South Témiscaming and Lake Kipawa. The branch went straight through Lumsden's Mills, allowing it to turn out huge quantities of lath, shingles and lumber. A bakery, office, dormitory, cooperage, blacksmith shop, storehouse and roothouse were built at Lumsden's Mills, plus a hydro-electric plant and powerhouse at the dam, a schoolhouse for the children of his work crews (Mr. Lumsden hired the teacher and prescribed the Ontario curriculum, despite the fact that the school was in Quebec), plus about twenty houses, which were rented out to some of the mill hands at a rate of $5 a month. There were now about 160 people living at Lumsden's Mills, and stables for about 60 horses. At nearby South Témiscaming, which was still commonly called Gordon Creek, there were storehouses, a cookery and a machine shop, as well as a railway station near the wharf, but South Témiscaming had barely one-third as many inhabitants as Lumsden's Mills. The Lumsden company (which was never incorporated) also built wharves and warehouses on both Lake Temiskaming and Lake Kipawa, and eventually hotels and boarding houses as well. As an additional enterprise, Lumsden developed a small farm with a dairy on the Ontario side of the river, near the modern village of Thorne.

Alex Lumsden died in 1904, a very rich man. His passing coincided with the end of the lumber trade around Lake Temiskaming. The last square-timber drives, we are told, left the lake in 1895, and in 1925 the editor of the New Liskeard *Speaker* would comment that lumbering had practically ceased in that area twenty years previously, thus doing the local farmers in Quebec out of their primary market for produce. Logging continued on the lake, but most of the cutting was now inland, around the Montreal and des Quinze Rivers and the Lake Kipawa watershed, and even there, most firms, including J.R. Booth, phased out their operations by the mid-1920s. In 1941, the Booth Company would even return to its Kipawa limits and build another large sawmill on Tee Lake, close to the former Lumsden's Mills. In addition, small mills would continue to cut for local needs, including the McCamus and McKelvie sawmill at New Liskeard, C.O. Foster's mill at Haileybury, the Gauthier mill at St-Bruno-de-Guigues, the Talbot mill at Laverlochère, and the Boucher mill at Fugèreville, plus a few more at Ville-Marie, but all of them would be gone by the 1930s. A few more would appear at Fabre and Laniel in the 1940s, and as recently as 1975 extensive log drives would continue from the des Quinze River down the Quebec side of the lake, but these would be pulpwood logs bound for the paper mill at South Témiscaming, a subject to be dealt with in Chapter 6. In the meantime, agricultural settlement had been developing by degrees in the North, with major consequences for the boat services, and this must constitute the next portion of our story.

Lumsden Line Steamers
LAKE TEMISKAMING

The Lumsden Line
letterhead features
pictures of the Meteor
(top), Argo and the
Bellevue Hotel. Courtesy
Mattawa Museum

Alexander Lumsden.
Courtesy Mr. Alex MacLaurin

CHAPTER 3

STEAMBOATS
AND SETTLEMENT

Although men may have set foot in what is now Timiskaming as early as 8,000 years ago — shortly after the last sheets of glacial ice retreated from the area — they did so only to hunt for food. Much later, during the 17th century, they also came in pursuit of furs, which to the Europeans meant employment, profit and wealth, and to the natives access to manufactured goods (and sometimes liquor) and European guns, without which they might find themselves at a disadvantage against hostile tribes. Red and white men alike fought wars over beaver pelts. The fur trade, however, produced no permanent settlements except a few posts like Fort Temiskaming and its satellites, which often had small gardens close by. The trade itself was deemed incompatible with colonization. During the 19th century, the lumber trade brought hundreds of men into the region, but lumbering by its very nature was transitory, and, once the desirable timber was gone, the lumbermen simply moved on. Permanent settlement, based on agriculture, had to wait until the 1880s.

All the early European settlers entered Témiscamingue by following the Ottawa River, and took their impetus from the Roman Catholic Church. Initially, the Church was interested only in mission work. Discounting the ill-fated Jesuit missions in Huronia during the 17th century, we can date the inception of settlement to 1834, when a mission was established near the old Hudson's Bay Company post at Mattawa, where there was a small Nishnabi encampment. From there, several intrepid priests at once began working among the Ojibwas, Algonquins and fur traders as far north as Fort Albany. No one else lived in the North then. European settlements in the true sense of the word did not exist west of Pembroke.

It was the Oblates who were most instrumental in bringing *colons* to Témiscamingue. This order was founded in France, primarily for mission work, and by the 1840s it had become interested in Canada. The first Oblates landed at Quebec City in 1841, and soon pressed on to Montreal and beyond. By 1844, Père Louis Laverlochère was paddling vigorously from Lachine up the Ottawa River, up Lake Temiskaming, and over the height of land to the Moose River, visiting encampments everywhere. By 1848, he had opened a mission on the Albany River, making up in zeal what he initially lacked in experience. In time Monseignor Joseph Eugène Guigues, the first Catholic bishop of Ottawa (himself a member of the order), assigned the Oblates the colossal task of bringing the gospel to the natives as far north as Hudson Bay!

It was a very hard life the priests led. Few "civilized" amenities were available. Until 1850, steamers plied only as far as the Chenaux, or Snows, rapids, about 50 miles west of Ottawa; beyond that, travel was exclusively by canoe or snowshoe. Only their faith and convictions could sustain them through the poorest food, the cruellest blizzards, the most turbulent streams and the longest portages. Shortly after 1860, the emphasis was placed on Lake Temiskaming, where Père Pian called for a permanent mission. As a result, three missionaries, including Father Pian, paddled north from Mattawa in 1863, and founded the St. Claude Mission on the Ontario side of the lake, opposite Fort Temiskaming. A chapel was soon built and a farm established, while a hospital, school and orphanage were opened by the Grey Sisters. Meanwhile, some converts were made among the natives. The coming of Christianity, like most gifts from the white man, was a mixed blessing to the Nishnabis, in that the priests solemnly warned them that many of their ancient beliefs and customs were sinful in the eyes of God — notably polygamy. It is only fair to add, however, that the priests were often the truest friends the native people had.

By this time, as we have noted, hundreds of lumbermen were pushing into the region, but very few farmers. This is not surprising. The country was frustratingly remote, and most men were aware that the granite ridges and thin leaf-mould soils of the Canadian Shield, coupled with long, cold winters, offered few prospects for agriculture. Mattawa, which stands at the confluence of the Mattawa River and the Ottawa River, was the original gateway to Témiscamingue. Yet as late as 1869 it had only four families: those of Noah Timmins, who had arrived in 1859 and was soon to become the town's foremost retail merchant; Amable Dufond, who gave his name to a nearby stream; and two Protestants working for the Hudson's Bay Company.

Yet settlement was growing. By 1875, there were reckoned to be about 500 Roman Catholics and 100 Protestants residing in the Mattawa district, of whom perhaps 150 lived in Mattawa itself. The village now had four stores and one hotel. In 1877, a bridge was built across the Mattawa River, and by then Noah Timmins, backed by all the local businessmen, was helping Captain Mulligan to put the steamer *Mattawan* into service between the village and Des Joachims. Soon afterwards, the Canadian Pacific Railway came through on its way to the West, and in the process all but wiped out the steamer services along the Ottawa River.

The coming of the railway also turned tiny Mattawa into a boom town. Though the navvies moved on as the line pushed west towards Callander, the hotels of Mattawa were soon swarming with travellers and lumbermen eager to take advantage of the area's prospects. Soon Mattawa had a roller grist mill, a tannery, a sawmill, a hospital, a newspaper, four schools, four churches, seven hotels and a population of 1,400, of whom about 76 percent were French-speaking Catholics. In 1885, Mattawa was incorporated as a village, and in 1891 as a town, with Noah Timmins as the first mayor. In July of 1895, following a close vote (held under highly controversial circumstances), it lost out in a bid to become the district seat of Nipissing. The winner was the upstart town of North Bay, itself a by-product of the Canadian Pacific Railway. This was not the last setback the little community would sustain at the hands of its neighbour.

For the time being, however, Mattawa was still the gateway to Témiscamingue, and as settlement and sawmills followed the railway west towards Lake Nipissing, some of it inevitably also diverged northwards. Besides, the timing was auspicious. The Province of Quebec needed more lands for farming. The St. Lawrence Valley and the Eastern Townships were largely filled up, and the advent of semi-mechanized farming had reduced the need for numerous hands on the family farm. The factories of Montreal and Quebec City could not employ all the surplus labour, and soon many French Canadians were emigrating to New England, looking for land and work. Obviously, those who left for the United States were bound to be assimilated. Nor did the rest of Canada afford many opportunities, as English Canadians poured steadily into the prairies, rapidly engulfing the small Métis communities there. French Canadian nationalists grew alarmed. It looked as if their entire culture was in danger. As early as the 1870s, a priest named Père Labelle began pointing forcefully towards the empty Laurentian Highlands to the north, including Lac St. Jean and the Chicoutimi region, which, he argued, should be opened up for industry and settlement to keep settlers Catholic and French. Later, as Mattawa became readily accessible, the same reasoning was applied to other regions, including Témiscamingue.

There were already Europeans in residence around Lake Temiskaming. A few had arrived as early as 1860, selling their surplus crops either to the Hudson's Bay Company or to the lumber camps. A handful of Norwegians had settled around the Montreal River, while a few more groups were working for Olivier Latour at the mouth of the Kipawa River and the Petite Blanche. In 1871, an Irishman from Dunvegan, James Kelly by name, who had been employed at the St. Claude Mission, left to build a hermitage across the lake, thus becoming the first settler at the Baie-des-Pères, which was sometimes called Kelly's Bay. In 1874, he was joined by Frère Joseph Moffette, who began clearing a farm at Baie-des-Pères. The Nishnabis called him "Mayakisis" ("with the sun"), because he was always up before dawn. Long before anyone else, Moffette became convinced of the region's agricultural potential, but for years he was a voice crying in the wilderness.

They were not entirely alone. A few more whites and people of mixed blood settled on Mann ("Burnt") Island and College Island in northern Lake Temiskaming, while about twenty Irishmen were located around the mouth of the Blanche River by Père Jean-Marie Nédelec, one of the most tireless of the missionaries. Besides these, there was a Nishnabi reserve at Tête-du-Lac ("head of the lake") near the mouth of the des Quinze River. By 1880, there were perhaps 500 people living around Lake Temiskaming, most of whom were lumbermen, and in 1877 the Quebec government decided to survey a township, called Duhamel, encompassing Baie-des-Pères and Fort Temiskaming. Further activity was stimulated in 1883, when Edward V. Wright, an Ottawa lumberman, began working a silver mine north of Baie-des-Pères, which the De Troyes expedition had noticed nearly 200 years earlier. Several settlers moved to the area of the mine, which by 1885, had yielded about ten tons of ore, but the second shipment was swamped and lost at Deux Rivières while being rafted to Ottawa.

About 1881, some of the missionaries became interested in colonizing the eastern side of Lake Temiskaming and creating a whole new Quebec. They began bombarding their bishops with letters praising the country, and soon the bishops became infected with their enthusiasm. In 1882, Monsignor J. Duhamel, who had himself visited Lake Temiskaming the previous summer, sent Père Charles Alfred Paradis, another Oblate from France, to take a closer look. On October 26, 1884, Père Paradis, along with an agent for the Canadian Pacific Railway and three others, took the train to Mattawa, paddled up to Gordon Creek, caught the steamer *Mattawan* and managed to reach the Mission on the 30th. They called at Fort Temiskaming, where they were warmly welcomed by the factor, C.C. Farr, and his wife, and met several local settlers, including Frère Moffette. In his report, Paradis observed that the soils north of Fabre were generally of an alluvial clay loam, quite free of stones and eminently suitable for agriculture. He also noted that the rugged hills around the lake's north end were only isolated peaks, and that there were extensive plains beyond them, offering sufficient space for perhaps 40 new parishes. Aside from early frosts, the main problem was the fact that the Ottawa River drops a total of 54 feet from Lake Temiskaming down to Mattawa, and some of those waters are turbulent. After taking some measurements, Paradis proposed that the boulders and glacial debris clogging the first two stretches of the Long Sault rapids be cleared away, and that a dam be built downstream at Les Érables. This would lower Lake Temiskaming by 22 feet and raise the level of the Ottawa River by 32 feet. As a result, the Long Sault and Montagne rapids would be drowned and the navigable portion of the lake lengthened by about 25 miles, leaving a gap of only seven miles between Les Érables and Mattawa (to be covered by rail). It would also expose thousands of acres of potential farming lands around the north end of the lake. Paradis returned home ecstatic about this potential new Eden and urged his superior, Père Pierre Édouard Gendreau, Procurer of the College of Ottawa, to visit the region. He did, and agreed that Témiscamingue looked even better than Chicoutimi.

As a result, a new organization called La Société de la Colonisation de Lac Temiskaming [*sic*] was established in Ottawa on December 12, 1884, under the auspices of Bishop Duhamel. Père Gendreau was elected president. The group's immediate objective was to settle the new townships of Guigues and Duhamel, on the northeast side of the lake and, to begin the process, two brochures were circulated, extolling the soils of the region and the advantages of colonization.

The new society also began buying up land and clearing it, and meanwhile drew up the terms of settlement. Members were to receive 100 acres for the price of $100, to be paid by installments. They would then be issued tickets indicating the locations of their lots and would receive letters patent once they had complied with strict duties of settlement: they must take possession of their land within six months, reside there at least two years, clear a minimum of six acres and build a dwelling at least twenty feet by sixteen in size. (These terms

BIRD'S EYE VIEW OF MATTAWA FROM MOUNTAIN.

were meant to discourage speculators.) Lands could also be purchased for $20 an acre, or $10 if burned over. The first arrivals in Duhamel found most of the area there in that condition, following a forest fire in 1872. The land patents did not include the right to sell timber, since the various lumber companies had already purchased limits in the area, but the settlers were permitted to use whatever timber they needed for buildings and fences. Usually, in cases of disputes over timber, the Oblates supported the settlers against the lumbermen.

The first new settlers — all six of them — arrived at the Mission as early as September 1883, on board the *Mattawan*. Here they were welcomed and given practical advice before moving on. Many of them were poor, and therefore worked for a time for the Oblates to earn money or gain a little practical experience. Some also spent the winters in the lumber camps. Farming methods were quite rudimentary at first, and even by the turn of the century, it was a lucky *colon* who could afford a mechanized harvester. Yet gradually the forests were turned into farms, despite the summer scourge of mosquitoes and black flies and the long cold winters and autumn frosts that sometimes ruined the crops. By 1885, some 850 acres had been cleared, and in 1886, there were 153 white people and 160 Nishnabis living round Fort Temiskaming and the head of the lake, with another 94 living further south. Some 65 newcomers arrived that same year.

Meanwhile, the Colonization Society was not idle. With the help of Père Labelle, it was advertising as far away as France and Belgium, with the result that 64 responded. Among them was Lucien-Napoléon-Bonaparte Wyse, an engineer and promoter of the Panama Canal project. (Wyse was also a grand-nephew of the Emperor Napoleon himself.) In the summer of 1886, along with his wife and two sons, Wyse paid a visit to Canada and took a tour of Témiscamingue.

They arrived at the Mission on August 24th, aboard the steamer *Argo*, which Alex Lumsden had kindly provided for the party, which also included Père Gendreau, Frère Moffette, and Pierre Bouillame (or Boulianne), a local contractor. The *Mattawan* was also on hand to accompany them to Baie-des-Pères, where the locals —who then numbered seven families — were just finishing Mass. After an impromptu welcome, Wyse resumed his trip north on the *Argo* to visit the Wright Mine and Chief's Island, which he had purchased. Here the Grey Sisters had a good rustic dinner prepared, which Captain Ernie Jones and his three young sons were invited to share. They returned to the mission by sundown, while the following morning the *Mattawan*, under Captain Charles Morin (himself a new arrival at Baie-des-Pères) took the Wyse party several miles up the Blanche River, and thence up the des Quinze River as far as the rapids. After a short stroll ashore, the group reboarded the steamer, which returned to the mission by 10:00 P.M. Wyse left for the Long Sault on the *Mattawan* the following day and afterwards returned to France, where he published a report enthusiastically praising the colonization scheme. Yet he never returned. Perhaps he became soured by a regrettable quarrel that sprang up between the French settlers and the Colonization Society several years later. The society ran short of funds, and therefore ceased to clear land and build houses, which, to the French, seemed like a betrayal. They accused the society of favouring the French Canadians and of lending its funds at interest to build a railway, and they demanded their money back. The matter was not formally settled until 1903, by which time the society agreed to remit its unsold lots in Guigues and Duhamel to the Crown, which paid the arrears in taxation and sold the lots, using the proceeds to reimburse the French. Nonetheless, some of the French settlers stayed in Canada.

By the time of the Wyse visit, the Colonization Society was already tackling the most vexatious of its problems: how to make the new Eden accessible. Getting to Mattawa was no longer a problem, thanks to the Canadian Pacific Railway, but how were the new settlers supposed to reach Lake Temiskaming? Only a few miles upstream from Mattawa were the La Cave rapids, with more to follow at Les Érables and La Montagne, all interspersed over a distance of just fifteen miles. The Lac de Sept Lieues or Seven League Lake then offered a respite, but beyond that stretched the Long Sault, a set of six rapids spread over as many miles. Of all those rapids, Les Érables was considered the most dangerous and the Long Sault the most laborious. Indeed, the difficulties with the route were so troublesome that some travellers preferred to portage overland to Lake Beauchenes and thence to Lake Kipawa. On Lake Temiskaming itself, transportation was much less difficult, thanks to the *Mattawan* and the *Argo*, but there were still no control dams to regulate the water levels, with the result that the steamers were prone to run aground in the autumn when the waters were low. Furthermore, Lake Temiskaming, with its long expanses of open water, lying in a valley that tends to funnel the northwest winds right through it, is notorious for sudden storms that can whip up big waves with little warning. In short, it can be very dangerous, especially for small craft.

Various proposals for transcending the upper Ottawa River were suggested. Père Labelle advocated a railway from Montreal to St-Jérôme, past the headwaters of the Lièvre and Gatineau Rivers to Lake Temiskaming, but the society chose the much cheaper expedient of utilizing the river itself, by steamboat wherever possible and by land using trams or railways wherever not.

As a first step, it appealed to both the federal and provincial governments for funds, and soon had enough money (some voted by the Ontario government) to build a set of horse-drawn tramways around the rapids at La Cave, Les Érables and La Montagne, apparently by 1885. (All three were placed on the Quebec side of the river.) The next step was to implement the Paradis plan of damming Les Érables and clearing the Long Sault, but a team of government engineers concluded that the scheme would cost far too much. The society, now short of funds, began to consider the idea of a narrow-gauge railway to bypass the Long Sault, and on July 20, 1886, La Compagnie de Chemin de fer Témiscamingue (known in English as the Lake Temiskaming Colonization Railway) was officially chartered by the Privy Council, and authorized to build past the Long Sault and to operate the tramways, bateaux and scows downstream. More subsidies from the federal and provincial governments were promised, and soon contractor Pierre Boulianne (now of Baie-des-Pères) had a crew of 100 men at work, under the overall direction of engineer Paul T.C. Dumais.

The railway was opened with great éclat around May 20, 1887. Bishop Duhamel was on hand with other dignitaries to bless the occasion. By June 9th, the entire system was in operation.

The actual railway, when first built, ran just 6.2 miles past the Sault, though later it would be lengthened. The gauge was only 36 inches, a standard duplicated by only two other railways in Eastern Canada: one at Sydney, Nova Scotia, and the other north of Montreal. The line had only a single locomotive, appropriately called the *Gendreau*, which first arrived at the south end of Lake Temiskaming on August 12, 1886. Presumably horses were still in use until then. In 1891, Father Gendreau resigned as president of the company — a post he probably found rather uncongenial — and soon took charge of the mission at Mattawa.

To complete the connection between Mattawa and La Cave, the line used a small steamboat and a scow. The steamer was apparently the *Charlotte*, which was later to go to Lake Kipawa. As noted in the previous chapter, the *Charlotte* was a 37-foot screw vessel registered at 9.42 tons. She was already six years old when the Lake Temiskaming Colonization Railway bought her in the fall of 1886. She was assigned to Captain George Lamothe, who was also responsible for the entire southern end of the forwarding service.

The records are vague about how the next lap of the service was run. A Captain Montreuil was in charge of the La Cave–Les Érables section, but no steamer is mentioned. Perhaps we should infer that the old-fashioned bateau, propelled by poles, was in use for a time. Above Les Érables, the company launched another small steamer, the *Lottie*, a 40-foot screw vessel listed at 8.52 tons. Built at Aylmer, Quebec, in 1885, the *Lottie* was a single-decked craft with a fantail stern. Père Gendreau bought her in March of 1886, then for some reason resold her in April to Olivier Latour. This was probably a mere formality, since by September she was officially the property of the Lake Temiskaming Colonization Railway. She took on the short stretch between Les Érables and La Montagne, under the command of Captain Ben Boulianne.

On the Lac de Sept Lieues, the line used a third steamer called the *Émerillon*. Little is known of this vessel beyond the registry record, which tells us that she was built at Trois Rivières (Three Rivers) in 1883, that she was 40 feet in length, had a 6-hp engine, a single deck, and a round stern, and registered 13.16 tons. The railway officially bought her in December 1886, and entrusted her to Captain Mulligan — probably Bernard Mulligan, who had imported the *Mattawan* to the upper Ottawa River ten years earlier. The *Émerillon* was the largest of the three boats, and had the longest route, plying to the foot of the Long Sault to connect with the little railway.

On Lake Temiskaming itself, the company built its largest and finest vessel, *La Minerve*, which, in her own brief time, became known as the "Queen of Témiscamingue." *La Minerve* was a composite steamer, with a steel frame and a hull planked in tamarack cut along the Blanche River, at the head of the lake. Fitted out at the Long Sault (now South Témiscaming), she was built under the direction of Captain Charles Morin of Baie-des-Pères, who had lately been running the *Mattawan*. Once again, it was Pierre Boulianne, along with a crew of twenty men, who carried out the actual construction. The new steamer was a double-decker, with a length of 104.6 feet and a rather ample beam of 23.8. According to local tradition, she was a sternwheeler, which seems distinctly possible, given that her stern was square. If so, she was one of a very rare breed in Eastern Canada, as sternwheelers were almost always confined to large shallow rivers such as the Red River and the Mississippi. She was powered by a 100-hp compound engine manufactured at Pointe Lévis, Quebec, and registered 111.49 tons. By May of 1887 she was ready to run.

No record of her début has been found, but we may be sure that *La Minerve* received a spirited send-off on her inaugural trip, with the usual assemblage of musicians, dignitaries, and Oblate fathers making speeches blessing her departure. She began making trips every Tuesday, Thursday and Saturday to the new settlement at Baie-des-Pères and other points on the lake, and soon proved capable of speeds of ten to thirteen knots. She also carried the mail once a week, but by popular demand this was soon increased to twice a week. Except for the *Argo*, she was the only steamer on Lake Temiskaming, since the *Mattawan* had just been taken back to Mattawa to provide a link with the Canadian Pacific Railway. *La Minerve* was, in effect, her successor.

The return of the *Mattawan*, which now belonged to the Lake Temiskaming Colonization Railway, led to a reorganization of the upper Ottawa River steamer service. Though the records are inconsistent, it would appear that the *Charlotte*, which was no longer needed north of Mattawa, was moved up to the stretch between Les Érables and La Montagne, and that the *Lottie*, which had formerly been on this route, was moved back to the La Cave-Les Érables run, where seemingly there had been no steamer operating. (A later source places the *Charlotte* on Seven League Lake, but it seems more likely that the larger steamer *Émerillon* remained in use there.) In 1893, as noted earlier, the Lake Temiskaming Colonization Railway bought the small steamer *Toneata* from Alexander Lumsden, but how she fitted into the schedule is unknown.

The Lake Temiskaming Colonization Railway and its boats provided the first organized transport to and through the Témiscamingue district. Before then, the region was virtually isolated, except by canoe or snowshoe (unless one could catch a ride on a passing lumber tug), and the importation of heavy merchandise was nearly impossible. Even with the boat and sleigh service, the area remained almost inaccessible for two or three months of the year, when the ice was too thick for navigation and too thin for snowshoeing. At such times the settlers had to make do entirely by themselves.

Commercially, the new route represented an extension of the trading corridor up the Ottawa River from Montreal, and at first most imports to the district came from the island city. Thanks to the Lake Temiskaming Colonization Railway and the Canadian Pacific Railway, travel time from Montreal to Baie-des-Pères had been cut from five days to three.

Settlement was now advancing steadily. In 1885, there were only 37 families residing in Témiscamingue; by 1892 there were 251. Of these, nearly half settled in Duhamel Township around Baie-des-Pères, while 28 more settled in Guigues, 45 at Tête-du-Lac, and nineteen more to the south at Fabre and the Long Sault. Baie-des-Pères with its fine sheltered harbour located two-thirds of the way up the lake, was always the hub of the colony, and by 1886, though it had barely 50 inhabitants, the community already featured two sawmills, a grist mill, a church and a large store, opened in the spring by André-Elzéar Guay, a notary from St-Jérôme. A hotel, stables, a forge and a hospital were also under way, while that same autumn Mr. Boulianne took on another contract, to build a wooden wharf for the government at La Pointe, on the south side of the bay near the mills. When a post office was opened at the budding village, also in 1886, it was decided to call it Ville-Marie in honour of the patron of the Oblates of Mary Immaculate, though the old name hung on for about another decade. In 1886, too, it was decided to move the old mission from across the lake to Ville-Marie, since the original location on the Ontario side had ceased to be convenient. By the winter of 1887, it was entirely abandoned.

The rise of Ville-Marie and the growth of settlement both led to the demise of Fort Temiskaming. The old Hudson's Bay Company post, for over 160 years a lonely outpost of European civilization amid the Laurentian hills, faithfully provisioning Nishnabis and white men alike, now declined with the fur trade and those dependent on it. Unrestricted trapping had wiped out most of the fur-bearing animals, while disease and liquor introduced by the white men were wiping out the Nishnabis. With amazing resilience, though, they managed to survive as a people. The fort was no longer the local headquarters of the fur trade; with the coming of the Canadian Pacific Railway up the Ottawa Valley, the Hudson's Bay Company transferred that role to Mattawa House in 1882. Another setback was the opening of Mr. Guay's store at Ville-Marie, four miles north, which forced the Hudson's Bay Company to move its own store there to counter him. Fort Temiskaming now became a secondary outpost, and in 1902 it would be abandoned entirely for Haileybury. Today, although the site has been purchased and groomed by Parks Canada, little remains of the old fort except a few stone chimneys and the historic cemetery. The coming of "civilization" has killed it.

In the midst of the expanding new settlements, *La Minerve* plied regularly, bringing in small groups of settlers, transporting groceries and freight and delivering the Royal Mail. She was also used for special excursions, often arranged by the Colonization Society, and recreational trips. On June 27, 1887, she and the *Argo* both hosted the first local St-Jean-Baptiste celebrations at the old mission; the visitors gathered from all parts of the lake to find the buildings gaily decorated. Nor was this an exclusively Catholic event; the local Nishnabis and the Hudson's Bay Company men were also invited to attend, and did. The day featured canoe races and sporting events, while the two steamers conducted a cruise up to Tête-du-Lac and paid a visit to Édouard Piché's farm, the oldest in Guigues Township. We also hear of a special grand Mass being held at the mission on August 21st, conducted by Bishop Duhamel of Ottawa and Bishop Lorrain of Pembroke, who had both come especially for the occasion. Once again, the two steamboats did their part, bringing in boatloads of Nishnabis, some of whom came from as far afield as Lake Temagami, Lake Kipawa and Lake Abitibi. *La Minerve* is also said to have transported limestone from Burnt Island to Ville-Marie to be sold to the colonists.

The steamer did not always enjoy clear sailing. Late in her maiden season when the waters were low, she managed to go aground at Fort Temiskaming and damaged her propulsion plant. This meant a trip to the only suitable shipyard then on the lake: Alex Lumsden's facilities at Opemicon. Precisely what happened next is uncertain. The Lake Temiskaming Colonization Railway was probably disheartened by the setback, and it is also doubtful whether the ship was making a profit. Perhaps there was not enough money available for repairs. Perhaps (most likely) her owners fundamentally did not want to be in the boat business. Whatever the reasons, the Lake Temiskaming Colonization Railway decided to sell the big craft in March of 1888 to Lumsden. The smaller steamers used downstream were not included in the deal.

Mr. Lumsden's business career was moving into high gear. His logging interests were prospering so much that he was making plans to open his own sawmill on Gordon Creek (Lumsden's Mills). His tug, the *Argo*, was then doing almost all the towing on Lake

ABOVE:

Fort Temiskaming in 1928.   Courtesy Société d'histoire d'Amos,
600 PH1-12-23

BELOW LEFT:

*Scene at North Temiskaming (now Notre-Dame-du-Nord),
circa 1900.*   Courtesy Société d'histoire d'Amos, 166G FCC-2-12-3

BELOW RIGHT:

Steam locomotive Gendreau, *of the Lake Temiskaming
Colonization Railway.*

Temiskaming. Presumably, when he bought *La Minerve*, it was on the understanding that he would continue to use her to serve the settlements. Why he decided to assume this responsibility is uncertain. He may have figured that *La Minerve* would make a useful reserve towboat in between her passenger trips. Or he may have wished to control navigation on the lake; the *Argo* was his and he was about to build the *Dora*. Probably he sensed that colonization was the trend, and concluded that catering to the public might prove a profitable new side venture. Almost certainly he knew of A.P. Cockburn of Muskoka, who was developing the Muskoka Navigation Company into the largest and most successful inland steamboat operation in the country. The two men had much in common. Both were self-made businessmen, both were Liberal Presbyterians, and both were involved in the timber trade. It is not known whether Cockburn and Lumsden ever met, but the former often had to visit Ottawa to attend to his parliamentary duties, and the Lumsden family is said to have taken holidays in Muskoka. On her death in 1907, Mrs. Lumsden would leave a substantial bequest to the tuberculosis sanatorium at Gravenhurst. Whatever his reasons, Alex Lumsden took over *La Minerve*, ran her for the 1888 season, then had her remodelled at Opemicon Depot and registered anew as the *Meteor*.

The steamer *Meteor* was destined to become a legend on Lake Temiskaming, though initially she was a rather modest double-decked all-purpose vessel, with an open bow and a bank of cabins on the upper deck behind the wheelhouse. She seems to have been little altered from *La Minerve* beyond her propulsion system; if *La Minerve* was indeed a sternwheeler, the *Meteor* was screw driven, with a round stern instead of a square one. Nevertheless, the *Meteor's* dimensions were initially almost identical to those of *La Minerve* — 105 feet in length by 23.8 in beam — and her register tonnage was reckoned at 115.68 rather than 111.49. Her engine, too, was unchanged, and she was now licensed for 130 passengers.

For the next nine years, the *Meteor* carried most of the passengers and much of the freight on Lake Temiskaming, though little is known of her early years. No doubt she had to face drifting ice, followed by seas of sawlogs every spring, plus thunderstorms and the occasional gale or blizzard as she battled her way to and from Ville-Marie, her lower deck packed with freight and the upper hosting groups of hopeful *colons*, hardy lumberjacks and parties of visitors. She must have experienced occasional groundings and broken propellers while trying to cope with the shoals and debris amid fluctuating water levels every season. Her passengers must have groped around in crowded quarters during inclement weather, especially if they had to spend the night on board, since cabin space was surely very limited. Probably few complained. Her crews must have known many a weary hour, wooding up the bunkers and loading and unloading cartons, bales and sacks of merchandise (often into scows or small boats where there were no docks), and cleaning up after the horses and cattle. They must have experienced many a chill, dark night on a lonely lake with only a coal-oil lantern for light and fellow crewmen for company. Lumsden, her owner, must have wondered periodically whether the new service would ever pay; only four families moved into Témiscamingue in 1888. But all this is mere conjecture, since none of her log books or any other detailed records survive. In September of 1894, however, the Toronto *Globe* reported that the four steamers on Lake Temiskaming were all very busy, as scores of families had lately arrived from Quebec, New England and other parts of the United States, as well as from Muskoka and Parry Sound. That same year, C.C. Farr noted that fares on the *Meteor* and the Lake Temiskaming Colonization Railway came to $4.50 one way from Mattawa, plus 85 cents extra per hundredweight of freight. He also remarked that Captain W. Percy was especially noted for his courtesy and kindness to his passengers.

Meanwhile, colonization continued. The society was now assisted by other groups, such as the Montreal Merchants' Colonization Society, which sponsored immigration to Guigues Township, and the St. Hyacinthe Colonization Society, which did the same in Fabre. In 1888, the village of St-Bruno-de-Guigues emerged, and four years later Lorrainville followed, about five miles inland from Ville-Marie. Before the turn of the century the villages of Laverlochère, Béarn and Fabre were on the map, and soon afterwards Fugèreville, St-Eugène-de-Guigues and

Guérin. In 1910, the little village of Nédelec was founded, about nine miles north of Tête-du-Lac. All of them were named after missionaries or leading Catholic clergy. The "Nouveau Québec," as Témiscamingue was often called, did not always enjoy prosperity. Autumn frosts damaged the crops in 1888 and again in 1894, and in 1890 a slump paralysed the lumber trade, leaving the camps almost idle for a few years. The Wright silver mine likewise shut down in 1890, depriving the settlers of another customer for their crops. However, by 1893, the various lumber companies, including Klock, Moore, Gillies Brothers, McLachlin Brothers and J.R. Booth were active again, and so were the sawmills at the Rivière de la Loutre (Otter River) and Ville-Marie. Ville-Marie itself now had several stores and a bakeshop, while Pierre Boulianne opened a hotel in 1894. That year, Témiscamingue formally became a separate district in Quebec, with A.E. Guay acting as mayor. When Ville-Marie itself became an incorporated village in 1897, Mr. Guay assumed the mayoralty of it.

In the meantime, another small village was slowly developing at Tête-du-Lac, at the mouth of the des Quinze River. The Nishnabi had been granted a reserve there, but between 1885 and 1892, 45 more families (mostly white) moved into the region. By 1890, the settlement had a school and a church, and soon a post office followed (1896), under the appropriate name of Nord-Témiscamingue, or North Temiskaming. For a time, the main feature at the village was the Klock Company farm and depot, but soon after the turn of the century, Thomas Murray, one of the leading businessmen of Pembroke, envisaged a whole new town there, perhaps even bearing the name of "Murray City." Accordingly, he bought up a lot of the Nishnabi lands, surveyed a town plot, and opened the first store in the community. Despite its becoming a regular port of call for the steamers, however, no city developed there, only an attractive little town. Nor did the new name stick; although Murray managed to make his own choice official, the idea did not go over very well with the French Canadians, and in 1908, they petitioned successfully to have the old name restored. Much later, during the 1930s, it would be changed again, this time to Notre-Dame-du-Nord, though English Canadians still commonly refer to it as North Temiskaming.

Thus, by the turn of the century, the region of Témiscamingue was becoming well populated, and soon some of the settlers were spilling over into Ontario, particularly the fertile valley of the Blanche River. At the far end of the lake, meanwhile, more exciting developments were under way. A through railway was coming!

That line was the Kipawa Subdivision of the Canadian Pacific Railway. Although records about the old Lake Temiskaming Colonization Railway are sparse, it would appear that it soon became quite profitable; according to *La Sentinelle*, the Mattawa French-language newspaper (September 20, 1895), the rail and boat lines were handling so much freight and lumber by 1891 that the company was invited to sell its charter to a new company, charged with building an unbroken line from Mattawa to Lake Temiskaming. That the Canadian Pacific was ready to build such a branch indicates that it, too, was impressed by the scope and development of the Témiscamingue market. In January 1891, the Canadian Pacific Railway, by mutual agreement, took over the Lake Temiskaming Colonization Railway and began the reconstruction. The 40-mile spur proceeded very slowly; the terrain was rough, and in places the roadbed had to be blasted out of the sides of sheer granite cliffs. Besides that, money was tight; the early 1890s were not good times. Nevertheless, by May 1894 the new branch was completed almost as far as the Long Sault, and on the 19th we hear of the *Mattawan* being used to transport a locomotive across the river on a scow, thus contributing to her own obsolescence. By November, the new line was completed, except for a bridge to span the river. This was not finished until the spring of 1896, and until then the little *Mattawan* was still busy filling the gap. This is almost the last we hear of her.

Initially, the new spur ran only to the head of the Long Sault, to what is now South Témiscaming, at which point it used the same roadbed as the former Lake Temiskaming Colonization Railway. Soon, though, it was extended to Lumsden's Mills and by 1903, it reached Lake Kipawa. Naturally, it eliminated all the slow and costly portages and transfers of the makeshift Lake Temiskaming Colonization Railway and reduced travel time from

ABOVE:

Crew of steamer Meteor, *at South Témiscaming around 1894.* Courtesy Mr. Gilles Amesse, 158G PH1-7-53

MIDDLE:

Scene at Ville-Marie, Old Wharf. Courtesy Mr. Gilles Amesse, 56/84 S.H. PH1-7-5

BELOW:

Wabi River, New Liskeard, circa 1910. The Meteor *appears at left. At the river mouth is a dredge with the* Dora. *It may be the Silverland next to them.*

Mattawa to Ville-Marie to a single day. The line was also immensely beneficial to the lumbermen, on both Lake Temiskaming and Lake Kipawa, and to the Lumsden Steamboat Line, which now enjoyed a year-round link with the outside world. The former Lake Temiskaming Colonization Railway and its trams were, of course, dismantled. No one knows what happened to the *Gendreau*, but perhaps the tiny locomotive went to some other narrow-gauge line, such as the Montfort Colonization Railway, which was opened north of Montreal in 1893. Similarly, the little steamers which had done the lion's share of the work on the route soon disappeared. The entire fleet was sold on February 26, 1897, to the Canadian Pacific Railway, which had little use for them. The *Charlotte*, as we have seen, was immediately resold to Patrick Kelly and spent her last few years on Lake Kipawa. The *Émerillon* was dismantled in the fall of 1897 and her hull abandoned at Snake Creek. The *Toneata*'s fate is unrecorded, except that she was out of existence by 1902. The *Lottie* fared better; she seems to have been remodelled and used as a ferry around Mattawa, and was inspected as late as 1907, but sometime soon afterwards she burned while beached just above Explorer's Point, near the town. The old tug *Mattawan* is said to have met the same fate at the same time in the same fire; both vessels were out of commission at the time. An anchor from one of these pioneer steamers is preserved in the Mattawa Museum today. So ended the boat services on the uppermost portion of the Ottawa River.

On Lake Temiskaming, by contrast, the steamers were just entering their heyday. Alex Lumsden was now running the *Meteor*, *Argo*, *Dora* and *Beaver* and though the last three were tugs, all would sometimes take passengers. South Témiscaming, too, showed a few more signs of life. Only a small Catholic chapel, a halfway house catering to lumbermen, and a few shanties existed there before the Canadian Pacific Railway arrived, but the railway built some sheds and a spur at the water's edge. A caboose served as the station until a proper one was constructed. For his own part, Lumsden opened an office with a cookery and a boarding house for the boat crews, plus another shipyard across the river, on the Ontario side (perhaps because there was no room for it near the docks). A store and post office were also opened at the wharf, but otherwise growth remained slow at South Témiscaming until the coming of the paper mills in 1917.

In the meantime, what had happened in Ontario? Was Ontario doing nothing about its lands in the Clay Belts while Quebec was opening up a new frontier and creating "le nouveau Québec"?

Not quite, although for some time the Ontario government showed scant interest in Timiskaming. This was hardly surprising. During the 1860s, '70s and '80s, Ontario, anxious to find new farm lands, had attempted to open up the wilderness region stretching from Georgian Bay to the Ottawa River, north of the Trent and Severn Rivers, with generally disastrous results. The whole tract, including Haliburton and Renfrew Counties and the Districts of Muskoka, Parry Sound and Nipissing, lies within the rocky ridges of the Canadian Shield, and (with some exceptions) the settlers who were induced to try farming there were soon forced to abandon the attempt. Many were ruined in the process. Humiliated by this colossal failure, the government was not very keen on tempting Fate a second time. The Shield extended relentlessly on to Lake Nipissing and beyond, and so far as anyone knew, it continued right up to Hudson Bay. It took the efforts of a few very persistent souls to convince the authorities that this was not so.

One of the first champions of Timiskaming was Captain Bernard Mulligan, who had been commanding steamboats around the upper Ottawa River for nearly twenty years. In 1881, Mulligan toured the north to verify reports of good soils and possible mineral wealth. He returned home enthused by what he saw, and soon led a delegation to Queen's Park, but the Commissioner of Crown Lands remained sceptical, and quoted reports from the Hudson's Bay Company that the land wouldn't grow a hill of potatoes, even if every one were supplied with an overcoat! Mulligan angrily retorted that the Hudson's Bay Company had very good reasons for not wanting to see any kind of settlement in Timiskaming, but his protests fell on deaf ears.

A more famous — and flamboyant — colonizer was Charles Cobbald Farr, whose name will always be indissolubly linked with the rise of Haileybury. C.C. Farr, as everyone called him, was born in England in 1851. As a youth, he displayed great athletic vigour, a strong love of Nature, and a rather reckless fondness for taking risks. He studied at Cambridge, but failed to secure an appointment to the Civil Service of India, and in 1871 he decided to seek his fortune in Canada. Here he was advised to try the Muskoka District, which was just being opened up for settlement. Arriving at Bracebridge, he tried his hand at various trades, such as smithing, trapping and hotel keeping, but none of these ventures prospered, and also, as a young English "greenhorn," he was frequently the victim of chicanery and practical jokes. Indeed, at times he might have starved but for the timely arrival of a little money from home. In 1872, he joined a government survey party working at Killarney, on northern Georgian Bay, and from there he worked his way up to Lake Nipissing. Soon afterwards, he joined another survey team that was preparing to demarcate the exact border between Ontario and Quebec from the head of Lake Temiskaming . Here, in the winter of 1873, he got his first glimpse of Matabanick ("the place where the trail comes out," as the Nishnabis called the future site of Haileybury). Even then, as he gazed upon the forested slopes forming a gentle declivity down to the shores and offering a magnificent view from its summit, a resolution was forming in his mind that "if ever I get the opportunity of making a stake in my life, it will be there."

The survey team carried out its assignment, chopping a line straight north midway between the mouths of the Blanche and the des Quinze rivers. The work gave young C.C. Farr a chance to study the country, and soon he became convinced that much of it was suitable for farming. Stopping at Fort Temiskaming on his return, Farr was told that a man of his calibre ought to be working for the Hudson's Bay Company. The Chief Factor at the post promised to plead his cause, and in August 1873, he received word that he had been accepted. After a brief apprenticeship, he was made factor at the post at Fort Kipawa.

Farr spent his next nine years at Fort Kipawa. He soon learned the Nishnabi tongue and frequently paddled out to the native camps and engaged in trading, hunting and fishing. The life was less rugged and arduous than his previous existence, but it was often lonely, except when groups of shantymen showed up in the wintertime or when his employees celebrated a Christmas party. Sometimes Farr also ran big canoe loads of furs down the river as far as Pembroke. In 1878, he was given permission to marry the girl of his dreams, Miss Georgina Probyn, whom he had met at Pembroke in 1873, and soon he brought his young bride to the isolated Kipawa post. While still at Fort Kipawa, Farr occasionally wrote to the Toronto newspapers praising the possibilities of the North, but the Hudson's Bay Company soon gave him an emphatic hint to keep quiet about it.

In 1882, Farr was promoted and took charge of Fort Temiskaming. This gave him further opportunities to explore the country and assess its prospects. Meanwhile, he had never forgotten Haileybury — or Humphrey's Depot, as it was then called, after a local squatter who sold hay to the lumbermen — and in 1885 he purchased 30 acres from him. Two years later his colleague, P.T. Lawlor, established himself there, and meanwhile Farr continued to lobby the Mowat government to open up Timiskaming, sometimes trekking down to Mattawa on snowshoes to catch a train to North Bay and Toronto. At first, the results were negligible, but finally, in 1887, the Department of Crown Lands agreed to survey eight townships around the northwest corner of Lake Temiskaming, including Bucke, where Haileybury now stands. Less than two years later, C.C. Farr abandoned his secure livelihood with the Hudson's Bay Company and prepared to head north.

On May 13, 1889, the Farrs moved out of Fort Temiskaming. They had arranged to take the *Argo* up to Matabanick, where C.C. had built a log shanty, but the tug failed to arrive and the party — including Mrs. Farr, her little daughter and six others — left in a red punt called a pointer and a canoe with their most essential possessions. The weather was windy, and the pointer was nearly swamped at Paradis Bay, but the little group reached their new home safely, though at first they had to sleep on the floor. Three days later, the *Argo* arrived, bearing the furniture, some fruit trees and strawberry plants, plus C.C. himself and two others. The very next day, a bush fire nearly burned the house down, but fortunately the grounds had already been cleared and the building was saved. The first church services, the first baptism, the first marriage ceremony and the first local court case were conducted in that house, and in 1890, a post office was opened, called Haileybury after the public school Farr had attended in England.

The growth of Haileybury was very slow at first. For five years, the Hudson's Bay Company steadfastly opposed the new settlement, and Farr had to bring in all his supplies and provisions from Mattawa. Even his friends called him a visionary and a dreamer. By 1891, he had a farm with livestock, plus a sawmill and some storehouses, but few settlers came, and the depression of 1891 certainly didn't help. In the winter of 1892-93, Farr resolved to try another tack; he made one more trek to Mattawa, took a train to Toronto, and arrived at the office of the Honourable Arthur Sturgis Hardy, who was then Commissioner of Crown Lands and later Premier of Ontario. Hardy, who was expecting him, looked at the rustic-looking Englishman still wearing his moccasins, and asked in an irritated voice, "What do you want, Farr?"

C.C. replied, "I want to open up that country of Northern Ontario."

"How can we open it up?" asked the Commissioner.

"By writing out a pamphlet," rejoined C.C.

"Who will write that pamphlet?" asked Hardy.

"Sure, I will," replied Farr.

Hardy shrugged, as if unable to think of any more objections, and said, "Well, write the pamphlet, and Mr. Yeight, my secretary, will correct the grammar, if you send the manuscript to him, and … he will make arrangements for the publication of it."

Farr went home jubilant, and soon had his pamphlet drafted. It stressed the agricultural prospects of Timiskaming, noted that there were lumber companies ready to buy crops, and mentioned the mining and touristic potential. It also pointed out that there were now four steamers on the lake to assist with transportation. In 1893, the pamphlet received its first printing, and that same summer a Crown Lands agent was sent to Timiskaming.

The results were disappointing. A few more settlers arrived and took up land at such places as Dawson Point, the mouth of the Wabi River and Haileybury, where a church and school were soon being contemplated. But this was a mere trickle compared with the Quebec side, and by the end of 1894, Haileybury still possessed only four houses. Frustrated by this state of affairs, C.C. Farr paid another visit to Montreal and Toronto in the fall of 1895, and again called at the Crown Lands office. When Hardy saw him, he asked, "What do you want now?"

"Mr. Hardy," rejoined Farr, "I thought that, seeing how hard appears to be the work of populating this great North West of Timiskaming by relays of our own Canadians, I might induce some other fool Englishmen like myself to come and share with me what you call the starvation of the impossible north."

"How are you going to do it?"

"By the usual method, namely pamphlet."

Wearily, with an air of 'here we go again' Hardy replied, "Well, I will give you seventy dollars and you can get out your pamphlet."

Farr reached Liverpool on what he later described as a cattle boat on Christmas Eve and arranged to get his pamphlet printed. It was meant to appeal to adventurous young men seeking a change, and it sold like hotcakes. The Canadian Pacific Railway, the Allan Steamship Line and the Dominion Line were soon clamouring for copies. Farr accompanied all this by a lecture tour, chiefly in his native East Anglia. The following year, he returned to Canada with a few dozen English settlers and reported to Hardy. Despite some nasty insinuations spread by the Conservative opposition, the federal government (now Liberal) was impressed with Farr's efforts, and proposed to reward him by granting him eight dollars a head for every immigrant he brought in, provided that affidavits were supplied. Farr refused the offer, with the comment, "I'm not importing cattle!"

As the newcomers settled in, the population of Haileybury rose sluggishly to 55 by 1899. It now contained a hotel, a blacksmith shop, an Anglican church and a general store and weather station run by Farr's cousin, Paul A. Cobbald. But there was still no sign of a railway, for which Farr had been campaigning for years, and worse, the sawmill burned in August 1898 (though it was soon rebuilt). Worse still, a party of 150 visitors on a government-sponsored free excursion on May 28, 1901, probably aboard the *Meteor*, steamed right past Haileybury, which had no dock, and unloaded its passengers at an upstart new settlement at the mouth of a muddy yellow stream called the Wabi, after a local Nishnabi chief called Wabis, who often hunted, fished and trapped in the area.

That Haileybury might have to face competition from other centres was borne home to Farr by John Armstrong, a native of Chaffey Township, in Muskoka, who stopped by in August of 1893. Armstrong had been invited by Hardy to go to Timiskaming, check the country out, and open a Crown Lands office if he saw fit. Himself interested in a new start in life, Armstrong asked Farr if he'd be willing to sell Haileybury. Naturally, Farr refused, and explained that his settlement was the stake of his life, and that he intended to develop a town there. Armstrong agreed that the site was magnificent, then added that he would obviously have to hunt for a new farm elsewhere. Farr gave him a canoe and some provisions, which were later paid for, and Armstrong paddled up to the mouth of the Wabi River, about five miles north. Here he found a solitary log house in a clearing of five acres on the north bank, kept by William Murray of Haliburton and his sister, who had arrived two years earlier. The land looked very good, Armstrong noted, with none of the rock or loose stones so abundant in the south, and there was plenty of spruce, tamarack, cedar, balsam, poplar, whitewood and birch in the bush. Satisfied, Armstrong surveyed both sides of the river and began selling lots at twenty-five cents an acre. Meanwhile, he reported very favourably on the land, and was soon appointed Crown Lands agent, a position that ought to have gone to Farr. Nonetheless, the two men got along well, although over the following winter Armstrong confided that he himself was considering another townsite, either at Dawson Point or at the mouth of the Wabi River. Thus began the long rivalry between Haileybury and New Liskeard.

The growth of New Liskeard was likewise very slow at first, and indeed, for a time it was touch and go what its name would be. When the post office was opened in 1896, it was named Liskeard by George Paget of Bristol, England, one of the first settlers, in honour of a friend who hailed from the market town of Liskeard, Cornwall. However, the mail, alas, was delivered only as far as Haileybury, and Liskeard's unlucky postmaster was paid a paltry fifty cents to walk or row to the older settlement three times a week to collect it — a sum that hardly even paid for his meals. There wasn't even a road of any sort connecting the two places until William Murray blazed a trail. Also, more problems arose as mail for Liskeard sometimes ended up at the little village of Leskard, near Port Hope, and for a time the name was changed to Thornloe, after the local Anglican bishop. However, the change was not universally welcomed, and after much bickering, the name was changed in 1902 to New Liskeard. The name of Thornloe was transferred to another little hamlet about ten miles farther north.

Meanwhile, by 1895, Mr. Armstrong had opened his Crown Lands office and induced the government to build a little hostel for immigrants. Deciding that lots of 320 acres were too big, the agent advised the government to sell half-lots only. An uproar resulted when he further recommended that the original settlers be required to surrender half their lands, but this proposal was soon dropped.

By 1896, the advance of settlement had pushed the frontier eight to ten miles up the Wabi River and seventeen miles up the Blanche, while a stumpy, muddy "road" had been started north from the river mouth. (The locals called it "Calamity Gulch" on account of all the wagon spills that took place.) It was greatly to Liskeard's advantage that, unlike Haileybury, it had a river offering an easy route to the interior, and likewise that the mouth of the Wabi River provided a harbour of sorts for the local steamers — although at first, there was no wharf and fluctuating lake levels often made it impossible for the *Meteor* to enter the

ABOVE:

Steamer Meteor, *flagship of the Lumsden*
Line.   Courtesy Mr. Gilles Amesse

BELOW LEFT:

Wharf at Fabre (Quebec).   Courtesy Mr. Gilles
Amesse, 812 PH7-4-1

BELOW RIGHT:

Railway depot at (South) Témiscaming.
Behind the station is the steamer Meteor.
Courtesy Mr. Gilles Amesse

estuary. Also in 1896, a teacher from Durham, Ontario — Angus McKelvie by name — arrived in company with Tom McCamus, a druggist from Bobcaygeon. The pair soon formed a partnership and built a badly needed sawmill at the mouth of the river. The local farmers cut the trees and hauled or floated them in, and soon some of the rough-hewn shanties in the area were dressed up with false fronts. In 1897, another newcomer, Samuel McChesney, collected a dollar from each of the local families (which netted $22 in total) and built a pontoon bridge over the Wabi River to link the two halves of the settlement. As an unexpected consequence, Armstrong soon found cattle crossing the bridge and eating his grain. To prevent this, he put a stile across the end of the bridge — which in turn prompted some local boys to cut the south end of the bridge loose one night. By the next day, the whole structure was out on Lake Temiskaming, which really made the fur fly! However, the following year the government built a proper wooden bridge across the river, the iron portions of which were delivered by steamboat.

By 1897, Liskeard (Thornloe) was firmly established with a store on both sides of the river, and another building that served as a combination church and school. Nonetheless, there were still only six houses, and as late as 1899 Thornloe was described as just a rural post office. But things were looking up. The Ontario government was now interested in opening up the Clay Belt lands in Timiskaming, partly as a means of relocating some of the impoverished farmers of Muskoka and Haliburton. Soon it was offering free excursions to the head of the lake to let people see for themselves; in May of 1901 alone, 125 took up location tickets. In 1898, a Presbyterian church was built at Liskeard, to be followed by an Anglican church in 1899, and Baptist and Roman Catholic churches by 1903.

Meanwhile, settlement was creeping up the Blanche River. The original Irish settlers were soon followed by French Canadians, who founded the hamlets of Brethour and Belle-Vallée. Before 1900, too, an old Englishman named Ulysses Henry Thomas proceeded about seventeen miles up the river by canoe, there to establish his home in a little two-room cabin set in a tiny clearing. So began the village of Tomstown. Soon other landings downstream were on the map, including Judge and Hilliardton, while in 1905 Jack Pearson established Pearson's Landing, which likewise became a local post office.

At first, the Blanche River settlers were extremely isolated, except for the passing of lumberjacks and log drivers employed by the Booth and Eddy Companies, with only the steamer *Clyde* available to bring in supplies and mail at irregular intervals. In 1901, however, the government sponsored a farming expedition to Tomstown, with positive results. Typical were the experiences of the McFarline brothers, Robert and Malcolm, who came, looked and selected farm sites for themselves, returning the following year. When a third brother, James, brought in his wife, child, horses, cattle and furniture aboard the *Meteor* in 1903, they arrived at Haileybury on a rainy night to find no wharf, no fit road to Liskeard and no room at the hotel. The family had to bunk in with a cousin. Fortunately, a small steamer called the *Geisha* had just started to ply from Liskeard up to Tomstown, and this allowed the McFarlines to proceed farther without any more trouble. But the Blanche River settlements were hampered for years by quagmire roads in the spring and fall, and by log drives that often clogged the river and prevented the farmers from exporting their crops or receiving the mail.

Meanwhile, how were the steamers doing? Presumably their fortunes fluctuated with the ebbs and flows of lumbering and immigration during the 1890s, which suggests that the early years of the decade were not good for them. However, we are told that, by 1894, the boats were busy; over 60 families moved in that year, mostly to Quebec, swelling the overall population to more than 1,000. Until they became more or less self-sufficient, the new settlements imported cattle, horses, crates of groceries, furniture and clothing, sides of beef, drums of coal oil, bundles of tools, bags of cement and the occasional plow. Bulk cargoes, such as lumber, were usually carried in scows. Hay was a vitally important commodity until the new farms could produce their own. To the small groups of lonely settlers struggling to clear the land and eke out a living, the whistle of the distant steamer was about the most welcome sound in the world. During the winters, their only contact with the outside world was by sleighs and horse teams down the lake, and it was not uncommon for such teams to encounter air holes where the current was strong, and go through the ice and be lost. For about six weeks in December and January, and again from late March to early May, traffic between Timiskaming and the "front" ceased altogether. Thus, settlers on both sides of the lake stocked up with plenty of provisions in the fall while the boats were still running, and hoped for an early opening of the navigating season in the spring. One winter, meat ran short in Liskeard, and the people were reduced to living on beans — and game, if they could catch any. Another year, nails ran short, another time it was underwear, still another time it was kerosene, with the result that people had nothing but candles to illuminate their homes and only fireplaces to provide heat. It was said that many couples got so cold that year that they usually bedded early for the night — and the result was a bumper crop of babies the next fall! Although the ice was usually gone from the lake by the last week in April, occasionally (as in 1893, 1895, 1899 and 1900) it stubbornly hung on into May, even as late as the 16th. Small wonder, then, that everyone anxiously peered down the lake after the spring breakup, watching for the distant plume of smoke that told them "The steamboat's coming!"

Until 1899, the *Meteor* was the only passenger steamer on the lake. Ordinarily, she would call at Haileybury, Liskeard and North Temiskaming on Tuesdays, Thursdays and Saturdays, and return to South Témiscaming on the alternate days. Both ways, she would usually dock overnight at Ville-Marie. As calling places, both Haileybury and Liskeard left much to be desired, Haileybury because it was open and exposed to all the winds, and Liskeard because the entrance to the Wabi River was shallow — sometimes too shallow —which forced the *Meteor* to stop at Sharp's Bay, about a mile south. Neither village had a wharf, and for years the ship had to anchor offshore and unload all her freight into scows and pointers; if no small boats were available, the lifeboats might be used. Unloading the small boats could also be unpleasant, especially in cold, wet weather, and the soggy clay shorelines of the Wabi River were slippery. As a result, many a handler heaving heavy bags of oatmeal would end up in the mud or the lake. Another problem was the drives of logs every spring, which might delay shipments for hours or result in a broken propeller — which could put a steamer out of service for days. Nonetheless, when the steamboat arrived, people would usually drop whatever they were doing and flock down to meet her, to claim their merchandise and greet the newcomers.

Although the Timiskaming settlements depended almost entirely on his boats, Alex Lumsden saw no need to improve or expand his fleet, except in the towing line, until 1896. By then, however, the Laurier era had started, coinciding with one of the most prosperous intervals in Canadian history. Immigrants were soon pouring in, factories were humming, and ambitious railway schemes were in the air. In short, people felt invigorated and optimistic. Some were discovering Timiskaming, too. One group arrived at Haileybury in drizzling rain in the summer of 1896, to discover only a rustic settlement overlooking a shoreline strewn with rocks and stones. This prompted one member of the party to remark that, if this was the "promised land" the government was sounding off about and offering for fifty cents an acre, he was going straight back to Toronto, since he could get plenty of land like that in Muskoka for nothing! Half an hour later, though, the steamer entered the mouth of the Wabi River, where the amazed newcomers found abundant clay loam soils and no sign of rocks anywhere. It was unfortunate for Haileybury that it happens to lie at the southern edge of the Clay Belt, rather than at its centre, as C.C. Farr had imagined.

Thus, by the end of 1896, Mr. Lumsden decided that he needed a larger ship to cope with the growing number of immigrants, and therefore ordered the *Meteor* drydocked at Opemicon. Here she was cut in half, lengthened by 25 feet, and completely rebuilt. The new *Meteor* was quite the largest vessel yet seen on Lake Temiskaming. She was now 130.5 feet in length (not counting the fantail) by an ample 27 in beam, and drew 7.4 feet of water. These proportions made her very safe and steady, even in the roughest weather. She now registered 203.62 tons and grossed 299.43. Her engine was a brand new 165-hp compound Bertram

ABOVE:
Steamer Meteor, *leaving Ville-Marie.*
Courtesy Mr. Gilles Amesse, 590 PH1-7-1

MIDDLE:
Steamer Temiskaming, *as a scow.*

BELOW:
Steamer Temiskaming *(third version).*

model, giving her speeds of up to eighteen miles per hour — though it was noticed that the engine's pulse sometimes made china creep across the dining room tables. Wood was still used for fuel, which continued to require periodic stops for more, but soon after the turn of the century she was burning coal, which was cheaper and more compact, and could be delivered by rail. Unlike most steamers of her size and type, the *Meteor*'s engines and boiler were both hidden below the main deck, leaving space amidships for staterooms, including some for the captain and the female crew. The main deck also housed the galley and the first- and second-class dining rooms, the former set near the stern. At the forward end of the deck there was a baggage room and storage space for freight, including horses and cattle. Often, lumberjacks and poorer immigrants who could not afford cabins had to sleep on the deck wherever they could find room. Lice were sometimes a problem. Mr. Lumsden was always very touchy about this issue, and gave strict orders that, at the very least, the first class rooms were to be kept free of vermin, especially when priests were aboard! The upper deck featured a smoking lounge for the gentlemen (ladies, by definition, did not smoke!), twelve staterooms for those who could afford them, and an elaborate sitting room aft, with red velvet divans and a piano. A clerestory with narrow windows along the sides helped brighten up the cabins. The bridge, of course, carried the wheelhouse and lifeboats. Eleven crew members, including three waitresses who also doubled as chambermaids, were usually required to crew the ship, which was now licensed to carry 305 passengers.

The *Meteor*'s début may have been delayed, since she was launched only on August 14, 1897, and seemingly completed her maiden voyage to Liskeard on October 17th. She was now under the command of the tall, amiable Captain Redmond of Mattawa, who was usually in charge until 1904. Whether Mr. Lumsden was aboard for that trip is uncertain, though we hear that she caused quite a stir when she first sounded her shrill whistle and hove to at the mouth of the Wabi River. Among those attracted to view the stately new ship were about 40 Nishnabis, who had never seen such a marvel before. They were invited aboard, and sat quietly in the lounge until it grew dark. Unknown to them, the *Meteor* featured another novelty never before seen in Timiskaming — electric lights. Suddenly, the captain flicked the switch and turned them on. The startled native people lost their usual stoic calm and jumped up in alarm; then, catching on, they laughed, a little sheepishly.

As before, the *Meteor* ordinarily left the wharf at Témiscaming around 4:00 P.M. on Mondays, Wednesdays and Fridays, following the arrival of the train, and would steam straight north, stopping at Opemicon Depot, the Montreal River, Quinn's Point and Fort Temiskaming, and in response to flag signals, before gliding into Ville-Marie at sundown. Bright and early at 6:00 the following morning, she would set off for Haileybury, with possible stops at Paradis Bay, Brown's Point and Martineau Bay; then proceed to Liskeard and North Temiskaming, again with possible stops at Dawson Point, Windy Point, Guigues landing and perhaps the old Wright Mine, before retracing her route back to Ville-Marie for the night. The day after, she would return to the foot of the lake. Of course, she and the other steamers always ran as late as the season would allow, and thus risked being cut off by ice at season's end. At least once the *Meteor* had to spend a winter at Haileybury, where men were kept busy cutting the ice around her hull at regular intervals.

Although accidents to the *Meteor* were infrequent, it is reported that she once had trouble at Haileybury, probably in 1899, when Captain Redmond ran her in too close to shore. The bow grounded and, try as he might, Redmond could not back her off again. Shifting the cargo towards the stern didn't help. In the distance, though, people could see the *Argo*, towing logs near Chief's Island. The *Meteor* whistled for help, but there was no response from the tug. Finally, a few of the *Meteor*'s crew set off across the lake in the pointer usually towed along for emergencies, and despite choppy waves whipped up by a southwest wind, they eventually intercepted the *Argo*, which secured her tow, came over to help, and soon pulled the *Meteor* free.

By this time, immigration was so brisk that new people were arriving every trip, and the *Meteor* could no longer cope with the crowds. In April 1899, as noted earlier, Mr. Lumsden bought the steamer *Clyde* and used her for a combination of towing, freighting and taking passengers. (The *Meteor* never towed.) Just a few weeks earlier, he had also purchased another new steamer called the *Témiscamingue* or *Temiskaming*, a sidewheeler built at the foot of the lake in 1898 by Louis Lacouture, a Montreal shipbuilder. The *Temiskaming* was a double-decked, round-sterned, all-purpose vessel, with an 80-hp walking-beam engine. Her original dimensions are unknown, but judging from photographs, she was probably about 120 feet in length. As a paddlewheeler, she apparently did not handle very well. Observers noted that she was listing somewhat on her maiden trip to North Temiskaming. Presumably she was meant to be a tug and freighter, but her owner soon ran short of cash and mortgaged her twice in the summer of 1898 to John S. Gillies. The following April, she was sold to a shadowy corporation called the Lake Témiscamingue Navigation Company of Ottawa, which never seems to have done a day's business. Just nine days later (April 14th), the vessel was resold to Alexander Lumsden — to become his eighth steamer on Lake Temiskaming.

The next few years of the *Temiskaming* are obscure. At an unknown date — perhaps immediately — Lumsden had the vessel's machinery removed, and according to one report she was briefly demoted to a mere scow, used in tow of the *Argo*. However, by 1901, we find her back in service as a propeller steamer, still retaining her overhanging decks. Her new engine was a 21-hp compound built at Point Lévis, Quebec. She was now commanded by Captain Blondin, who had lately been running the *Clyde*.

The *Temiskaming* was now the *Meteor*'s running mate, plying the same route but on alternate days. She would leave South Témiscaming on Tuesdays, Thursdays and Saturdays, while her sister was at the far end of the lake. Both would arrive at Ville-Marie in the evenings. This meant that the Timiskaming communities were now favoured with a boat service daily, except Sundays, and no doubt a daily mail as well. The *Temiskaming* had a few staterooms, but she was more of a freighter than a passenger steamer, and her interior appointments had none of the opulence of the *Meteor*'s.

A story is told about a bet made between Captain Blondin and Captain Redmond at Ville-Marie around 1901. It seems that Blondin wagered $50 that he could arrange to unload a scow filled with sixty 260-pound barrels of salt pork in two hours or less, using just one man to do it, along with four others to keep clearing the wharf. To Redmond this seemed a very safe bet, but he did not reckon on Blondin's secret plan, which was to offer a big burly teamster named Pierre (Pete) Le Lièvre a full day's pay plus one "square face" bottle of gin to do the job. With that kind of incentive, Le Lièvre, a 26-year-old giant of a man, had the scow unloaded in just one hour!

Another, less savoury, incident took place on the *Meteor* around 1903. The ship was coming up the lake with a certain Ben McKenzie and his son on board. The McKenzies were prone to become violent when drunk, and were generally considered "bad medicine." On this trip, perhaps under the influence of liquor, the older man picked a quarrel and started to beat up a Lebanese immigrant named Michael Abraham, who was engaged in selling cheap jewellery. The captain was summoned, but he could not break up the fight. The hapless Abraham might have been killed had Mrs. Redmond not come down from the bridge brandishing a revolver. A warrant was issued for McKenzie's arrest, but the constable at New Liskeard had no enthusiasm for carrying it out. Then Kalil (Big Pete) Farah, another Lebanese newcomer, who had just completed the Hotel Canada in town, offered to execute the warrant himself if sworn in as a constable. He was. "Big Pete," who weighed 260 pounds, then proceeded straight to McKenzie's house, arrested him with no trouble, and brought him back to town in a buggy. The son was picked up the following day.

Boisterous behaviour was not uncommon on the Temiskaming steamers at that time, especially when parties of lumberjacks were aboard. Although there were some exceptions, to many "jacks," getting "loaded up" when off duty was part of life, and one day a group of these characters, reeling, carousing, singing and hiccuping, staggered ashore at Haileybury and made a general nuisance of themselves. The magistrate collared them, confiscated part of their wages, and put them back on the boat. When some of the other passengers remonstrated and asked how the authorities could justify the fines, they were told in no uncertain terms, "Because we want sidewalks." By 1912, the town was able to pay for ten miles of wooden boardwalks.

Except for a few little-known private steamers in use around Ville-Marie — including Captain Bergeron's *Étoile-du-Nord* (1888), Frère Moffette's *Sarto*, Captain Montreuil's *Santa Lucas*, the *Santor* and the tug *Jean-Baptiste*, built in 1889 to help service François-Xavier Coursol's sawmills — the Lumsden Steamboat Line enjoyed a monopoly on Lake Temiskaming, and was doing an immense business. In 1901, 445 settlers moved into New Ontario (which may have netted the boats $3,842.50 in fares alone), and on May 16, 1902, about three weeks after the ice broke up, we find the *Argo* following the *Temiskaming* into New Liskeard, carrying fifteen rail carloads of freight. As the boat service grew and took on a life of its own, Lumsden apparently assigned it to his son John, but in the meantime he was also building his own wharves, including one at North Temiskaming (valued at $500), two at New Liskeard (each valued at $600) and another at South Témiscaming (valued at $2,500). As early as 1903, we hear of a government dredge at work, clearing out the mouth of the Wabi River so that the *Meteor* could dock safely, while five years earlier Lumsden engaged Captain Morin to lengthen the wharf at Ville-Marie. Ville-Marie itself was now a thriving village, rising in terraces around the Baie-des-Pères, while Haileybury was finally starting to look like a town. Its population rose to 200 in 1901, and 464 by 1904. C.C. Farr, who had invested so much vigour and dedication coaxing his colony into being, could now enjoy the fruits of his labours. For the first time in his life, he was growing wealthy by selling off lots, and he was now editing his own newspaper, the *Haileyburian*. In 1904, Haileybury became a town, with P.T. Lawlor as its first mayor. Farr himself would become mayor in 1906, by which time the population had jumped to 1,228. New Liskeard was booming too. By 1902, it had fourteen stores and a population of 500. The following year, it was likewise incorporated, with John Armstrong becoming its first mayor. By 1905, the town had two large hotels and a population of 1,500. Nonetheless, for a time its growth would be slower than that of Haileybury.

The Lumsden Steamboat Line, meanwhile, was going out of the towing trade. Lumbering was now in decline around Lake Temiskaming, and in any case the Upper Ottawa Improvement Company, which had been formed in 1870 to tow logs for all the lumber companies downstream from Des Joachims, was now interested in extending its services farther north. In the fall of 1902, Mr. Lumsden sold his largest tug, the *Argo*, which had been in service for 20 years, to the Upper Ottawa Improvement Company, and the following spring, as mentioned earlier, he also relinquished his two alligators, the *Mink* and the *Beaver*. The *Mink* and the *Beaver* continued to ply for several more years but the *Argo*, which was probably getting worn out, was dismantled in September 1902, and her hull sent down the Long Sault rapids. The following year, her massive walking-beam engine was installed in a large steel-hulled tug built to replace her. In 1904, the Lumsdens apparently built a second, smaller, *Argo* at Turtle Portage on Lake Kipawa to tow and take passengers, but this vessel — which was only 87 feet by nineteen — lasted just one season, during which it was evidently moved to Lake Temiskaming. There she burned at Haileybury on October 17, 1904.

The *Argo* was not the only Lumsden steamer to fall victim to fire. The same fate befell the *Comet* in 1902. This vessel is something of a mystery today; her registry has not been found and no photos have turned up. All we know is that she was a screw-driven freighter and scowboat that was also licensed for 50 passengers. She is said to have grossed 144.92 tons, and to have been built around 1900 to assist the *Meteor*; Mr. Lumsden evidently liked astronomic names. The Témiscamingue *Gazette* routinely noted her arrival at New Liskeard at 2:00 A.M. on May 13, 1902, with a new scow in tow, as if there were nothing unusual about it, but otherwise we know only that she met with disaster about a mile north of Opimica Narrows, apparently on August 22, 1902. Sparks from the funnel seem to have ignited a cargo of hay, which was no doubt being towed alongside in the scow, and before anyone noticed it the blaze was out of control. Captain Burley hastily ran the vessel ashore, where the crew abandoned ship, but the steamer became a total loss. Alex Lumsden spoke of rebuilding the *Comet*, but evidently he changed his mind and imported the steamer *Jubilee* from the St. Lawrence River instead.

The *Jubilee* was built at Portsmouth (now a suburb of Kingston) in 1897, in the year of Queen Victoria's celebrated Diamond Jubilee — which probably accounts for her name. The vessel was originally 65.8 feet in length by 14.4 in beam and registered 36.63 tons. She was a screw vessel, with only one deck and a square stern, and was powered by a second-hand high-pressure engine. Apparently she was used as a freighter or workboat around Cornwall until Lumsden brought her (by rail, no doubt) to Témiscaming in the spring of 1903. He seems to have had her rebuilt at once and lengthened to 84.2 feet. She was also fitted out with a second deck, and registered anew at 78.29 tons. The *Jubilee* entered service in 1903, on the same route as the *Meteor* and the *Temiskaming*, often with a scow in tow. With only a 15.4-foot beam, she proved somewhat top heavy, however, and a strake of timber was attached to her sides near the waterline to make her more stable.

Like most of the other boats, the *Jubilee* had at least one anxious moment at the Long Sault rapids, which begin several hundred yards below the wharf at South Témiscaming. (Until 1911, there was no control dam at the rapids.) One day the steamer, under Captain Morin, was starting to leave Témiscaming when a sawlog jammed against her propeller, immobilizing her. Within a few minutes she was caught in the current, which began carrying her back towards the rapids and certain destruction. The captain, who was very excited, yelled in French to a deckhand to drop the anchor at once. The deckhand grabbed the anchor, then shouted back that there was no line attached to it. The flustered skipper told him to drop it anyway. The deckhand obeyed, and that was the last anyone saw of the anchor! Meanwhile, the steamer was drifting back faster and faster amid the eddies; the captain, frantic, tried reversing, then forwarding, then reversing the engines again and again. Just when it seemed that all was lost, the log finally slipped loose, the engine room bell rang "full ahead" and the *Jubilee* crept forward out of danger.

Meanwhile, Alex Lumsden had come up with a new idea: to go into the resort business. Sometime around 1900 he constructed the Bellevue Hotel at Témiscaming, on the slopes directly above the steamboat wharf. The Bellevue was an elaborate three-storey mansion with broad verandahs, and an annex close by, containing a recreation hall with bowling lanes, a billiard room and a ballroom. A golf course was also started across the river. The big hotel was perhaps inspired by the resort-building boom in Muskoka, which was providing unparalleled prosperity for the Muskoka passenger steamers, but the Bellevue actually featured two luxuries that few Muskoka resorts could yet afford: electric lights, powered by the nearby generators at Lumsden's Mills, and pure spring water. Milk and fresh meat were supplied by an experimental farm across the lake. The big hotel charged rates of $2.50 per day, then equivalent to about two days' wages, which, needless to say, was beyond the means of most incoming settlers, who were more likely to spend the night at Boulianne's hotel, in a tent or a wagon, or on the deck of a waiting steamer. The Bellevue was designed to appeal mostly to American anglers and sportsmen, and no doubt it was built with the blessing of the Canadian Pacific Railway, which was making considerable efforts to advertise the region's attractions. Despite everything, the hotel failed to transform Lake Temiskaming into another Muskoka. The setting was remote, bathing and swimming were difficult on account of the log drives, and the place was bedevilled with blackflies and sandflies. During the 1920s, prohibition paralyzed it, and it soon passed on to other uses.

Incredible though it may sound, the ever-active Mr. Lumsden had taken on yet another venture, in addition to his mills, his boats and his hotel: a career in politics. The Ontario Liberal Party had held office since 1872, and was looking for prominent new candidates to infuse fresh blood into the government. Since Lumsden was now one of the leading businessmen in Ottawa (still his place of residence), a number of Liberals asked him to run. Lumsden hesitated. He was a very busy man, and unaccustomed to wearing fancy clothes or making speeches, and furthermore, he was not really well known in his home city, despite

ABOVE:

Train at Haileybury Station, 1912.

Courtesy Haileybury Fire Museum

BELOW:

Charles Cobbald Farr, founder of Haileybury. Courtesy Haileybury Fire Museum

his contributions to charity. The Ottawa *Free Press* even got his name wrong when reporting his attendance at the Liberal nomination meeting on February 19th, 1898. There, in the presence of Premier Hardy (as he now was) and Prime Minister Laurier, Alex Lumsden made a trenchant speech, spiced with poetry, in which he apologized for his lack of rhetorical skills, praised the ladies as mistresses of the homes and hearts of men (at a time when women were still denied the vote), and noted his 53-year effort to advance the prosperity of Ottawa. He promised to devote the same zeal to politics, praised the Queen's recent Diamond Jubilee celebrations, and lauded the integrity and beneficence of the Ontario government. The speech went over very well, and Lumsden was congratulated and sworn in as one of the two Liberal candidates for the City of Ottawa. His next few days were full of hectic campaigning and speechmaking. The Conservatives found him a difficult man to attack, since he had no political sins to atone for. They tried to portray him as an unwashed shantyman who had somehow done well, while suddenly becoming very concerned about the well-being of working men themselves. To a heckler who sneeringly offered to buy him a decent suit of clothes, Lumsden caustically replied that he wasn't "tailor-made"! He felt no shame in his working-class origins, and said so.

The election was held on March 2nd, with the result that the Hardy government was sustained, although by a narrow margin. In Ottawa, traditionally a Tory town, Alex Lumsden won by over 200 votes, though the other Liberal candidate went down to defeat. As a Member of the Legislative Assemby, he seems to have proved a forceful speaker and a logical debater, and was even considered for the job of Minister of Public Works.

From his vantage point in the Ontario legislature, Mr. Lumsden was soon listening to some very interesting developments from Timiskaming. At that time the Clay Belt communities had no land links whatever with the south, and for five months of the year they were isolated. They wanted something better. In 1898, Angus McKelvie of New Liskeard and a neighbour walked the length of frozen Lake Temiskaming, took a train to Toronto, and asked the government to open a road to the north. The following year, they were back, making the same request. When nothing happened, John Armstrong and the Reverend T.E. Pitts made another try in 1900, bearing a petition for grants to open "a good stage road to North Bay." When this likewise failed, Armstrong and McKelvie returned to Queen's Park in 1901, this time to ask for a railway. They met some of the members in a caucus room and eloquently stressed that the North was Ontario's treasure chest, with vast, untapped resources in timber, minerals and farming land, all just waiting for the iron horse.

At last the agitations bore fruit. Although it caused an uproar in the legislature, the government agreed to send ten exploratory parties, each including a surveyor, a geologist, and a timber estimator, plus guides and packers, to conduct a massive survey of the enormous tract of lakes, rivers and muskeg from the Ottawa River north to the Albany River, and to see if a railway was warranted. The teams noted the forest wealth and found some evidence of mineral outcroppings, but the greatest surprise of all was the discovery of a second great Clay Belt stretching over 16,000,000 acres in the Cochrane region, far to the north of Timiskaming.

The results of the surveys were tabled at the next session of the legislature, and the verdict was favourable. However, although various lines, such as the Nipissing and James Bay Railway and the James Bay Junction Railway, had been chartered during the 1880s, no capitalists were prepared to finance them — which is hardly surprising, since the population was very sparse, the resources unproved, and the white pine disappearing. Besides, according to one estimate, a railway to Timiskaming would cost about $6,600,000 — then a staggering sum. Nonetheless, the Ontario government, now headed by Sir George Ross, who had succeeded Hardy in 1899, felt committed to its northern colonies, lest the settlers should desert Timiskaming for Manitoba, and consequently it favoured a railway, even if it meant that the province would have to pay for it. But the government's majority was very slim, and many M.L.A.s denounced the idea of a line into the "God-forsaken North," running hundreds of miles through impossible country to nowhere. Could such a proposal pass? Here Armstrong and McKelvie tried their hand. Being Liberals, they decided not to approach the Tory leader, Sir James Whitney, and instead used their efforts to win over the Toronto Board of Trade, which then approached Whitney, who agreed not to oppose the measure. On January 15, 1902, the Honourable Frank Latchford, Minister of Public Works, tabled a bill for the Temiskaming and Northern Ontario Railway.

That the proposed railway would tap Lake Temiskaming was clearly implied by its name, but for a time it was uncertain what route it would take or when it would start. The Canadian Pacific Railway preferred, of course, to see its own very profitable spur from Mattawa extended into the region (which would mean up the Quebec side of the lake), and in this it was supported by both Montreal and Ottawa. Elsewhere, however, the interests of Toronto and much of southwestern Ontario favoured a line from the small railway town of North Bay — which was already linked with Toronto by the Grand Trunk. It was a classic case of two major metropolitan centres seeking new arteries of trade to the same hinterland by different routes, and in this case Toronto won.

The dilemma facing Alex Lumsden was very serious. As a loyal son of Ottawa, Lumsden was expected to oppose the new line from North Bay, which was also likely to ruin his flourishing steamboat line. On the other hand, his party was generally in favour of it, and besides, Lumsden knew the sentiments of the Timiskaming settlers, who greatly preferred a railway from North Bay to an extension from Mattawa. At first, he inclined to the Mattawa connection, but then changed his mind and voted for the Temiskaming and Northern Ontario Railway, explaining that he felt that this would serve the North better, and besides, any extension of the Canadian Pacific Railway spur would go through a desolate rocky wilderness before it reached the Clay Belts. It was a public-spirited decision, but it probably cost him his seat in the election of 1902. The Tories accused him of being ineffectual and betraying the interests of Ottawa, among other things. Lumsden defended his stand and the government's record, but the Conservative muckraking stuck, and he lost his seat on May 29, 1902. Mr. Lumsden accepted defeat philosophically, taking comfort from the fact that at least the Ross government survived, albeit with a majority of only five. The province was swinging towards Toryism.

Meanwhile, the Temiskaming and Northern Ontario Railway received official sanction on March 17, 1902, and on May 10, the first sod was turned by Mr. Latchford at North Bay amid a volley of cheers. It was impossible for the new line to proceed straight north on account of the long, high escarpment fringing the edge of town, but after some dispute it was decided to run it east past Trout Lake and up the gap of the North River valley. Zigzagging past post-glacial lakes and mounting hairpin curves through ravines, gullies and muskegs, it climbs 600 feet in twenty miles. Originally, after crossing the Marten River, it was slated to go around Caribou Lake, but, thanks largely to the determined efforts of a flamboyant Scotsman named Daniel O'Connor, the route was changed to tap the eastern arm of Lake Temagami instead — of which more in Chapter 5. The line was scheduled to reach New Liskeard a distance of 110 miles, by the end of 1904, and though it was initially dubbed the "Time No Object" railway, it managed to meet that deadline. By 1903, the contractor, A.R. Macdonell, had completed 65 miles of roadbed and 35 miles of track.

The new railway was, in fact, being pushed from both ends simultaneously. Over the winter of 1902–03, huge quantities of rails, ties, tents, tools, provisions and dynamite were stockpiled at South Témiscaming, to be hauled north to Haileybury in the spring by the *Meteor*, *Temiskaming*, *Clyde* and *Jubilee*. There it was laboriously unloaded into pointers to be taken ashore. Once again steamboats were being used to hasten their own demise. From Haileybury, the supplies were hauled overland by horse teams as far as the Montreal River. At that time, there was nothing to be seen in any direction except solid bush. Hundreds of horses were also brought in, mostly to pull the scrapers used to make cuttings through ridges of clay, and with the horses came mountains of baled hay — all of which was scowed into Haileybury by boat. One local settler, who had tried to take the *Temiskaming* down the lake on a trip to North Bay in the summer of 1903, only to find the vessel quarantined because someone aboard was supposed to have smallpox (which turned out to be fly bites!), decided to walk down the railway right of way instead. He noted that ties were already being laid at Latchford, where the line crossed the Montreal River, and rails at Mile 103 near Long Lake, about eight miles farther north. That same season, the tracks reached Haileybury, just as C.C. Farr had dreamed they would, and by September of 1904 there was steel to New Liskeard. Already the roadbed was being extended farther north, deep into the Clay Belt. On January 16, 1905, the first section of the Temiskaming and Northern Ontario Railway was officially opened, as a paying train completed its first run.

The coming of the railway was an event of such momentous importance that northeastern Ontario has never been the same since. The line forever revolutionized the economy of the North. In its wake came spectacular mineral discoveries and several unprecedented mining booms — of which more in the next chapter. It also gave the lumber companies new opportunities for expansion, and eventually led to the founding of the pulp and paper industry. It opened up new markets for farmers. It created new towns and employment for hundreds of men. It transformed people's lives by breaking the annual isolation of winter and putting Timiskaming in regular touch with the south all year round. Inevitably, too, it shifted the major routes of commerce, so that the North ceased to be a remote dependency of Ottawa and Montreal and instead became a direct dependency of Toronto. The ancient water corridor of the Ottawa River had been augmented by a land corridor, which at once became paramount — as land travel always does.

Alexander Lumsden, who had unselfishly refused to oppose the Temiskaming and Northern Ontario Railway, was not obliged to witness what the railway would do to his steamboat line. By 1904, he was 60, and showing little diminution of his formidable energies. Always he had seemed hale and hearty, and never was he ill a day in his life. But in fact, his unceasing workload was slowly killing him. The reckoning came on the morning of August 4, 1904. Having just completed arrangements for a summer holiday at the Bellevue, in the hope that it might revive his wife, (who was then in poor health), Mr. Lumsden was suddenly seized with chest pains at his home on Stanley Avenue in New Edinburgh. Alarmed, his daughter and sister placed him in bed and summoned a doctor, but the pain rapidly grew worse, and by the time help arrived he was almost comatose. Despite all efforts, the stricken man soon lost consciousness and passed away shortly before noon. The medical verdict was heart failure.

The news made the front pages of the Ottawa newspapers, and it was reported that over 100 carriages gathered at his home for the final solemn procession to Beechwood Cemetery. Among those in attendance were Sir Wilfrid Laurier, the Mayor of Ottawa, and several of the lumber kings, including F.H. Bronson, David McLaren and J.R. Booth. However, his son, two daughters and a brother-in-law were the chief mourners, Mrs. Lumsden being too ill to be present. Mr. Lumsden was eulogized as a "quiet, unassuming, hard-working citizen" and a generous benefactor to his church, a man with the courage "to speak what he thought, and execute what he willed." All of his acquaintances knew him as a dynamic entrepreneur, but relatively few had known the kindly, gentle, often charitable human being behind the somewhat gruff façade. One of those who did was Wilfred Campbell, who later wrote several stanzas in memory of his friend.

Certainly Alex Lumsden had been a consummately successful businessman. At the time of his death, he owned stocks and bonds in 23 companies and banks, plus properties in Ottawa, extensive timber limits, most of Lumsden's Mills, most of the major wharves on Lake Temiskaming, the Bellevue Hotel and more buildings at Témiscaming, another hotel with a wharf and a storehouse at Kipawa, plus his Fair View Farm opposite Témiscaming and much more. Indeed, his total assets were inventoried at $935,042.70, all of which was left to his wife. Not bad for a working man who had started out in life with only a few dollars.

The Lumsden Steamboat Line, as such, outlasted its founder by just one and a half years. Margaret Lumsden kept the ownership of the boats until February of 1906, but in the meantime she assigned the management to her son John, who was also given the lumber business. The assets of the Lumsden Steamboat Line, not counting the docks and storehouses, were assessed at $32,050 when Alex died. Of these, the *Meteor* was valued at $12,800, the *Temiskaming* at $5,500, the (second) *Argo* at $4,000, the *Jubilee* at $2,000, and the *Clyde* (which was close to its end) at a mere $800, while the two Lake Kipawa tugs, the *R. Hurdman* and the *Otter*, were listed at $3,500 and $1,000 respectively. A balance of $12,940 was still owing on the Temiskaming steamers, and another $8,345 on the Kipawa boats. In addition, the line possessed five scows, six wharves, the depot at Opemicon with its maintenance yards, the ways for the steamer *Argo* and miscellaneous supplies.

On or about April 28th, the *Meteor*, now under the command of Captain Albert Gaul, opened the navigation season with a call at Haileybury and New Liskeard, running on essentially the same timetable as in former years. But this time there were no crowds of eager people flocking to greet her. Instead, the public reaction was casual, if not completely indifferent. They now had trains calling once a day from North Bay, sometimes bringing in 125 new arrivals every trip. With direct access to Toronto, no one was particularly interested in ordering shipments by way of Mattawa — except at Ville-Marie, which still had no railway. How much revenue the displaced steamboat line lost in 1905 is no longer known, but it is certain that New Liskeard, for one, was never a profitable port of call again; previously it had been the most remunerative. If anything, more freight was now shipped by boat from New Liskeard than was shipped to it. Indeed, the company kept only three ships in regular service in 1905: the *Meteor*, *Temiskaming* and *Jubilee*. The *Clyde* had been taken to Lake Kipawa, the *Dora* sold as a tender to the *Dredge Queen* and the *Argo* (II) destroyed by fire. The day of the steamboat was far from over on Lake Temiskaming, but in essence the best days came to an end in 1904.

By the winter of 1905–1906, the Lumsdens decided that there was very little future left for their steamboat line, and made plans to sell it off. On February 15, 1906, Mrs. Lumsden formally sold the *Meteor* and the *Jubilee* to Joseph Arthur Larochelle of Mattawa, a long-time employee who was supervising the formation of a new firm called the Temiskaming Navigation Company. The *Temiskaming* was sold the following day and within a month all three had been reassigned to the new company. The yards at Opemicon Depot were sold to the Upper Ottawa Improvement Company. John Lumsden kept the tugs on Lake Kipawa, and even built another one, the *Emma Mac*, in 1910. She and the *Otter* were ultimately sold, probably around 1917, when their owner retired from the lumber business, while the *R. Hurdman* was scrapped in 1915. Her whistle was installed on the *Meteor*, producing a chiming sound when the old and the new were blown together. Thus ended the Lumsden Steamboat Line, concluding seventeen years of faithful and indispensable service to the settlements of Timiskaming.

Steamer Prima *(centre) with the* Belle *at Charlton (see page 131).* Courtesy Englehart & Area Museum

CHAPTER 4

STEAMBOATS
AND MINING

THE COBALT BOOM: (1903 ET SEQ.)

I t all started on September 17, 1903, at Mile 103 of the new Temiskaming and Northern Ontario Railway, around the northwest shore of a small pool called Long Lake. According to a popular legend — and when has History ever been able to discredit a good story? — Alfred Larose, a French-Canadian blacksmith from Hull, Quebec, who was working with the railway crews, happened to be sitting down to have lunch when he spotted a pesky fox peering at him. Irritated, Larose grabbed a pick and threw it at the creature. He missed, but the pick rebounded off a nearby rock outcropping with a peculiar ringing sound. Intrigued, Larose went over for a closer look, and found himself staring at a vein of flinty, lustrous pink ore. Might this stuff be valuable … ?

Larose broke off a specimen, which he later showed to his boss, Duncan McMartin, a subcontractor on the railway. McMartin thought it might be native copper, and, though doubting its value, he agreed to have it assayed by the Bureau of Mines. The experts diagnosed it as kupfer-nickel, a rare mineral that indeed looks like copper, and in 1904 they sent out a skeptical geologist, Willet G. Miller, to take a closer look. Miller examined the veins Larose had seen, and also studied some other finds made on August 7, 1903, by two lumberjacks, James H. McKinley and Ernest Darraugh. These consisted of veins of flaky white stuff, so pliable that a knife blade could dent it. The geologist pronounced it native silver, and estimated its consistency at 4,000 to 8,000 ounces per ton. In other words, a ton of this ore should be worth about $2,500 to $5,000. Convinced now that this was just the tip of the iceberg, Miller boldly painted a sign reading, "Cobalt Station, Temiskaming and Northern Ontario Railway," and mounted it on a tree. The name caught on instantly.

Meanwhile Alfred Larose had not been idle. On his way back to Hull, he stopped at Mattawa and showed his specimens to Noah Timmins, whom he had met when the Canadian Pacific Railway was being extended to South Témiscaming. Timmins, whose father had founded Mattawa, was then part-owner of one of the largest stores in town. Having done some prospecting himself since 1889, he knew something about ores, and realized that Larose's samples contained high-grade silver. Immediately he telegraphed his half-brother Henry in Montreal to get in touch with Larose and buy a share of his claim. Eventually the Timmins brothers ended up with a one-quarter interest, for which they paid $3,500. Noah Timmins himself hurried up to Long Lake (now Cobalt Lake), where he found a local fire ranger disputing Larose's claim. The argument was finally referred to the Ontario Department of Crown Lands, which decided in favour of Larose. Like most discoverers, Alfred Larose did not create his own company or open his own mine. Instead, he transferred his claims to a syndicate consisting of Duncan McMartin and his cousin John, David Dunlop, a Mattawa lawyer, and the Timmins brothers, for the handsome sum (as it then was) of $30,000. Thus was born the famous Larose Mining Company, which soon sank a shaft and struck a rich vein of silver nearly 100 feet below the surface.

These developments did not pass unnoticed. In the fall of 1903, a Haileybury sawmill owner named E.C. Wright, whose father had started up the Wright Mine on the Quebec side of Lake Temiskaming in 1883, heard of the Larose find and came over to Mile 103 to see for himself. He was soon joined by his brother, and the following year they discovered what became the Drummond and Jacobs silver mines. Similarly, in October of 1903, a French Canadian named Tom Hébert, who had been a logger for the J.R. Booth Company before joining the Temiskaming and Northern Ontario Railway, stumbled upon a rich vein of silver near Cobalt Lake. He showed some specimens to Arthur Ferland, who had just purchased the Hotel Matabanick in Haileybury. Ferland had them assayed, discovered their value, and obtained the backing of some officials of the Temiskaming and Northern Ontario Railway. Then a New York financier, E.P. Early, saw Ferland's samples and eventually bought out the entire group for $250,000. Early then organized the Nipissing Mines, with capital authorized at $6,000,000. Meanwhile, a group of Buffalo financiers led by Dr. H.N. Miller, having prospected for some time in Coleman Township (near Cobalt) without finding anything, tried sinking a 50-foot shaft near the lake. They found little, but in 1904, they tunnelled 20 feet deeper, then drilled horizontally another 100 feet. Then — presto! — they struck it rich. Within just a few more months the Century Mine had extracted about $100,000 in silver ore, and by 1908 this would eclipse $300,000.

More examples could be cited. An English prospector named W.G. Tretheway, having read of the first Cobalt strikes, came to Haileybury in 1904, where he met Wesley Mackay, who had made a find near Long Lake. Tretheway explored further, staked some claims of his own, then returned to Toronto and secured the financial backing of Colonel R.W. Leonard of St. Catharines. The result was the Coningas Mining Company, which became the richest producer in Cobalt. As early as 1904, the new camps were exporting ores valued at $136,218, mostly to smelters in the United States.

The Cobalt finds were the first important discoveries of precious metals in all of Eastern Canada, but it took some time for Wall Street to react to the news. Perhaps the attention of the mining world was still caught up with the spectacular gold strikes in the Klondike, just a few years earlier. But as claim after claim was registered near Cobalt and the mines started pouring thousands of dollars into the pockets of promoters and the coffers of Canada, speculations on the New York Stock Exchange began to grow lively, then frantic. Lumbermen, oil magnates and financiers staked millions of dollars to open up the silver fields, and by the summer of 1905 Cobalt was in the limelight of world mining news. Prospectors with weather-beaten faces, set jaws and slouch hats poured in, bringing tents, packsacks, camp stoves and canoes — to be followed by blacksmiths, miners and workmen. Every train was packed, and nobody bothered to wait for them to come to a stop before surging off. Some found treasure in short order; others searched for years and found nothing. A tent city sprang up in tiers among the stumps, scrub and slash on the rocky hills around Cobalt Lake, where only a few years earlier lumber magnates such as J.R. Booth and the Gillies brothers had been sending their loggers. Soon shacks began to replace tents, as the railway sent in trainload after trainload of fresh-cut lumber from the south. Clotheslines appeared everywhere, along with soap and washbasins as the men tried to keep moderately clean, while a hundred campfires glowed by night. It was soon obvious to the Temiskaming and Northern Ontario Railway that a townsite was needed, but when bidding day arrived there was perfect pandemonium, as new arrivals vied with squatters to offer fabulous prices for small lots. By 1906, Cobalt was in full swing. On March 30th, the New Liskeard *Speaker* noted that the bustling town had sprouted stores, boarding houses, one large hotel and two bank branches, plus six lawyers' offices, where just a year earlier there had been only one small store and one boarding house. Thirty-two new mining companies were registered in 1906; in 1907 the number jumped to 233, but needless to say many of them were fraudulent, as the usual array of grafters, crooks and confidence men swarmed in with the miners. By 1908, a total of $6,020,249 in silver ore left Cobalt by rail.

Initially it was possible for the miners to operate using only sledgehammers, two-handed drills, hand winches, buckets and dynamite. However, as surface finds grew scarce, more extensive and elaborate machinery became necessary — which usually drove prospectors straight into the arms of outside monied men. By 1910, electricity revolutionized mining at Cobalt, as the Hound Chutes on the nearby Montreal River, plus Fountain Falls and Mattabechewan with its 300-foot drop, were all harnessed to produce hydro-electric power. As a result, the mines could be electrified and the stamp mills powered. It also meant that electric aerial trolleys could now be used to convey ore from the pits to the crushers in the concentration plants. In addition, an ingenious new plant was built at Ragged Rapids (also on the Montreal River) to produce unlimited quantities of air at high pressure.

By 1914, Cobalt was a noisy, gutsy community with perhaps 20,000 inhabitants. It was not a very pretty place, with its ugly frame buildings perched precariously on denuded granite hills. Its muddy zigzag streets and boardwalks often cut right into the rock (sometimes with mine shafts running directly beneath them), and its growing slag heaps spilled into Cobalt Lake, while dozens of stark headframes stood like sentinels guarding the wealth beneath. Yet, despite its rough image, there were very few robberies or crimes of violence, and as a rule a consignment of ore could be piled up at a wharf or railway platform without anyone touching it. Liquor was legally prohibited at Cobalt, as it was in all mining towns, although illegal stills — known as "blind pigs" — flourished in the area for years. But to its partisans it was "the best old town" in the world; the lyrics of the "Cobalt Song" echoed from many a hotel or pool-hall in the evenings, pouring scorn on any place not lucky enough to be Cobalt. After all, how many other towns had added $300,000,000 to the wealth of Canada in just ten years?

It was lucky for Haileybury that it was just over five miles from Cobalt by rail, and therefore far enough removed for liquor to be legal. Indeed, the town soon reaped enormous benefits from the sensational silver discoveries at its back door. Its population, which stood at a mere 464 in 1904, jumped to 1,228 by 1906 and 2,265 by 1909. As of 1906, Haileybury had five churches, two hotels, two saloons — where many a mining deal was concluded — a school, about twenty stores, and perhaps a hundred homes. A disastrous fire in August of that year burned out most of the business section, but the buildings were speedily rebuilt, this time of stone or brick. A thick crust of gentility soon settled over Haileybury, as many a millionaire who had made a fortune at Cobalt retired there to build a gracious home overlooking Lake Temiskaming.

It goes without saying, of course, that the completely unexpected discoveries at Cobalt revolutionized the fortunes of the railway. The Temiskaming and Northern Ontario Railway had been undertaken as a developmental line, which initially offered passenger service just three times a week, utilizing one locomotive and two old coaches obtained from the Canadian Pacific Railway and the Grand Trunk. A trip along the serpentine track from North Bay to New Liskeard took twelve to fifteen hours. But as word of the Cobalt camp leaked out, the "Muskeg Express" — as some termed it — quickly turned into the "Cobalt Flyer," as the new railway groped to find enough rolling stock to handle the rush. Right from the very beginning, the Temiskaming and Northern Ontario Railway paid dividends, and by the winter of 1905, it had six locomotives (plus four on order) and ten passenger cars (plus five on order), providing service once a day. The company also purchased about 260 freight cars (mostly flatcars) handling an average of 875 tons daily. Seldom had the provincial government ever undertaken a more profitable or productive venture. The line was already advancing beyond New Liskeard, and in August of 1906, it announced plans for three new branches, including a two-mile spur to Haileybury wharf and a five-mile spur from Cobalt to Kerr Lake, through the Gillies Company timber limit.

Though the Temiskaming and Northern Ontario Railway was deriving enormous profits from the mining industry, the same was not true for the Temiskaming steamboats. Had Cobalt been discovered a few years earlier, before the railway came, it might have been a different story. Nonetheless, steamers did play a modest role in the Cobalt boom, bringing in prospectors and supplies, notably tools, machinery and hydro poles from South Témiscaming and farm produce from Ville-Marie, and taking out the occasional cargo of ore. However, it was not at Cobalt proper that the boats were destined to play an important role, but at some

ABOVE:

Cobalt Station, T.&N.O. Railway, circa 1907. Courtesy National Archives of Canada, PA 52767

MIDDLE:

Nipissing Mines, Cobalt. Courtesy Mr. Allan Richardson

BELOW:

Steam launch Little Roxy, *on the Blanche River.*

of the outlying areas, such as Elk Lake, Larder Lake, South Lorrain, and later Rouyn-Noranda, where more finds followed in the wake of Cobalt.

In the meantime, galvanized by the Cobalt boom, settlement was spreading rapidly in Timiskaming. The Blanche (or White) River formed an admirable route of entry through miles of good farming lands, and some pioneers were paddling and trekking even farther, up the Englehart River. By 1900, a few were established at the foot of Long Lake, about 36 miles northwest of New Liskeard, where the village of Charlton now stands. At the same time, prospectors were pushing northwards into the rockier terrain around Wendigo and Larder Lakes. The railway was not slow to follow. Without a pause the crews began laying track beyond New Liskeard, across the relatively level plains of the Clay Belt, and on to the emerging hamlets of Thornloe, Earlton and Heaslip. A major construction site developed at the Blanche River, about midway between Charlton and Tomstown, where a large viaduct was required to span the river. The campsite proved permanent and grew into another town, which in 1906 was named Englehart, after Jacob (Jake) Englehart, a millionaire oil-company executive who had just been named Chairman of the Temiskaming and Northern Ontario Railway. The town that bore his name was soon selected as a division point.

At this point, we must pause for a more detailed look at the boat services on the Blanche River.

STEAMBOATING ON THE BLANCHE RIVER: (CIRCA 1889–1906)

The lower seventeen miles of the Blanche River flow through the heart of the Clay Belt and forms a fine navigable appendix to Lake Temiskaming — at least for vessels of shallow draft. Inevitably, it became an important route of entry for the early settlers, who resorted to punts, rafts, canoes and dugouts to make headway. They made their living as best they could by selling their meagre surpluses to the lumber companies or the Hudson's Bay Company, or by working in the logging camps.

Very little is known about the beginnings of steam navigation on the Blanche River. In Chapter 3 we noted that the steamer *Clyde*, built by the Gillies Lumber Company in 1888, was reputedly the first steamboat to ascend the river, but she probably did so only on occasion, to bring in men and to provision the lumber camps. Most of the time she was out towing on Lake Temiskaming. A few of the little-known private steamers around Ville-Marie, such as the *Étoile-du-Nord* and the *Jean Baptiste*, may have made the occasional trip up the Blanche River during the 1890s, but there are no records to prove it.

In the case of the steamer *Little Roxy*, we are on firmer ground. She was built at Ville-Marie in 1896, by Captain Morin for Samuel Rothschild, who owned a hotel in the village. She was a large, handsome launch, measured 41.7 feet, registered 6.88 tons, and featured a clipper bow and a round spoon stern. She had an upright 4-hp engine and could go ten miles per hour. Her owner apparently used her to ferry men and supplies to the old Wright Mine, where a bit of fitful activity was still going on prior to 1903. But she was also used as a scow-boat, a passenger boat, an excursion vessel and even as a fishing tug. Occasionally she would run up the Blanche River to Tomstown, while the local settlers would wave her over or paddle out to meet her if they wanted anything. Her masters included Captain Morin and Captain Charles Tassé, who later moved to Haileybury. The *Little Roxy* was still operating out of Ville-Marie as late as 1908, but afterwards she is said to have been taken to Larder Lake, where she finally foundered.

Another steamer that served briefly on the Blanche River was the *Olga*, a little screw launch with a wooden canopy, which belonged to a Mr. D. Hammond of Haileybury, who built the Hotel Matabanick around 1901. The boat was apparently unregistered, and her year of construction is unknown. However, an advertisement in the Temiscaming *Gazette* reveals that Captain Hammond's little tug made weekly trips up the Blanche River by May of 1902, and that the "charming little craft" was also available for charters. Business, we are assured, was brisk, but the service did not last long. In 1903, Mr. Hammond decided to sell his hotel and leave Haileybury for the West. (He soon had cause to regret this move, because his son-in-law Arthur Ferland, who took over the Matabanick, was soon to make a killing from the Cobalt boom.) The steamer meanwhile went to Robert Herron of New Liskeard, who was then the agent for the Rideau Lumber Company. Herron used the vessel as a workboat, with a little scow in tow, both of which he entrusted to his brother Elmer. Soon afterwards, the boat temporarily came to grief while docking at Dawson Point on a windy day. Her scow struck the wharf and caused her to capsize and sink in shallow water. No one was hurt, but Mr. Herron was not very pleased when he arrived. Gradually the boat was dragged ashore and bailed out, and soon was back in service. After the railway arrived, Bob Herron went into the livery business, connecting with the trains at New Liskeard station, before becoming a successful contractor. Elmer, in turn, left for Calgary. No one recalls what happened to the *Olga*.

Another small steamer dating from this period was the *Scotchman,* a 45.6-foot tug built at Carleton Place in 1904. Grossing 25.91 tons, this vessel was imported by Daniel Lang of Sturgeon Falls, former owner of the *Osprey*, who had secured a licence for commercial fishing on the Quebec side of the lake. Repeating his practices on Lake Nipissing, Lang laid long fish traps using pound nets and piles driven in by pile-drivers mounted on scows. The *Scotchman* was used to tow the scows and check the traps. Occasionally she was also chartered to take spectators to the ball games between New Liskeard and Haileybury, or to sweep logs and refuse around the Blanche River.

The results were much the same as on Lake Nipissing. For a time Lang was able to bring back scowloads of pike and sturgeon, and soon the lake was depleted. As the fish stocks fell, the Quebec government cancelled the licence. Then Mr. Lang died, and his sons showed no interest in fishing. The *Scotchman* lay idle at Haileybury, until Captain Ted Guppy purchased her and took her by rail to Lake Abitibi, where she was rebuilt and put to work for the Abitibi Power and Paper Company in 1917.

The Blanche River settlements, meanwhile, still needed a boat service, and fortunately someone was ready to provide it. That man was Captain Fred Hendry.

Frederick William Hendry was born in Toronto on December 27, 1873. He came by his boating instincts honestly; his father, John Hendry, was a prominent local boat-builder who, amongst other things, built the 50.9-foot schooner *Geisha* in 1900, which he used around Toronto harbour. Young Fred married and took a job in a nearby machine shop, but probably he also served at times on his father's boat. However, around 1902 he decided to strike out on his own.

Why he chose to come to Timiskaming can only be conjectured. Perhaps he had read about New Ontario in the newspapers, and sensed opportunities there. Presumably he came north on an exploratory trip to size up its prospects. He must have decided that they were good, because he formed a partnership with Francis Stockwell Brickenden, a Toronto butcher who in his younger days had served as a blacksmith, then (at the age of nineteen) as a bugler in the short campaign to suppress Louis Riel's Northwest Rebellion in 1885. The two then laid their plans.

First, Fred Hendry arranged with his father to lease or purchase the *Geisha* in 1903. Her two masts and rigging were removed at Toronto, and she was remodelled and fitted out with a second-hand 1.4-hp high-pressure Doty steam engine (which may have been installed in the North). In May of 1903, she arrived at South Témiscaming on a Canadian Pacific Railway flatcar, and was soon steaming up to Haileybury for the first time. After that, it was said that she never had an idle hour, except during the winter. The same month, Hendry formally secured his own master's ticket, and soon he and Brickenden were shuttling freight, passengers and mail, mostly from New Liskeard up the Blanche River as far as Wilson's Landing, a mile beyond Tomstown. From Tomstown a rough road ran westward to what soon became Englehart and Charlton.

The *Geisha* was a round-bottomed craft with a ten-foot beam, a single deck and a round stern. She registered 13.40 tons and was licensed for 25 passengers plus all kinds of freight, though her owners quickly started building scows to handle the bulk cargoes. Perhaps John Hendry was engaged to help. Though there are no records to prove it, we may rest assured that the new steamer was welcomed by the Clay Belt communities; those on the river had probably never had the benefit of a regular and dependable service before, and at every landing people would crowd down to the shore when they heard the *Geisha*'s whistle. It was probably at this time that post offices were opened at Hilliardton and Tomstown, and since Hendry and Brickenden had managed to secure a mail contract, it is not surprising that they named their new operation the White River Mail Line.

The *Geisha* was a staunch and seaworthy craft, and could buck almost any kind of weather. Many a time anxious Haileyburians would watch her set off, rolling amid the waves of a "chop sea" on Lake Temiskaming and sometimes follow her progress with binoculars, though she never failed to get through safely. Once, we are told, a gust of wind almost blew her over off Windy Point, but the passengers had the good sense to rush to the upper side of the vessel and thus saved the day. Indeed, throughout her first two seasons she only once missed completing her daily trip. Her main difficulty was not stormy weather but logs and deadheads. Although the white pine was mostly gone, companies such as Booth and Eddy were still driving thousands of spruce logs every spring, and sometimes into the summers as well. Furthermore, the log drivers acted as if they owned the river, and gave scant consideration to the boatmen. Nonetheless, the new service paid, partly thanks to the vigour of Hendry and Brickenden, and partly because there was nothing else available.

In 1904, the pair were back, this time with two steamers. With the help of Hendry senior, they had built a second vessel at New Liskeard over the winter. This was the *Blanche*, a shallow-draft twin-engined screw steamer about 45 feet in length and listed at 18 tons, although she grossed 30. Her exact dimensions are unknown. She had a round stern and twin decks for most of her length, but was open at the bow — probably because the river steamers almost always had to manage without docks (which would have been demolished by the log drives in any case). Like the *Geisha*, she was painted white, and, by 1906, was licensed for 40 passengers, though much of her work consisted of towing scows. Since Frank Brickenden also obtained a master's certificate, it is likely that he assumed command of the *Blanche* while Captain Hendry remained on the *Geisha*.

That the White River Mail Line was becoming more aggressive and was starting to compete with the Temiskaming Navigation Company (the successor to the Lumsden Line), is evident from a timetable published in the Temiskaming *Herald* in 1905. The *Geisha*, we are informed, leaves New Liskeard at 7:00 A.M. daily except Sundays, and calls at Haileybury, Judge (on the lower Blanche River), Hilliardton and Tomstown, returning at 6:00 P.M. The *Blanche* provides a Sunday service, leaving New Liskeard at 7:30 and Haileybury at 8:00, crossing over to Ville-Marie by 10:00 and staying until 2:00 in the afternoon, then returning to Haileybury by 4:00 P.M. and to New Liskeard by 4:30. Otherwise, she is available for picnics, excursions and special engagements. Both boats take freight, passengers and mail, and will tow or deliver freight between any points.

Still, the business prospered, and in 1906 the White River Mail Line was operating three steamers. Its new vessel, the *Gipsy*, is said to have been built at Toronto, although local sources agree it was at New Liskeard. Perhaps the hull was imported by rail. The *Gipsy* was 51.8 feet in length (56 overall) by 12.5 in beam and drew a modest 4.4 feet of water. Like the *Blanche*, which she rather resembled, the *Gipsy* had two second-hand engines, delivering 2.4 hp. Perhaps the river boatmen preferred twin-screw vessels for ease of manœuvring on confined waters. Besides, if one propeller were to be broken on a log, the second was always there. The *Gipsy* registered 23.82 tons, which made her the largest vessel of the Blanche River fleet.

She was not yet ready to sail by May of 1906, when the other two steamers — both improved — were back in service, but by late June she started her runs to Tomstown, under Captain Hendry's command. On Dominion Day we find her running an overnight excursion from New Liskeard to Tomstown, which now had a hotel, and by midsummer she had assumed the *Geisha*'s main route, leaving New Liskeard six days a week at 7:00 A.M. (and Haileybury 40 minutes later) and arriving at Tomstown at 12:30. Meanwhile, the *Geisha* was handling parties of prospectors heading for Wendigo and Larder Lakes with their baggage supplies and canoes — and also running groups of berry pickers down to Martineau Bay in midsummer. Unluckily, the weather was so dry that season that by September the *Gipsy* could no longer reach Tomstown, and a punt had to be used to complete the run. For the same reason, the vessel was pressed into service on Labour Day to run an emergency trip down Lake Temiskaming as far as the Kipawa River, to rescue about 130 Methodist church excursionists, including children, who found themselves stranded because low waters prevented the *Meteor* from docking there to pick them up. (The group had left New Liskeard that morning on the *Temiskaming*.) Once the *Gipsy* arrived, the people were ferried out to the big ship without any trouble, but they did not get home that night until 9:30 — which was hard on the children.

Despite logs and low waters, the Blanche River steamers seem to have operated with few serious accidents — except one. On the morning of May 12, 1906, just days after the season opened, a humiliating mishap befell the *Geisha*. The little steamer was approaching Haileybury (which now had a small dock) with a number of passengers and a consignment of hay and freight on board, when someone caught one of her lines and snubbed it fast, before the vessel had stopped moving. She gave a lurch, and careened toward the dock. The hay tumbled over and landed in the water, along with several of the passengers, while the steamer filled with water and sank to a depth of about 35 feet. Everyone got off quickly, some without even getting wet, except a woman and her baby, who happened to be inside the cabin. Realizing the situation, Captain Hendry immediately went after them and managed to get them out, though he had to duck the child under water to do it. The only casualty was the captain's dog, which was unfortunately chained inside the cabin. The hay, now floating, was retrieved and sold at once, while the embarrassed boatmen promised to make good all the other losses. The *Geisha* was raised two days later and towed back to the Wabi River, where the owners had their yards. The following day she was back towing logs as if nothing had happened.

Although the White River Mail Line had been a great success, it did not remain in existence very long. Events in Timiskaming were moving much too fast during those dynamic decades to allow any boat service to function long without disruptions, and the Blanche River route was no exception. By 1906, the railway, advancing steadily northwards, passed through the new hamlet of Heaslip, just a few miles west of Tomstown, and by September of 1907, the Tomstown mail was arriving overland from Heaslip. Even before then, however, the White River Mail Line had already passed into history. It had been swallowed up by a new company laying ambitious plans for many parts of the North.

THE UPPER ONTARIO STEAMBOAT COMPANY:

There seemed no limit to the possibilities of Timiskaming after the turn of the century. Trainloads of new settlers arrived almost daily, while prospectors fanned out in all directions from Cobalt. Soon there were exciting new reports of gold discoveries around Larder Lake, up the Montreal River, and around Gowganda Lake. As always in such situations, there was a crying need for new transport services, and with a growing number of venturesome men moving in, it is not surprising that some of them were studying the problem closely.

In the forefront was Captain Hendry, who noted with keen interest the growth of settlement around Long Lake, on the upper Blanche River, and the new influxes of gold seekers frantic to reach Gowganda and Larder Lake. All this seemed too good to miss, and soon a truly ambitious scheme arose in the captain's mind: why not form a new company to provide boat transport services to all four localities — and perhaps in the process channel the profits back into the local scene rather than into the pockets of Toronto profiteers?

Such an enterprise was more than Captain Hendry and his partner could accomplish by themselves, and therefore he began discussing the scheme with William John Blair, a prominent local engineer, businessman and mining speculator who had just succeeded Angus McKelvie as Mayor of New Liskeard. Soon others were drawn in, and by February of 1907, the new enterprise had been incorporated as the Upper Ontario Steamboat Company. Its objects were primarily to transport passengers, freight and mail on the Blanche River, Long Lake, the Montreal River and, of course, Lake Temiskaming. The company secured a federal

FACING PAGE, ABOVE:
Steamer Meteor, *on the ways at Moore's Cove (July 1916). Alongside is the steam tug* Scotchman. Courtesy National Archives of Canada, PA 130089

BELOW LEFT:
Steamer Geisha, *at Pearson's Landing, Blanche River. Note the cow at the stern.* Courtesy Muskoka Steamship & Historical Society

BELOW RIGHT:
Captain Frederick William Hendry.

charter, no doubt to allow it to operate in Quebec as well as Ontario. Its capital was authorized at $99,000, divided into 1,980 shares valued at $50 each. W.J. Blair became President, Captain Hendry Vice-President and Frank H. Norris of New Liskeard Secretary-Treasurer. M.R. Jennings of New Liskeard, M.P. Wright of Haileybury, J.D. Kingston of Latchford, J.J. Faran of Murray City (North Temiskaming) and Frank Brickenden were directors. Norris was engaged to act as manager for 1907.

The Upper Ontario Steamboat Company lost no time making its plans. For the opening season it proposed to run four steamers on Lake Temiskaming and the Blanche River, three on the Montreal River and one each on Long Lake and Larder Lake, plus a stage service from Tomstown to Boston Creek on the Temiskaming and Northern Ontario Railway, about 22 miles north of Englehart. Offices were planned at Haileybury and Latchford, with the head office in temporary quarters in the New Liskeard post office. A large new immigrants' hostel was built on the south side of the Wabi River, complete with kitchen facilities. The company also bought out Captain Hendry's White River Mail Line, including its three steamers and its lifeboats, pointers, docks, tools and warehouses, for $20,000 — half of it paid for in shares.

Like most of the local steamer services in the North, the Upper Ontario Steamboat Company started out with a surge of vigour and enthusiasm, but, although many of its shares were subscribed, none of its sprawling operations was destined to last very long. All four of its disconnected branches, responding to urgent but short-lived needs, burst forth like flood waters after a storm, only to dry up again in the hot sun of changing circumstances. Only the Montreal River division ever generated much momentum, and that for only six years. Nevertheless, the new company would provide a big boost to the rapid growth of several parts of Timiskaming.

For convenience, we shall follow the fortunes of each of the company's four divisions separately, beginning where we left off — on the Blanche River.

THE UPPER ONTARIO STEAMBOAT COMPANY OPERATIONS ON THE BLANCHE RIVER: (1907–1908)

The new line proposed to continue Captain Hendry's service on the Blanche River, using two boats to connect with the trains at Haileybury and New Liskeard, as well as a stage line from Tomstown up to Larder Lake. By March of 1907, it was decided to move the *Geisha* overland to Larder Lake to serve the new mining camps. To replace her, the company authorized Captain Hendry to purchase two shallow-draft steam vessels, one to join the *Blanche* and the *Gipsy* on the river, and the other to run charters on Lake Temiskaming. Additional vessels were purchased for the Montreal River.

The new Blanche River steamer was the *St. Antoine*, a large wooden yacht built on the St. Lawrence River at St. Antoine, near Verchères, Quebec, in 1898. The *St. Antoine* was originally 51.4 feet in length by 8.9 feet in beam, with a single deck, a round stern, a lounge cabin on either side of the engine room, and an unusual circular wheelhouse. She registered 9.78 tons and had a powerful 10-hp triple-expansion engine, giving her speeds of up to twenty miles per hour — very fast for the times. She was purchased by the Upper Ontario Steamboat Company on May 13, 1907, and within a month she arrived at New Liskeard to begin her runs to Tomstown. Along with her came the *Wenona*, a large 66-foot steel-hulled yacht with a similar engine and very handsome fixtures. She registered 17 tons and, like the *St. Antoine*, came originally from the St. Lawrence, though her registry is unknown. She was intended mainly for charters, but in fact spent most of her time on the river. (Winters were usually spent at Dawson Point.) Both vessels were on hand for the first boating regatta ever held at New Liskeard, on July 19, 1907. The *Wenona* served as the official boat during the events (which came off splendidly), while the *St. Antoine* raced all four of the local gas launches and beat them easily, despite a handicap of six and a half minutes. (The stately *Meteor* of the Temiskaming Navigation Company was also present to take 200 visitors from the American Institute of Mining Engineers on an afternoon charter, followed by a moonlight cruise.)

The Upper Ontario Steamboat Company boats were apparently quite busy during 1907 and 1908; we hear of one particular tow, consisting of a million feet of timber, undertaken for the Brethour Milling Company from Pearson's Landing to Haileybury in August 1907. Only occasionally did they have trouble. On Dominion Day 1907 — when New Liskeard was inundated with nearly 1,200 visitors from miles around for the sports and festivities — the *Wenona* was cruising down to the Notch near the mouth of the Montreal River, with perhaps 40 excursionists aboard, when she was caught in the rough waters for which Lake Temiskaming is notorious. Worse still, the steam pump failed, and the faltering vessel was soon wallowing helplessly in the troughs of the waves. Just as the situation was starting to look distinctly unpleasant, the *Meteor* hove into sight and towed the disabled craft to Ville-Marie. By that time, the engineer had managed to get the pump working again, and the *Wenona* was able to return to New Liskeard under her own power.

That was not the last of the *Wenona*'s troubles that year. On October 15th the vessel sank at her moorings while docked for the night at the south side of the Wabi River. She was raised within a week, none the worse for her ducking, but the cause of the mishap was never determined.

In the meantime, exciting new mining developments south of Cobalt helped to engender a little fleeting prosperity for all the boat lines. In September 1907, a prospector named Charles Keeley, along with two partners, staked a claim to some fresh silver deposits in the Lorrain Valley, close to the mouth of the Montreal River. By the following spring the Keeley Mines Company Ltd. was formed, and when so august a personage as Dr. Beattie Nesbitt, the immaculate President of the Farmers' Bank of Toronto, arrived in Haileybury, complete with his silk hat and gold-headed cane, to write a cheque for $1,000, backing the new company's bonds, the result was another rush, this time to South Lorrain. More claims were staked, and soon the Lorrain Valley was being touted as the new Cobalt.

Unlike Cobalt, South Lorrain was not located directly on the railway. However, the new mines were mostly within about three miles of Lake Temiskaming and a steamboat base was promptly established at Maiden Landing, at the mouth of Maiden's Creek, which soon developed into Silver Centre Landing. At first there was no wharf, and the boatmen had to use a long gangway to reach the shore, but by 1910 a small dock had been built, plus a large boarding house or "hotel." Soon the Landing also had a school and perhaps a dozen families in residence. From the depot, a wagon road wound its way up a long incline so steep that each horse team could make only one trip a day overland to the mines. Not until 1913 would the government begin opening a new road from North Cobalt to South Lorrain.

The Lorrain boom was of relatively short duration. Only a few mines like the Keeley proved really profitable, and then not until the 1920s. Still, huge quantities of fuel and power-line poles (to say nothing of other commodities) were delivered to Silver Centre Landing for a time, but though this apparently provided some business for the Upper Ontario Steamboat Line, most of the profits seemingly went to its rival, the Temiskaming Navigation Company, which had larger vessels and controlled the docks at the far end of the lake. In June of 1908, for example, the first shipment of ore from the Keeley Mine (about fourteen tons) left on the steamer *Jubilee*, bound for a smelter at Marmora. Competition from the older line was already forcing fares down on Lake Temiskaming, and even more disheartening was the news that a third steamboat company was being formed at Haileybury to cash in on the Lorrain boom. On top of all this, another misfortune struck the *Wenona* on November 6, 1908. The unlucky vessel was docked at Ville-Marie, when a gas launch belonging to Frère Moffette, the esteemed colonizer of the New Quebec, exploded nearby and set the steamer ablaze. Prompt action plus the vessel's steel hull saved her, but not before $250 in damage had been done. For reasons such as these, the Upper Ontario Steamboat Company decided to abandon its branch on Lake Temiskaming and the Blanche River at the end of the season of 1908 and to concentrate on the more profitable Montreal River division. Most of its vessels on the lake were soon transferred to other waters. So ended the second organized attempt to operate a regular steamer service from New Liskeard.

ABOVE:

The Collingwood Hotel at Larder Lake. Courtesy Mr. Allan Richardson

MIDDLE:

Haileybury wharf, circa 1904. The steamer at right seems to be the Wenona. In front of her is the Temiskaming.

BELOW:

Scene at Elk Lake City (October 1908). In the centre is the little steamer Shoofly. The vessel at the right may be the S.&Y.

STEAMBOATING ON LARDER LAKE: (CIRCA 1907–1924)

It was in 1906 that prospectors from Cobalt first spotted the flecks of yellowish metallic ore while panning around the north shore of a small irregularly shaped lake about five miles in length, located 39 miles due north of New Liskeard. Men called it Larder Lake because of the great abundance of lake trout to be found there. When the ores were assayed and found to be pure gold — almost the first gold discoveries in Northern Ontario — the rush was on. After the sensational finds at Cobalt, anything seemed possible. In no time at all a flotilla of as many as 60 canoes was bound for Fitzpatrick's Landing on the northwest shore of the lake, as scores of men swarmed in with their packs and gear to get a piece of the action. Most came north from Tomstown via Wendigo Lake, undergoing eleven risky portages over a distance of seventeen miles, but others chose the 23-mile overland trek from Boston Creek on the Temiskaming and Northern Ontario Railway. Despite the fact that almost everything had to be imported, men kept arriving, and even the advent of winter failed to chill the ardour. Before the year was out, 4,000 claims had been staked, some in the snows, and Larder Lake was hailed as the new Yukon. Already tents were giving way to wooden buildings, as a townsite was laid out in November 1906 at Fitzpatrick's Landing, which was soon renamed Larder City or Larder Lake.

Obviously, the new camp needed provisions on a steady basis, and by January of 1907, a mail service, run by Jack Wilson of Tomstown, was busy hauling sleighloads of snowshoes, toboggans, foodstuffs, hardware, stoves and dynamite every day. By May a "hotel" or halfway house had been opened at Larder City, which soon afterwards featured a barber shop, bake oven, Methodist parsonage, and a stamp mill as well.

The Larder rush was exciting news to Captain Hendry and his syndicate, and indeed was one of the main reasons for the formation of the Upper Ontario Steamboat Company. By March of 1907, the ambitious new line was planning to run its boats to connect directly with Wilson's stages. It also proposed to move the *Geisha* to Larder Lake itself.

That was no mean feat. The *Geisha* was nearly fourteen tons burden and over 50 feet long. Furthermore, she was then at her winter quarters at Dawson Point, about 40 miles from her new destination. Nonetheless, it was decided to proceed at once, before spring, since the "road" north from Tomstown, though fairly level, was hardly worthy of the name and would turn into a morass after the snow melted. The engine and boiler were removed and the vessel loaded onto sleighs, while a local man was hired to move her. The party and its teams of horses then set off over glare ice for Tomstown, but en route one of the sleigh runners broke in two. A new one was obtained, but meanwhile Nature dumped another six inches of snow on everything. Soon the contractor ran short of money and quit. Hendry and Brickenden then took over, and got the boat to Tomstown, but after that they had nothing but trouble as their unwieldy load kept bogging down in the snow drifts. Finally they decided to cut the vessel in two, and by this desperate expedient they at last brought her to Larder Lake in early April. Here the ex-schooner was rapidly reassembled and relaunched in time to fire up the boiler on April 17th. That day she steamed from the falls on the Raven River into Larder City for the first time, to be greeted with gusty cheers.

With the opening of the lakes came another surge of prospectors, and soon there were 50 teams of horses on the Larder trail, cadging in supplies, although by August the forwarders were obliged to do all of their freighting from Tomstown by canoe, since the road had become too soft to handle any load in excess of half a ton. Meanwhile, the *Geisha* was busy shuttling back and forth, bringing men and provisions over the last leg of their trek from Tomstown, and unloading them at campsites everywhere. She was not the only boat on the lake. A 30-foot motor launch called the *Maple Leaf* was brought in about the same time by the Tighe Brothers outfitting syndicate, and others soon followed. A large dock and several warehouses were built at Larder City, which soon had a permanent population of 95, of whom only five were women.

Apparently the *Geisha* was quite busy on her new route — at least for a year or two. She was particularly useful on windy days, when the lake grew too rough for canoes. She was also in demand for the occasional pleasure trip on Sundays or civic holidays. In the meantime, plans were under way to build a dam on the Raven River, about one and one-half miles downstream. The purpose was primarily to provide power, but one of the effects was to raise and stabilize the lake levels. By 1909, the dam was completed.

The *Geisha*'s prosperity did not last. She was scarcely even launched before a second road was being built to Larder Lake, this one from Boston Creek, a distance of 23 miles. Heavy rains in the fall of 1907 delayed construction but by 1908 the road was opened, allowing supplies to be teamed in directly from the railway depot — which had been renamed Dane after one of the railway commissioners. The route from Tomstown collapsed immediately, resulting in severe losses to the Blanche River steamers as well as to the *Geisha*.

But the greatest disappointment proved to be the gold deposits themselves. The Larder Lake mines were soon found to consist of low-grade ores, most of which could not be exploited profitably at the time, given the remoteness of the site and the shortage of wood and coal for fuel. By 1909, many of the camps were being abandoned, while the newspapers trumpeted the marvellous new finds at Gowganda. Only the Goldfield Mines still hung on, keeping the settlement moderately alive, but it could do little until after 1924, when a branch of the Temiskaming and Northern Ontario Railway, pushing east from Kirkland Lake towards Rouyn-Noranda, Quebec, went through Larder Lake. The Goldfields Mines passed to Proprietary Associated Goldfields, thence in the 1930s to Omega Mines, when they finally began to pay. Meanwhile, the Kerr-Addison Company, which had been sitting on the old Reddick-Maxwell claim, also helped bring Larder City back to life, opening a sawmill, a shingle mill and a planing mill at the beach as sideline operations. Kerr-Addison also created the nearby village of Virginiatown for its workmen and staff, though Larder Lake itself remained the commercial core.

The *Geisha* did not last long enough to participate in these developments. By the spring of 1909, the Upper Ontario Steamboat Company, having lost faith in the potential of Larder Lake, sold her to Messrs. McLaughlin and Guilfoyle, a pair of merchants at Larder City, who ran her for at least one more season and perhaps longer. By 1913, however, she was listed as "not in commission," and shortly afterward she was gutted by fire — whether purposely or accidentally is not known. For years, her burned-out skeleton could be seen submerged near the end of the street at the east side of the village, with the boiler still in place. A local family has her compass. Around 1920, a second steamer — perhaps the *Little Roxy* — was imported and used, along with several motorboats to tow logs to the Kerr-Addison sawmill for about four seasons. With her disappearance went the last vestige of steamboating on Larder Lake.

STEAMBOATING ON THE MONTREAL RIVER : (CIRCA 1907–1950)

The scene on the Montreal River from 1906 until 1912 was probably the closest thing to the Klondike that Ontario ever knew. As in the Yukon, the alluring prospect of buried riches accessible only by a major river was to bring thousands of prospectors, and their attendant hangers-on, in motley flotillas of every sort of craft, battling their way into a wilderness that had previously been known only to Nishnabis, trappers and lumbermen. There were, of course, several differences. The Montreal River was far less remote than the Yukon, the lure here was silver rather than gold, the rush was of shorter duration, and the route to the mines ran upstream rather than down, and over a much shorter distance.

The Montreal River is one of the largest tributaries of the Ottawa River. Taking its source from the vicinity of Shining Tree, amid the hills of the northern Sudbury District, it first angles northeast, then follows a natural fault line southeast for about 55 miles to what is now Bay Lake, at the modern town of Latchford, before resuming its way southeastward over churning rapids and through deep gorges (now flooded) on its way to Lake Temiskaming. Wandering parties of Nishnabis had used the river for centuries, and after them, fur traders, some of whom were trying to circumvent the Hudson's Bay Company. It retaliated by opening a post called Fort Matachewan about 80 miles upstream from Lake Temiskaming, where the river becomes narrow, and then another during the 1880s at Fiddler's Point on Portage

Bay near Latchford. Around 1905, the Fiddler's Point post burned down, and the factor, James Mowatt, moved upstream about ten miles to farm at a spot soon to be known as Mowatt's Landing. (One of his sons, Duncan Mowatt, would serve as pilot on the Montreal River steamboats.) By the 1890s, too, the lumber companies were moving in, notably Booth and Gillies, felling and floating out softwoods that frequently took two years to reach the sawmills on the Ottawa River. Over a third of them never made it. Neither the fur trade nor the lumber trade led to any permanent settlements, nor were any steamboats used on the river during this period; the current alone sufficed to move the logs.

The muffled placidity of the Montreal River region was suddenly disrupted in the summer of 1903, as the Temiskaming and Northern Ontario Railway crews began a roadbed to the rapids at the exit from Bay Lake. A Mr. Legris and his family at once built a store there to cater to the railwaymen. Even so, there was nothing at the bridge site as late as April 1905, when the Empire Lumber Company moved in from Quebec to build a mill, plus quarters for the mill hands. By then, though, the Cobalt boom was on, and prospectors were already fanning out towards the Montreal River. Within months the word got out that Leo Erenhous of Haileybury had found silver near a spot called Bear Creek, about 51 miles upstream from the railway crossing, where the river widens out just enough to be called a lake — Elk Lake. By 1906, another rush was on. Hundreds of claims were staked, and soon several mines were actually in production. The solitary Indian wigwam noted at Elk Lake in 1903 gave way to a veritable city of tents, and "Elk Lake City" started to look like a new Cobalt.

All this, of course, meant a surge of activity at the railway crossing at Bay Lake, which was now the gateway to the Montreal River region. Almost overnight another new town appeared, which was named for Frank Latchford, the Public Works Minister who had been such a staunch supporter of the railway. By June of 1906, the infant town of Latchford already had two hotels, five retail stores, a few churches and two sawmills. This was only the beginning, and soon there were over seventeen stores along its muddy, stumpy main street, plus boarding houses and pool halls. Even the scourge of fire, which struck the town with depressing frequency during the early years, failed to stem the vigour. Within a very short time the community, with over 1,000 permanent residents, seceded from Coleman Township and became Ontario's newest incorporated town, largely at the prompting of the hotel owners, who wanted licences to sell liquor.

The thousands of impatient silver seekers, clamouring to reach the Elk Lake camps in May of 1906, swarmed into Latchford in droves, bringing canoes, punts and rowboats or requisitioning just about anything that would float. But navigating the river was not easy, least of all with bulky cargoes. There were no charts of any kind, and no control dams to regulate the water levels. Worse still, the route was interspersed with boulders, strong currents and rapids in several places. The first and longest of these — located seven miles upstream from Latchford — was Pork Rapids, which surged and foamed over a distance of roughly half a mile. Beyond Pork Rapids lay a long, uninterrupted stretch of 29 miles to Flat Rapids, where the river dropped 1.7 feet in about 150 yards (or 5.7 feet at extreme low water). Only three and a half miles beyond Flat Rapids lay Mountain Chutes, where the full force of the Montreal River boils down through a narrow twisting gorge, dropping 7.2 feet in just a hundred yards. From here, one could proceed the remaining twelve miles to Elk Lake without interruption, and, indeed, go fifteen miles farther to Indian Chutes. From that point, it was possible to reach Gowganda Lake by canoe — with difficulty. With no facilities to help them, such as horses and wagons at the three portages, and no powerboats except a few motor launches hastily brought in to Latchford, the men had to be self-sufficient and self-reliant.

So much excitement did the Elk Lake rush entail, that the Ontario government started to open a wagon road from Earlton to the upper Montreal River as early as the winter of 1906–07. But at New Liskeard, the newly formed Upper Ontario Steamboat Company, rightly assuming that a mere road would never be adequate for the immense volumes of traffic, was already studying how to adapt the river as a new artery of commerce. With Captain

Hendry doing most of the field work, the company soon concluded that, unless the Montreal River could be dammed at Latchford to enlarge Bay Lake and drown Pork Rapids, it would be necessary to bypass them with a 2,850-foot tramway on the west bank. For Flat Rapids, a horse-drawn sleigh, or stoneboat, was suggested, and at Mountain Chutes another tramway. In the meantime, of course, teams of horses would have to suffice. Docks and warehouses would be needed too, as well as dining facilities at the portages. (This would require some co-operation from the lumber companies, which controlled most of the shores.) And, naturally, steamers would do most of the transporting, with scows to handle the bulk cargoes.

At the very onset (February 1907), the new company decided to put at least three steamers on the river, and Captain Hendry was authorized to buy them. For the first leg of the run, from Latchford to Pork Rapids, he selected the *Aileen*, a sturdy single-decked screw vessel registered at 23.60 tons. She was about 67 feet in length by 12 in beam, and licensed for 40 passengers. (Later she would be enlarged.) She was registered at Kingston, although the actual record has not been found, and may have come from the St. Lawrence, like the *Wenona* and the *St. Antoine*. However, by July of 1907, she was in service at Latchford. The following year she was assigned to Captain Rassmus (Ross) Hansen, a veteran steamboat man from Gravenhurst who had lately commanded the steamer *Kenozha* for the Muskoka Navigation Company. John A. McCaw, the son of Captain McCaw of North Bay, acted as engineer. In the meantime, the company put up an office and boathouse at Latchford (probably housed in the same building), plus a few docks, all located near the modern marina site. An agent was hired to bill freight and sell tickets, canoes and boats. So far, so good.

The *Aileen* did not remain on the Latchford run for long. By August 1907, she had been hauled past Pork Rapids to ply the long stretch ending at Flat Rapids. At times when the waters were high, to the delight of her owners, she actually succeeded in running right up Flat Rapids to Mountain Chutes, but at least once — probably in 1908 — she had almost reached the top of the rapids when the current prevailed and swept her down again, stern first. The vessel tossed about in the foaming river, but remained undamaged.

Her place on the lower stretch of the river was taken by the *Myrtle*, a 67-foot screw steamer lately purchased from Orillia. Little is known about this vessel today, but no doubt she was a single-decked craft, painted white, like the others, with a black stack, a red waterline and black trim. By midsummer of 1907, she was running from Latchford three times a day, usually starting around 10:00 A.M. after the arrival of the morning train. The railway built no spurs to the docks, but horse teams and drays were available to move freight to and from the boats.

Above Flat Rapids, the company installed a small screw steamer called the *Lena May*, which had been built at Penetanguishene in 1906. The *Lena May* was only 35 feet in length and registered just 4.46 tons. She had the usual round stern and a 0.5-hp engine, and is said to have carried her wheelhouse atop the amidship cabins. No doubt her owners were content with her small size because her route was a mere three and a half miles, and she could easily make several trips in the time that her running mates could do one. It is also claimed that this portion of the river was too strewn with boulders and sandbars to allow larger vessels to be used.

On the last leg of the route, the line placed a fourth steamer called the *S.&Y.*, which was built at Kingston in 1904, and seems to have briefly preceded the *Aileen* on the Pork Rapids to Flat Rapids run. Like that of the *Myrtle*, the register of the *S.&Y.* has not been found, but we know that she was a screw vessel, grossing 26 tons, and that she was licensed for 40 passengers. She is said to have been 64.8 feet in length by 11.1 feet in beam, and to have carried her wheelhouse on her deck rather than on top of the cabins. She took her name from her builders, Messrs. Selby and Youlden. It usually took about an hour and twenty minutes for her to reach Elk Lake, and no doubt she received a royal welcome on her first arrival. Nonetheless, she developed a reputation for being unstable when heavily loaded, thanks to her narrow beam, and Captain Hansen, for one, considered her unsafe and refused to command her. Eventually she was to confirm those fears.

Thus, by August of 1907, the basic service on the Montreal River was in place. Not all of the prospectors used the steamers, of course. Large flotillas of canoes were known to leave

ABOVE:

Scene at Latchford, 1907.

Courtesy House of Memories Museum, Latchford

MIDDLE:

Steamer Aileen.   Courtesy Haileybury Fire Museum

BELOW:

The King George Café, Pork Rapids, Montreal River.   Rev. W.L.L. Lawrence Collection. Courtesy Ontario Archives, S13643

Latchford every day. However, only steamboats could cope effectively with large cargoes, strong currents and the log drives, which were still sent downriver every spring. Soon the boats began supplementing their revenues by towing for the lumber companies. Also, since none of the steamers were big enough to provide meals en route, (except for their crews), the company arranged to have boarding houses built at Pork Rapids and Mountain Chutes. These were leased to various individuals and their families, who in turn provided simple meals for the prospectors, who might also be allowed to sleep on the floors, if necessary. (Usually travellers who left Latchford in the morning could count on being at Elk Lake by sundown.) In addition, one resourceful operator named Dan McLeod opened a cafe with ten tables in it, just above Pork Rapids. With his wife and two girls to assist, he baked his own bread, buns, cookies, cakes and pies, offering travellers all they could eat for fifty cents. Sometimes he would feed up to 175 people at a time. McLeod's restaurant was on board a houseboat; since his premises were floating, he could not be required to pay rents.

The Montreal River steamers plied until early November, by which time their main duties were bringing men home for the winter. It had been a most gratifying season. Up to 4,000 people had been active around Elk Lake that year. Hundreds of claims had been staked, and Elk Lake City itself, initially just a jumble of tents and shacks beside the river, crisscrossed by muddy paths meandering around the stumps, was already starting to sprout hotels, theatres, banks, stores and restaurants. Fresh discoveries of silver at Gowganda ("pickerel's tooth") Lake, about 25 miles west, in the autumn of 1907, only heightened the mining fever, though the effect was to lure many away from Elk Lake to Gowganda.

For the Upper Ontario Steamboat Company, the Montreal River route had been by far the most profitable of its divisions, and plans were under way to improve the service, especially the shipping of baggage. Henceforth bulk cargoes were transported by tugs and scows, while passengers and their effects were taken by unencumbered steamers. Perishable commodities, such as fruits, went on the faster boats. The Ontario government was already talking about improvements at Pork Rapids, but since there is no mention of dredging, this probably meant helping to build a tramway there.

These plans called for more scows and steamers on the route, and in 1908, Captain Hendry arranged to import at least two more vessels. One was the *St. Antoine*, which had been used the previous year on the Blanche River run. By mid-April, the vessel was at Latchford, being reassembled by a North Bay shipbuilder. It was probably at this time that she was lengthened from 52 to 69.2 feet, thus increasing her tonnage to 18.90. By May, when the ice broke up, the *St. Antoine*, licensed for 40 passengers, was ready for her new route from Latchford to Pork Rapids, sometimes under the command of William V. Reynolds, a captain from the Kawartha Lakes. A press correspondent who travelled on the *St. Antoine* in September described her as piled with canoes and baggage, and making remarkably fast time. (The *Myrtle* is no longer mentioned, perhaps because she was now towing scows.)

Around the same time, the company also transferred the *Gipsy*, previously on the Blanche River, to the Montreal River, to ply between Mountain Chutes and Elk Lake. With her went the *Adrelexa*, a 60-foot screw vessel which the company may have imported to Lake Temiskaming in 1907, along with the *Wenona* and the *St. Antoine*. Little is known of the *Adrelexa*, except that she registered about fourteen tons and could carry 40 passengers — like most of the company's vessels. She seems to have remained in service until 1912. The *S.&Y.*, meanwhile, was apparently taken downstream to share the Pork Rapids-Flat Rapids route with the *Aileen*, perhaps as a towboat, since the *Aileen* was seldom used in that fashion. Finally, we also hear of a tug called the *Alice*, which is mentioned as being in service around 1908, probably between Flat Rapids and Mountain Chutes, along with the *Lena May*.[3] Unless one of the boats had been retired, the company now had eight steamers on the Montreal River, and four more on other waters.

---

3   It is possible that the Alice was soon renamed the *Gow Ganda*: the register lists a 48-foot steamer of that name on the Montreal River in 1910, and notes that the 19.69-ton craft, which was built at Sturgeon Falls in 1907, was originally to have been called the *Alice*. Unfortunately, the record does not tell us any more.

The 1908 season was so busy that the line, even with double the number of boats, could hardly cope with the rush. An estimated 6,000 men pushed into Elk Lake and Gowganda that year, most of them dreaming of returning with bars of silver in their knapsacks. By that time, the straggling new village of Gowganda — then a one-street settlement of tents and log shanties on the northeast corner of Gowganda Lake — was staked for miles around. It was still accessible only by canoe from Indian Chutes, or by dog-teams in the winter, when temperatures sometimes fell to 50 below and hoarfrost covered everything, but by the end of 1908, a cadge road of sorts was opened from Charlton, west of Englehart, and soon up to 900 horse teams were at work while the ground was still frozen. As usually happens during a mining rush, nobody gave much thought to providing hay or water for the unfortunate animals, which were driven past their endurance and then left to die by the hundreds along the road. By 1909, Gowganda had a post office, a telegraph office, two drug stores, and eleven hotels — to say nothing of "blind pigs"! Already there were exciting reports that the Canadian Northern Railway was planning to route its Northern Ontario line through Gowganda.

In 1909, the Upper Ontario Steamboat Company decided to abandon all its other boat routes and concentrate its efforts on the Montreal River, and therefore moved its offices from New Liskeard to Latchford. It now proposed to operate four scows and seven steamers as far as Stoney Creek, about fifteen miles beyond Elk Lake City on the route to Gowganda. To assist, it would bring in the *Wenona*, its last remaining vessel on Lake Temiskaming. Most accounts agree that the trim little propeller was put on the short Flat Rapids to Mountain Chutes run, presumably in concert with the *Lena May*. A guidebook published that same year says the company was using one steamer (the *St. Antoine*?) with a scow on the run from Latchford to Pork Rapids; three more (the *Aileen, S.&Y.*, and *Alice*?) plus a scow from Pork Rapids to Flat Rapids; two more (the *Wenona* and the *Lena May*?) plus a scow from Flat Rapids to Mountain Chutes; and two more (the *Gipsy* and the *Adrelexa*?) with a scow from Mountain Chutes to Elk Lake. Two additional steamers and another scow were contemplated for the run up to Stoney Creek, but we do not hear of any being used. The same guidebook confirms that there were now horse tramways in place at all three portages, plus restaurants and accommodation, and that returning travellers could reach Latchford in time to catch the evening trains — although in truth the trains never waited for the boats. It was not unusual to find six to seven carloads of freight piled up daily at Latchford station during the navigating season because, despite the competition of stages running overland from Earlton and Charlton, Latchford was still the gateway to Gowganda from May to November. On her maiden trip during the 1909 season (May 19th), the *St. Antoine* left town with 75 passengers aboard, leaving hundreds more behind at the wharf. The company now employed about 70 men, most of whom were locals except for the boat captains and engineers. (Beyond Elk Lake a local resident named Calixte Bastien ran an ungainly little steamboat of his own up to Indian Chutes, perhaps the *Shoofly*, from Lake Nipissing.)

What was it like to take a trip up the Montreal River during the hectic days of the silver stampede? Fortunately a few eyewitnesses have left us colourful reports of their experiences, and a few more old-timers can still remember the glory days. They speak of long trains lurching and whistling around curve after curve and mile after mile of meandering railway line through the unending bush, until at last the open expanse of Bay Lake comes into view and the conductor shouts, "Latchford, next stop!" No sooner does the train shudder to a halt than throngs of passengers pour forth from every vestibule and crowd towards the baggage cars to retrieve their gear from the trucks piled high with canoes, crates, packsacks, tents and other paraphernalia needed for survival in the bush. Among them are fly-by-night businessmen, a few painted lady entertainers headed for honky-tonks and dance halls, and — most numerous of all — hundreds of miners and prospectors in high-top elk boots or shoepacks, loose laced shirts and broad-brimmed hats, with coats slung over their shoulders. All scramble eagerly to get on with the search for buried treasure. Amid all the hustle and bustle, as men don their packsacks and swing canoes over their heads, the tension in the air is heightened by the shrill whistle of the distant steamer, and rapidly the motley procession picks its way over the

ABOVE:

Scene at Banker's Bay, Gowganda.
Courtesy Gowganda & Area Museum

BELOW:

Steamer St. Antoine, on the Montreal River.
Courtesy Elk Lake Museum

bouldery hill crest towards the floating log dock, where the *St. Antoine*, with steam hissing from her safety valves, wheezes and belches wood smoke from her stack, impatient to depart.

Then follows a mad scramble for tickets. Since the steamer can carry only a small portion of the crowd, failure to get one means a least a day's delay. Local residents mingle with the newcomers, offering them advance tickets at twice the price (a practice known as "scalping"), then console those left behind with helpful hints as to the best hotels and bars in Latchford. Meanwhile the steamer, loaded to or above capacity, sounds her whistle once more, casts off, pulls back and bears away into midstream and up the broad reaches of Bay Lake (then much smaller than it is today), her deck and railings jammed with spectators eager to observe the new land where fortunes can be made by grubbing in just the right places.

By now the morning mists are rising, and the emerging sun starts to dispel the chill in the air. Soon, off to starboard, the lake broadens out into a deep bay — Portage Bay — where canoes loaded with pelts have lately been transported across to Sharpe Lake and thence to Matabanick (Haileybury), on their way to Fort Temiskaming. Nearby, on a jutting headland half hidden by the bush, is the Jumbo Mine where a number of men might get off. Soon everyone on board hears how this mine had already killed two men without producing much silver. But despite all this, the prevailing mood is jovially optimistic, and presently someone produces a fiddle or a mandolin, whose squeaky strains accompany the deep bass voices of the miners and the shrill tones of the ladies in a rollicking song.

Meanwhile, the river gradually narrows, as the captain in his peaked cap threads his vessel past drifting logs and deadheads, around curves with a growing current, and past rocks and sandbars. Farther aft, the grimy engineer adjusts the valves and connecting rods or shouts orders to a sweating fireman who endlessly chucks four-foot bolts of cordwood into the voracious maw of the firebox. About seven miles upstream, at the mouth of Trout Creek, someone points out the distant headframes of the Edison Mine, so named because the famous inventor Thomas Alva Edison himself put money into it — with little return.

Then, about 40 minutes after departure, the whistle toots once again as the *St. Antoine* approaches a clearing beside a backwater on the west side of the river, where stands a log house or two, a gently sloping tramway with steel rails on rough ties emerging from the bush, and a makeshift dock. To the right may be glimpsed the churning waters of Pork Rapids, gurgling past the boulders vainly trying to block the flow. Here it's "Everybody out!" Some of the men head over to Bill Michael's house for refreshments while their packs are loaded onto the tramway truck, but most follow their freight across the half-mile portage past the rapids. By now, people are more than ready for lunch at Dan McLeod's houseboat on the other side, the signal being the tinkle of a triangle. But the food has to be gulped down quickly, because soon a shrill whistle blast announces that the steamer *S.&Y.* has finished loading and is ready to board passengers.

With lines cast off, the *S.&Y.* starts rolling and bobbing in the current as her propeller churns furiously to get a grip. Failure to make headway means being swept down into the rapids, but somehow she always escapes. The little steamer then proceeds up the longest stretch of the river for about three and a half hours past drifting logs, rocks and sandbars. Thick, silent, impenetrable bush hugs the shores almost everywhere, thrusting branches out over the water. Here and there, one might spot a flock of ducks swimming close to shore, or perhaps a solitary moose calmly browsing on lily pads, ignoring the boat. Around a bend, the river broadens out to reveal Mowatt's Landing to the right and, nearly opposite, the silvery cascade of Mattawapika Falls, the outlet from Lady Evelyn Lake. The steamer might stop here in midstream to allow a few prospectors to launch and load a canoe, and then perhaps head over to the Landing to drop off mail and supplies to old Thomas Moore, the long-time agent for the Hudson's Bay Company and father-in-law of James Mowatt. Then she is off again. And the men strike up acquaintances and talk, mainly about the weather, the country, the bugs and the prospects of finding silver.

On and on, the *S.&Y.* wends her way, stopping occasionally to leave provisions at a campsite or drop off a few more prospectors at the mouth of some narrow creek leading to a lonely camp in the bush, amid shouts of "Good-bye, boys — and good luck!" Prospecting is a rugged business in a land like this. As one narrator continues:

> Here the river narrows. The shores are thickly wooded to the very water's edge, the green shadows mirrored in the clear depths. The tracery of the trees flecked with dancing sunspots the glassy surface of the stream. Then my eye shifted to the shoreline and the mysterious movement of the undertow. A stone's throw from the prow the waters recede from the bank as though answering some hidden force in the hollow depths, disclosing yards of riverbed along the shallow shore, the water rippling inward as it ran. Then, caught by the swell, at the stern the waters were thrust backward in long graceful curves that broke upon the far-off beach, a rhythmic water-play one could watch mile upon mile. [4]

The whistle re-echoes amid the lofty forests as Flat Rapids comes into view. At this portage, some 36 miles from Latchford, conditions are a lot more primitive than at Pork Rapids. Instead of a horse-drawn lorry on a tramway, there is only a boulder-strewn trail here, and a stoneboat drawn by mules. The portage itself is much shorter — only about 600 feet — but the steamer at the other end (the *Lena May*) is tiny, with only a miniature vertical boiler. Even with a small scow and a couple of pointers to assist, she can scarcely handle the cargo, let alone the passengers, and everyone either has to climb on top of the boxes, kegs and duffel bags, scramble onto the woodpile, or await the next trip. It is not uncommon for the top-heavy tug to slosh water over her gunwales as she chugs drunkenly along, especially at a curve, where turns are required and the towline grows taut. The men make wisecracks and ribald comments while wondering whether the steamer — or the scow — is about to turn turtle. (This actually happened once, around 1908, when the scow lurched over and spilled men, canoes, barrels and bales of hay into the water. But there were no fatalities, and soon everyone either made it to shore clinging to flotsam and jetsam, or were picked up by their friends. The *Lena May*'s run was mercifully short, and took only about 20 minutes.)

By the time the steamer reaches Mountain Chutes, it is mid-afternoon. Here the river really comes to life, with foaming white water spilling down over a distance of 100 yards. As the steamer draws up to the shelving rock in the lee of the falls, willing hands start unloading the cargo to the boulder-strewn shore. The portage here is only 660 feet, but this time it is steeper, with nothing but a home-made jumper drawn by an ox to haul everything up to Mountain Lake. Since several trips are invariably required, travellers may have time for another quick lunch at Frank Hartzske's log boarding house, but again, at such a remote site the food leaves a little bit to be desired. If an omelette seems a little soupy and tastes funny, someone will explain that the eggs were laid by sick hens, and if the tea tastes like tannic acid, well, what could anyone expect in the bush?

By sundown the people and their provisions are safely loaded aboard the *Gipsy* for the last leg of their journey. The reedy river soon widens out. Mountain Lake, though only an enlargement of the river, is broad enough, and sometimes rough enough, to swamp a canoe. A glance rearward reveals how the lake got its name. To the southeast stands a tree-clad cone-shaped mountain, catching the final rays of the setting sun. With darkness falling, the flickering lights of scores of campfires appear on the adjoining hills, and one might glimpse a lantern in a passing canoe. Finally, a triple whistle signal confirms that the lights in the distance are those of Elk Lake City. As the steamer slowly draws near, lights bobbing ashore congregate at the wharf, each one becoming a lantern in someone's hand. The low murmur of voices is punctuated with cheerful greetings as old friends and partners recognize one another. Once again, the steamboats have maintained the lifelines to Latchford.

Although several mines — including the Beacon, Crown Jewel and Silver Queen — were already erecting headframes around Elk Lake, most of the prospectors were now bound for

---

4   MacDougall, J.B.: *Two Thousand Miles of Gold*, Toronto, 1946

Gowganda This meant proceeding another twelve miles up the Montreal River to Stoney Creek by canoe or motorboat, and then enduring a canoe trip with seventeen portages up to Gowganda Lake, or trekking about 35 miles overland on a cadge road containing over 250 curves! Already by April of 1909, there were reputedly some twenty gas boats on Gowganda Lake, plus a single steam launch called the *Atalantis*, which is said to have arrived by sleigh from Charlton in March. Nothing more is known of this vessel, unless she was identical with a small steam-powered workboat that was still operating from Craig's sawmill at Gowganda as late as the 1940s, hauling gravel, feed and provisions in a scow. The remains of the steamer now lie sunk in front of the sawmill site, perhaps with the machinery intact. In any case, the Gowganda rush proved brief. Although over 60 claims were actually worked, by August of 1909, the *Canadian Mining Journal* reported that the Gowganda silver veins were irregular, and that transport facilities were woefully inadequate. (Gowganda never did get a railway.) By 1910, the village was quiet again, and Elk Lake too. Not until 1925, when two mines were busy and more claims staked, would Gowganda enjoy a partial comeback.

Despite the problems, the Upper Ontario Steamboat Company's service had been a great success. But success usually breeds emulation, and the Montreal River scene was no exception. From the very start (1906), there were gas motorboats on the river, and by 1907, the Joy brothers, Albert and Lester, had a string of inboard launches in service, taking both freight and passengers. The "Joy rides," however, did not last more than a year or two. By 1909, William Kervin of Callander was trying to run a twice-daily service with his own line of motorboats, while Messrs. Brown and Maxwell of North Bay likewise introduced a fleet of pointers (presumably motorized). That same year, a Toronto syndicate called the Richardson Navigation Company was planning yet another line of 40-foot motorboats on the Montreal River, to be equipped with cushions and electric lights. Finally, a local merchant from Elk Lake was said to be using a gas boat and pointer for his own provisioning.

The gas boats had a few advantages over the steamers, in that they were sometimes a little faster and could disembark from the docks more quickly. But they could not carry large cargoes or provide much shelter during bad weather, nor could they cope very well with the Booth Company logs. In 1910, the New Liskeard *Speaker* noted that the mail to Elk Lake was frequently delayed for exactly that reason. Hence, to the steamboat company, the motorboats were something of a nuisance, but nothing more. We also hear of a few independent steam vessels: the *Jean*, which is mentioned as surviving a grounding at Latchford in 1908; the *Polly*, which transported for some Elk Lake merchants in 1909; and the *Gertrude B.*, which was intended to freight in supplies from Flat Rapids in conjunction with a nebulous concern calling itself the New Alligator Line, which in July of 1909 claimed to be able to move 20 tons of freight per day from Latchford — though whether it ever did so is unknown.

Far more disquieting was the news, confirmed early in 1909, that a rival steamboat company was being formed at Latchford. This concern, known as the Montreal River Navigation Company, is believed to have been another of the enterprises of John R. Booth. In fact, it is not clear from the existing records whether J.R. Booth had anything directly to do with the new company, except that he undoubtedly sold or leased to it some of his surplus boats. Quite possibly he was a major player behind the scenes. The President of the company was Herman Humphrey Lang, who was then Mayor of Cobalt, where a street still bears his name, while the General Manger was A.G. Smith of Latchford, who had been employed on the Booth Company log drives for several years. "Eb" Smith was a vigorous sort, often seen on the boats hunting up business.

In any event, before the ice broke up in mid-May of 1909, the Montreal River Navigation Company already had at least two steamers on the Latchford to Elk Lake route. Both of them were flat-bottomed steel-hulled passenger tugs, which the Booth Company had imported to Latchford in 1907 to take provisions and horses (up to six teams at a time) to the lumber camps. It was a very simple matter for a new company to lease or charter these tugs, import a few more, build a few docks, and provide their own horse teams at the transfer points. Then it was ready to compete with the Upper Ontario Steamboat Company.

The two tugs were the *C.J. Booth*, which grossed 86 tons and registered 55, and the *J.F. Booth*, which was larger and grossed 90 tons. Both were sidewheelers, about 75 feet in length, and licensed for 100 passengers each. This made them both larger and slower than the Upper Ontario Steamboat Company boats. The *C.J. Booth* took the Latchford to Pork Rapids run, while the *J.F. Booth* plied from Mountain Chutes to Elk Lake, each crewed by a captain, mate, engineer, fireman, one or two deckhands and a cook. For the central section of the route, from Pork Rapids to Flat Rapids, the new line imported a screw steamer called the *Empress*, of which little is known, while a small screw yacht called the *Agnes* handled the short run between Flat Rapids and Mountain Chutes. Grossing only 14 tons, the *Agnes* was licensed for just eighteen passengers. According to the Toronto Shipping Register, a fifth steamer was acquired by the spring of 1910, if not earlier. This was the *Champion*, a 69-foot passenger screw vessel of 28.31 tons, built at Orillia in 1904 and previously used on the Severn River and Sparrow Lake as a water taxi to the resort hotels until her owner went bankrupt. She no doubt joined the *Empress* on the long stretch between Pork Rapids and Flat Rapids. Like its rival, the Montreal River Navigation Company assured patrons that its steamers reached Latchford in time to connect with both the northbound and southbound trains, that dinners at popular prices would be arranged en route, and that the boats always reached Elk Lake in time for supper. "No pains or expense have been spared in furnishing ample facilities to meet the requirements of the anticipated rush this coming summer," promised an advertisement in 1909.

That season was probably the busiest ever on the Montreal River. Even with twelve or thirteen steamers on the route, travellers had to get their tickets at least three days in advance. An estimated 10,000 people worked seasonally in the area. So impressed was the government with the volume of business that it ordered studies to investigate building a lock at Mountain Chutes and/or a dam at Latchford to raise the levels of Bay Lake and perhaps drown out Pork Rapids. Meanwhile, the two boat lines jockeyed furiously to get the better of each other. Both provided horse teams to move freight and baggage from the railway depot to their respective docks. Both employed agents to shout above the babble of voices, promising cheaper rates and faster service. Both tried loading their vessels as quickly as possible, in the hope of getting off ahead of the others. And both tried the suicidal technique of slashing fares.

Once on the river, the screw steamers of the Upper Ontario Steamboat Company had a slight advantage over the Montreal River Company's sidewheelers, but still it was always a race to the portages to see who could get to use the tramways first. Not uncommonly, one steamer might overtake a rival, then blow her whistle, demanding, "Move over and let me pass!" Usually the slower boat would oblige, because, despite everything, relations between the rival boat crews were fairly friendly. Both companies helped to host a number of visiting M.L.A.s in September, and both did a little log towing on the side. The Upper Ontario Steamboat Company also secured a mail contract in 1909, which entailed teaming from Charlton to Elk Lake during the winter. But despite the rush, both lines were in trouble before season's end. Besides some competition from the independents, there was concern about a road opened from Uno Park, near New Liskeard, to Mountain Chutes in August 1909. More disquieting still were rumours that the Gowganda silver strikes might be turning into a fizzle. But most critical of all was the fact that both companies ran up a deficit that year on account of their ruinous rate wars.

As a result, by the spring of the next year the two firms agreed to bury the hatchet and amalgamate. Each kept its own name and its own property, but starting in June of 1910, they published joint advertisements, announcing that their boats would leave Latchford daily at 9:45 A.M. (connecting with the Toronto special), and arrive at Elk City by 3:30 P.M. Returning, they would leave Elk City at 7:00 A.M. and 12:00 noon, and be at Latchford by 1:30 or 6:30 P.M. (These fast through trips were for passengers only. Freight was now handled separately.) The Upper Ontario Steamboat Company still had seven steamers, and its new partner, four. Herman H. Lang was now the President of the joint venture, "Eb" Smith was General Manager, and W.J. Blair was Vice-President. Captains Hendry and Brickenden hung around

for the rest of the season, but both soon returned to New Liskeard, Hendry to take up a new career on a steamer of his own on Lake Temiskaming.

The 1910 season opened on April 18th, and finished on November 19th. It was moderately profitable, and by late June, the boat lines had managed to move out 30 tons of ore in bags, from the Millerite Mines near Elk Lake. But the mining companies could not remain content with a forwarding service that required three portages; either these would have to be eliminated or some other system devised. Also, Mr. Booth's log drives remained a problem, although the lumbermen tried to minimize this by engaging two tugs to tow their log booms, one at either end, so that when a passenger steamer appeared, the tug at the aft end could try swinging the boom to one side to let the other vessel pass. Another worry was the growing disillusionment with Gowganda. Mining fever was subsiding, or, rather, it was moving on towards Porcupine Lake. New finds near Shining Tree and Fort Matachewan brought larger crowds in 1911, when the boats, in response to the trains, delayed their departure for Latchford until 11:00 A.M., but even so, the Upper Ontario Steamboat Company decided to sell its largest steamer, the *Aileen*, to the newly formed Nipissing-Pontiac Steamboat Company of New Liskeard in the spring. The vessel was soon moved to Lake Temiskaming, leaving only the *S.&Y.*, the *Alice* (?) and the *Champion* on the long stretch from Pork Rapids to Flat Rapids. Another problem was the bridge at Elk Lake, which was initially a floating log structure, prone to sink under people's feet. Later, barrels were substituted, but apparently there was no provision to allow steamers to proceed farther upriver to Stoney Creek. Only by September of 1911 was a revolving bridge (partly of steel) completed, thus freeing one of J.R. Booth's side-wheelers, which had been stranded upstream for the duration.

The Montreal River Boat Lines were no doubt heartened by the fact that the Ontario government was building a dam at Latchford to raise the waters of Bay Lake by nine feet. By 1912, the new structure was nearing completion, giving the boats the prospect of steaming directly to Flat Rapids, a distance of 36 miles. But all hopes were dashed in March, when the Temiskaming and Northern Ontario Railway voted to build a new branch line from Earlton to Elk Lake, a distance of 30 miles, at an estimated cost of $180,000, much of which was to pay for a steel bridge across the river at Mountain Chutes. (The railway soon regretted this move, because the Elk Lake branch did not prove very profitable.) By October, all the grading was completed. There was no way that the river steamers could compete with trains, and glumly the two boat lines accepted the fact that the 1912 season would be their last.

And so it proved. That year, also, a mishap befell the steamer *S.&Y.* This vessel had always been considered suspect, given her tendency to roll when loaded up, and besides, rumour had it that she was used to smuggle liquor in a secret compartment hidden away at the bow. In any event, old-timers agree that one day a log got caught in her propeller somewhere below Flat Rapids, and soon the stern was holed. As the water gushed in, the captain made for the shore. The bow reached the bank just as the engine failed, but the crew all got off safely. A line was secured to a tree, but soon it snapped and the *S.&Y.* slid back into the stream and sank in about 30 feet of water. Only the bow remained visible. Her owners, confident that they would soon be out of business anyway, made no effort to salvage her.

The first train rolled into Elk Lake on February 4, 1913, and the whole town turned out to welcome it. A triumphal arch was set up over the main street, and a new spike and key made of native silver presented to Chairman Englehart and the railway commissioners. An elegant sleigh pulled by two fine prancing steeds took the dignitaries around the town, and the happy day culminated with a dinner at the Flat Iron Building.

It was a different scene at Latchford No longer was it the gateway to Gowganda, and indeed the tiny town has never been the same since. Though the Bay Lake dam was completed in 1913 — too late to benefit the boats — there was little cause for rejoicing. In 1914, the Empire Lumber Company dismantled its plant, and soon the impressive King Edward Hotel followed suit. Its contents were sold to Cobalt. People moved away, stores closed, the school shut down and the Town Council ceased to function. Even the local Chinese restaurateur closed shop, leaving a sign that he might be back in five or six months. For a time it seemed that Latchford was doomed to become a ghost town. Then, happily, by the 1920s a few of the sawmills were re-established, breathing a little life into Latchford, and today — though none of the mills survive — the town has started to benefit from the tourist trade. Lately, some local entrepreneurs have revived the boating tradition, by running excursions up the scenic river in motorized canoes.

Steamboating survived on the river after 1912, mainly in the form of towboats for the lumber companies. The *J.F. Booth* reverted to the Booth Company, which moved her to Elk Lake to transport horses and provisions and to tow logs from the vicinity of Matachewan. She was probably still there in 1924-25, when the North Bay *Nugget* speaks of a steamer making regular trips to Indian Chutes and Long Portage on the way to Matachewan. Interestingly enough, she was again taking passengers and diamond-drilling machinery, since gold had been found in the region, but within a short time trucks were able to reach Matachewan. Her sister ship, the *C.J. Booth*, on whose decks the people had sometimes "tripped the light fantastic" on a moonlight cruise, continued to tow for the Booth Company for one more season (1913), but was then partly dismantled, loaded onto railway flatcars and moved away. We have already noted her activities on Lake Kipawa during the 1920s. The steamer *Agnes* was sold and taken to the Mattagami River, around Timmins (where we shall find her in the next chapter), while the *Gipsy*, in true nomadic fashion, left Elk Lake on a flatcar to go to Charlton and operate on Long Lake. Captain Hansen went with her. The *St. Antoine* was abandoned on the ways just above Pork Rapids, and then largely submerged when the rapids were flooded out. The wreck is clearly visible, with the boiler still in place. The rest of the Montreal River steamboats simply vanished into oblivion, and are presumed to have been abandoned or scuttled. The Upper Ontario Steamboat Company continued to file tax returns for another two years, then it, too, disappeared. The last steam vessel on the river was a screw-driven alligator called the *Beaver*, which was owned by the Murphy Lumber Company of Latchford. The boat, later gas powered, was sold elsewhere after the Murphy sawmill burned in 1957. So ended the days of steam on the Montreal River.

STEAMBOATING ON LONG LAKE: (1906–1922)

Before we leave the Upper Ontario Steamboat Company, we must pause for a brief look at its short-lived division on Long Lake, on the upper Blanche River, and the unspectacular boat services that followed it there.

The Long Lake chain begins at the village of Charlton, about seven miles west of Englehart. The lake, which was practically created by the dam built at Charlton in 1908, extends about 40 miles northwest, following a fault line parallel with that of the Montreal River about 28 miles to the west. The central portion of Long Lake is known as Lake Kinagami (short for Kinagami-ja-jing) up as far as Pickerel Narrows, about 30 miles upstream from Charlton, and the far end is called Kushog Lake. Part of the land adjacent lies within the Clay Belt, which made it a natural magnet for settlers early in the century, but Long Lake also played a modest role in the Gowganda silver saga.

The first white settlers, pushing northwards from Lake Temiskaming, arrived at Long Lake in 1901. The exit from the lake, offering excellent water power amid good farming land sloping gently down to the water, seemed ideal for a town, and by 1904, a townsite was being laid out at the local farm. One of the early settlers wanted to call it Aura Lynn ("Golden Falls") but instead it was named Charlton, after the M.P. for Norfolk County. The new town, located initially on the south side of the Blanche River, grew rapidly and soon sprouted a post office (1905), sawmill and hotel (1906), then a drug store, public library and telegraph office by 1909. A school and two churches followed, and soon hydro-electric power was being generated there. (An attempt was made to develop a rival townsite called Broadwood on the lake about a mile west, but with little success.) In August 1906, Charlton held its first municipal holiday, with races, sports and a dance, plus canoeing on Long Lake.

ABOVE:

Elk Lake City. In the foreground is the steamer Shoofly.
The unknown vessel leaving town may be the S.&Y. or the
Adrelexa. Courtesy Elk Lake Museum

BELOW LEFT:

Steamer C.J. Booth at
Latchford. Courtesy Mr.
George Burk

BELOW MIDDLE:

Steamer C.J. Booth leaving
Latchford. Courtesy House
of Memories Museum

BELOW RIGHT:

Steamer Gipsy, on
Mountain Lake.
Courtesy Elk Lake Museum

The only fly in the ointment was the Temiskaming and Northern Ontario Railway's decision to bypass the community in favour of Englehart. By September 1908, Charlton had its own spur, which was built to the opposite side of the river. The resulting real-estate boom in that quarter speedily led to the emergence of West Charlton. In 1915, the community formally became an incorporated town.

In a growing pioneering and logging region, with the usual dreadful roads, it was inevitable that someone would consider founding a boat service. Transport concerns suddenly became more urgent when silver was discovered at Elk Lake in 1905 and then Gowganda a few years later. It was quickly realized that the distance from Englehart to Elk Lake by way of Charlton and a portion of Long Lake was only half as long as up the Montreal River from Latchford, and a winter road was immediately blazed overland from Decou's Landing, about seven miles west of Charlton, to Elk Lake. Teaming followed, almost all of it by sleigh. Over 600 of them were in use that first winter, often hauling boilers and heavy machinery. Only one trip per day was possible.

Meanwhile, there was already a boat service on Long Lake. In the spring of 1906, a man named J.J. Kelly brought in two gas launches and founded the Long Lake Navigation Company, while the Dominion government voted $2,000 to clear out the snags in the route at Long Lake Narrows, two miles upstream from Charlton, and also at Hooey's Narrows, Pope's Narrows and Pickerel Narrows. Even with these improvements, navigation is tricky on Long Lake, not only because of the valleys, which produce wind tunnels at odd angles, but also from "black fogs" that tend to descend at night. Despite these inconveniences, the two motorboats were able to run as far as Kushog Lake, and Kelly was already contemplating a small passenger steamer for 1907.

He never carried out his plans. In March, the Upper Ontario Steamboat Company, which was just getting started, bought him out and engaged Frank Hamilton Brickenden, the eldest son of Captain Brickenden, to import the steamer *Britannia* to Long Lake.

The *Britannia* is something of a mystery today, in that neither her registry nor any inspection reports about her have ever been found. On the other hand, the register does list a steamer called the *Prima*, which was owned by the Upper Ontario Steamboat Company in 1907 (when Long Lake services were founded), but there is no further mention of her until 1913 — which seems odd. The *Prima* was a handsome 34-foot screw launch built in Toronto in 1898 and rebuilt in 1906. She registered 5.13 tons, and was powered by a high-pressure 1.2-hp engine. From 1907 until 1910, there are repeated references to the *Britannia* operating on Long Lake, but then she disappears and the *Prima* reappears. The obvious conclusion is that the *Prima* and the *Britannia* were one and the same vessel, and that the temporary change of name was never made official. This conclusion seems even more likely when one examines the photographic record. We shall proceed on this assumption.

Manned by a crew of two or three, the *Britannia* (*Prima*) began plying on Long Lake in the spring of 1907, along with the two motorboats, mainly between Charlton and Decou's Landing but also to the other new settlements up the lake. Sometimes she also handled fishing and hunting parties or brought some of the local people in to Charlton for a Saturday evening dance, in which case several trips might be necessary. For a time, an elderly, jovial tobacco-chewing skipper named Captain Vincent, a veteran from the Great Lakes, was engaged to command her.

Despite competition from various private motorboats, the Long Lake steamer service seems to have earned a modest profit for a few years. Here, too, the Upper Ontario Steamboat Company imported and sold canoes and skiffs as a sideline. By the fall of 1908, dredging was under way, the dam at Charlton was completed, and docks had been built at Charlton, Decou's Landing and Zeta, a tiny postal settlement up the lake. Also by then, the trains had started to run, but at first the service consisted of nothing more than a few way-freights that simply dropped off their cargoes and left.

The Upper Ontario Steamboat Company operated its Long Lake division only until the fall of 1909. Its reason for abandoning the service seems to have been the provincial government's decision in March of 1910 to spend $30,000 on a permanent road from Charlton to Elk Lake, bypassing Decou's Landing. This meant that the Long Lake boats would no longer share in freighting along this route. Another discouragement may have been the old bugbear of sawlogs, since by now the Booth Company was busy cutting timber around Long Lake. In June of 1910, the *Britannia* — now owned by Frank Brickenden Junior and his brother Ted — bent her propeller shaft while bucking logs, but fortunately there were now a couple of marine railways at Charlton. The Brickenden brothers seem to have carried on with the *Britannia* for just one year, trying to subsist on the local trade. Apparently it wasn't enough, because they sold the boat and left in 1911.

During the next two years there is no certain record of any steamer being used on Long Lake, though there were definitely motorboats, pointers and bateaux, which were like double-ended 30-foot rowboats equipped with 50-hp engines, used mainly to gather logs. Then, in May of 1913, we find the *Prima* being used by her new owners, the Sparkman brothers, Louis and Victor, to take provisions for settlers — in their rather happy-go-lucky way. By the spring of 1916, however, the vessel was reported dismantled near Charlton.

By this time, log towing was becoming the main activity on Long Lake, thanks partly to local initiative. A speculator named Dominic Legault, who dabbled with limited success in several enterprises at Charlton, also became a late entry into the lumber trade and the teaming business, setting up bush camps and creating a demand for peeled pulpwood. It was he who purchased the *Gipsy* from the defunct Upper Ontario Steamboat Company sometime after 1913, and brought her in from Elk Lake to tow and transport. The *Gipsy* was four times the size of the *Prima*, and probably the largest steamboat ever to appear at Charlton. Captain Hansen came along to command her for a few years, before leaving for the Porcupine country, where he passed on at a ripe old age. Captain Vincent also returned from Cochrane to serve on her a little later.

The *Gipsy* was not alone on the lake. Another large steam launch, called the *Belle* — which may have been built at Port Burwell in 1896 — was also imported as a workboat during this period. She was about 44 feet long and registered 7.7 tons. She changed owners frequently, and was converted into a gas boat around 1920. Similarly, the tug *King Edward* (24 tons gross), which had previously been in service on Lake Nipissing, was imported by the Beaver Board Pulp Company, which was engaged in towing thousands of cords of pulpwood into Charlton, where it was hauled ashore using conveyor belts and peeled using a water-drum pulp peeler. Finally, around 1918, Thomas Foulke, the son of a Sturgeon Falls lumberman, returned from the war and imported a splendid steam vessel called the *Navarch*, which had been built in Boston in 1892 and used by the Canadian government as a revenue cutter on the Great Lakes. After chasing smugglers and bootleggers for several years, the *Navarch* served a term on the Bay of Quinte, near Belleville, on the fisheries patrol. As might be expected, she was a very speedy craft, with a double-expansion 5-hp engine, brass tubes and fine fittings, although, alas, the beds and mirrors in her cabins were removed at Charlton, and a new plank deck laid to protect her from the loggers' spiked boots. She was used to tow booms and take provisions up to the camps, returning to Charlton every night. With her round bottom and easy manoeuvring ability, the fourteen-ton vessel could climb right over a log boom. She towed a lifeboat behind her, and sometimes her crew would go hand over hand under the towrope to reach the boat and take a swim.

The *Navarch* experienced a few mishaps on Long Lake. Once she was drydocked at Charlton with engine trouble, which was soon traced to some tubes that had split and were taking in lake water. The vessel, still equipped with a condenser for use at sea, was now adapted with a feedwater pump to use the local water. Another time, one of the chains on a log boom got caught around her propeller shaft, and wound in so tightly that the hook couldn't be loosened. It took one deckhand eighteen hours and endless dives to cut the thing loose.

Sometime before 1920, Dominic Legault abandoned the pulpwood business and left for Kirkland Lake to become a real-estate agent. His tug, the *Gipsy*, was sold and taken back to her original home on Lake Temiskaming. Thus she escaped the great disaster that was soon to fall upon the unlucky town of Charlton.

On the warm, sunny morning of October 4, 1922, smoke was observed west of Long Lake. There had been a number of bush fires that fall, and initially no one thought much of it. But the smoke, fanned by winds engendered by the fire itself, rapidly grew denser as flames shot through the bush and sparks ignited more fires. By noon, the hamlet of Zeta had been burned out, and by mid-afternoon the conflagration had reached Charlton itself. People helplessly fled or took to the lake; five perished, plus more in the surrounding countryside. About 70 refugees crowded into the powerhouse, which was built mostly of concrete. A baby boy was born during those desperate hours. By 4:00 P.M., it was all over. Every building in Charlton, including all the mills, warehouses, and the railway station, as well as over 700,000 cords of drying pulpwood, were destroyed, along with the *Navarch* and the *King Edward*, which were moored at their docks. The former steamer *Belle* then happened to be up at Saunders Lake, beyond Lake Kushog, and hence escaped the disaster. Nothing was left standing except a single residence and the powerhouse itself. (The same inferno also destroyed the town of Haileybury and many other centres, but in northern Timiskaming it is still grimly remembered as the Charlton Fire. Englehart somehow escaped with little damage.)

Charlton never recovered from the catastrophe. The ruined mills were not rebuilt, the generating station was shut down, and the population, which had stood at 900 or more before the fire, now shrivelled to 130. Later the railway spur was dismantled, and in 1969 even the post office was closed — in the name of improving the service! Today Charlton is a sleepy, scattered little village, with one or two stores and many vacant lots. Of late, it has started to revive a little, with the growth of a cottage community on Long Lake. But of the short-lived steamer service, nothing remains — save a few pictures, and vanishing memories.

THE TEMISKAMING NAVIGATION COMPANY AND ITS RIVALS: (1906–1917)

We must now return to Lake Temiskaming and observe the fortunes of the steamers there in the post-railway period. In the pulpwood towing line, this means essentially the operations of the Upper Ottawa Improvement Company, which for convenience are discussed separately in Chapter 6. In the passenger and freighting business, it means, basically, the history of the Temiskaming Navigation Company and a few operators who either followed it or tried to compete with it.

The Temiskaming Navigation Company was the direct successor to the Lumsden Steamboat Line, and was officially incorporated on February 20, 1906, with authorization to raise $99,000 in capital shares. Through the efforts of Joseph Arthur Larochelle, its first manager, in mid-March of 1906 the company secured title to the *Meteor* (Lumsden's flagship), plus the *Temiskaming* and the *Jubilee*, though this entailed mortgages on the first two vessels totalling $18,120 — roughly what the two steamers were deemed to be worth in 1905. The company also obtained the Lumsden wharves at (South) Témiscaming, Ville-Marie, North Temiskaming and New Liskeard, and probably other supplies and assets as well. It did not acquire the small steamer *Clyde*, which was probably sold and taken to Lake Kipawa about this time, nor the Bellevue Hotel nor the shipyards at Opemicon. Usually the fleet spent the winters at the beach near Fort Temiskaming.

A few years after its inception, the new company also acquired a fourth steamer. This was the *Ville-Marie*, a mystery vessel which barely appears in the printed records at all. According to government sources, she was built at Ville-Marie in 1902, and registered in Ottawa, though the actual file has not been found. She is said to have been just 35 feet in length, and registered 27 tons, but if so, she must have been greatly enlarged; a photograph shows a double-decked screw steamer about 66 feet in length. The 1906 inspection report indicates that she was licensed for twelve passengers at that time. Old-timers recall that she had a towpost and a very noisy (low-pressure?) 2-hp engine. Presumably she was used largely for freighting around the Quebec side of the lake, and sometimes she called at Haileybury on market days, often under the command of Captain Morin. Beyond that we can say very little, except that she belonged to one Joseph Lavigne until 1910, and afterwards to John Lumsden. It was Lumsden who brought her into the Temiskaming Navigation Company.

At the company's inaugural meeting, held in Mattawa in March 1906, George H. Rochester, an Ottawa businessman, was elected President, with Martin J. Malone of North Temiskaming as Vice-President and Hector O. Tremblay of Ville-Marie as Secretary-Treasurer. Of the remaining directors, one was from Ville-Marie and three from Mattawa (perhaps because most of the company stock was held in those quarters), though within a few years two members of the Board — Tremblay and Dr. C.W. Haentschel — would move to Haileybury, and George Rochester would open a hardware store there. By 1909, too, a lumberman named Samuel McChesney would come to represent New Liskeard, along with Arthur Ferland of Haileybury. J.A. Larochelle was confirmed as General Manager, a post he would hold for seven years.

Not a great deal is known of Joseph Arthur Larochelle. His family stemmed from St. Anseline in southern Quebec, but nothing is known of his early life. Presumably he followed the Canadian Pacific Railway to Mattawa, where in 1889 we find him building a large scow for the railway. Before long he became works manager on the Lake Temiskaming Colonization Railway, and it was probably in that capacity that he paid his first visit to the future site of New Liskeard, along with a team of surveyors, around 1891. After the railway's absorption into the Canadian Pacific Railway, he seems to have gone to work for the Lumsden Steamboat Line as a builder and maintenance man. In 1892 he was elected to Mattawa's first council, where he proved himself a tireless promoter of the region's interests, and even after his appointment to the Temiskaming Navigation Company he continued to live in Mattawa, which for a time was headquarters of the line. As manager, he seems to have been honest and conscientious, but at least one former employee recalls him as meddlesome and prone to interfere with the activities of the boat crews. It is also said that he drank a lot on the side, though perhaps the misfortunes of his company were enough to induce that. To his credit, Larochelle got along well with the public and never behaved in an abusive way.

The Temiskaming Navigation Company must have seemed impressively strong, in that it was built on the foundations laid by the immensely successful Lumsden Steamboat Line and all but controlled navigation on Lake Temiskaming, except pulpwood towing. Yet it was formed after the best days of steamboating were already over. The coming of the Temiskaming and Northern Ontario Railway to New Liskeard in 1905 had not only broken the Lumsden Steamboat Line's monopoly, but it had also usurped most of the freighting and transport. Traffic on the Canadian Pacific Railway branch to (South) Témiscaming had fallen off drastically since then. The Temiskaming Navigation Company was based on the gamble that there would still be enough business on Lake Temiskaming to justify a steamboat service. After all, Ville-Marie and the other settlements on the Quebec side still had no railway, and the roads were terrible. Perhaps the Temiskaming Navigation Company could still offer rates competitive with the Temiskaming and Northern Ontario Railway (with the help of the Canadian Pacific). Besides that, the lake had some potential for touristic development, and new silver deposits were being found almost daily — who knew what the future might hold? And all the lake communities were still clamouring for a boat service.

The 1906 season started problematically. On May 2nd, the *Meteor*, packed with provisions, and again with the tall, dapper Captain Albert Gaul at the wheel, left South Témiscaming for Ville-Marie, only to find the lake still frozen beyond the old fort. After waiting all night for a change, she turned back. Three days later she tried again, but though the ice had shifted the day before, she still found the entrance to Baie-des-Pères blocked, and consequently steamed over to Haileybury. Though people were glad to see her, there was little of the excitement of former years. Two evenings later, the *Temiskaming*, under her former master, Captain Morgan Ernest Jones, likewise made her maiden trip of the season. As previously,

ABOVE LEFT:

The scourge of the north: a forest fire, circa 1909.

Courtesy Gowganda & Area Museum

BELOW:

Steamer Ville-Marie *at New Liskeard, circa 1906.*

Courtesy National Archives of Canada, PA 130071

ABOVE RIGHT:

Steamer J.F. Booth, bringing M.L.A.s to Elk Lake, 1909. Courtesy Gowganda & Area Museum

the *Meteor* sailed on Tuesdays, Thursdays and Saturdays, leaving New Liskeard at 8:00 A.M. for the return trips, while the *Temiskaming* plied on the alternate days. The *Jubilee*, presumably, was busy freighting.

In addition to her regular duties, the *Meteor* was in considerable demand for excursions. On June 3rd, under unusually hot skies, she took a large crowd to the end of the lake. On Dominion Day she took 175 Haileyburians and 15 Liskeardites on a cruise to the Kipawa River, where they picnicked beside the rapids. Later that evening she ran a moonlight cruise (with music) for the Epworth League, and so crowded was the vessel that some couldn't get tickets. About a week later there was a monster-sized St-Jean-Baptiste celebration at Ville-Marie, for which every available steamer was pressed into service, ferrying in crowds from both sides of the lake. (In those days there was a fair amount of fraternizing between French and English Canadians, who were both struggling to make homes for themselves in the bush.) More such outings followed during the summer, but the patronage tended to drop; perhaps the novelty was wearing off. The Canadian Pacific Railway likewise tried offering discount rates for excursions from Mattawa, but apparently with meagre results. On August 15th, we hear of the *Temiskaming* taking the Methodist Sunday School children on a picnic at the Kipawa River, then the favoured destination. They came back on the *Meteor*.

Complications developed during one cruise held in early September. The *Meteor*, we are told, left New Liskeard with about 130 passengers, under cool, rainy skies (which deterred others from coming), though the sun was out by the time she reached the Kipawa River. Then it was discovered that the steamer could not dock on account of the low water levels. Someone got a message through to Mr. Larochelle, who tried to arrange for a couple of small steamers to unload the people, but the telephone failed to work. As a result, the crowd was kept waiting for an hour, until Captain Hendry arrived in the *Gipsy* (which had not yet gone to the Montreal River) to effect a transfer. Once ashore, everyone had a good time picnicking amid the glens, or hiking inland to see the falls, or trying to fish. But the delay meant that the *Meteor* didn't get back until 9:30 P.M. The whole incident, of course, underscored the fact that there was no control dam at the foot of Lake Temiskaming.

Indeed, fluctuating water levels caused the boats a lot of grief. In May of 1906, the lake was so high that the *Meteor* almost ran over the little wharf at Haileybury one night, with the result that one of her wooden fenders got pinched between the hull and the dock and snapped. No one was hurt, and the local wharfinger soon had the damage repaired. By contrast, come early September the lake had drained so much that the big ship could no longer use the Wabi River dock at New Liskeard, and, once again, small boats had to be used to unload the cargoes. Some dredging had been done, but the estuary kept silting up because settlers and lumbermen had cut all the trees along the river banks.

Of course, fluctuating water levels were not to anyone's advantage. New Liskeard in particular was left with extensive mud flats every fall, and in late October 1908, we hear of the *Temiskaming* going aground on a mud bank. It took several small steamers some days to get her floating again. As early as 1906, the Department of Public Works was studying proposals for control dams at both ends of the lake, at South Témiscaming and the des Quinze River (mainly for the benefit of industries located further down the Ottawa River), but with characteristic bureaucratic sluggishness, no contract was actually let until March of 1909 — and even then, nothing could be done until the summer on account of flood waters that were so high in June that every wharf on the lake, except at New Liskeard, was reported to be under water!

This state of affairs nearly proved fatal to the *Temiskaming* during the summer of 1908. The sturdy vessel had just left Témiscaming one morning amid the pulp logs, when her pointer — which was taken in tow — was found to be missing. Captain Jones ordered the mate to stop engines while a boat was lowered and the pointer retrieved, but by then the steamer was caught in the current and carried sideways. The rapids were only about 300 yards away. Naturally, the Captain rang for "full ahead," but there was no response. A pulpwood log had been caught between the rudder and the propeller, jamming it tight. A young deckhand, Bruce Pringle, grabbed a fire axe and climbed over the stern and down the rudder chain.

Then, perching on the rudder, he began chopping away frantically at the log, seemingly with no effect. Meanwhile, the gushing sound of the rapids grew louder and louder, and soon white water was foaming under the stern. Just when disaster seemed certain, the log finally rolled loose and the engineer cranked the gears into reverse. Gradually, the steamer began to creep backwards up the channel, until finally she was out of danger.

As always when shipping was trying to co-exist with timbering, logs were a never-ending problem. On the open lake the steamers could usually avoid the logs, but in confined waters it was often survival of the fittest. Probably the worst spot of all was at the mouth of the Wabi River, where it sometimes took a month or more for the Booth or Eddy Company logs to float down to be bagged with boom timbers. A number of times, the steamer *Jubilee* was almost unable to reach the wharf, and once, in 1906, Captain Jones of the *Temiskaming* had to threaten to ram and break a log boom to get the lumbermen to clear some space for docking. Even on the open lake there could be problems. One autumn day in 1910 or 1911, the *Temiskaming* was heading south near the mouth of the Montreal River, when Bruce Pringle, who was now mate, suddenly spotted a deadhead from the wheelhouse. He swerved to avoid it, only to strike another log submerged under the first one. After the impact, the steamer began to vibrate alarmingly — which indicated that the propeller had been damaged. As a result, Pringle took the ship home at a mere four miles per hour to avoid injuring the machinery. Once she was on the ways, an inspection revealed that two blades had been sheared off the propeller, but it took the crews just a few hours to bolt on new ones.

Sometimes logs could be the indirect cause of accidents. Twice during the 1907 season — on May 24th and July 24th — the *Temiskaming* struck a small boat in New Liskeard Harbour while trying to manoeuvre amid the logs, and on September 10th, the same thing happened to the *Jubilee*, which was groping past Messrs. McCamus and McKelvie's booms. All of these mishaps took place late at night. There were, of course, no lights set and no watchman on duty, since neither the navigation company nor the town wanted to pay the costs. Although the boat crews were hardly to blame, the courts fined the company over $100 in damages. This was particularly galling, because New Liskeard had almost ceased to be a paying port. On October 3rd, Mr. Larochelle wrote to the Board of Trade, explaining all this and asking it to do something about all the logs, canoes, boats and scows in the harbour. He also hinted that the Temiskaming Navigation Company might discontinue calling at New Liskeard if the lawsuits didn't cease. The Board, while not anxious to lose the boat service, did little more than express sympathy, although apparently lanterns were set in 1908 and 1909.

The problem of the wharves was gradually being rectified. There were good docks at North and South Témiscaming, while New Liskeard had two: one in the river and one just outside — though the latter could hardly be used when the waters were low. By 1907, the federal government built a very elaborate L-shaped wharf at Haileybury, complete with storehouses, offices and a waiting room. The structure, some 356 feet in length on its outer face, also served as a breakwater, and for the first time made Haileybury a safe place to dock. Some of the steamers helped to build the wharf by scowing in limestone from Dawson Point. In the course of these operations, the *Ville-Marie* is said to have gone aground on the footings and remained piled up for days. The town immediately made plans for a railway spur to run down along the lakeshore from the north, linking the wharf with the Temiskaming and Northern Ontario Railway, but thanks to internal squabbling, the spur, though started in 1908, was not completed until 1912. This move was not especially beneficial to the boats, since the effect was to feed more freight, especially logs, to the railway. By 1908, a good dock had been built at Fabre, south of Ville-Marie, and another soon followed at Point Piche, to serve the village of St-Bruno-de-Guigues; this came as an immense relief to the boat crews, who had long dreaded this exposed spot. At Ville-Marie itself, the old wharf at La Pointe, on the south side of the Baie-des-Pères, was upgraded in 1909, but the following winter a disastrous fire levelled that quarter of the community. The citizens then petitioned for a new wharf, to be located farther north, at the foot of the Rue Ste-Anne, close to the heart of the town. They got it in 1913. As at Haileybury, the new Ville-Marie wharf was an impressive structure, featuring sheds and warehouses. On the Ontario side, the government spent $3,000 for a dock at the mouth of the Montreal River, and $950 more for a small one at Dawson Point. The Department of Public Works also built a wharf and depot for its dredges at Moore's Cove, just south of New Liskeard.

Navigating problems were not the worst of the Temiskaming Navigation Company's difficulties. Much more serious was competition, and as if the railway were not sufficient in that regard, numerous attempts were also made to establish rival boat lines. Few of these intruders remained in business for long, but every time a new one appeared the result was usually a rate war, guaranteed to lead to losses for all.

From the very start, the company had to coexist with Captain Hendry's White River Mail Line. This line, operating mostly between Haileybury, New Liskeard and the Blanche River, acted as a sort of feeder to the Temiskaming Navigation Company, but its successor, the Upper Ontario Steamboat Company, was frankly out to scoop up as much business as possible from all over northern Lake Temiskaming in the interests of New Liskeard. As we have noted, the aggressive new company soon had four steamers in service, and probably captured much of the local business, especially in towing. Moreover, its vessels, being relatively small, could manœuvre fairly easily in crowded harbors like New Liskeard. When silver was discovered in South Lorrain in 1907, the two firms fought desperately to corner the action, but the older company had the advantage, in that it was well equipped to bring in large stockpiles of lumber, telegraph poles, machinery and fuel to Silver Centre Landing, using its handy connections with the Canadian Pacific Railway, plus foodstuffs from Ville-Marie. The steamer *Temiskaming* is said to have brought in 500 tons of coal in 1908 and 1909. Similarly, we hear of the *Jubilee* scowing fourteen tons of silver ore valued at $30,000 down the lake in June of 1908, with more to follow. (The Upper Ontario Steamboat Company had no convenient connections with any railway.) The rate war threatened to become totally impossible when a consortium from Haileybury chose to enter the fray in 1909. Soon the smaller, weaker Upper Ontario Steamboat Company began to falter, and in 1908 it withdrew the steamer *St. Antoine* to the Montreal River. The following year, it gave up completely on Lake Temiskaming and retreated to Latchford, taking the steamers *Wenona* and *Gipsy* there as well. This left it with only the *Blanche* on the local scene, and in 1909, this vessel was leased to the Temiskaming Navigation Company, which now assumed the added responsibility for service on the Blanche River.

The troubles of the Temiskaming Navigation Company did not end at this point. Late in the season of 1908, tragedy struck the *Temiskaming* in one of the worst disasters on any of Canada's minor inland waterways.

It was chilly on the morning of Tuesday, November 10th, when the *Temiskaming* left Haileybury on another routine trip to the foot of the lake. Passengers and crew alike shivered and blew their hands on the deck. The vessel was soon chugging along at normal speed, stopping at the usual places and occasionally responding to a hat or coat waved by someone on the shore who wanted a lift. About halfway down the lake she passed her sister, the *Meteor*, then northbound from Témiscaming. Continuing south, the steamer called at the Kipawa River to pick up a couple of hunters from Toledo, Ohio, who were on their way home, and later stopped at McLaren's Bay where she met the *Jubilee*. There were now about 25 people on board, including J.A. Larochelle, the manager. The ship was running about 20 minutes late, and apparently there was some concern about whether she could reach Témiscaming on time to connect with the train. The engineer, a Mr. Laverdure, was aware of this, though the officers would later deny that they had given him orders to make up for lost time. Otherwise, things seemed to be normal, although the mate, Philip John Gutcher of North Temiskaming, who was steering, noticed a lot of steam blowing off at McLaren's Bay.

About 30 to 40 minutes later, the *Temiskaming* sounded her whistle at Colton's Narrows. She was now only about six miles from her destination. Around 4:00 P.M. Captain Jones, who held a third-class engineer's certificate himself, paid a visit to the boiler room. He found one

ABOVE:

Steamer Jubilee
*at Haileybury
Wharf, circa
1908.* Courtesy
Mr. Gilles Amesse

MIDDLE:

*Steamer
Temiskaming
(third version),
with her pointer.*
Courtesy Mr. Gilles
Amesse, 192GA PH1-
7-29A

BELOW:

Steamer Meteor
*at Silver Centre
Landing.* Courtesy
Mr. Gilles Amesse,
35/84 S.H. PH1-7-11B

of the firemen on duty, a novice with only three months' experience. The engineer had apparently gone aft to get a breath of fresh air, leaving the senior fireman in charge. But the senior fireman, John Menard, had found a bottle of gin, and, feeling a little the worse for wear, was sleeping it off in the heat of the engine room, leaving the other man unsupervised. Observing that the valves were sometimes blowing off steam, Captain Jones checked the steam gauge for the boiler. It indicated about 137 lbs. pressure — quite normal. Apparently neither he nor the novice fireman noticed the level of water in the indicator tube, which would have told them that the boiler water was getting dangerously low — so low that the crown sheet of the furnace box was no longer submerged by hot water, and was therefore free to expand and overheat until the staybolts could no longer maintain their grip. The stage was set for disaster.

The time was now just a few minutes after 4:00. The steamer covered perhaps another mile. Then it happened. A tremendous roar erupted, and the whole boat, except for the bow, was suddenly engulfed in clouds of scalding steam. For several minutes no one could see a thing. From throughout the vessel came muffled cries and screams. Gutcher, stupefied, nonetheless had the presence of mind to swing the bow towards the Ontario shore, where it grounded gently on the beach. Presently lines were secured to trees.

Staggering through the hold amid the din and the blinding steam, Captain Jones finally encountered Bruce Pringle, the senior deckhand, and asked what had happened. Pringle yelled, "I think the boiler blew up!" The two men groped their way to the engine room, where they found everything in a shambles and the novice fireman grasping a pipe. As they moved to help him, the hapless man fell over. Captain Jones wanted to get him up on deck but Pringle, sensing that the man was dead, advised leaving him and trying to help those who might still be alive. In the engine room they found Menard with his head poking through a porthole in a desperate attempt to escape the hot steam. He was dreadfully scalded, with ribbons of flesh hanging out of his mouth and his head swollen to what seemed twice its normal size. The others got him out, but he survived for only about six more hours, dying in terrible agony. Meanwhile a hysterical waitress was screaming for help in the galley, and Pringle climbed down from the upper deck, opened a window and helped pull her up.

As the noise of the escaping steam died away and the survivors assembled on the upper deck, people began to assess the situation. At least one man was dead, two more were missing and several were badly hurt. Some crew members emerged from their quarters forward of the stokehold with coal dust impregnated into the raw flesh of their wounds. No one knew the condition of the ship, though amazingly she was basically intact.

As first aid was administered to the injured, it was decided to lower the lifeboats and take them to Témiscaming. As this was being done, someone shouted that he saw a man in the water swimming. Larochelle instructed Pringle to stay on board, since the steamer might be sinking and he would be needed. Pringle at first obeyed, but minutes later, when he heard that there was still a man in the water, he and Gutcher joined one of the lifeboat crews, with four others at the oars. The hands, alas, were too excited to row, so Pringle asked the mate to steer while he himself took an oar and moved to the bow. At last they began to make headway, and finally reached the exhausted swimmer. Pulling him into the boat, they found it was Charlie Ryan, one of the deckhands, who had been standing at the gangway with one of the American hunters when the blast occurred, blowing both of them into the water. He was taken back to the ship and into the saloon cabin, where the remnants of his clothes were cut away, taking some of his skin with them. He had superficial burns all over his body, and the outer rim of his ears were gone; that he survived in the freezing water so long seemed a miracle. The worst injured were removed on bedsprings placed across the lifeboats.

Meanwhile, the others began to leave the ship. Some of the passengers — who were mostly lumberjacks — waded ashore, clinging to the lines, and walked four miles south to the Guppy family farm, where they were kindly received. Two of the sons began rowing them across the lake to the depot in relays. This lasted well into the night. One of the lumberjacks was later found leaning against the station wall, mumbling unintelligibly. When taken inside and his clothes removed, he was found to be covered with blisters, with the bones showing in places. Yet he had walked four miles from the scene. The second American hunter, who had jumped overboard, was luckier, but he arrived with strips of flesh hanging from his lower legs. There were no doctors at Témiscaming or Lumsden's Mills, and though a train was summoned from Mattawa, it did not arrive until about 11:00 P.M. Two doctors came with it. In the meantime, the local people did what they could, using lard to cover the wounds for lack of anything better. Only by 3:00 A.M. did the victims reach the hospital in Mattawa. Altogether, four men lost their lives — including the unfortunate lumberjack at Témiscaming station — and several others never fully recovered. As Ted Guppy observed, "It was a bad night all around" — surely a gross understatement!

Once at the depot, Larochelle telegraphed the grim news to George Rochester, the president, who took the *Meteor* south from Haileybury the following day. The manager also wired the Ministry of Transport and asked what steps should be taken. The ministry, which was very strict about boilers, ordered an immediate official investigation. After questioning a parade of witnesses, including the inspectors, the inquiry concluded that the boiler had been quite sound, and that low water inside it had allowed it to overheat. Less easy to establish was why it happened. Both firemen were dead, and the engineer was in hospital, in no condition to answer questions. It was believed in some quarters that Laverdure had been aware that the water was running low, but, realizing that taking on more would only delay things further, he had decided to take a chance. But this hardly explains why he left his post shortly before the blast. He had worked for five seasons for the company, and everyone considered him competent. Bruce Pringle (who did not testify) suspected that Menard might have awakened, discovered the state of the boiler, and hastily turned on the feed-water pump, and that the cold water hitting the hot crown plate proved too much. Whatever the reason, Laverdure was never employed by the company again, and for that matter Captain Jones, who had spent three years on the *Temiskaming*, never returned either. His place was taken by the popular Captain McCarthy (Carty) Burns, who had previously commanded the *Jubilee*. His brother, Captain Dan Burns, had already followed Captain Gaul on the *Meteor*, though in fact the two brothers would often exchange ships. As for the *Temiskaming*, the explosion had blown two aft bulkheads loose from the hull, heaved up part of the promenade deck, and blasted four tons of coal in both directions throughout the hold. The boiler itself was a write-off, and worse, the insurance had just expired. But the ship was fit for salvage, and after a massive five-month rebuild she was ready to re-enter service in 1909.

The beleaguered Temiskaming Navigation Company was still not out of hot water. Despite the South Lorrain strikes it had lost money for the past two seasons, and though the Upper Ontario Steamboat Company was pulling out, another competitor was moving in to replace it. This was the Haileybury Navigation Company, which received its letters patent on December 2, 1908.

The new company was the brainchild of Absalom (Ab) Gibson, who first came to Haileybury around 1906 to drive a wagon team for the Vendôme Hotel, often to and from the railway station. Hearing of the South Lorrain silver finds, he quit his job, went prospecting, and staked a claim near the Keeley Mine. It proved valuable, and eventually earned a comfortable $40,000. But the mine was roughly three and a half miles from the lake, and, as usual, transport problems were onerous. Hence, Gibson formed a partnership with Hector McQuarrie, an honest, plodding notary who lived near Haileybury, plus a few other backers, to form a steamboat company to move freight, passengers and ore to and from town, and to trade with Ville-Marie. McQuarrie became Secretary, and Arthur Edward Way, of Haileybury, the Manager. Gibson also contemplated developing a new townsite at Silver Centre Landing, now the gateway to the Lorrain camps.

It is possible that the Haileybury Navigation Company did some business as early as 1908. There are a few vague references to three steamboat companies that year, and an Ottawa shipping register lists a steamboat as having been sold to a Haileybury man on June

ABOVE:

Steamer Temiskaming *with her pointer.*
Courtesy Mr. Gilles Amesse, 801 PHI-7-20

MIDDLE:

The Meteor *(left) and* City of Haileybury *at Haileybury Wharf.*
Courtesy Mr. Gilles Amesse, 813 PHI-7-51

BELOW:

Steamer Jubilee *at Haileybury, with an alligator at right.* Courtesy Mr. Gilles Amesse

20th. The steamer was the *Mahigama*, a single-decked screw vessel listed at 19.41 tons. With a length of 60.7 feet and powered by a second-hand upright high-pressure engine, the *Mahigama* had been built in 1899 at Fort William, Pontiac County, Quebec, not far from Pembroke. In 1903, she was sold to the Pembroke Navigation Company, which was then engaged in freighting and sightseeing cruises on that portion of the Ottawa River. Five years later, the vessel was sold to a Haileybury dentist named Joseph A.C. Crawford, who, in turn, resold her to the Haileybury Navigation Company in March of 1909, perhaps according to some previous arrangement with Gibson. An inspection report for 1910 alleges that the vessel was then in service on Lake Temiskaming but, curiously, she is never mentioned in the surviving newspapers from the area.

The operation, faced with fierce competition, can hardly have been profitable, yet in May of 1909, the Haileybury Navigation Company announced that it planned to have a second steamer running to South Lorrain in a month. The firm was as good as its word, and before the 21st, the new vessel had arrived — in pieces — from Toronto. She was called the *Silverland*, reflecting the dreams of her owners.

Although the *Silverland* was assembled at Haileybury, she is said to have been rebuilt from an earlier steamer, perhaps used on Georgian Bay. In any event, she was shipped north on three railway flatcars to Haileybury, where ten shipwrights went to work on her. The new steamer had a steel frame, a fantail stern, and measured 85.4 feet by 17. She was powered by a 13.5-hp fore-and-aft compound engine and a 150-lb. boiler that gave her speeds of up to eighteen knots — considerably faster than the ships of the Temiskaming Navigation Company. Gradually her superstructure took shape, until she was ready to be launched, stern first, by the beginning of the summer. She registered 52.70 tons and was licensed for 190 passengers. With her steel frame she could easily cope with the logs, but the public viewed her with mixed feelings. Some complained that she was narrow and top heavy, and prone to roll a lot when heavily loaded. Also, she apparently did not make a good scowboat, and was rarely used that way. One old officer also thought her windows were angled peculiarly. They looked fine when the vessel was on the ways, but distinctly queer and slanted when she was floating!

Commanded by the veteran Captain Blondin, who had lately been on the *Temiskaming*, the *Silverland* began plying twice a day from Haileybury to Silver Centre Landing, and sometimes to Ville-Marie and the Montreal River, taking men and provisions and some silver ore back to town. But Silver Centre Landing never developed into a metropolis, and South Lorrain never became another Cobalt. By 1910, the rush was over and soon most of the mines failed — which led to the ruin of Dr. Beattie Nesbitt and the Farmers' Bank of Toronto. The Haileybury Navigation Company went under too. In 1911 a New Liskeard critic was to imply that the firm, which had offered 1,600 shares on the market at $25 each, had, in fact, sold only 80 of them (for $2,000). Nevertheless, it had spent $21,000 on a steamer (or rather, two steamers), which had operated for four months and earned $8,000. The result: a loss of $13,000. Whether true or not, Ab Gibson and his partners decided to call it quits in March of 1910, and soon afterwards the Haileybury Navigation Company was merged with the Temiskaming Navigation Company, which thus acquired the *Silverland*. What happened to the *Mahigama* is unknown.

The 1909 season had been unusually frustrating for the Temiskaming Navigation Company. Not only was it facing competition from both the Haileybury Navigation Company and the Temiskaming and Northern Ontario Railway, but plans were also being made for yet another competitor in the passenger business: the Nipissing Central Railway. The Nipissing Central was to be an electric radial railway, similar to the suburban lines then running self-propelled trolley cars into and out of Toronto and other cities in the south. It was to run between Cobalt, Haileybury and New Liskeard, with options to extend its tracks to Silver Centre and North Temiskaming, Quebec, using power developed on the lower Montreal River. For this reason, the Nipissing Central Railway acquired a federal, rather than a provincial, charter, allowing it to operate beyond Ontario. This would later prove vitally important to the Temiskaming and Northern Ontario Railway, which — though annoyed by the little intruder — would end up buying control of it in 1911. Later, when the Temiskaming and Northern Ontario Railway, itself a provincial line, chose to expand into Quebec, it could do so using the Nipissing Central's charter. The Temiskaming Navigation Company likewise had no desire to see another railway gobble up what little business remained around New Liskeard, and in 1909 it tried to counter by proposing a radial railway of its own, to be called the Cobalt Range Electric Railway, to run from Cobalt to Haileybury and Gowganda, and perhaps even from Ville-Marie to connect with the new National Transcontinental Railway which the Laurier government was building from Quebec City through the Abitibi region to Winnipeg — anywhere except between Haileybury and New Liskeard. But in March 1909, the Haileybury Town Council — despite the opposition of the mayor and George Rochester, who was now a councillor — voted to give the Nipissing Central Railway the right to run its tracks along the streets of Haileybury, provided that the work was completed by the fall. Cobalt, fearing a drain of its population to Haileybury, hesitated to follow suit, but by May the Nipissing Central, starting midway at North Cobalt, began pushing its tracks in both directions. By October, the work was well advanced, and by April 30, 1910, the little trolleys were running, collecting 30,000 fares in the first nine days. Not until 1912, though, would the line be extended to New Liskeard, and during the interim Liskeard workmen would sometimes catch a steamer to Haileybury to make connections.

The navigating season of 1909 opened with the arrival of the *Meteor* at New Liskeard on May 14th, dodging ice all the way north. But the lake was in flood, and by June the steamer was able to sail up the Wabi River far enough to unload cargoes right behind some of the stores. But for the bridge, she could have gone inland as far as Uno Park. It must have given the Temiskaming Navigation Company some bitter satisfaction when the Temiskaming and Northern Ontario Railway trestle at Moore's Cove was washed out at about the same time, leaving the rails and ties dangling over the gap. Suddenly the steamers became indispensable again, ferrying back and forth between Haileybury and New Liskeard. But the railway speedily rebuilt the trestle.

At this time, the Temiskaming Navigation Companyhad six steamers in service. Besides the *Meteor*, *Temiskaming*, and *Jubilee*, it was running the *Blanche* up to Tomstown three times a week, returning the following day, and the *Ville-Marie* from Baie-des-Pères to North Temiskaming. All of the boats called at Haileybury, which was the company's headquarters. In 1909, the line also acquired another small auxiliary steamer called the *City of Haileybury*, a 67-foot single-decked screw vessel, which had been built at Kipawa the previous year for John Lumsden, who was still running his father's lumber business. Since Lumsden apparently had some connection with the Temiskaming Navigation Company, it may be that he sold the vessel to the line in return for shares. The *City of Haileybury* was a trim, handsome little craft, with a small saloon cabin, and licensed for 40 passengers. She registered 25.58 tons, and was considered one of the speediest vessels on the lake. C.C. Farr, who must have approved of her name, once implied in his old age that the *City of Haileybury* was actually a rebuilt version of the *Clyde*, which had gone to Lake Kipawa about 1905, and which disappears from the record just at this time. Though the circumstances are unknown, the boat was evidently moved from Lake Kipawa in the spring of 1909, and we may imagine that she was used mainly to trade between Haileybury and the ports of call in Quebec, perhaps to counter the *Silverland*. On October 4th, another tragedy struck, when her fireman was accidentally crushed between the steamer and the wharf at Fabre. Though he was transferred to the *Temiskaming*, the man died on board before a doctor could be reached.

This does not complete the Temiskaming Navigation Company's litany of setbacks in 1909. On September 3rd, it also lost the *Blanche*. The small steamer was docked at Pearson's Landing, where she was delivering a load of freight, including a new Massey-Harris binder set on the forward deck. It was midday, and the crew decided to have lunch on board before unloading. Suddenly, smoke was seen curling out of the engine room, and within moments the entire amidships was ablaze. The men hastily abandoned ship but, lacking firefighting equipment, they could do nothing. John Pearson himself sprang onto the deck, hoping to

single day, transferring from one ship to another in mid-lake. Let an advertisement for 1912 speak for itself:

NO RESIDENT OF OR VISITOR TO HAILEYBURY
Should fail to take a trip down Lake Temiskaming by
the magnificent boats of the TEMISKAMING NAVIGATION
CO., leaving Haileybury every morning.

A trip over the waters of this most beautiful lake is one to be enjoyed and not forgotten. The scenery throughout its whole length is diversified and never monotonous. Broad waters and narrow, but always deep; at places, shores rising to the hills in the background, but bold, precipitous and grand looking bluffs, forest-clad wherever tree can strike root, is the predominating feature. A couple of miles below Haileybury the Devil's Rocks rise perpendicularly out of the water over 200 feet high; from the top of the rocks a fine view of the lake and country bounding it can be had. Martineau Bay is noted far and wide for its blueberries and, in the old days, for its bears as well. Ville-Marie is prettily situated on Kelly's or Priest's Bay; is the centre of a prosperous settlement and the headquarters of the Oblate Fathers. The "Fort Narrows" is now reached, where Ontario and Quebec people can speak to each other from either shore. Fort Temiskaming is on the Quebec side; the Old Mission on the Ontario shore. Both are charmingly situated on the high ground with a splendid gravel beach, but running to sand farther along the shore on the Fort side. There is a dancing platform and a pavilion erected on the Old Mission side for the gratification of pleasure and picnic parties. Meals are served, and tents, blankets, etc. may be got. From both places a fine view is had up and down the lake. Silver Centre, a few miles below, has not a silvery look, but is interesting by reason of its mines. Fabre lies on the opposite shore.... Montreal River, about 26 miles from Haileybury, looks apparently low-lying, but the Great Beaver mountain, 1,200 feet high, is the background and dwarfs its surroundings. Kipawa River next shows up, with its volumes of wild water rushing down to the lake. The shores from Montreal River down to [South] Temiskaming are high, bold and imposing, well wooded. From the boat, looking over McLaren's Bay, a pretty landscape is to be seen. For the nonce at the bay, the bold shores recede and there is a gradual rise to the high land. Fields and bush lands, form the foreground, the high land some two miles distant, the background of the picture. Opemican Narrows is a narrow channel and deep, where Ontario and Quebec are but a few feet apart. It is a pretty spot, with the best of fishing. Green Creek is nearby, the outlet of Green Lake, noted for its speckled trout. An hour's run from here between high, rugged shores over the narrowest part of the lake, brings us to Temiskaming Station and the Canadian Pacific Railway.

One wonders how people could resist the appeal of such ads! But they could — and did. Though Lake Temiskaming has many dramatic views and fine vistas, in the main the scenery is not greatly varied or diversified and it lacks the wild ruggedness of Lake Temagami or the Muskoka District. Furthermore, it was accessible only by a roundabout dead-end railway spur to Témiscaming, or at faraway Haileybury and New Liskeard. In neither place did passenger trains ever run down to the local wharves. The lake is also prone to get rough with very little warning, and perhaps its yellowish-coloured waters are a deterrent to swimmers. And of course, at the best of times it is hours away from Toronto. For such reasons Lake Temiskaming never became a mecca for tourists.

It would appear that the Temiskaming Navigation Company actually had a profitable season in 1910. It was still the only economic lifeline to Ville-Marie and the settlements in Témiscamingue. Haileybury was a busy port, South Lorrain was booming, and competition on the lake was negligible. But once again, this situation did not last. New Liskeard merchants,

ABOVE:

Wabi River, New Liskeard, from a steamer.

Courtesy National Archives of Canada, PA 130080

MIDDLE:

Wharf and farmers' market, Haileybury. The boats appear to be the Lady Minto *(left), a chaland (house-boat), two scows, the* Scotchman *(centre), the* Meteor *(behind the shed) and the* Silverland *(right).*

Courtesy Mr. Gilles Amesse

BELOW:

View of Ville-Marie (new wharf), circa 1921. The steamers are the Silverland *(left),* Meteor, Temiskaming *(final version) and the* Bobs.

Courtesy Mr. Gilles Amesse

envious of the success of the Haileybury market, now decided that they wanted one of their own, and in this they were supported by the merchants and farmers of Guigues across the lake. Early in 1911, a deputation from Guigues and North Temiskaming, headed by J.E. Piche, a prominent merchant, paid a visit to New Liskeard to try to increase trade. To do this, they all agreed to push for a new wharf and a railway spur at New Liskeard and a bridge across the Blanche River. They also agreed to form their own boat line, to be called the Nipissing-Pontiac Steamboat Company after the respective districts in Ontario and Quebec it was to serve. (The Timiskaming district had not yet been detached from Nipissing).

The new company was organized in March 1911, with Captain Frank Brickenden — lately a partner in the Upper Ontario Steamboat Company — in the chair. Of the new directors elected, two, including Piche, were from Guigues, two more were from North Temiskaming, and five from New Liskeard and the Blanche River, and perhaps Haileybury and Ville-Marie. It obtained a Dominion charter, authorizing it to sell shares to a total of $40,000 of which one-quarter were actually issued. The headquarters were to be at New Liskeard, in the former office of the Upper Ontario Steamboat Company — not an auspicious location. A notary from Guigues was appointed to handle legal matters from the Quebec side. The company proposed to buy the wharf at Tomstown and a dock and storehouse at New Liskeard, and a 72-foot covered scow currently tied up in town. It also arranged to purchase the steamer *Aileen* from the Upper Ontario Steamboat Company and import it from Latchford. Haileybury snickered at the whole scheme and predicted that those involved would soon lose their shirts, as presumably the backers of the Haileybury Navigation Company had recently done. Significantly, New Liskeard's other veteran boatman, Captain Fred Hendry, decided to have no part in the venture either. Instead, he quietly arranged to bring in another vessel of his own.

When the *Aileen*, newly repainted, refitted, and re-engined, set off on her maiden trip from New Liskeard on the King's Coronation Day in June 1911, with several of the new company's directors and shareholders aboard, she seemed like a brand-new ship, although in fact she had seen four years' service on the Montreal River. Registered at 23.60 tons and licensed for 40 passengers, she would leave North Temiskaming every morning at 7:00, call at St-Bruno-de-Guigues around 8:15 and New Liskeard at 9:40, leave her scow and ply to Haileybury by 10:35 and back to Guigues at 11:10. At 11:20, she would leave for Haileybury, arrive at 11:50, and return to New Liskeard by 12:25. At 3:30 P.M., she would make a third trip to Haileybury, gather up any surplus freight, leave around 4:05 and return to Guigues by 4:50 and North Temiskaming at 6:15. (All this suggests that she could do only seven miles per hour with a scow in tow.) When the above schedule proved too tight, she began to leave earlier, at 6:15 A.M., calling at Haileybury first, and at New Liskeard by 9:00 A.M., and leaving in the afternoons at 2:00. This arrangement was apparently more convenient for shoppers. Her master that year was Captain Fred Marsh, another Muskoka mariner who had recently been handling some of the steamers of the Huntsville and Lake of Bays Navigation Company. But the following year, Captain Marsh left for Lake Temagami, and his place was taken by Captain J. Reamsbottom of Haileybury, who, in turn, was followed by Captain Ladouceur in 1913.

The *Aileen* was soon quite busy on her new route, importing scowloads of meat, butter, eggs, cream, buttermilk and garden produce, which were usually sold to the public right off the scow itself. She also helped to ship out silver ore from the Casey-Cobalt Mine near North Temiskaming. Nor did she ignore the recreational market. On August 17th we hear of her running a picnic cruise for the Literacy Society, up the Blanche River to Bolger's schoolhouse at Pearson. Despite her efforts, however, the attempt to build up a market in New Liskeard was not very successful, partly because the local farmers, having but recently arrived, had little to sell (unlike their Quebec counterparts, who had about a ten-year head start.) In September of 1912, Brickenden and Piche, after failing to get to use the old fire hall on the Wabi River as a building, tried opening a meat market in a former store, with uncertain results. The following spring Captain Brickenden — who had been in ill health — left New Liskeard with his wife to take up a new life as a fruit farmer near St. Thomas, Ontario. Later still, he would move to Florida and become a successful businessman before his death in 1952. It may be that his departure marked the end of the Nipissing-Pontiac Steamboat Company, which disappears from the local press around the same time. It was the last attempt by New Liskeard entrepreneurs to found a boat line. The *Aileen* carried on, sharing business with Captain Hendry's new steamer, the *Zara*, which was now plying on the Blanche River. During the winters, a stage line maintained connections with North Temiskaming and the Casey Mine.

It is doubtful that the *Aileen* was very profitable, given that she had three operators in as many years. In June of 1914, one T.J. McMullen was running her, still on the same route, but by the fall she had been transferred to Messrs. Wood and Gutcher (probably Jack Gutcher, once mate on the *Temiskaming*), who engaged Captain Hansen to finish the season. The following year, she was leased to Richard (Dick) Gibbins of North Temiskaming, later of Haileybury, who had become the manager of the Temiskaming Navigation Company. Gibbins assigned her a new route, taking mail, freight and passengers from Ville-Marie to Haileybury, Guigues, New Liskeard and North Temiskaming three times a week, again under Captain Ladouceur, who later transferred to the *Silverland*. Since New Liskeard was not served on the southbound route, it may be inferred that the market trips had become a thing of the past.

It was perhaps ominous that the *Aileen* had such a rapid turnover of captains. She was quite a narrow vessel, with a lofty wheelhouse, and later a former deckhand would claim that he noticed rotting timbers around the entrance to her cabin in 1915. Be that as it may, no one was expecting any trouble on the chilly morning of Thursday November 11, 1915, when she set off from Haileybury for the "Head" as usual, carrying 2,616 lbs. of pork, lard and drums of coal oil on her deck. Besides her crew of three, she was carrying one passenger, H. Lacasse, a storekeeper from North Temiskaming. The *Aileen* steamed past Dawson Point and continued northwards towards Windy Point and Chief's Island, one of the most dangerous portions of the lake. The weather, calm at first, soon turned windy and rough, though not stormy. The small steamer was never seen again.

The following day, an anxious telephone call from North Temiskaming confirmed that the *Aileen* had failed to make port. The Temiskaming Navigation Company at once sent the *Silverland* to conduct a search, and soon the grim evidence began to appear: several barrels of oil floating in the lake, plus an overturned lifeboat and miscellaneous flotsam and jetsam. That same day, the body of Mr. Lacasse was washed ashore at Sutton Bay, and the following June the deckhand's body was found. That of the master, Captain H. Kirby of Chatham, turned up in July. The engineer was never found, probably because he went down in his own engine room. It was generally suspected that the cargo had shifted suddenly in the waves, causing the steamer to roll over in deep water. The wreck was never found, but it was noticed that several families around Sutton Bay seemed to have plenty of kerosene over the following winter! One man was indeed fined for possession, and a few others briefly jailed. Next to the *Temiskaming* explosion, the *Aileen* disaster was the worst marine tragedy in the history of Lake Temiskaming.

By now the best days of steamboating were definitely over. The once-powerful Temiskaming Navigation Company was faltering, and on the local scene only the steamer *Zara* was still sailing from New Liskeard.

The *Zara* was another all-purpose boat, somewhat smaller than the *Aileen*. She was originally built at Port Rowan, Ontario, and registered at Port Dover. She may have been used as a fishing boat on Lake Erie. However, by 1911, Captain Hendry, who had lately left the Upper Ontario Steamboat Company, had arranged to buy and import the vessel, in partnership with Captain Bill Reynolds, a feisty little skipper who had once commanded the steamers *Golden City* and *Empress* on the central Kawartha Lakes. Then, after spending six years in Cuba, he had returned to Canada to serve on the Montreal River. It was a big day in New Liskeard when the new steamer arrived, and by mid-June she was ready for business, including charter cruises. Her main route was up to the Blanche River three times a week, with Captain Hendry at the helm and Reynolds at the engines. By the season of 1912, the partners also had two large scows, one mainly for hauling gravel from Windy Point, and a 73-foot covered barge for fuel and more perishable cargoes, such as hay.

The venture apparently prospered. The *Zara* and her scows transported anything and everything, including lumber, bricks, cement, produce and mineral ores. She is also said to have delivered the steel for a bridge at Judge on the Blanche River, in 1913. Sometimes she ran south on errands to Ville-Marie and Silver Centre. She was also in demand for picnics, especially to Pearson or Dawson Point, where she might be joined by other steamers and motorboats, and in the fall she took hunting and fishing parties. Then, in the spring of 1913, she was cut in half on the riverbank near the McCamus and McKelvie sawmill and lengthened by 12 feet for a new total of 63.4 feet, which nearly doubled her capacity. Now registered at 24.05 tons, she was like a new boat when she was relaunched in May. But her operations were often hampered by logs, especially on the Blanche River. On May 12, 1913, Captain Hendry found himself completely unable to ascend the river, and this occurrence was not unusual. The following season was just as bad, but the lumbermen didn't seem to care. They acted as if they owned the river. In May of 1914, the vessel struck a deadhead out in the lake, and had to creep home again for repairs.

Despite the logs, the *Zara* generally puttered about quietly and uneventfully. Only once did she become the focus of a spectacular incident. On the evening of June 22, 1912, the steamer, under the temporary command of Captain Brickenden was towing a scow loaded with tons of baled hay down the lake from North Temiskaming. Somewhere south of Chief's Island, a spark from the stack ignited the hay, which burst into flame. By the time the crew noticed it, the fire was out of control, and the order was give to cut the scow loose. This was done, but the blazing barge began drifting close to shore off Dawson Point. The fire was visible from as far away as Haileybury, and soon people were coming out in their motorboats to see what was happening.

The steamer's crew, meanwhile, grew fearful that the blaze might start a major fire ashore. They therefore drew close, and tried to scuttle the scow by punching holes in the side. Just when they seemed to be succeeding, the tug ran aground in the dark!

In the meantime, the *Meteor* happened to be out on a moonlight cruise, when Captain Burns spotted the blazing scow and steamed over to help. The ship manœuvred close, and the crew turned the hose on the scow, but while turning around the *Meteor* bumped into the side of the hapless *Zara*, which began to sink in shallow water. Captain Brickenden and the deckhand were easily picked up, but the engineer had to jump overboard in order to be rescued. The scow was finally towed away and allowed to sink. Happily, the *Zara* was not seriously damaged, and after a brief visit to the marine railway at New Liskeard she was soon running again.

The *Zara* still had about sixteen years of life ahead of her, but the days of the Temiskaming Navigation Company were about to run out. The line's revenues must have slumped again in 1911 and afterwards, thanks to the Nipissing–Pontiac Steamboat Company and the Nipissing Central Railway, which by 1912 was running trolley cars to New Liskeard every half-hour. There was no way that anyone else could offer a comparable service. Worse still, the roads were improving. In 1912 the one from Cobalt to Haileybury and New Liskeard was macadamized, and by 1913, there were eight automobiles in New Liskeard alone. People were soon using their new-found mobility to drive to picnics at Dawson Point or on the Blanche River — or they could go by motorboat. Very gradually excursions declined; people had seen the old sights often enough. Meanwhile, the lake levels continued to fluctuate. In May of 1911, the new coffer dams, intended as a prelude to a control dam at Témiscaming, collapsed and swept away the derricks, steam-shovels and much of the construction equipment. Worse followed in June 1914, when rising water pressure swept away three piers of the new dam, with the result that the waters fell eighteen inches in just a few hours. Not until March 1915 was the structure rebuilt and functioning. As a direct result of this setback, the *Meteor* struck a rock about a mile from North Temiskaming on the evening of June 14, 1914, and the captain was forced to run her ashore and beach her in shallow waters. By then, the water in the engine room was knee deep, but the engineer and fireman stayed at their posts.

ABOVE:

Steamer Meteor *at Ville-Marie. The vessel behind her seems to be the* Dora. Courtesy Mr. Gilles Amesse

BELOW:

Mystery steamer Wanakewan *at Ville-Marie, with the* Meteor *(1923).* Courtesy Mr. Gilles Amesse, 634 PH1-7-9

The *Temiskaming* was despatched to assist, only to go aground herself, and the company had to borrow an alligator from the Upper Ottawa Improvement Company. The *Meteor* was apparently repaired in time for a Sons of England moonlight cruise on July 9th; 175 people took part.

By 1910, having absorbed the Haileybury Navigation Company, the Temiskaming Navigation Company had seven or even eight steamers, probably more than it needed, and in 1911, it found the *Aileen* and the *Zara* usurping business at the north end of the lake. As a result, the company had to retrench. Probably it never used the *Mahigama*, which disappears after 1910, but the *Silverland* was too valuable to be left idle. She was put to work freighting and handling special cruises. But the smaller steamers began to go, quietly and obscurely. By 1913, if not earlier, the *Ville-Marie* was listed as "not in commission," and nothing more is heard of her. She probably went to pieces soon afterwards, forced out of service by the *Aileen*, which had more or less taken over her route. By 1913, too, the *City of Haileybury* was sold and taken back to Lake Kipawa, to resume her duties there as a tug and passenger boat. Similarly, the *Jubilee* is last mentioned in the fall of 1914, when she brought back the body of Captain Reamsbottom, who had accidentally shot himself while hunting near Silver Centre. The steamer, which was growing unseaworthy, seems to have been stripped and abandoned near Opimica Narrows. In 1915, the company may have leased the *Aileen*, but she was lost that same season.

Though the record is vague, it appears as if the sturdy old *Temiskaming* was rebuilt and scaled down in size around this time. Originally registered at 336.22 tons, she was rebuilt (perhaps after the 1908 explosion) to just 212.75 tons. Her new dimensions are unknown, but she was now considerably smaller than the *Meteor*. Starting in 1909, she was assigned to transport all of the cement used to build a control dam on the des Quinze River at the future village of Angliers, Quebec — a stupendous task, which required the vessel to be at the railhead at South Témiscaming by 7:00 every morning to collect bags of dry cement weighing 87½ pounds apiece. Each railway car carried about 600 of these bags, and the steamer was known to take two or three carloads at a time. For most of five seasons she did little else but ply back and forth from one end of the lake to the other, taking few passengers for the duration. Vital though the contract was, it was not enough to sustain the company.

No doubt the fleet dwindled in the face of falling revenues. In 1912 — rather ominously — the line had to secure a mortgage of $13,000 on the *Meteor* and the *Temiskaming*, just about the time that the mortgages owed to Mrs. Lumsden's estate were finally discharged. In 1913, the situation was nearing a crisis point. In the spring of the year J.A. Larochelle — for unstated reasons — resigned as General Manager, although he remained on hand as part of an *ad hoc* management committee for a time with George Rochester, Arthur Ferland and John Lumsden. As if to symbolize the retreat of the dying enterprise, the head office was now removed from Haileybury back to Témiscaming. Little more is heard of Larochelle, who seems to have taken another job at Témiscaming with the Canadian International Paper Company, which ran many boats to tow pulpwood logs in Quebec. In the end, he apparently left the north country for good.

In a desperate effort to retrieve its fortunes, the Temiskaming Navigation Company had hired William Kervin of Callander as manager, by the season of 1914. Kervin did his best, opening the season with the *Silverland* in mid-May, and soon following with the *Temiskaming* and the *Meteor*. He tried to cut costs and concentrate on paying business only, but it wasn't easy. In May, he lost a possible charter cruise with the *Meteor* because the sponsors wanted to operate the lunch counter on board, but the manager politely explained that there would be too little profit to the company if it didn't supply the refreshments as well. Result: no deal! Nonetheless, the *Meteor* received quite a few charters, usually to the Mission or to Martineau Bay. We even learn of an outing from South Témiscaming to the Mission on August 11th. By then, though, war had broken out in Europe, and as its realities began to sink in with mounting casualty lists, it helped to put the damper on excursions. In 1915, there is no mention of pleasure cruises until Dominion Day.

The war soon made men scarce, and wages rose accordingly. After just one season, Kervin quit, and for a time it seemed doubtful that the steamers would even sail in 1915. Then, in June, it was announced that Richard Gibbins of North Temiskaming had taken charge, and that the *Meteor* and the *Silverland* at least would ply, along with the *Aileen*, which he had leased separately. On July 1st, all three steamers took part in a monster picnic to Dawson Point, running across in relays; the proceeds went to the Red Cross Fund. About a thousand people took part, and were pleased to find that J.W. Fitzpatrick, the local landowner and lately President of the Nipissing Central Railway, had beautified the property with a dance pavilion and a boardwalk down to the dock, giving the site a park-like setting. The whole scene was repeated on August 21st, when nearly 1,500 employees of the Temiskaming and Northern Ontario Railway arrived in a special twenty-coach train from North Bay to picnic at the Point. Though some stayed in the towns, most went out on the lake, keeping the *Meteor* and the *Silverland* plying almost non-stop. The local people joined in the festivities, which included sports, a baseball game and a tug-of-war between the Temiskaming and Northern Ontario Railway and the Nipissing Central Railway. Both sides claimed victory. It was reported afterwards that the ladies of the Red Cross Society had made and sold over 1,000 meals that day.

Though the *Temiskaming* was apparently laid up after 1914, the *Meteor* and the *Silverland* continued to ply throughout the war, but they were now the only passenger ships on the lake. Gradually, reports of cruises peter out in the local press, and although the boats took part in Dominion Day festivities at New Liskeard in 1916, and even brought in spectators from Ville-Marie, many of the participants arrived by train, automobile and streetcar instead. People could now take a trolley to Sharpe's Bay, south of New Liskeard, for a picnic, or motor to Dawson Point or Fort Temiskaming.

In the spring of 1917, with scarcely a whimper, the Temiskaming Navigation Company — the successor to the Lumsden Steamboat Line and once the proud owner of six steamboats — decided to surrender its charter. No reasons were given for this decision, but evidently the directors were discouraged by rising costs and diminishing profits, and perhaps by rumours of an imminent railway extension to Ville-Marie. Probably they chose to withdraw before the situation got any worse.

The company's three remaining ships, the *Meteor*, *Temiskaming* and *Silverland*, were sold to Télésphore Simard of Pontiac County, Quebec, a Liberal M.P., who represented a new syndicate from Ville-Marie that was determined to save the steamboat service. Steamboating was by no means over on Lake Temiskaming, but it hadn't many more days to run.

THE VILLE-MARIE NAVIGATION COMPANY: (1917–1923)

La Compagnie de Navigation Ville-Marie, which represents the second-last serious attempt to operate a commercial freight and passenger service on Lake Temiskaming, was founded by interests in Ville-Marie and vicinity who were anxious not to lose their boat service, which, for them, still represented almost their only link with the outside world. Little is known today about its operations since, as with most defunct firms, all of its official records have long since been destroyed, and Ville-Marie itself had no newspapers to chronicle weekly events. All that remain are a few shipping registers, some inspection reports, a few local histories (usually not overly concerned with navigation), a few old-timers' recollections, and the occasional comment in some surviving Ontario newspapers. On these bases we proceed!

The Ville-Marie Navigation Company — to use its English name — was chartered under Quebec law on March 25, 1917. (It is also said to have acquired the charter of the old Temiskaming Navigation Company as well.) One of its first moves was to appoint as general manager a prominent local businessman named William (Welly) Chenier, who had many interests in Ville-Marie. The family was well thought of in town, and indeed a brother, Augustin, served as registrar and secretary of the navigation company. Welly Chenier himself was a well-established merchant, who owned, wholly or in part, a number of stores by 1908, when, at the age of 26, he helped to found the Ville-Marie Chamber of Commerce. Amiable, affable, bilingual and frugal, he seemed to be well suited to manage the boat line.

Meanwhile, thanks to Télésphore Simard (a civil engineer by training, who also happened to be Mayor of Ville-Marie at the time), arrangements were being made to purchase the three steamboats from the assignees of the Temiskaming Navigation Company. This entailed a $7,500 mortgage on the *Temiskaming*. By April 9th, the formalities were concluded, and the new company at once began to overhaul the boats. The *Temiskaming* apparently, was extensively rebuilt, but there are no signs of serious changes to the others.

The new firm inherited most of the staff and officers from the old. Captain McCarthy Burns continued to command the *Meteor*, while his younger brother Dan acted as agent for the company and generally looked after the maintenance of the boats. He may also have commanded the *Temiskaming*. The old schedules were apparently retained, with the *Meteor* sailing thrice weekly up and down the lake, alternating once again with the *Temiskaming*, while the *Silverland* (at least in 1918) plied from Ville-Marie to Haileybury six days a week, with calls at New Liskeard and North Temiskaming every second day. The northern communities noticed no disruptions in the service.

A few glimpses of the *Silverland*'s activities around this time have been provided by Mr. Émile Boucher of Témiscaming, who at eighteen served as a deckhand in 1918, when men were scarce. The little steamer set off on her maiden trip of the season on May 2nd at 7:00 A.M. under the command of Captain Arthur Kelly, a newcomer from Lake Kipawa, amid clear skies, a cold wind and three-foot waves. The vessel, as was her habit in rough waters, rolled a lot, and at times the rudder rose halfway out of the water. Soon all of the crew except Boucher were desperately seasick (being mostly landsmen), and many of them threw up. Captain Kelly, though anxious and none too comfortable himself, decided to let the lad steer up to Ville-Marie. The steamer arrived safely, though it took ten and a half hours to run from Témiscaming instead of the usual five. Soon she was busy, often carrying up to 175 bales of hay from Ville-Marie to Haileybury, and returning in the evening with the mail. Heifers and other livestock were sometimes included, and as many as 111 passengers. Boucher did not like the job; the work was so arduous that he lost 46 lbs. that season, and moreover he was continually harassed by two other crew members from Ville-Marie, who apparently resented him as an outsider. Hence, his first season on the *Silverland* was also his last.

A little is known of the *Meteor*'s operations during this period, though most of them were unremarkable. They included more excursions to the Old Mission, some Boy Scout cruises to McLaren's Bay and, starting in 1919, annual excursion picnics to the Montreal River by the employees of the Wabi Iron Works of New Liskeard and their friends, wives and sweethearts. Nonetheless, excursions from the town continued to decline, partly because New Liskeard was itself becoming a recreation centre. In 1919, the town finally got around to clearing away the brush and debris along its southern shores — and discovered that it had a lovely beach! The Beach Park was officially opened on July 22nd, and proved so popular that most people soon lost interest in taking a long steamer ride down the lake. Before long the railways were doing a good business bringing people in for picnics and as usual, what the railways gained, the steamers lost.

It was still possible to dine in style aboard the *Meteor*. According to the recollections of Mme Lucienne Paré, who as a young girl in 1917, followed her mother, Joséphine Racicot, as part of the steamer's galley staff, the breakfast menu consisted of crêpes, bacon and eggs and potatoes. Lunch featured ham, bacon, chops, or roast beef, with cake or pie for dessert. Dinner consisted of pork stew or chicken and vegetables, with cake for dessert. Fruits were also served, but only in the first-class dining room. The tab was fifty cents. All the food was supplied from a store in Ville-Marie. The atmosphere in the first-class dining room was very sedate, but second class, which was usually full of boatmen and newly arriving *colons* and their families, was invariably noisy. One of the girls on staff looked after each of the dining rooms, including dishwashing, while the third attended to the staterooms on the upper deck —

for $25 a month plus room and board. Joséphine, who became chief cook, received a comfortable $75. Her daughter Lucienne quite enjoyed her days "at sea."

Cruises continued from Haileybury and Ville-Marie. On July 10, 1920, the village of North Temiskaming had something special to celebrate: after an agitation of seventeen years, it had finally induced the government to build a double-spanned steel bridge across the des Quinze River. On opening day, some 289 rigs and 78 motor cars drove in from Guigues, Laverlochère, Lorrainville and other centres, along with 57 automobiles from Ontario. At 10:30, the *Meteor* and the *Temiskaming*, sailing together for once under sunny skies, steamed into town bearing another 600 people, including the band from Ville-Marie. After a parade to the church, a special Mass was held, followed by festivities and a banquet at the town hall. Later that season (August 23rd), the *Meteor* helped to entertain 200 visiting Ontario teachers, who had come to Haileybury to see the sights of the North. She also ran regular "grotto cruises" every year to Ville-Marie, starting in 1904, to allow pilgrims and sightseers from both sides of the lake to visit the shrine of the Virgin being developed on the "mountain" behind the town, and patterned after that at Lourdes, France. Every such pilgrimage involved a pontifical Mass, with solemn processions, benedictions and celebrations afterwards, including sometimes a moonlight cruise. And on July 22, 1922, the *Meteor* ran an unusual excursion, this time to take Ontario public school teachers down the lake to Témiscaming to see the new giant pulp mill and company town being developed by the Riordon Company — of which more in Chapter 6. This was inevitably an overnight trip, with some of the participants putting in at the Bellevue Hotel, and others taking staterooms on the *Meteor*. Few would have guessed that this excursion would prove to be one of her last.

Only a few weeks later, a tragic incident took place as the *Meteor* was leaving Ville-Marie for Haileybury. On board was a Russian railway navvy who had been engaged to work on the Canadian Pacific Railway branch at Kipawa. The fellow was considered dangerous, having just been sentenced to a year in jail for striking another man with a crowbar, and was on his way to Bryson manacled in the custody of a constable. He boarded the steamer calmly, but before the gangway door could be closed, he deliberately stepped off and fell overboard. Apparently having second thoughts about suicide in the cold waters, he struggled desperately to stay afloat. Meanwhile, the steamer stopped engines and a boat was lowered … but then the struggling ceased. About 125 passengers witnessed the incident.

The Ville-Marie Navigation Company must have been mildly prosperous during this period, because it actually acquired a fourth vessel. This was the *Bobs*, a 26-ton screw tug with a six-hp engine and a steel-framed hull. Little is known of this craft, except that she was built at Parry Sound in 1900 and fitted out with some accommodation for passengers. In 1905, she went to Lake Temagami, where we shall find her in the next chapter, but by 1920 she was in service with the Ville-Marie Navigation Company, mainly on the market run from Ville-Marie to Haileybury. She also assumed mail deliveries, perhaps in succession to the *Silverland*, which is said to have been growing unseaworthy. A sailing schedule dating from this time lists all four steamers in service, with the *Meteor* now sailing the full length of the lake three times a week and spending the nights at Haileybury and Témiscaming. The *Temiskaming*, now based at Ville-Marie, was looking after the local stops at the north end of the lake, and connecting with the 4:00 P.M. trains at Haileybury daily except weekends. The schedules for the *Bobs* and *Silverland* are not specified. Finally, around 1921 the company obtained the *St. Bruno*, another mystery vessel, which seems to have shared the local service with the *Bobs*; a photograph shows the two of them wintering together near Fort Temiskaming. In 1923, however, the *St. Bruno* was apparently moved to Lac des Quinze — of which more later.

Before the end of the 1922 season, the *Meteor* and the *Temiskaming* both became minor parties to another tragedy, this one of catastrophic proportions.

The weather was generally hot and dry in Timiskaming during the autumn of 1922. Nonetheless, farmers continued to burn brush in the area after September 15th, as they had a right to do, despite the objections of the fire rangers. Annoyed, the farmers appealed to the local boards of trade to remove the meddlesome rangers, and this was done in the townships

ABOVE:

Steamer Zara, *at Windy Point, Lake Temiskaming.*

BELOW LEFT:

Steamer Silverland *(left), with the* Meteor *at Haileybury.*

BELOW RIGHT:

Steamer Temiskaming *at North Temiskaming (Notre-Dame-du-Nord). The vessel is in her final version, circa 1918.* Courtesy Mr. Gilles Amesse, 85APCC PH1-3-3

northwest of the lake. In late September several bush fires were noticed, but no one was worried; people in the North were used to fire scares. True, Haileybury had suffered a very serious fire in August 1906, in which most of the business section had been destroyed, but this had started locally at a time when most of the town was built of wood. It was also true that a major fire had swept the Porcupine country and burned out the town of Cochrane in 1911, with the loss of 70 lives. And everyone remembered the Matheson Fire of 1916, which had burned out 500 square miles and killed 280 people. But these fires had started in pioneer regions up north. It surely couldn't happen again, not in the south. However, as a precaution, a firebreak was slashed through the bush near Haileybury.

By the beginning of October, smoke from the west was hanging over Haileybury, and growing denser every day. By the morning of the 4th, the town was full of smoke, but there was still no feeling of urgency when the *Temiskaming* left dock as usual for Ville-Marie and places south. There might have been, had people known that several local fires had joined into one that was racing through the dry underbrush near Constance Lake, creating its own wind as it swept towards the town.

By noon, however, the fire bell began clanging, as men hurried with hoses, buckets and shovels to check a blaze near the railway tracks. For several hours it looked as if they could do it. But alarm was mounting. At 2:30 the school children were sent home, and by 3:00 people started to leave town. Automobiles jammed the road to Cobalt, along with wagons and buggies, and though headlights were turned on, the smoke was so dense that many went into the ditch or bumped into those in front. Meanwhile, around 3:30, the hoses spread across the tracks were severed by a northbound train, and soon the roof of the railway station was ablaze. Then the power lines burned and the power went off. The trolleys on the Nipissing Central Railway ground to a halt and two were left stranded. Winds blew at 40 miles per hour, throwing embers onto rooftops. Houses everywhere burst into flame as if ignited spontaneously. There was little panic, perhaps because the heat was not too great, but the confusion was terrific. One thing was now clear, though: nothing could stop the fire.

All over town buildings were starting to burn. Around 4:00 the Anglican parish hall caught fire, then within another ten minutes the Vendôme Hotel was ablaze. Stores containing explosives blew up. A bank building built of sandstone melted like wax. The Roman Catholic cathedral, which had cost $125,000, disintegrated in the heat. At the hospital, three patients died, one on the operating table, but the nuns and nurses remained calm and managed to evacuate the rest before the hospital likewise took fire. Everywhere there was smoke, darkness, and chaos.

While about 1,500 refugees fled to Cobalt and Latchford, and others groped north to New Liskeard, the fire drove about 600 more down to the wharf. This seemed fairly safe, but then someone remembered the drums of gasoline stored there. These soon exploded into sheets of flames, and now the wharf was ablaze too, even ahead of the buildings behind it. The crowds were driven into the water, which was choppy and bitterly cold; some swam out a quarter of a mile or more. Others were luckier and climbed into canoes, punts and motorboats. Twelve families found refuge on a scow, which was propelled away to the Devil's Rock, out of danger. No one could turn his face towards the town on account of the heat and the sparks. Within two hours, it was all over, and the fire burned itself out in South Lorrain. Fortunately, the wind shifted to the northwest, which helped to save about 40 residences at the north edge of town; it may also have saved the fugitives at the lake from being suffocated. But by 6:00 P.M. only a single house was still standing in the southern part of Haileybury. Ninety percent of the town, including three hotels, three banks, the court house, the recorder's office, six churches, two schools, a convent and about 500 homes lay in ruins. Eleven citizens perished.

Things were not much better elsewhere. North Cobalt was almost wiped out, though somehow the storage barns of the Nipissing Central Railway survived. Farther north, the communities of Thornloe, Uno Park, Heaslip, Hilliardton, Tomstown and Charlton were burned out, along with half of North Temiskaming. About 50 people lost their lives. Over sixteen townships and hundreds of farms were razed, and thousands of people were left homeless. Thirteen homes and the flour mill in west New Liskeard were destroyed, but the citizens managed to hold the fire at the railway tracks and use buckets and wet blankets to keep the rooftops from catching until the wind shifted. Had the fire jumped the tracks, New Liskeard would have shared the fate of Haileybury. Within just a day or two, the weather turned cold and dumped snow on the stricken region, intensifying the misery.

Where were the Temiskaming steamers at this time of crisis? Apparently doing their rounds as usual, but with a difference. The *Temiskaming* had called at Haileybury that morning, but there was no rush to get aboard, despite the smoke. By the early afternoon, though, the pall became so intense that the captain decided to pay an unscheduled return visit to Haileybury. By that time, the situation looked chaotic, but there was still no rush to leave. Nonetheless, a large number of people, including the patients at the hospital and many frightened children, were evacuated by boat to Ville-Marie. The steamer was preparing to make a third trip, but visibility was almost nil, and meanwhile the wind arose. All she could do was continue her rounds. The *Meteor* was then on her way north from Témiscaming when she encountered her sister ship and got the grim news. Captain Carty Burns, who lived at Haileybury, was anxious about his family, but he, too, could make little headway beyond Ville-Marie until after dark. By the time the *Meteor* arrived at the ruined dock, there were few people in sight and the town was practically gone, but the captain found his family, now homeless, and took them and any others he could find to Ville-Marie. For some time afterwards, the Burns family lived aboard the *Meteor*. The ship was back the following afternoon, thus helping to dispel rumours that she had gone down with 200 refugees on board. Nonetheless, some parents did not find out until three days afterwards that their children were at Ville-Marie.

After the initial shock lifted, people swung into action. Relief committees were formed at Cobalt, Englehart and New Liskeard. Motorists began driving about, distributing supplies and bringing in the destitute. The railways offered free passes to the victims, and within 48 hours, relief trains were on their way from Toronto. Boots, clothing, food, lumber and other donations began pouring in, along with about 80 old Toronto streetcars, which were turned into emergency housing. Power was soon restored, and by late October the Nipissing Central Railway's trolleys were again running between Haileybury and Cobalt. The provincial government promised to carry Haileybury's debenture load for five years, and to rebuild the schools and courthouse. Premier E.C. Drury himself sent a wire of "spare no expense" plus a personal cheque for $500. By November, despite a succession of snowstorms, eleven stores had been largely rebuilt, but it was not until the fall of 1924 that the Town of Haileybury seemed close to normal again.

The steamers played a modest role in the recovery. At Haileybury itself, they could do little, especially since the wharf was not properly rebuilt until the fall of 1924, but they ran food and provisions to North Temiskaming and the Blanche River until the freeze-up. One of the most urgent needs was to erect shanties and rebuild barns for the livestock and stock them with hay, and here the boats were invaluable. On October 24th, the *Zara* towed her first scowload of building lumber up to Hilliardton, and repeated the process until December. In 1923, we hear of her transporting timbers and a pile driver for a new bridge at Tomstown, assisted by various launches. By this time, too, the *Gipsy* — now assigned to Captain Gutcher — had returned to her old waters from Charlton to assist with freighting and scowing. To a press correspondent the sight of the busy steamers and launches looked just like the old days, when settlement was first starting on the Blanche River.

By the spring of 1923, the Ville-Marie Navigation Company must have been wavering between going out of business or making a fresh start on other waters. On Lake Temiskaming the future looked bleak. There had long been rumours that the Nipissing Central Railway might extend its tracks to North Temiskaming, or even to Ville-Marie, using power to be developed on the des Quinze River — or that the Canadian Pacific Railway might decide to extend the spur from Témiscaming to some point on the des

ABOVE:

Steamer Temiskaming
(final version), at
Haileybury. Andrew
Merrilees Collection, courtesy
National Archives of Canada,
PA 142387

BELOW:

Captain Rouleau (left),
manager Welly Chenier
and Captain Kelly on the
Meteor, *circa 1920.*

Quinze, if not all the way north to Rouyn, where exciting new discoveries of gold deposits were being made. Gold at Rouyn might spell new navigating prospects on the des Quinze River and new markets for farmers, but a railway on both sides of Lake Temiskaming could only mean the end of the lake steamers.

As early as 1906, just after the Temiskaming and Northern Ontario Railway was on its way, the Canadian Pacific Railway ordered a survey for an extension to Opemicon. In April 1911, another survey was ordered for a line between Mattawa and the new National Transcontinental by way of Ville-Marie. Such a move would siphon off business from the Abitibi country and Témiscamingue to Ottawa and Montreal. Still the railway wavered, wondering if the returns would justify the costs. Then the war intervened, and plans were put on hold. What transformed the entire situation was the discovery of gold around Lake Osisko in 1922, confirming the importance of earlier finds in the region, and by 1923 the rush to Rouyn was on. From the railways' viewpoint, the question was simply this: which line would get there first? The fact that the Northern Canada Power Company was planning a massive hydro-electric plant on the lower des Quinze River, primarily to provide power for the new mines and smelters at Rouyn, only confirmed the Canadian Pacific Railway's resolve to extend the Témiscamingue spur north to the river at once.

By the spring of 1922, work on the new 97-mile branch was under way. By September, the line was open as far as Fabre, a distance of 40 miles, and the roadbeds even farther. To the bitter disappointment of Ville-Marie and Lorrainville, the railway bypassed them by five miles on account of engineering difficulties; Ville-Marie would have to make do with a local spur. Guigues and North Temiskaming were also left out. The line's terminus was to be the new power dam on the des Quinze River, which was expected to become a major new industrial centre. New Liskeard likewise hoped for an extension to come its way, but in vain. Compounding the discomfiture of the doomed steamboat line, the Quebec government started building a road from Témiscaming to Ville-Marie in 1922, though in fact it would take years before it was adequate for automobiles. Ontario still had no road of any kind to Timiskaming.

The new railway was extended at a rather leisurely pace, but by September of 1923, it was opened to Laverlochère and Ville-Marie. The little town, which had awaited the iron horse for over 40 years, now welcomed it with joy and fanfare. Finally, on March 10, 1924, service was inaugurated to Des Quinze, where already a new town was springing up, soon to be christened Angliers.

It was with these developments in mind that the Ville-Marie Navigation Company made its plans for the 1923 season. The *Meteor* and the *Temiskaming* both sailed that year, but not the *Silverland*. On February 2nd, she was sold for $7,500 to Captain John Cunningham of Kipawa, who had earlier purchased the *City of Haileybury*. That spring, the little steamer, now fourteen years old, was taken on two railway cars to Kipawa to finish her career on the lake of that name.

Captain McCarthy Burns remained with his beloved *Meteor* right to the end, but in 1923, following the retirement of his brother Dan, the old *Temiskaming* was assigned to a newcomer, the gentlemanly Captain Jean Baptiste Chartier, who had lately been commanding the large steamer *G.B. Greene* on Lac Deschênes. His son, John Roméo Chartier, became mate and pilot on the *Temiskaming*, and it was in that capacity that he attracted the attention of a shy young girl named Yvette during a special grotto cruise from Haileybury in May of 1925. Yvette had been raised in a convent, and didn't especially like boats, but with the ingenuity of love at first sight, she managed to think of an unobtrusive way of attracting the attention of the handsome young officer. When stormy wet weather drove all the other girls into the cabins, Yvette remained forlornly outside on the deck. The mate naturally noticed her, and with true Gallic chivalry he invited her into the wheelhouse. Thus began a long courtship, and five years later they were married.

An interesting incident is still vaguely remembered in connection with Captain Chartier's command. During the 1920s, Ontario, yielding to the wave of prohibition then sweeping the United States, voted to go "dry" while Quebec remained "wet." Human appetites being what they are, bootlegging soon became an exciting way to make a profit — for those clever enough not to get caught! By the year 1923, a strange old steamer called the "Wawakewan" appeared on the lake, ostensibly to trade between the two provinces. (This vessel was perhaps identical with the *Wanakewan*, which was built at Kingston in 1910 for the Rideau Steamboat Company of Ottawa. The *Wanakewan* was 70.2 feet in length and registered 44 tons.) In any event, the police became convinced that her real business was rum-running, and Captain Chartier was ordered to intercept her and bring her to Ville-Marie. This he did without incident, and seemingly the impounded vessel was then left to sink and fall apart at Ville-Marie.

By the end of the 1923 season, the Ville-Marie Navigation Company decided to concentrate its future efforts on the des Quinze River, where it already had a steamer and two motor launches in service taking prospectors up to Rouyn. On Lake Temiskaming, the only future seemed to be in freighting and carrying the mail between Haileybury, Ville-Marie and other centres. Hence it was decided to keep the *Temiskaming* and the *Bobs* in service, the former on a schedule from North Temiskaming to Guigues, Haileybury and Ville-Marie, with occasional stops at Dawson Point, New Liskeard, Martineau Bay and Paradis Bay, where there were farms and a government wharf. The stately old *Meteor* may have been put in reserve at Ville-Marie for a time, but apparently she was never in commission again. Captain Burns, unwilling to leave the waves, acquired the old steamer *Gipsy* at Guigues with the idea of freighting ore from Silver Centre to Haileybury, but after a busy initial season the mines began shutting down and business languished. By 1926, the captain gave up, and soon the twenty-year-old vessel was beached at Haileybury and left to deteriorate. In 1931 she was finally cut up for firewood.

The *Meteor* did not last that long. As she lingered on and grew shabbier, hope for her revival diminished, until in 1926 the inspectors condemned some of her side planking, below the waterline. She could still have been repaired, and in November she was taken, in tow of a launch, from Ville-Marie for what proved to be the last time. She was supposed to join the *Bobs* at the Old Mission, but in transit the old ship swung around and grounded on the Ontario side of the Mission Narrows. The lake levels were dropping, and though tugs from the Upper Ottawa Improvement Company were brought in, they could not get her off. Still intact, she languished on the gravel bottom amid the boulders over the winter, but with the spring breakup the ice shoved her higher up. Salvage was now out of the question, and a local man was given permission to extract what he could. The upper works were torn apart for the sake of the wood, and the steel "sleigh-shoeing" strips that protected the rubbing strakes of her main deck were unbolted and recycled, but it proved impossible to remove her engines and generator. One lifeboat was fitted out with an engine, the other was scrapped. The hulk remained at the Narrows for another year, but in June of 1928, the logging booms caught on it, and consequently the remains were dynamited. So ended the *Meteor*, for 37 years the queen of Lake Temiskaming. Her steering wheel is now at Ville-Marie, and her capstan is said to be at a nearby tourist camp beach.

Her old running mate, the *Temiskaming*, died just a short time earlier. Unlike her sister, the *Temiskaming* remained active to the last, still running excursions and freighting, sometimes still to the foot of the lake. As late as July 10, 1925, a moonlight trip from New Liskeard — the first in several years — attracted so many patrons that some had to be turned away, and the steamer had to cancel a stop at Haileybury. On September 19, 1926, we find her taking the fire department staffs from New Liskeard, Haileybury, and Cobalt for a day of postponed Labour Day celebrations at Ville-Marie. By that time, however, the Ville-Marie Navigation Company no longer owned her; the vessel, now 27 years old, had been sold in July to a building contractor from Ville-Marie, and it is likely that the company itself wrapped up its affairs about the same time. The manager, "Welly" Chenier, took up other business activities, including pulpwood contracting and a new supply centre at Rouyn, but he remained active in the affairs of his home town right up until his sudden death from a heart attack in 1945, at the age of 63. One of his sons would establish a local bus line, known as Meteor Transport Limited.

THE LAST OF THE TIMISKAMING STEAMERS: (1926–1939)

With the passing of the Ville-Marie Navigation Company, the last flickering steamer services on Lakes Temiskaming and Kipawa were left to die a lingering death. The days of the *Temiskaming* had already run out. In the late afternoon of November 3, 1926, the old steamer docked at Haileybury for what was expected to be the last trip of the season. On board was a consignment of cargo, including some drums of oil. She was scheduled to call at North Temiskaming the next day, then return and pick up some more freight for Ville-Marie before entering winter quarters, but for the moment Captain Chartier went to see a movie at Cobalt, leaving the engineer in charge. Most of the other hands likewise went ashore.

Around 8:00 P.M., tragedy struck. Fire broke out in the ship's oily hold. The engineer raised the alarm and people came running — including the captain — but it seemed impossible to put the fire out. To save the wharf and its storehouses, the burning steamer was cut loose and towed away. It was a calm night, and the blazing vessel slowly drifted northwards, eerily like a Viking funeral. For hours, half the town of Haileybury watched her receding into the distance on a voyage of no return. Sometime around 11:00 P.M. she went down off Dawson Point. Everyone knew that he was witnessing the end of an era.

In an ironic twist of fate, the steamer *Silverland* met a similar fate barely six months later. This little ship had arrived at Kipawa in 1923, where she was jacked off the two flatcars onto the waiting slips to be launched sideways. However, that night a train came in and struck the flatcars, jerking the steamer loose and into the lake. An alarm was raised, and men hurried to the scene — to find the *Silverland* rocking from side to side, but undamaged. Many sections of the vessel proved to be rotten, though, and she was drydocked for an overhaul. A team of carpenters from Arnprior stripped her down to the main deck and rebuilt all of her superstructure along much the same plan as before, except that she no longer had a hurricane deck, and the pilothouse was now mounted on the second deck.

The *Silverland* was promptly put to work, scowing supplies to Laniel for the Canadian Pacific Railway plus provisions for the new hydro-electric dam there. She also scowed freight for the lumber companies, sometimes in concert with the *City of Haileybury*, usually with one scow between the two steamers and two more on the outsides, in the following arrangement: scow-steamer-scow-steamer-scow. Sometimes she continued to take passengers, mostly hunters and fishermen, to and from their camps. The Cunningham brothers, Robert and Orval, usually operated the *Silverland*, while their father commanded the *City of Haileybury*. Unlike the *City of Haileybury*, the *Silverland* with her steel-framed hull could easily cope with logs and climb right over the booms. Winters were spent on the ways at Kipawa, using horses on a treadmill to pull her out.

As it turned out, the *Silverland* plied Lake Kipawa for only three seasons. Early in her fourth, it happened. She was moored at Kipawa on the evening of May 7, 1927, with a cargo of hay on board, and the crew bedded down for the night. The hay ignited, and within moments flames were shooting up to the promenade deck. The captain, awakened in time, raised the alarm and roused the engineer and deckhand, who were sleeping below. All three took to their heels in their nightshirts. Fanned by a breeze, the fire engulfed the steamer and quickly spread to the two warehouses on the dock, which housed about 60 drums of gasoline. One by one they exploded in a gigantic fireball, illuminating the entire scene. Men gathered to fight the flames, and in time they were joined by a Canadian Pacific Railway pump train rushing in from nearby Gendreau, but even so, there was little they could do. By dawn, the steamer, the docks and the sheds were a total loss, then reckoned at nearly $75,000. The steel frames of the *Silverland* were hauled over to the point facing Kipawa village, where they rusted for many a year. Captain Ted Guppy once considered using them in a new vessel he was planning for Lake Temagami, but gave up the idea when advised that the top plates would have to be rerolled because they were warped. Finally, the remains were cut up for scrap.

Her small running mate, the *City of Haileybury*, outlasted her by a few more years, until the Depression struck and the lumber companies pulled out. The *City of Haileybury* probably ran for the last time in 1930, but was then hauled out of the water and left to rot and fall apart; later the engines were scrapped. Such was the ignominious end of steamboating on Lake Kipawa.

On Lake Temiskaming, only a few steamboats still carried on. Captain Hendry continued to run the *Zara* up and down the Blanche River until about 1928, sometimes accepting rather unusual assignments — such as towing away the old bridge at Hilliardton, which had been wrecked by ice in the spring of 1921. But business petered out as the roads improved and trucks took over the transporting business, and the little *Zara* probably sailed no more after 1928. She was then beached at the mouth of the Wabi River, and soon fell apart — the usual fate of redundant steamboats. Captain Hendry left the lakes and opened a seed grain store in New Liskeard, which he operated until about 1939, when failing health forced him to retire. Soon afterwards he died, on April 30, 1941, at the age of 68, and was buried in New Liskeard, whose interests he had done so much to promote.

Rather surprisingly, a few more efforts were made to run a boat service on Lake Temiskaming. In May of 1922, a group of businessmen, headed by William Short of Cobalt and his friend Alec Lorne Herbert, opened a boat livery at Haileybury, under the title of the Lake Temiskaming Boat Company. They rented canoes and skiffs, sold gasoline, and sometimes took parties of fishermen out to Burnt Island or other places in one of their three motor launches. The operation proved profitable, only to be wiped out in the fire of 1922. In 1927, Captain J.B. Chartier, lately master of the *Temiskaming*, bought the steamer *Bobs* from the vanishing Ville-Marie Navigation Company, hoping to use her to take freight and passengers, only to be denied a certificate because the vessel was judged top heavy. The *Bobs* then went to Lake Abitibi, where she capsized on the Whitefish River in 1928.

Another attempt was made in 1926, when a group headed by M.B. Saunders of Haileybury bought the charter of the old Temiskaming Navigation Company, which was apparently still held by the Ville-Marie Navigation Company. Saunders himself became the managing director of the revived company, with the active support of Fred Arnott, an energetic speculator who was then, among other things, developing Camp Timkipp for tourists near the mouth of the Montreal River. The new line established a regular schedule, from Haileybury to Ville-Marie, where freight agents were employed; perhaps others were engaged at Fabre, Guigues and Silver Centre Landing.

To provide the actual service, the company imported a large cruise boat called the *Keego*, which had been built at Toronto by the Polson Works in 1905. The *Keego*'s early years are obscure, but she seems to have been taken to Lake Temagami in 1909, of which more in the next chapter. Apparently she was originally a steam vessel, but the earliest official record, dated 1909, assigns her a four-cylinder gas engine made in Buffalo that same year. This was later exchanged for a two-cycle Fairbanks-Morse diesel in 1914. At this time she was shortened from 63 feet to 58, and her tonnage reduced from 15.74 to 13.91. She had a ten-foot beam, drew six feet of water, and is said to have had a steel frame and a heavy lead keel for stability. She also featured one deck and an elliptical stern, and was licensed for 25 passengers.

The *Keego* was imported from Lake Temagami in the spring of 1926. Entrusted to veteran Captain Carty Burns, who had just abandoned the *Gipsy*, she was assigned a thrice-weekly schedule, from New Liskeard to Haileybury, Ville-Marie and Silver Centre, returning to Haileybury in the afternoons for another trip to Ville-Marie and back. (On the alternate days she plied mainly between Haileybury and Ville-Marie.) The round trip cost $2. In August of 1926, we hear of her running a shuttle service to and from Dawson Point for the Wabi Iron Works' annual picnic, but after that the owners ceased to advertise in the *Speaker*, and apparently contented themselves with the Ville-Marie run, where she had a mail contract.

ABOVE:

View of Notre-Dame-du-Nord (North Temiskaming). The tug at the left may be the Wabis.   Courtesy Mr. Gilles Amesse, 156G PH3-2-5A

BELOW:

The Meteor *and* Temiskaming *at winter quarters, Fort Temiskaming.*   Courtesy Mr. Gilles Amesse, 45/84 S.H. PH1-7-18

The *Keego* was in some demand for excursions, and sometimes took parties of Boy Scouts and Girl Guides and other groups on fishing trips to McLaren's Bay. But she was considered top heavy, and was none too popular as a passenger vessel. Whenever she encountered rough waters, which happened frequently, she would roll and pitch alarmingly. One time, while returning from a Y.M.C.A. camping trip to the Bay, she was beset by waves that pounded over her forward deck, and soon almost all of the 43 passengers were violently seasick. Some huddled miserably in the lounge, sucking oranges and lemons and vomiting; others, having been ordered out of the wheelhouse, retched over the railings. Luckily, no one fell overboard. Such incidents did little to enhance the vessel's reputation.

In 1928, the *Keego* found an unusual group of customers, when the Burdon Picture Company engaged her to make runs to the Montreal and Kipawa Rivers, where scenes were being shot for a movie called *The Silent Enemy*. (The "silent enemy" was starvation, which all too often was the fate of many unhappy Nishnabis.) Her main business, however, was delivering 45-gallon drums of gasoline costing $13 apiece, plus a handling fee of $1.50; customers found this cheaper than making trips to town. In 1937, she also began to transport ore from the Nipissing Lorrain Mines in South Lorrain, but once again, the operations there were of brief duration. For a long time, she was assisted by a large 39-foot motor launch called the *Kipawa*, which sometimes ran on the des Quinze River.

The (revived) Temiskaming Navigation Company was able to pay its way, but it never issued any dividends, and little by little its business declined. Captain Burns retired around 1929, having commanded boats on the lake for nearly 20 years, and went into the hotel business around Latchford, though he would return briefly to act as titular captain of a passenger boat on Lake Temagami for one more season, shortly before his death in 1958. In 1929, the Great Depression struck, and persisted for a whole decade. In 1931, the construction of a new road to the Old Mission ruined the need for a boat service there, while improved roads to Quebec eroded the business even further. The company staggered on until about 1939, but finally gave up and sold the *Keego* to the Indian Affairs agent at Nipigon, Ontario. (The *Kipawa* went to the McIntyre Gold Mines of Timmins.) After that, the only commercial vessels left on Lake Temiskaming, whether steam or diesel, were those used by the Upper Ottawa Improvement Company for pulpwood towing, a subject discussed in Chapter 6. The Age of Steam was almost over in the North.

STEAMBOATING ON THE DES QUINZE RIVER: (CIRCA 1911–1927)

Before we close this chapter, we must say a few words about the short-lived boat services on the des Quinze River, if only because the Ville-Marie Navigation Company briefly had a hand in them.

La Rivière des Quinze (or "River of the Fifteen," referring to the fifteen portages up to Lac des Quinze), forms the main continuation of the Ottawa River beyond Lake Temiskaming. As such, it has been used as a canoe route from time immemorial. The De Troyes expedition followed it on its way north to capture the Hudson's Bay Company posts on James Bay in 1686. Quinze Lake itself extends north nearly 40 miles from Angliers, and east a similar distance to Lake Expanse (now Lac Simard). From there, above Sturgeon Rapids, the Ottawa River extends north to the junction with the Kinojévis River, from which it is possible to reach Kinojévis Lake, Lac Routhier, and Lake Rouyn.

It is said that a steamer was put into service on Quinze Lake as early as 1888, presumably to tow logs and assist the settlements around Fugèreville and Latulippe, but nothing more is known about it. Soon after the turn of the century, however, matters became more urgent. In 1906, just after the Cobalt boom set in, a couple of prospectors from Ville-Marie — Auguste Renault and Alphonse Olier — found gold deposits around Lac Fortune (which they named), about fourteen miles west of the modern city of Rouyn-Noranda. More finds followed, and in 1911, another prospector named Edmund Horne, operating from Kirkland Lake, discovered some "likely looking rocks" near Lake Osisko (or Lac Tremoy), barely a mile from Lake Rouyn. These finds prompted a pair of boatmen, Captain Larry King of North Temiskaming and

Willie Polson (or Poisson) to form a partnership to move men and supplies to the new gold fields. By June, the King and Polson Steamboat Line was advertising that its stages left Ville-Marie daily at 9:00 A.M. for Kinojévis Depot on Quinze Lake, a distance of about twenty miles over very rough roads. From there, around 1:00 P.M., the steamer *Margata* would sail to Lake Expanse and the upper Ottawa River. She could go no further than Sturgeon Rapids, a distance of 30 miles, but already there were motorboats in service, perhaps beyond the rapids. In the meantime, a government dam was started on the des Quinze River — with the help of the *Temiskaming!*

The King and Polson Steamboat Line had a very brief existence. Lake Rouyn was frustratingly remote — about 80 miles from Quinze Lake — and the value of the Osisko gold deposits remained in doubt for many years. The outbreak of war in 1914, coupled with financial constraints, meant that little could be done for a decade. Besides, there was immediate competition in the transport business. In April 1911, the McEwen brothers of New Liskeard announced that they were putting two gas boats on Quinze Lake, and founding their own stage service to Ville-Marie, connecting with the Lake Temiskaming steamers. A report in the New Liskeard *Speaker* (April 28, 1911) even hints that there was already a steamer running beyond Sturgeon Rapids. Amid all these difficulties the King and Polson Steamboat Line soon gave up, and by 1914 Captain King seems to have accepted command of the *Wabis*, an alligator owned by the Upper Ottawa Improvement Company on Lake Temiskaming.

Edmund Horne did not give up. Still prospecting by himself, by 1917 he became convinced of the importance of the Osisko deposits. In time he found backers, and by 1922 he found some rich veins near Lake Osisko, which proved to be an extension of the same geological formation that runs through Larder Lake and Kirkland Lake. More discoveries followed quickly, and by the year's end a pair of American geologists, Thompson and Chadbourne, formed the Norcanda ("Northern Canada") Mines Company Ltd., which was soon shortened to Noranda. Noah Timmins Jr., who had already made a fortune with the Hollinger Mines in the Porcupine region, now induced his company to advance $3,000,000 in debentures to Noranda Mines. It was to prove a very profitable investment.

But not immediately. Aside from a solitary log cabin, built by Joseph Dumulon of Ville-Marie in 1922, there was nothing at Rouyn. Any prospectors would have to bring in their own food and shelter. There was no mail service and no transport facilities, although the Dumulon family was building several pointers and barges for that purpose in 1922–23, a service they had to abandon by 1924, on account of competition from the Ville-Marie Navigation Company. Power for the new mines was also lacking, but already the Northern Canada Power Company was building a huge new dam at Angliers for the purpose of supplying cheap power to the Porcupine, Kirkland Lake and Rouyn, even though no one knew whether the Osisko finds would "prove their mettle." Nonetheless, hundreds of men were impatiently waiting to find out in the spring of 1923. By May, after the ice broke up, the stampede was on.

There were four possible routes to Rouyn. One was from Amos, the nucleus of the new Abitibi settlements then developing around the National Transcontinental Railway line in Northern Quebec. This entailed a trip by rail from Cochrane to Amos, and thence up the lengthy Harricana River by steamer or motorboat, through several lakes and across a tramway to the Kinojévis River. The second route was from Dane on the Temiskaming and Northern Ontario Railway, overland to Larder Lake and Lake Fortune. The third route was from the new dam site at Angliers up Quinze Lake. The fourth, and preferred, route was from Haileybury to Ville-Marie by steamer, and thence overland to Gillies Depot (now occupied by the Riordon Company and renamed), and up Quinze Lake.

The scenes were chaotic. A few automobiles and trucks were now available to reach the Riordon Depot, but the boat services were hastily organized and generally inadequate. The motor launches were not big enough to take all the cargoes, and rival operators were not disposed to help one another. Fuel often ran short, and the boats were bedevilled by pulpwood logs. Some gold seekers brought their own canoes, but at best it always took several days to paddle to Rouyn, and often longer when the upper Ottawa River was in flood. Forest fires

ABOVE:

Main Street, Haileybury, after the fire of 1922.

MIDDLE:

C.P.R. train at Angliers (Quebec), circa 1924.

Courtesy T.E. Draper Museum, Angliers 427

BELOW:

Steamer Silverland *entering winter quarters at*

Kipawa.   Courtesy Mr. Gilles Amesse

were a constant threat, especially in 1923. Still, despite the odds, by July over a thousand men were busy combing an area of 10,000 square miles and staking claims all the way across to the Ontario border. Rouyn itself became a wild and woolly mining town, and by 1925, it had a post office (housed in the Dumulon family store), a hotel, a chapel school, a bank, and about a hundred log houses. Liquor flowed freely, but all other luxuries were scarce.

Right in the middle of the transport scene was the Ville-Marie Navigation Company, which was still running the *Meteor* and the *Temiskaming*, and making its last bid for survival. By June of 1923, it had placed a large motorboat called the *Sunshine* on Quinze Lake, and a second, the *Swallow*, to ply above Sturgeon Rapids. It also imported the steamer *St. Bruno* from Lake Temiskaming to share the route on Quinze Lake. By early June, the company was (sometimes) able to provide a daily service, leaving Ville-Marie at 7:00 A.M. and reaching the gold camps, hopefully, that same evening. The fare was $9 to the rapids and another $11 to Rouyn.

Such trips could be adventurous. On August 28th, the *St. Bruno* broke her propeller on a log on Quinze Lake, and had to be hauled ashore for repairs, tying up large shipments of freight and passengers. Much worse befell the *Swallow* on the morning of June 3rd. The launch was just setting off from Sturgeon Rapids with sixteen men aboard, plus a heavily laden pointer and several canoes in tow, when the engine malfunctioned in midstream. As the boat and its flotilla began drifting backwards, nine of the men sprang into the trailing canoes and struggled to get them ashore. They succeeded, but they could not secure the launch. With seven men still aboard, the *Swallow* swept wildly through the rapids, tossing and plunging. Then she crashed onto a rock, throwing four of the men into the seething waters. One was hauled back aboard and rescued, while the engineer managed to swim to shore, but the other two drowned. The shattered boat meanwhile swung clear and sank in shallow water below the rapids. Apparently she was a total loss, along with the pointer and all the freight. Rather tardily, the Quebec authorities ordered a deflecting boom to be placed across the river above the Sturgeon Rapids. The company, meanwhile, put another launch on the river.

Despite all the problems (including competition), it is likely that the Quinze boat service paid in 1923. But it could not last. In August of that year, the Quebec government announced plans for a new road from Quinze Lake to Rouyn, and by 1925, the road was a reality — although driving it was an exercise in courage and endurance. Another road was opened from Macamic, on the National Transcontinental Railway (now a part of the Canadian National) to Rouyn about the same time, and by 1927, it was fit for motor vehicles. Meanwhile, the Temiskaming and Northern Ontario Railway was starting a branch from Swastika through Kirkland Lake towards the gold camps. Progress was delayed by the opposition of the Quebec government, which was not keen about seeing an Ontario line invading the gold fields. When the railway finally reached Rouyn in 1927, it had to do so under the charter of its dependency, the Nipissing Central Railway, which was authorized to build into Quebec. Meanwhile the Canadian National Railways had built its own branch in from Taschereau by October of 1926, though this did not prevent Rouyn from becoming dependent on Toronto. Complicating the transport scene even further, in May of 1924, the Laurentide Air Service — for the first time ever in Canada — began operating a flying boat from Angliers to Rouyn three times a week, and soon it was extending its flights to Haileybury wharf. The plane, although limited in its transport capacity, could reach Rouyn in just 45 minutes. Under these fast-changing circumstances the des Quinze boat services were doomed, and though men and supplies continued to use the water route until 1927, little more is heard about the Ville-Marie Navigation Company, which ceased to exist in 1926. Soon the only remaining steamboats on Quinze Lake were a few tugs engaged in towing pulpwood logs.

Rouyn flourished. In 1924, Noranda Mines decided to exploit the Horne mine, and create a town close by. Over a hundred other companies invested in the operations, and in 1926, Noranda became a town and Rouyn a village. Much later, they would be merged to form a single city. A smelter was started in 1926, and soon power lines were opened from Angliers.

Today, Rouyn-Noranda is a regional capital, and still one of Canada's leading producers of gold, silver and copper.

STEAMBOATING ON THE HARRICANA RIVER: (CIRCA 1919–1936)

Though steamboating was dying out in Timiskaming, it survived a little longer in the Abitibi region, where the Harricana River system became a prime route for both settlers and prospectors.

Ever since the discovery of the second great Clay Belt across northern Ontario and Quebec, French-Canadian nationalists had dreamed of a second Témiscamingue beyond the Laurentians. Once again, the Roman Catholic Church took the lead. Idealizing the agrarian past as a spiritualistic Golden Age, and condemning the present as the Age of Mammon, the Church — in the words of an eminent French Canadian historian, Michel Brunet — wanted a static society, far removed from the corrupting temptations of city life and mechanization. It hoped to achieve this in the Abitibi country, where its children might remain uncontaminated by forestry, mining and big business. The building of the National Transcontinental Railway across the Clay Belt from Quebec City to Winnipeg made the colonization scheme feasible. Work started in 1907, and by 1912 the line was opened from Cochrane to Amos, on the Harricana River, though it was not until 1916 that regular service was inaugurated from Amos to Quebec City.

Until 1910, the only inhabitants of the Abitibi region were small groups of Nishnabis, a few Oblate missionaries, and a handful of men working for the Hudson's Bay Company. However, thanks to vigorous promotional efforts, settlers began to trickle in, mainly from old Quebec. The first arrivals came by boat up the des Quinze River and had founded Amos by the fall of 1910, but most of the later newcomers simply came by train and took up lands along the railway. By 1912, La Reine and Taschereau were on the map, to be followed by Authier and Villemontel (1913), Macamic and Senneterre (1914), Barrault (1916), LaSarre (1917), and others. By 1914, there were 983 people in Abitibi (a figure that swelled to 13,172 by 1921), and despite the short growing season, 2,000 acres under cultivation. As elsewhere, there were lumber camps and road construction projects to help keep men employed. From the start, Amos was always the focal point for the colony.

Almost immediately, the rivers became side arteries of settlement. In the forefront was the Harricana (meaning "biscuit river" in Algonquin), which flows northwards into James Bay over a distance of 360 miles. Above Amos, the river is navigable for small boats, and periodically widens out to form a succession of shallow lakes, including Lac LaMotte, Lac de Montigny (also called Lac Kienawisik or Lac Blouin), Lac Senneterre, Lac Malartic and others. Together they constitute one of the longest navigable inland waterways in Canada (about 175 miles), and they soon allowed settlement to bulge 30 miles southward from Amos to LaMotte village by the 1920s. Naturally, boat traffic became very extensive, and not infrequently the people of Amos, St. Mathieu and LaMotte held picnics on Lorette Island on Lac LaMotte. Sawmills proliferated, and soon several of the owners had their own boats to tow logs to the mills. Thus Frank Blais of Amos ran the *Vermillion*, Alfred Fortin the *Petit Voileau*, Ernest Massicotte the *Monson*, and the Beauchemin brothers the *Toque* ("fur hat"). These vessels were probably all motorboats.

In the meantime, gold deposits were discovered in the Cadillac geological formations extending from Rouyn east to Lake Malartic and beyond. This provided a powerful new incentive for navigation. The war almost paralyzed progress for a time, and until 1920, vessels of deep draft were unable to proceed more than four miles south of Amos. But then the Department of Public Works built a small dredge, which soon removed the impediments and then went on to clear a passage past the source of the Landrienne River, at the entrance to Lake Malartic. Already a new firm, called La Compagnie de Navigation d'Amos, was being organized in April 1919 to run boats upstream to the new mines around Lake Kienawisik.

Docks and storehouses were built, and soon tugs, motorboats and *chalands* were busy delivering food, supplies and mail three times a week to the Martin, Caseo, St. Maurice and Benjamin Molybdenite mines, and also to ferry in prospectors heading for Rouyn. Two years later, another boat line was established by Maurice Benard for the same purpose.

Little is known of the early Harricana steamboats. The main one, probably owned by the Amos Navigation Company, was called the *Harricanaw*, and is described as a modern vessel, some 70 feet in length by 30 in beam and capable of carrying 100 passengers, but nothing more is known of her. Others included tugs such as the *Clemence*, owned by Charles St. Pierre of Amos, which was running in 1924, and the *Colin S.* Another was a scowboat called *Tit Willow* (17 tons), which served as a tender for a large *chaland*, or barge, which the owner, Alfred Fortin of Amos, was now using to haul cattle, hay, fuel oil, electric drilling equipment and everything else, starting around 1928. According to an article in the North Bay *Nugget*, by July of 1925 there were no fewer than sixteen steamers and 250 gas launches on the route, plying as far as Lake Malartic, where a tramway provided a link with the Kinojévis River. The steamers are said to have ranged from 40 to 115 feet in length — probably an exaggeration.

In 1928, a new consortium, headed by Stanley Siscoe, was opening up a gold mine on Siscoe Island on Lake Blouin. This spelled opportunity for Captain Iréné Yergeau, who had come to Amos six years before to run boats for the Beauchemins. Yergeau resolved to build a large new steamer to ply to the Siscoe Mine. The vessel was ready for launching in March of 1929. With a length of 87 feet and a beam of 18, the steamer *Siscoe* was the largest ever seen on the Harricana River. She could take 70 tons of freight at speeds of twelve miles per hour. She was also equipped to carry passengers in some degree of comfort, in that she had a lounge for first class, cabins for second, and a dining saloon. By 1929 she was in regular service, plying to St. Mathieu, LaMotte, Rivière Héva and Siscoe Island on Mondays, Wednesdays and Fridays, following the arrival of the trains. Later she also assisted in the establishment of the Lamaque, Perron and Sullivan mines, which in turn helped to create the new towns of Bourlamaque and Val d'Or. A trip one way took about six and a half hours and cost $2.50. Captain Yergeau was something of a character, and was popularly known as "le bonhomme caribou."

The Siscoe Mine was in operation by 1929, and was soon producing 1,000 tons of ore a day. All this was taken in scows to Amos to be refined in Ontario. The boats ran from April to early November, and were sometimes known to unload provisions on the ice if they couldn't approach the wharf. For lack of any roads, the mining company used the river as a highway — which meant that the entire operation was dependent on the *Siscoe* and the *Tit Willow*, although in 1931 the firm deserted Captain Yergeau in favour of a Captain Kelly, who undertook to provide cheaper service with his own steam tug, the *Ruth B. Kelly*. Docks were built to receive fuel oil, machinery and supplies, while Siscoe Island became a self-contained community, with homes for the miners, a school, a curling rink, and even a golf course. It was the first settlement in the region of Val d'Or.

Soon after the Siscoe Mine opened, the Depression struck, and before long most of the sawmills shut down. But bad times only led to an expansion in mining; indeed, the mines were to do much to carry the country through the grim years of the 1930s. In 1934, Sullivan Consolidated Mines Ltd. opened a very profitable mine just east of Siscoe Island, and in the process created another mining village, called Sullivan Mines. This company also built a large vessel to furnish and provision its mines, and to run excursions. The boat, called the *Sullivan*, was launched at Amos in the spring of 1935. A wooden twin-screw diesel masquerading as a steamer, the motor vessel *Sullivan* was 75.9 feet in length by 19.2 in beam, registered 156.6 tons, and was powered by two 4-cycle Fairbanks-Morse engines, giving her speeds of fourteen miles per hour (a little faster than the *Siscoe*). She was assigned to Captain J.B. Chartier, now of Montreal, who had once commanded the *Temiskaming*.

The *Sullivan* began a thrice-weekly service from Amos to Sullivan Mines, often carrying 125 passengers and 70 tons of freight. Aside from groundings, she rarely had trouble, although once she managed to collide with a smaller motor vessel, the *Nahma*, which was

being used to take milk and other commodities to Bourlamaque. The *Nahma*, slashed through the side, sank at Sullivan wharf and became a total loss, although fortunately there was no one aboard at the time. In the winter, everything had to be delivered across the ice by tractors, horses and dog teams.

The *Sullivan*'s life was very short. By September 1936, a road of sorts was opened from Amos to the new town of Val d'Or, a few miles south of Sullivan Mines, and soon trucks and buses were successfully pushing through the dust or the mud to reach the mines. The following November, the Canadian National Railways opened a new line from Senneterre to Val d'Or, and later to Rouyn. Supplanted, the *Sullivan* was sold and taken back to Amos, where she was allowed to sink near the railway bridge. Her engines were sold to the Beauchemins. The *Siscoe*, likewise displaced when a causeway was built to Siscoe Island, was tied up and converted into a restaurant at Rivière Héva, and later used as a chicken coop. Eventually she fell to pieces. She and the *Sullivan* were the last large vessels on the waterway. With the possible exception of the occasional lumber tug, steamboats thus disappeared from the Harricana River.

~~~~~~~~

In such a manner the steamers served the mining operations in Timiskaming and Abitibi. It remains only to describe their services to tourism and to the pulp and paper industry.

≈≈≈

STEAMBOATS
AND TOURISM

A s in so many other parts of the province, steam vessels played a leading part in the growth of tourism and recreation in northeastern Ontario. This role was inevitably limited in most localities, because Timiskaming has never been a prime recreation region or tourist region — although the amount of boating activity on Lake Temiskaming itself has been growing in recent years.

Part of this chapter has already been written. We have noted earlier how Alex Lumsden built the Bellevue Hotel at South Témiscaming around 1900, in an attempt to lure American sportsmen to the Lake Kipawa region, with very limited success. We have also observed how the *Meteor* and her sisters conducted picnics and moonlight cruises on Lake Temiskaming, especially after the railway came through in 1905. Perhaps the amount of business lost to the railway allowed more time for tours. If anything, the *Meteor* was probably unsurpassed as a recreation ship in Timiskaming. Yet there was one area where steamers were used almost exclusively to serve tourists and recreationists, and that was Lake Temagami.

STEAMBOATING ON LAKE TEMAGAMI: (1903–1944)

Lake Temagami is probably the most famous lake in Northern Ontario, traditionally for the rugged grandeur of its scenery and the excellence of its hunting and fishing, and more recently because of long-standing aboriginal land claims and disputes between environmentalists and the lumber industry. Geographically, the lake lies west of Lake Temiskaming, wholly within the Nipissing District, and has an area of roughly 78 square miles. On the map it looks like a gigantic inkblot squeezed into a fantastic shape, with enormously long arms and bays reaching out in almost all directions from a very small centre. Some of the arms stretch over 12 miles, and overall the lake extends about 28 miles from north to south, and about 22 miles from east to west. Yet it seldom exceeds two miles in width, and it is bedecked with over 1,200 rocky little islands. All this gives Lake Temagami 570 miles of shoreline, of which about 200 miles are insular. The lake is 965 feet above sea level, and forms the headwaters for the Lady Evelyn and Sturgeon River watersheds. Formerly Lake Temagami used to drain northward into the Montreal River by way of Lady Evelyn Lake, and southward into Lake Nipissing by way of the Temagami and Sturgeon Rivers, but today only the southern outlet continues to function; the link with Lady Evelyn Lake was blocked off by the Spanish River Pulp and Paper Company in 1918.

The name "Temagami" (also written Timagami, Timagaming or Temagamingue) means "lake of the deep waters," and indeed some parts are said to reach depths of 400 feet. The lake lies wholly within the Canadian Shield (which accounts for its magnificent scenery), and hence has never supported a large permanent population, although groups of native people — perhaps the ancestors of the Teme-augama Anishnabai of today — are known to have arrived there at least 5,000 years ago. They led a hand-to-mouth existence, hunting, fishing and gathering, and, much later, trading furs with both the French from the St. Lawrence and the English at James Bay. In 1834, the Hudson's Bay Company opened a tiny post on Temagami Island, mainly to discourage rival traders, but in 1876, it was moved to nearby Bear

FACING PAGE:

Motor vessel Aubrey Cosens V.C. *at Camp Keewaydin, Lake Temagami.* Courtesy Mr. Jack Guppy

ABOVE:

Steamer Belle of Temagami.

Courtesy Ontario Archives, S12876

BELOW:

Dockyards at Temagami Village, around 1912. In the centre is the steamer Bobs. The vessel to the left may be the Temagami, while the departing steamer may be the Marie. Courtesy Ontario Archives, S13541

Island, the largest on the lake. The Bear Island post would remain open as late as 1974. In 1898, the first mail came in from Lake Temiskaming.

Despite its isolation, several observers were convinced that Lake Temagami had great potential for tourists, especially the sporting variety. As early as 1894, C.C. Farr, who knew the lake well, was convinced that someday it would excel Muskoka and abound with cottages and resort hotels. All that was needed, in Farr's opinion, was a railway to make it accessible (and to continue north to Haileybury, as well). Five years later the Canadian Pacific Railway, anxious to increase business on its branch to South Témiscaming, issued a pamphlet entitled *Timagaming: A Glimpse of the Algonquin Paradise*, which tried assiduously to foster the mystique that Lake Temagami was an unspoiled virgin wilderness teeming with fish and game. The "silent waters" of Lady Evelyn Lake, it claimed, "are but a setting for islands that seem to float on its molten surface." Getting there was not easy, though; it involved a 35-mile trip by steamer from Témiscaming station to the mouth of the Montreal River, thence a trek up the Matabichewan River to Bass Lake, Rabbit Lake, Whitebear and Snake Lakes, and a portage to the tip of the Northeast Arm of Lake Temagami.

It usually requires an entrepreneur or two to launch any new venture or trend, and in the case of Temagami tourism the honour goes overwhelmingly to one man. His name was Daniel O'Connor.

Dan O'Connor was born at Pembroke, Ontario, in 1864, and was apparently the eldest of several children. The family was Scottish in descent, Catholic in religion, and mostly Liberal in politics. Of Dan's early years hardly anything is known. We first hear of him around 1886, by which time he had moved to Sudbury, following the railway. Sudbury was then a rough-hewn shanty town that had sprung up in 1883 close to Lost Lake (now Ramsey Lake) as a Canadian Pacific Railway work camp, but its future was already assured by the discovery that it was sitting on one of the world's richest bodies of copper/nickel ore. The Canadian Copper Company was incorporated as early as 1886, and by 1889 a smelter was operating at nearby Copper Cliff. (At first only the copper was considered valuable, until about 1908, when it was discovered that nickel alloyed with steel produces excellent rails and armour plating.) At Sudbury, Dan O'Connor soon became prominent in the lumber trade and opened a sawmill, but, not content with that, he also, with a partner, became the proprietor and manager of the White House Hotel, the third, and then the finest, to be erected in town. His main interest was mining, however, and by 1890 he had registered a claim in Denison Township. Many more were to follow. In 1892, with characteristic thoroughness, he organized a mineral exhibit at the Toronto Industrial Exhibition and also joined the Sudbury Board of Trade.

By now he was recognized as one of the most vigorous citizens of Sudbury, and was elected to the council for McKim Township. When Sudbury became a town in 1893, O'Connor sat as a councillor, and the following year he ran for mayor. Curiously enough, religion was the main issue in the election, and even more surprisingly in a largely Protestant community, O'Connor won (by a scant three votes), mainly on the basis of his personal popularity, and by appealing to a combination of Catholics and moderate Protestants. As mayor, Mr. O'Connor presided over the passing of many useful bylaws pertaining to policing, street repairs, stray animals, a waterworks and sewage works, electric lights and other matters crucial to a town that was barely ten years old. He did such a good job that he might have been re-elected by acclamation, but already Dan O'Connor had his mind set on other things, and declined a second term. When a banquet was held in his honour at the White House in January 1895, over 70 prominent Sudburians attended.

Having left politics and sold his hotel, O'Connor reverted to his main love: prospecting. He was convinced that there was "gold in them thar hills," and gold, as he often used to say, "is where you find it." This drew him farther and farther north. He was soon staking claims around the Vermilion River, where placer gold was discovered north of Sudbury in 1891, and also around Lake Wanapitei, where more gold was found in 1894. In 1898, he spent seven weeks around Lake Temagami, where he discovered the iron-ore body that would later give rise to the Sherman Mine, close to the tip of the Northeast Arm of the lake. He then persuaded the Ontario Bureau of Mines to investigate further, but nothing was done to mine the ores, because there was no railway in the area, and because the site, which was within a forest reserve, remained off limits until 1902.

By now Dan O'Connor had become aware that Lake Temagami could produce wealth in a very different way. It could, he decided, become a sportsman's paradise. Deer and moose were plentiful, the fishing was excellent, and the scenery splendid; lumbering had made few inroads there. All that was needed were the three As: advertising, accommodation and accessibility. When, in 1902, he heard that the Temiskaming and Northern Ontario Railway was being promoted to provide a link between North Bay and the Timiskaming settlements, his mind was made up. Confident that the railway would tap Lake Temagami at the tip of the Northeast Arm, he moved to that area, erected a few log buildings, and immediately made plans for a hotel, to be called the Ronnoco ("O'Connor" spelled backwards), which he proposed to finance partly by selling some of his mining claims.

But then things threatened to go very wrong. O'Connor found out that the railway wasn't planning to tap Lake Temagami at all. It was projected to take an alternative route, around Caribou Lake. Determined not to be thwarted, Dan O'Connor headed straight to Toronto, where he ardently pleaded with the railway executives at least to come up north and see Lake Temagami for themselves. Eventually they agreed — on condition that O'Connor provide a steamboat to tour the lake.

As it happened, O'Connor already had a steamboat. It was a large launch called the *Marie*, which was completed at Toronto in July of 1902 for his wife, Mary Ann Bourke. The *Marie* was 33.5 feet in length, had one deck and a fantail stern, and registered 3.74 tons — ample to carry a party of railway executives. The problem was how to move her to Lake Temagami. There were no roads to the lake, and Dan O'Connor decided to wait until the following winter. The little craft was taken to Lake Temiskaming by rail, put on a sleigh and dragged up the lake over the ice to the mouth of the Montreal River. From here she was hauled up the Clay Hill portage to Bass Lake, thence to Snake Lake, Rabbit Lake and finally over the divide to Lake Temagami. Sixteen horses were required for the feat, and the portages had to be cut and brushed out especially for the purpose. By the following season (1903) she was ready to run, and perhaps helped to ferry provisions and personnel to Camp Temagami, the first of many on the lake, established by Arthur Lewis Cochrane of Upper Canada College on an island in the South Arm that same year. At last the railwaymen arrived, and Dan O'Connor was ready for them. He took them on a cruise around Lake Temagami, showing them all the sights, and that evening wined and dined them, until finally, very late at night, when the gentlemen were all in an extremely good mood, everyone agreed that the railway must come to Lake Temagami. And so it did. By the summer of 1904, steel was laid to the site of Temagami village. A post office was opened, with O'Connor doing the honours.

But the busy Scot was already proceeding with new plans. Once assured that the railway was coming, he secured the backing of William George Gooderham, a leading Toronto businessman, plus two lawyers, Alex and David Fasken, and several others to form a company initially called the O'Connor Steam Boat Company Limited but speedily renamed the Temagami Steamboat and Hotel Company. The new firm was chartered under Ontario law on September 1, 1905. David Fasken became the President, W.G. Gooderham Vice-President, and Dan O'Connor General Manager. The syndicate at once completed the Ronnoco Hotel, barely a few hundred yards from the new Temiskaming and Northern Ontario Railway station, and followed this up with two more resorts: the Temagami Inn on Temagami Island, near the centre of the lake, and the Lady Evelyn Hotel on the North Arm, near the portage into Diamond Lake. Of these, the Ronnoco was designed essentially for stopover traffic, while the other two were more luxurious. The Temagami Inn was built of logs, while the others were both three-and-a-half-storey wooden structures with mansard roofs. When completed they could take a total of 550 guests. They offered fishing and canoe trips, fine meals, good liquor and the occasional party or ball, but they charged very high rates: $2.50 to $3.50 per day. As a side venture, O'Connor organized the Temagami Canoe Company, which provided canoes, guides and equipment for visitors who did not care for hotels. The Temiskaming and Northern Ontario Railway was so impressed that, in 1906, it set up direct links with the Canadian Pacific Railway and the Grand Trunk Railway at North Bay, thus allowing passengers from Toronto to reach Temagami in ten hours. It also built an especially ornate station at Temagami, complete with a restaurant, and arranged for trains to halt there for twenty minutes to give passengers time to get out and eat.

Of course, the operation required steamers to bring the guests to the more distant hotels. Initially, the company had only the *Marie*, which probably could not hold more than fifteen passengers, but as early as June 1905, it had acquired at least two more vessels: the *Spry* and the *Wanda*. Of the *Spry* little is known, except that she grossed 13 tons, was about 36 feet in length, and licensed in 1906 for ten passengers. The *Wanda* was a 65-foot screw yacht, built at Kingston in 1899, and registered at 26.25 tons. She had two masts, one deck, a round stern, and a 7-hp compound engine, which — in view of her rather narrow 10.5-foot beam — probably gave her quite a respectable speed. She was based in Toronto when O'Connor bought her in his own name in January 1905, and by the following spring she was handling groups of up to 30 passengers on Lake Temagami.

By an odd coincidence, a second *Wanda* arrived on the lake in 1905, but her name was immediately changed to the *Temagami*. This vessel was another yacht, 70.5 feet in length, registered at 12.2 tons, and fitted out with a steel frame and an elliptical stern. She was built at Toronto in 1898 for Timothy Eaton of department store fame, and used for commuting and recreational cruises on the Muskoka Lakes — until she lost a race with another yacht, despite her very powerful 9.6-hp triple-expansion Polson engine. The vessel was then sold to a short-lived consortium known as the Temagami Navigation Company, which was attempting to build its own hotel on Bear Island. This company also imported another big composite screw vessel called the *Bobs* (26 tons), which had been built at Parry Sound in 1901, and used hitherto by the Parry Sound Lumber Company. Named after Field Marshal Lord Roberts of Boer War fame, the *Bobs* likewise arrived at Temagami in 1905, and was soon vying for business with the Temagami Steamboat and Hotel Company steamers. But the volume of business could not sustain two boat lines. Worse, the Bear Island hotel scheme collapsed in 1908, amid wrangling between the Ontario government and the Hudson's Bay Company over who really owned the island. It is also unlikely that the Temagami Navigation Company's vessels were welcome at the Temagami Steamboat and Hotel Company hotels. As a result, the luckless line gave up in the spring of 1909, and sold the *Temagami* (and probably the *Bobs* as well) to its rival.

Undeterred by this competition, the O'Connor line had been building docks and storehouses, and adding more steamers to its fleet. In 1905, O'Connor acquired the *Beaver*, a 36-foot steam yacht of 1.87 register tons, built at Kingston four years earlier. She had the usual single deck and round stern and a 3-hp engine, and was licensed for ten passengers. This gave the company a total of four vessels. Even this was judged insufficient, and late in 1905 it was decided to build a really large passenger steamer, one which would dwarf every other vessel on the lake. The new ship would be almost 100 feet in length — big enough to carry at least 300 passengers. She would have two full decks plus a hurricane deck, a round stern and an iron frame. She would be powered by a brand-new compound steam engine and a steel Polson Works boiler operating at 143 lbs. pressure, delivering a net 16.6 horsepower. She would be a beautiful vessel, the pride of the lake. She would be the *Belle of Temagami!*

The contract for building the *Belle of Temagami* went to the Pontbriand Company of Sorel, Quebec, for the sum of $18,000. The frames were probably fabricated at Sorel, but the vessel was actually built at Temagami. Her hull planking was three inches thick. On July 5, 1906, she was launched with a good deal of éclat. The O'Connors of course were present, and very likely Mary Ann was given the honour of breaking the customary bottle of champagne. The steamer was put through her sea trials and began plying at once, though her registration was delayed until August 1907, because the company could not immediately pay the costs of construction, and the builders would not certify her until the bills had been paid. The certificate gave her extreme dimensions as 107.6 feet by 22.6, and set her register tonnage at 101.25.

Commanded initially by the genial Captain Albert McKenney, who would later take charge of various steamers on Lake Nipissing, the *Belle of Temagami* began a daily service from Temagami village to the Temagami Inn, Bear Island, and up the North Arm to the Lady Evelyn Hotel. She also stopped as required at Camp Temagami and Camp Keewaydin, an American boys' camp founded on Devil's Island on the North Arm in 1904. She took a crew of five — the captain, mate, engineer, purser, and a fireman for stoking coal — plus a cook who sublet the restaurant concession on board. Sometimes she ran excursion cruises, but these were usually just part of her daily scheduled runs, except for the occasional evening trip to Bear Island. In the spring she might take parties of fishermen to their favourite haunts, and in the autumn there was the deer-hunting season, when she would usually return with a pile of carcasses on her main deck.

On August 1, 1906, a special train brought about 200 Oddfellows from Timiskaming down for a tour of Lake Temagami, which most of them had never seen. They were impressed to find a considerable village developing at Temagami, including a new church, school, the Ronnoco Hotel, and a cluster of tents occupied by prospectors and Nishnabis. They were even more impressed with the *Belle of Temagami*, which rode steadily on the waves, even with several hundred people aboard. Better still was the unspoiled scenery, still unmarred by the axe or the scourge of fire. Serenaded by a band, the visitors toured the lake, calling at the rustic-looking Temagami Inn, which the steamboat line had recently completed to the tune of about $40,000, before arriving at the Lady Evelyn Hotel shortly after noon. The Lady Evelyn Hotel was a charming place, set amid scenic groves, and boasting 108 beds and its own water works. The steamer afterwards brought them back to catch the 5:00 P.M. train. A few weeks later, the Timiskaming Old Boys held their own excursion on the *Belle of Temagami*, with free tickets for the press; about 60 attended. C.C. Farr came along to entertain with stories about some of his experiences on the lake 25 years earlier. He pointed out an island where he had been obliged to wait out a passing storm, and another called Broom Island, where an Indian had trimmed a cedar tree to look like a broom, and where an Indian of 135 lbs. had once murdered a stalwart of 180 lbs., and what happened to him, and so on. The group enjoyed themselves immensely, and voted their thanks to Mr. O'Connor at the end.

The *Belle of Temagami* — sometimes called the *Temagami Belle* or just the "Belle" — proved both popular and efficient. In 1907, she took the American Institute of Mining Engineers to spend a weekend at the Temagami Inn and the Lady Evelyn Hotel, following their visit to Cobalt and New Liskeard, and the following year she hosted the American Association of Passenger and Ticket Agents on a tour of the lake. On August 3, 1908, she was well-nigh overwhelmed by a monster-sized Oddfellows excursion from New Liskeard. Although the weather was not the best, about 350 attended, in the belief that the *Belle of Temagami* could carry at least 400. In fact, she was usually licensed for 175, and since the smaller steamers were absent up the lake, part of the crowd, including the band, had to remain in Temagami. Those who took the cruise had hoped to hold their sporting events at Bear Island, only to find the grounds there unsuitable for the purpose. Consequently, some events were postponed until the return to the village. But the crowd still enjoyed themselves, and some afterwards claimed that one could catch up to 46 fish on Lake Temagami in just 30 minutes.

Of course, the *Belle of Temagami* had the occasional mishap. Fluctuating water levels were not a serious problem after 1910, when the Cobalt Hydraulic Power Company installed dams at the two outlets of the lake, but there was always the risk of an undetected shoal. Captain Ted Guppy would later recall a time around 1912, when she ran aground at full speed on the rocks between Camp Keewaydin and the Lady Evelyn Hotel. Getting her off

ABOVE:

Temagami Inn, Lake Temagami. Courtesy
Mr. Jack Guppy

BELOW:

*Lady Evelyn Hotel, Lake Temagami, circa
1910.* Courtesy Mr. Jack Guppy

proved very difficult. Floating piers were placed on either side, and jacks and beams were brought in, but jacking sometimes served only to lift her up, rather than slide her backwards. As a result, the unsupported stern developed a droop until it was rebuilt around 1930.

Although Temagami never lived up to its potential to rival Muskoka, tourist accommodation continued to grow, thanks largely to promotional efforts by the government and the railways. Sometime after 1905, John Turner, who had founded the original Hudson's Bay Company post at Bear Island in 1876, also developed a modest boarding house on the island, which he called Wisini Wigwam or Lakeview House. Under the direction of his wife, affectionately known as "Granny" Turner, the Lakeview House took about 50 guests every summer. The Turners also provided canoes and organized fishing trips and the occasional dance, which attracted guests, campers, cottagers and even the local Nishnabis. Bear Island soon became the social centre for the entire lake. A post office was opened in 1909 and the Hudson's Bay Company co-operated by turning its post into a general store, selling tents, blankets and other supplies to tourists. The company even considered establishing its own steamer service, but drew back when it noted the shortness of the season and the lofty expectations of the public, which imagined that the company could afford the very best of everything. Around 1913, another resort called the Wabikon was opened on nearby Temagami Island, and was soon taking nearly 200 guests (mostly American). The Wabikon thus became the largest resort on the lake.

Meanwhile, there was a growing demand for cottages, and in 1905 the Ontario government adopted the policy of leasing lots on some of the islands for that purpose. The leases ran for 21 years, but were available for renewal. In 1906, some 34 leases were granted, many to Americans, a figure that rose to about 50 by 1914. Few were issued during the war, but afterwards the number rose considerably, until by 1927 about 160 cottages and campsites had been established. Until the 1920s, most cottagers and campers relied on the lake steamers to get around, but after that, motorboats became more common.

For the moment, however, the steamers reigned supreme and the Temagami Steamboat and Hotel Company continued to expand its fleet. Late in 1908, the line purchased the *Chance*, a 43.1-foot screw yacht built for an Ottawa resident in 1895 and afterwards removed to Kingston. Registered at 1.54 tons, the *Chance* had a spoon stern and no decks. The following season the company acquired yet another vessel, the *Keego* (15.74 tons), a Polson yacht built at Toronto in 1905. The *Keego* was 63 feet in length, with one deck and an elliptical stern. She was apparently built as a steamboat, but in 1909 she was refitted with a four-cylinder gas engine from Buffalo, which made her the first motor vessel in commercial service on Lake Temagami. In 1914, she was rebuilt and fitted out with new engines.

Even this did not seem to be sufficient, and in May of 1909 the Temagami Steamboat and Hotel Company — which had just absorbed its rival, the Temagami Navigation Company — prepared to launch its tenth vessel. This craft was not a mere yacht, but a large new passenger and freight steamer, registered at 24.70 tons. She was 71.5 feet in length by 12.6 in beam, and powered by a 12-hp triple-expansion engine. She had a bank of cabins set amidships on her deck and an elliptical stern. On May 24th, she was christened the *Queen of Temagami*, and launched before a large crowd of people, many of whom had arrived on a special train. The day, which marked the official start of the tourist season, also featured canoe and motorboat races, plus a grand ball at the Lady Evelyn Hotel. The Temagami Steamboat and Hotel Company was now at its height. For a time there was even speculation that it might establish a link with the Upper Ontario Steamboat Company's boats on the Montreal River during the Gowganda silver rush, by running a vessel on Lady Evelyn Lake, but nothing came of the idea.

It is not known whether the *Queen of Temagami* and her smaller sisters sailed on regular fixed schedules, or simply in response to demand, but for years it was common practice for most of the fleet — led by the *Belle of Temagami*— to steam out of Temagami village in procession after the arrival of the morning train and wend their way down the Northeast Arm to the central part of the lake, then disperse to their respective destinations. Nor is it clear how long some of the smaller vessels remained in service. In 1912, the company is said to have been running six boats, and since the *Beaver* and the *Marie* both disappear from the record before that time, it seems likely that the ones still in service were the *Bobs*, *Chance*, *Keego* and perhaps the *Wanda* — and of course the *Queen of Temagami* and the *Belle*. According to the inspection reports the *Chance*, *Spry* and *Wanda* were out of commission in 1913–1914, while the *Temagami* — not listed after 1910 — was sold to a trio from Haileybury in the spring of 1916, perhaps to be used for prospecting, though by 1920 she was reported dismantled. In short, service was being drastically curtailed even before the war.

Why was this so? One factor in the decline may have been the early departure of Daniel O'Connor himself. Always restless and active, the pioneering entrepreneur was much more keen about founding ventures than sustaining them, and as early as 1907 he was dropping hints that he would soon leave the management of the steamboat company to some of his partners. By July of 1907, a Captain Malcolmson was managing the line, and by 1912, a Mr. Irwin. Long before then, Dan O'Connor sold out his one-third interest in the company and the "Laird of Temagami," as many called him, left the village he had founded to resume prospecting. By 1912, he had gone to Connaught, a once-prosperous lumber town on the Frederickhouse River, in which vicinity he found deposits of nickel ore. Later still, he discovered some promising gold veins in what became the Ronnoco and Cleaver Gold Mines. Always he forged ahead of the railways, and repeatedly sold his claims at a profit and ploughed the proceeds back into the North, opening new stores, sawmills and mines. Ever kindly, he frequently came to the aid of destitute trappers, prospectors and Nishnabis. As late as 1925, he was back exploring the iron ranges north of Temagami, and dreaming of exporting ores down the French River, which he hoped to tame with locks and control dams. Finally, he retired and settled down at Connaught. Death in the form of double pneumonia finally overtook him in hospital at Timmins on March 29, 1933, at the age of 69, and he was laid to rest at the family vault in Sudbury. His wife, a daughter, two sisters and a brother survived him. Many tributary cables and telegrams poured in at the time of his funeral, but perhaps the most fitting was the one which declared that, "He had unfailing faith in the destiny of Temiskaming, and his name will always live among the builders of Northern Ontario." A street in Temagami village still bears his name.

His former steamboat line did not outlive him. Though the records are scanty, it appears that the overextended Temagami Steamboat and Hotel Company was disappointed in the returns from the tourist trade. The lake was too far from Toronto to attract really large crowds (which was fine with many cottagers and campers), and the tourist season was short. As a result, the hotels seemingly did not pay; the Lady Evelyn had barely a dozen guests when it burned on the afternoon of July 4, 1912, without any loss of life. The big hotel, which had cost nearly $30,000, was never rebuilt. Luckily there was some insurance. The Temagami Inn reverted to the Faskens, who could not make a success of it. Around 1914, they sold it to the American Baldwin Locomotive Company, which proposed to use it as a retreat for its executives, but then the war intervened and spoiled the plan. The Inn did not reopen until l920. So depressed did the tourist trade become that the graceful *Belle of Temagami* had to be laid up at Muddy Water Bay, remaining idle for at least five years. Soon only a few of the boats were running, and in September of 1918 the *Queen of Temagami* was sold and taken to Lake Nipissing, there to become a supply boat for the mercantile firm of Michaud and Levesque of Sturgeon Falls until l923, when she went to Lake Temiskaming. The Temagami boat service was nearly dead.

It was revived in 1918 by a new firm known as the Perron and Marsh Navigation Company. One of the partners, Oderick Raphael Perron, was a native of Hull, Quebec. Along with some of his relatives, Perron came to Temagami during the war years, and in 1922, caused quite a stir by building the first propeller-driven motor sled ever used on the ice of Lake Temagami, using a surplus V-8 Liberty water-cooled engine. It worked very well. His colleague, Frederick George Verny Marsh, was one of the sons of Captain George Marsh of Huntsville, founder of the Huntsville and Lake of Bays Navigation Company. Born at

ABOVE:

Temagami Village, after the coming of the Ferguson Highway. The Belle of Temagami *is at the wharf. The hotel Ronnoco is at right.*

BELOW LEFT:

Captain Ted Guppy, aboard the Aubrey Cosens V.C.   Courtesy Capt. Ted Guppy

BELOW RIGHT:

Daniel O'Connor, the "Laird of Temagami."
Courtesy Sudbury Public Library

Cannington in 1870, Fred Marsh had learned seamanship and navigation on his father's steamers. When the Huntsville company was reorganized in 1906, after his father's death, Fred, not caring much for the new owners, moved to New Liskeard, where in 1911 he took charge of the *Aileen* for a season before moving to Temagami. Here he began operating some of the local steamers, until 1918, when he formed his partnership with Perron. At first they had only launches, but in November 1919 they managed to buy the *Belle of Temagami*, plus numerous other supplies left over from the Temagami Steamboat and Hotel Company. As a rule, Captain Marsh commanded the *Belle* during this period, while Perron ran the office. Two of Perron's relatives, Joe and Eugene, sometimes acted as engineers, while a boat builder named Louis Poulin took charge of repairs and maintenance.

By now the *Belle of Temagami* was the only steamer left on the lake. The *Bobs* had gone to the Ville-Marie Navigation Company by 1920. Under Perron and Marsh, the *Belle of Temagami* was used mainly on the North Arm route, plying to Wabikon, Bear Island and Camp Keewaydin. Most other destinations were serviced by launches.

The tourist industry enjoyed a vigorous revival after the First World War. The Temagami Inn changed hands and reopened in 1920. Among other things, it featured stables, a power plant, a sewage system, guest cabins, ballroom and square dancing, and over 100 canoes with local guides, including Nishnabis, available for fishing. By 1929, it was taking up to 200 guests, mostly Americans. In 1926, Arthur Stevens, who first took charge of the railway restaurant in 1905, established the Temagami Outfitting Company to provide canoes and camping gear for visitors. He also bought and refurbished the Ronnoco Hotel. Also in 1926, Gordon S. Gooderham, son of W.G. Gooderham of the Temagami Steamboat and Hotel Company, founded Camp Chimo for adults at the entrance to the South Arm. This was followed in 1929 by Arthur Judson's Camp White Bear, a private resort on an island in the Southwest Arm. More modest accommodations were available at Friday's Lodge, which was opened by a Nishnabi family of that name on the mainland a little north of Bear Island. On the island itself, "Granny" Turner was still running the Lakeview House, where country hoedown square dancing was the rage every Tuesday and Saturday evening. It is said that the worst weather couldn't deter the boats from coming. By 1929, there were about eight resorts on Lake Temagami, all of which were doing well.

One more adult lodge dating from this period was Camp Accouchiching, which was opened in 1920 on two islands deep in the South Arm. It featured a fine beach, log buildings, tents and an outfitting service. The owner, George N. Allabough of Omaha, Nebraska, was a Swiss fur speculator who also founded a short-lived enterprise called the Temagami Fur Company. From about 1920 to 1923, the Temagami Fur Company is known to have run a boat — reputedly the *Keego* — on regular trips to Camps Temagami and Accouchiching, and other sites in the south end of the lake. If he was using the *Keego*, Allabough must have leased her from the defunct Temagami Steamboat and Hotel Company, which still officially owned her until the spring of 1922. At that time, however, the *Keego* was sold to Perron and Marsh, and soon afterwards the Temagami Fur Company went bankrupt. Around 1927, Allabough sold Camp Accouchiching and left the area.

The camps, both youth and adult, were flourishing. In July of 1925, Father Paradis, the former Oblate colonizer of Temiscamingue, now 77 and still holding weekly services at his little church on Bear Island, estimated that nearly 1,000 visitors were flocking to all eight camps on Lake Temagami every summer. Many former campers were also building cottages, usually clustered around the camps. Regattas were popular. Although motorboats were becoming common, and a few wealthy cottagers were using seaplanes, most continued to depend on the commercial boat lines.

Press comments from the period agree that the *Belle of Temagami* was extremely busy, and very comfortable. In 1924, for the first time, she was chartered by the Northern Ontario Summer School to take about 60 young people from the railway depot to a tent site on Bear Island for a week of camping, recreation, sports and Bible studies. The following season the school was held at Friday Point, and included in the festivities was a cruise all around the lake. Towns from Timmins to South River were represented. In June of 1928, she took the Simcoe County Council and several M.L.A.s on a tour of Lake Temagami, and the following July she hosted nine Orange Lodges on a monster-sized afternoon cruise to celebrate the "Glorious Twelfth." A flotilla of launches escorted the graceful *Belle* down the lake. Many of the participants came by car, since the Ferguson Highway from North Bay had been officially opened in July 1927, making it possible — for the first time — for adventurous motorists to drive from Toronto to Temagami in a day. (The highway was not paved until 1937.) In 1925, the Perron and Marsh Company secured the contract to deliver the mail to the new post office at Wabikon.

Prosperous though it was, the Perron and Marsh Company was hardly ever free from competition. Seemingly, there were many camp operators and cottagers who resented the near monopoly of the boat line and welcomed rivalry. Initially this came from the Temagami Fur Company, but by 1922 the Perron and Marsh Company consolidated its position by acquiring the *Keego*, which was now the only sizeable vessel on the lake besides the *Belle of Temagami*. The company also enticed Captain Edwy (Ted) Guppy, who had been running the *Keego* for Allabough, to stay in command of her on the South Arm run.

This arrangement did not last long. Within just a year Captain Guppy decided to go into business for himself and start competing with his former employers.

Ted Guppy was born in Wise Township, Ontario, very close to South Témiscaming, in 1893. His family had migrated up the Ottawa River by boat, intending to farm, and had settled on 60 acres near the south end of the lake. Ted, however, decided that he wanted to be a boatman, and as early as the age of twelve he joined the crews on one of the Lumsden alligators. A year or so later, he went to Lake Kipawa to work as a deckhand on the tug *Emma Mac*. Then, around 1908, he moved to Haileybury and began crewing on the Temiskaming Navigation Company steamers. Later still, at the age of sixteen, he and Captain James Ladouceur went north to Lake Abitibi to serve on the *Mistango*, a huge alligator owned by the newly formed Abitibi Power and Paper Company. Captain Ladouceur did not remain long, and Ted Guppy was groomed to succeed him. He soon obtained his tug papers and spent five years working around Iroquois Falls; we shall hear more of him there in the next chapter. Then he moved to Temagami and took charge of the *Keego*. When the Temagami Fur Company went bankrupt, Guppy attempted to buy the *Keego*, but failed. Perron and Marsh engaged him to run the boat for them, but Ted had ideas of his own.

Early in 1924, Guppy secured the financial backing of A.L. Cochrane, the owner of Camp Temagami, and a few other prominent summer residents, and founded a new Temagami Navigation Company. Then he scouted around for a suitable boat, and arranged to buy the *Iona*, an impressive 14-ton steam yacht previously in service on the Muskoka Lakes. The *Iona* had been built at Hamilton, Ontario, in 1907, for a Pittsburgh steel magnate who liked to spend his summers at a cottage near Beaumaris on Lake Muskoka, but in 1918 she was exchanged for a big Ditchburn Company motor launch. For several years the yacht remained idle at a boathouse in Gravenhurst, until Captain Guppy arranged to buy her. The Ditchburn Company apparently gave her an overhaul before she was shipped by rail to Lake Temagami to ply to the tourist camps in the southern portions of the lake.

But Guppy soon ran into a snag. Captain Marsh apparently pointed out that the regulations now required a special certificate for commanding a passenger boat. So Ted Guppy went to Toronto, paid a fee, and discovered that he was expected to pass an examination in the use of charts and compasses. Not having this knowledge, he took a quick course at the Nautical School, passed the exam, and returned home with his ticket. The way at last was clear.

The *Iona* was a fast, graceful vessel with a 14.7-hp steeple compound engine, and was capable of taking twenty or more passengers. She began a daily 25-mile run from Temagami to Wabikon, Camp Chimo, Camp Temagami, and Camp Accouchiching in direct competition with Perron and Marsh. For a time it was doubtful whether either operation would pay, but as the pressure mounted Captain Guppy managed to find a few more backers. Finally, Perron and Marsh decided to abandon the South Arm service, and to sell the *Keego* to the newly reconstituted Temiskaming Navigation Company in the fall of 1926. About the same time, the genial Captain Marsh, who had operated six boats in the North over a period of seventeen years, now withdrew from his partnership with Perron and moved to Midland, where he became active in civic activities and the Masonic Lodge. On December 21, 1940, he died in Toronto, at the age of 71. Oderick Perron had to carry on with the help of some of his relatives. Lake Temagami was now effectively divided between the two boat lines.

Captain Guppy ran the *Iona* for eleven years, and rarely had any trouble with her. One evening, though, he took the vessel to Camp White Bear on the Southwest Arm around 11:00 P.M. Afterwards, they proceeded towards the snye channel leading towards the centre of the lake. It was a dark night, and clouding up, and the captain had to steer by compass. At one point he remarked to the engineer, "There should be a rock around here someplace." Then — crunch! "That must be it!" observed the engineer, who then went forward to check for damage. He found no sign of any, but the boat remained caught on the rocks for about two hours and didn't get back to Temagami until about 2:00 A.M.

The boats carried on into the Depression and survived it, mainly because they were indispensable. Few new resorts were opened during that dismal decade, but several more camps (mostly American) were established, including Camp Wanapitei, which was moved from the lake of that name to the North Arm in 1931. The *Belle of Temagami* at once extended her routes up to Sandy Inlet to service it. In 1933, Camp Wabun, an offshoot of Camp Keewaydin, was opened at Garden Island, near the centre of the lake. Wigwasati was established near the entrance to the Southwest Arm in 1930, and Northwoods in 1937, deep in the Southwest Arm. By 1939, there were seven boys' camps on the lake, mostly specializing in canoe trips. The first successful camp for girls, Cayuga, was established on an island in the Northwest Arm in 1940.

Despite all this, the Depression years were difficult for the boat lines. Captain Guppy tried to reduce expenses by converting the *Iona* into a diesel during the 1930s. Meanwhile, Oderick Perron, who had obtained his own certificate, took charge of the *Belle of Temagami* for a time, though her seasons were confined mainly to the summer months. Around 1932, he engaged as engineer Mike Pritchard, who had served for many years on the tugs on the Magnetawan River. This once led to complications. Soon after the season opened, the *Belle of Temagami* was approaching Bear Island one day, and the captain rang the signal to reverse engines. Pritchard, who was used to right-hand engines, accidentally put the gears in forward instead. As the steamer rapidly bore down on the wharf, the Nishnabis scattered. The captain tried to swerve and minimize the impact, but the ship rammed the wharf, sliced off several crib logs, and struck a canoe shed. The damage was extensive, but luckily not to the boat. Another time the *Belle of Temagami* was running an evening excursion to Temagami Inn for what was expected to be a long stay. Captain Perron, Pritchard and the fireman all went ashore, where they were shown around and offered a few drinks. Then the whistle blew, signalling an early departure, and the crew hastened to return. The ship was already backing out amid high winds when the fireman discovered that the boiler pressure was down to 80 lbs. and dropping. He stuffed in some more wood, but the pressure continued to fall. Desperate, he tried throwing kerosene into the firebox. The fire rebounded with a roar, but gradually the pressure began to climb. Fortunately the steamer had to back out slowly for a considerable distance from the dock, and by then there was sufficient steam up for the trip home.

The *Belle of Temagami* had other troubles during those years. One winter the oakum in some of the seams of her hull loosened and allowed the steamer to sink at the winter quarters at Muddy Water Bay, west of Temagami. The owners decided there was nothing they could do until the spring. Then attempts were made to raise her, using pumps and scows with beams — in vain. Finally a crew was summoned from Port Colborne. A diver sealed all the portholes and openings and pumps powered by donkey engines were put to work. Finally, the *Belle of Temagami* agreed to rise from the bottom and float. She was towed over to Camp Ahmek and completely cleaned up and overhauled, at a cost of $3,000. This included jacking up the superstructure and rebuilding the entire stern, which was drooping by about eleven inches. The frames all had to be refabricated and the hull replanked. Once completed, the *Belle of Temagami* was good for at least another dozen years.

Sometime after 1928, Perron decided to engage a new captain for the *Belle of Temagami*, and hired Bill Reynolds, who had lately run the engine of the *Zara*. Having commanded steamers all the way from the Kawartha Lakes to Lake Temiskaming for over 30 years, Captain Bill was in no mood to retire. He was a cheerful, quiet little man, good with children, and always ready with a joke or a yarn about his numerous adventures. He was especially noted for his parrot, Loretta, which he had picked up in Cuba, and which regularly screamed out "Bob!" in the course of a cruise.

Most of Captain Reynolds's trips on the *Belle of Temagami* were uneventful, but one run during the 1930s made a vivid impression on the entire crew. It happened in midsummer, when the *Belle* was taking about 140 boys to Camp Keewaydin. They all arrived safely, but it was on the return trip that things became interesting. Around Bear Island the winds arose, and a hailstorm set in. Captain Reynolds turned the vessel's bow into the wind, but the driving ice pellets broke the wheelhouse windows, and both the captain and the mate were badly cut by splinters of broken glass. As the steamer rolled and pitched, the water-holding tanks on the bridge fell over. The pipes broke, and water gushed all over the deck. Some of it seeped down into the stokehold around the funnel, giving the fireman a soaking. By the time the storm abated, several other windows had been smashed. Everyone was rather relieved that there had been no passengers aboard when it happened.

In the meantime, Oderick Perron was finding the task of looking after the company boats and service and running the office too much, and presently formed a new partnership with James Ross Sproat. A native of Seaforth, Ontario, "Jack" Sproat had come to Temagami to work as a clerk at the Friday Silver Mine near Black Bear Lake. When the mine failed to produce much silver, Sproat left to run the office for the Perron and Marsh Navigation Company. He also became an officer of the Temagami Lakes Association, which was founded in 1931 primarily to preserve the beauties of the natural environment around the lake. Nonetheless, he soon ceased to get along well with the Perrons, who came to distrust him profoundly.

By 1934, Oderick Perron's health was failing, and he left to spend the winter at West Palm Beach, Florida. There, on February 26, 1935, he died, without leaving a will. Sproat borrowed money from the banks, putting a mortgage on the *Belle of Temagami*, and proceeded to buy out Perron's heirs. He also gained some backers and formed a new company called the Temagami Boat Company, of which he held most of the shares. Chartered as of May 7, 1934, the company's objectives were transportation, boat building, storage, marine-engine sales, dock and cabin construction, and outfitting. Hyacinthe Reinhold Valin, a North Bay lawyer who had been looking after Perron's estate, became the nominal President, and Sproat the General Manager. Soon afterwards, Sproat also managed to get control of Captain Guppy's Temagami Navigation Company. His chance came in 1936. It seems that, around 1935, the *Iona* had been engaged in towing two heavily loaded scows, when one of them began leaking and sank. The other one lurched, and the cargo rolled off into the lake. (The incident was witnessed by the crew of the *Belle of Temagami*, which was then passing by.) This led to a costly court action, and Captain Guppy was ordered to pay for the damages. Soon afterwards, he sold his business to Sproat, using some of the proceeds to pay off his backers.

Nonetheless, Ted Guppy's sailing days were by no means over. He continued to run some of the boats for the Temagami Boat Company, usually the *Belle of Temagami* herself. Captain Reynolds was put in charge of the *Iona*. It is said that he was sometimes known to boast that the *Iona* was the fastest boat on the lake — until a local resident challenged him to a race in his new inboard motor launch. They raced from Bear Island all the way to Temagami, but in the end the motor launch won by about half a mile. Two weeks passed before Reynolds would speak to his challenger again.

ABOVE:
Steamer Belle of Temagami, *at a camp on Lake Temagami.* Courtesy National Archives of Canada, C37619

BELOW:
Captain William V. Reynolds on the Aubrey Cosens V.C.

Meanwhile, Jack Sproat consolidated control over the Temagami Boat Company and bought out the remaining shareholders. But the company made only modest profits, and was generally run on a shoestring. The outbreak of the Second World War in 1939 only made things worse, since gasoline was rationed, and many people could no longer afford either to come to Lake Temagami or to send their sons to camp. Sproat also refused to do business with the Milne Lumber Company, which had opened a sawmill near Temagami in 1935, because of a personal feud with David Milne. (In 1937, the Milne Company began towing booms of logs by itself on Lake Temagami, though it was careful not to do this during the summer months, when cottagers were around.)

By 1944, Sproat had definitely had enough of the Temagami Boat Company. Not only were the docks and wharves at Temagami growing dilapidated from lack of maintenance, but the *Belle of Temagami* and the *Iona* were becoming unseaworthy too, and needed a refit. Sproat was not interested in doing either. Instead, he persuasively talked the Temiskaming and Northern Ontario Railway into taking over the boat services, an arrangement that was officially ratified by August 21, 1945, after the railway's charter had been duly amended to allow it to take on this role. As a result, the Ontario Northland Boat Lines was formed as a division of the railway, which itself was renamed the Ontario Northland in 1946. Sproat then left Temagami to go into the deep-freeze business at North Bay.

By this time the age of steam was over on Lake Temagami. The *Belle of Temagami*, now 39 years old, was the only passenger steam vessel left anywhere in Northern Ontario. The Ontario Northland Boat Lines was initially prepared to give her a refit, but the master shop superintendent, Norman Wickens, felt that she was too big and persuaded the railway to that effect. As a result, the *Belle* and the *Iona* were both scrapped at Muddy Water Bay in the late summer of 1945. The steel portions were removed, cut up, and sold, and the wooden parts burned. To soothe local sentiments, the railway promised to build a new *Belle of Temagami*, but it never did. Instead, it imported the ex-steamer *Modello* from Lake Nipissing.

As noted in Chapter 1, the *Modello* was already 30 years old by the time she was shipped north by rail in 1945. There she was again re-engined, and fitted out with a pair of compact 60-hp diesels. As a result, she floated too high and became top heavy. Consequently, she had to be ballasted with several railway rails, each cut into four pieces. Like the *Belle of Temagami*, she developed a drooping stern from being left unsupported when hauled out of the water.

Commanded by Captain Guppy, the *Modello* took over the *Belle of Temagami*'s route to Bear Island and the centre portion of the lake, with motor launches to service the outlying arms. But she was already old when she arrived, and she gradually became less and less seaworthy. In addition, her diesel engines sometimes gave trouble. One night she experienced a breakdown while taking 115 boys to camp. The captain sounded the air whistle, and finally a lowly outboard motorboat arrived, and took the ex-steamer in tow. Another afternoon around 1:30, both engines gave out about half a mile north of Bear Island because of dirty diesel fuel, and the vessel started drifting in a stiff breeze. An anchor was dropped, and a full 250 feet of chain played out, but the boat kept drifting and dragging the anchor along the bottom. The engineer was about to lower the second anchor, but the deckhand warned him that this one had only three feet of chain attached — for show! Meanwhile, the boat kept whistling for help, and soon a fleet of small boats arrived. Even that was not the final humiliation. The gears of the capstan used for winching in the anchor had been mangled on some previous occasion, with the result that the vessel had to be towed to Bear Island with the anchor still dragging. Once she arrived, it took six men to hoist the anchor by hand. In the meantime a barge was summoned, and finally one engine was started, allowing the *Modello* to return to Temagami at half speed.

On yet another occasion that same season, the *Modello*'s engines broke down around 11:30 at night while the boat was returning to Temagami. Once again, an outboard was engaged to tow her, but in the meantime the deckhand was ordered to have the anchor ready for lowering to keep the stern from swinging in the channel. Suddenly the boat stopped moving, and the small boat in front started swinging helplessly from side to side, going nowhere. The deckhand had dropped the anchor prematurely, without waiting for orders. This time, the anchor worked only too well.

Despite such problems, the *Modello* plied regularly for about eleven years. In the meantime, the Ontario Northland Boat Line tried hard to promote tourism on Lakes Nipissing and Temagami, and even extended the routes and services. It rebuilt the docks at Temagami, and briefly operated (and then sold) the old Ronnoco Hotel, which became the Minawassi in 1946. And it built up a fleet of eleven boats. These included the *Ramona*, the *Vedette* (which usually plied to the Southwest Arm), the *Grey Owl* and the *Ojibway*, a recycled Second World War crash boat which could reach any part of Lake Temagami in two hours.

Next to the *Modello*, the company's largest acquisition was the *Aubrey Cosens, V.C.*, a former sailboat used originally on the St. Lawrence River and the Atlantic. Named after a famous war hero from Latchford, the *Aubrey* was remodelled and recommissioned at Temagami in 1947, and fitted out with new cabins, a canopy and two diesel engines. She assumed the North Arm run until the retirement of the *Modello*, with Captain Reynolds at the wheel. (Reynolds retired shortly afterwards, and died at New Liskeard in 1952 at the age of 80.) In 1954, the Ontario Northland Boat Line obtained its last vessel, the steam yacht *Naiad* from the Lake of Bays. A magnificent craft with a clipper bow decorated with gilded scrollwork and a fantail stern, the *Naiad* was 68 feet in length, registered 19.74 tons, and looked like something designed for royalty, with her mahogany planking and plate-glass windows set at a rakish angle. She had been built in 1890 for a Hamilton wool magnate who used her on Lake Rosseau, but latterly had become the plaything of a wealthy boat fancier on the Lake of Bays. She arrived at Lake Temagami fully equipped, even down to her flags, pennants and lockers, but was immediately converted to diesel. She was also speedily deprived of the little brass cannon mounted on her foredeck, because her engineer, Robert Boudray of North Bay (nicknamed "Silent Sam" on account of his tendency to be otherwise), kept concocting gunpowder and firing it.

Soon after the *Naiad* entered service, Charles Humphrey of Temagami, who was crewing on her, grew very annoyed because the boat line failed to supply the vessel with a proper flag. Finally he found and raised a Japanese pennant. The manager, Jack Swan, was very indignant, but he took the hint and ordered some new flags.

The lovely *Naiad* was assigned to Captain Sam Cody, a Nishnabi from James Bay, who operated her on a temporary ticket, valid only for Lake Temagami. He handled her well, but on one occasion while coming to dock, he managed to split one of the support posts at the Temagami wharf with the bronze-tipped spear of the vessel's bowsprit. The bowsprit of course broke off and was never replaced. Captain Cody later left the region and went west to Edmonton.

By 1955, the *Modello* reached the end of her days. Captain Guppy found her hull so badly rotted that he refused to take her out again, and shortly afterwards she was dismantled and burned. Guppy then took over the *Aubrey Cosens* until he suffered a stroke in 1965. He returned as nominal skipper in 1966, while the mate, Ivor Smith, did all the work, but then retired and spent his last years as a much-respected citizen of Temagami. He died in 1972.

By that time the Temagami boat service was dead. Several factors combined to kill it. One was the endless proliferation of private motorboats, which allowed cottagers to get around the lake at their own time and convenience; some even used seaplanes. Another was the decline of the resorts. By about 1960, the public seemed to prefer private cottages to the more communal life of the hotels, and besides, the resorts now seemed too rustic and lacking in modern comforts and conveniences. Roughing it in the bush was no longer in style. By 1963, electric power was extended to the hub of the lake, allowing some of the resorts to modernize, but many others had to shut down — or convert themselves into youth camps. Some lodges began promoting the autumn deer hunt or winter ice fishing, but soon there were no deer left around Temagami, and few fish. In 1958, following the opening of a copper mine

ABOVE:

Dockyards at Temagami Village. In the foreground is the launch Ojibway, *with the* Ramona *at left and the* Grey Owl *at right.* Courtesy Mr. Jack Guppy

BELOW:

Steamer Iona, *leaving Temagami Village.* Courtesy House of Memories Museum, Latchford on Temagami Island, a new road called the Temagami Mine Road was opened to the hub of the lake, south of Temagami village. Cottagers now began driving the extra twelve miles and bypassing the village completely. As a result, accommodation in Temagami declined, and in 1973 the Minawassi Hotel — once the Ronnoco and still one of Temagami's leading landmarks — burned to the ground after some years of dereliction. Regattas and excursion cruises faded out, and by 1963 the Ontario Northland Boat Line cut back its services, amid rumours that it was planning to abandon the boat business entirely. Reputedly, the railway hoped that Temagami village would incorporate itself as an improvement district, and when the villagers refused — fearing the costs — the Ontario Northland resolved to do nothing more for Temagami, and let the sheds and repair facilities deteriorate.

At the end of the 1965 season, despite protests from the camps and resorts, the Ontario Northland Railway sold the Temagami boat division to the Shell Oil Company. Included in the deal were the *Aubrey Cosens*, the *Ramona*, the *Grey Owl* and the *Ojibway*. The Shell Oil Company, however, was interested only in acquiring a site for a service centre. Of necessity it ran the boats for one more season, then leased them to a private concern called the Temagami Development Company, which built a new dock and parking lot at Boat Line Bay on the Northeast Arm, miles from the village. Even this service soon lapsed, and the boats began disappearing.

In 1966, the *Aubrey Cosens*, having rammed a dock, was retired from service. Two years later she was hauled out on the slipway and her engines removed. The presiding engineer, a very opinionated fellow, ignored orders to pump the water out of the bilges first, with the result that the keel broke during the move. The *Aubrey Cosens* was then trucked down to Marten River, where it was proposed to turn her into a cocktail bar. But the hull was found to be saturated with engine oil and the scheme was abandoned. Soon afterwards she was destroyed by fire.

The *Naiad* met a similar fate. In 1966, she was condemned out of hand after a hasty inspection and cut up with chain saws. Only when this process was well advanced was it realized that she had a steel frame, and could easily have been repaired. By then it was too late, and the once proud craft was burned. About fourteen feet of the bow were spared, and afterwards went to a Toronto man who had long been enamoured of the vessel. He also acquired her steam engine and other relics, which have lately been returned to Muskoka. Little else remains of one of Ontario's most celebrated yachts.

Today, except for the raucous noise of motorboats and snowmobiles, Lake Temagami is quiet, and it seems the Nishnabis, after a long struggle, have finally won their battle to have their ancient land claims acknowledged by the Ontario government. Though disputes continue between environmentalists and extractive industries, the region is still prime canoe country, and in a few places virgin forests still remain. Camps and cottages still abound, and some resorts still survive. But of the graceful little steamers that did so much to make the present recreation scene a reality, nothing remains except some musty old records, a few photographs, and receding memories.

PLEASURE STEAMERS ON LAKE TEMISKAMING: (circa 1902–1914)

Lake Temiskaming is also known to have had a few private pleasure steamers, but very little is known about them, and in any case few residents had the time or the money to indulge in such luxuries.

One exception was Kalil (Big Pete) Farah, a husky, popular Lebanese immigrant who came to New Liskeard in 1900 and became one of the town's most active citizens. Among other things, he founded the community's first hotel, known as the Hotel Canada, and later became instrumental in taking over the Long Lake Power Company and bringing electricity to town. Shortly after his arrival, Mr. Farah imported a steam yacht called the *Swan*, which he used both for recreation cruises and — reputedly — to run groups of passengers to and from North Temiskaming. The *Swan*'s registry has not been found, and hence little is known of her.

The New Liskeard *Speaker* mentions her only in June of 1906, when Hendry and Brickenden accepted a contract to raise the vessel, which had sunk near the mouth of the Wabi River on account of spring ice. Apparently they failed, because the yacht remained on the bottom until August, when she was finally raised by another contractor. It is not known whether the *Swan* was used again, and in any case the restless Farah moved to Toronto in 1913. A street in New Liskeard was named in his honour.

Another private launch, which may have started out as a steamer, was the *Jinnie M.*, which was owned by C.C. Farr. Again, little is known of the vessel, except that she was a motorboat in later life. In 1905, we are told that Farr and various others took the *Jinnie M.* up to Murray City (North Temiskaming) on a summer outing, and that, on the return trip, they took the shortest and riskiest route back to Haileybury — past the mazes of the Devil's Snye to the very tortuous Corbeau channel at the mouth of the Blanche River. Here they had some good luck. Amid the mud flats they found a Nishnabi drawing his pack and canoe ashore. Circling in the wind, they hailed the Indian and offered him a ride down the lake. He accepted. The canoe was lashed alongside, and the man boarded the steamer, fascinated by the machinery. When she reached a mud flat, the native, who knew the waters exactly, guided her around it. The Nishnabi was Basil Antoine, who had conducted the Farrs to Kipawa on their wedding trip 27 years earlier!

The *Jinnie M.* was used for several years. Just once — in August 1913 — she is mentioned in the New Liskeard *Speaker*, when she helped to rescue a five-year-old girl who had been lost on Burnt Island for several days. The following year, on November 25th, C.C. Farr died, quite unexpectedly, of a throat infection at the age of 63, and was buried at Haileybury. Many attended the funeral of the man who had done so much to found and nurture settlement in the North. Nothing more is heard about his yacht, though one of her name signs is now in the Haileybury Fire Museum.

Aside from a few boats noted earlier in Chapter 3, no other private pleasure steamers are known from Lake Temiskaming.

PLEASURE STEAMERS ON THE MATTAGAMI RIVER: (CIRCA 1914–1925)

The only other region in northeastern Ontario known to have been served by excursion steamers is the Mattagami River, in the Porcupine country around the town of Timmins.

Timmins and the various "towns" round it — including Porcupine, Golden City, South Porcupine, Pottsville and Schumacher — were all by-products (some temporary) of the Porcupine gold rush of 1909. The region took its name from an island that looks like a porcupine, located in the Porcupine River. Although camps were first set up around Porcupine Lake as early as 1896, it was not until 1908 that gold was discovered. By 1909, prospectors were forsaking Larder Lake for the Porcupine in droves, and soon claims were staked at what became the Dome and Hollinger gold mines, among the richest in the world. Many other finds followed, and in 1911 a townsite was laid out beside the Mattagami River. It was originally called Hollinger, after Benny Hollinger, but the name was soon changed to Timmins after Noah Timmins, who became the first president of Hollinger Mines. Despite a number of disastrous conflagrations, including the Porcupine Fire of 1911 and the Matheson Fire of 1916, which destroyed nineteen buildings at Timmins, the camps flourished, and they eventually exceeded Cobalt at least 35 to one. It is said that by 1922 the Porcupine had produced $100,000,000 in gold, and it is still going strong today. Cobalt, by contrast, was already declining by 1916.

Although Porcupine Lake was teeming with boats by 1911, none are known to have been steamers. Hence steamboats could have played no part in saving the lives of the hundreds of people who had to flee to the lake when fire swept through Golden City, Pottsville and Porquis Junction in July of 1911. In any case, the Timiskaming and Northern Ontario Railway opened a spur from Porquis Junction to Timmins that same year. However, there may have been a steam vessel or two on Night Hawk Lake, a little east of Porcupine, towing logs for the local lumbermen and taking freight and passengers. In 1924, a firm called the Connaught Navigation Company, managed by a D. Warren, was running a boat (probably a motor launch) from Connaught station on the railway to Night Hawk Peninsula, where another gold mine was in operation, and to other sites on the Frederickhouse River. The duration of this operation is unknown.

The Mattagami River itself hosted two steamers for over ten years. The river is hundreds of miles long and drains ultimately into the Moose River near James Bay, but the navigable portion around Timmins extends only about 22 miles, from Wawaitin Falls at the exit of Lake Kenogamissi to Sandy Falls, about seven miles downstream from town. As settlers, prospectors and lumbermen began flooding the area around 1909, the river was swarming with boats, and soon plans were afoot to build power dams at Wawaitin and Sandy Falls. This spelled opportunity for Alexander Lee Casselman, a boatman from Mattagami Heights, and in the spring of 1914 he imported the steamer *Agnes* to the north country.

The *Agnes* was a 55-foot yacht, registered at 9.86 tons. We have already encountered her on the Montreal River in 1910, where she plied until 1913, and by the time she went to Timmins she was sixteen years old. Casselman probably used her for anything that paid, including log towing, scowing sand and provisions up the meandering stream to Wawaitin Falls for the Wawaitin Power Company, and the occasional recreation cruise. But the river was bedevilled with booms and sawlogs, which often made navigation almost impossible, and in 1917 Casselman sold the vessel to his neighbour, John J. Power, a lumberman who carried on with the boat service. In July of 1920, we find him taking the Cercle Thériault picnic in relays from Timmins to Sandy Falls. Altogether at least 250 people took part.

On September 27, 1920, the *Agnes* was destroyed by fire, under unknown circumstances, but within just a few months Mr. Power purchased an elegant new steamer to replace her. This was the *Minga*.

The *Minga* was a larger yacht, some 56 feet in length, and registered at 13.43 tons. Built at New York City in 1903, she spent seven years on the Muskoka Lakes before she was shipped in from Montreal by rail in early November. She had one deck, an elliptical stern, a steam-heated lounge cabin and even a little kitchen. With an overall length of about 60 feet, she could take parties of up to 50 patrons in style and comfort, and was used almost exclusively for the passenger trade.

The *Minga* was launched on April 21, 1921, and began plying six days a week from Timmins to the Northern Canada Power Company dock above the Redsucker River, making various stops along the way. She was in great demand for charters and excursions, by such groups as the Caledonian Society, the Rebekahs, the Boy Scouts and the Oddfellows, and became a veritable institution on the Mattagami. Not infrequently she had a fiddler or a harpist aboard (or, failing that, a gramophone) to provide music on a cruise. On July 27th, for the first time ever, a regatta was held on the river, with the usual sports, canoe tilting and boat racing, but the *Minga* and the Town Band were the star attractions. By 1923, she even had a running mate, the *Irene*, which seems to have been a motorboat.

Popular though she was, the *Minga* did not sail for long. She was often hampered by logs, and the competition of gas motorboats. As late as 1926, there was still no dock at Mattagami Landing. Patronage was sometimes discouraged by cool or rainy weather, especially in 1922. In addition, the novelty of the cruise began to wear thin, and by 1924 she was seldom being mentioned in the local press. Then, on September 12, 1925, tragedy struck. The vessel was hosting an early-evening tea party for some of the social set of Timmins, who were bound for Sandy Falls to join their friends at a picnic, when a prominent lawyer named D.W. O'Sullivan stepped backwards to sit on the railing. Unluckily, there was no railing behind him, only the entrance gate, which was guarded simply by a chain. He lost his balance and fell overboard, but despite the freezing waters he started to make for a nearby timber pointer. Then, to the horror of the onlookers, he sank. Several men dived in to help, but it was too late. The outing was of course cancelled, and three hours later the body was recovered.

ABOVE:

M.V. Aubrey Cosens V.C. *on Lake Temagami.*

Courtesy Muskoka Steamship & Historical Society

BELOW LEFT:

View of Timmins, circa 1912.   Courtesy National

Archives of Canada, PA 30044

BELOW RIGHT:

Steam yacht Minga. *The vessel appears here from her days on the Muskoka Lakes.*   Courtesy Muskoka Steamship & Historical Society

Perhaps the *Minga* herself died as a result of this mishap, which may have cost her her passenger certificate. Possibly she remained in use a while longer, but there is no further mention of her in the newspapers, and her final fate is unknown. And so the brief episode of steamboating petered out on the Mattagami River.

~~~~~~

By the 1940s, all the steamboats in Northern Ontario were gone — except a number of tugs used in the pulpwood business. Their story constitutes our concluding chapter.

Steam yacht Naiad. *This fine vessel finished her career as a diesel on Lake Temagami.* Courtesy Muskoka Steamship & Historical Society

CHAPTER 6

STEAMBOATING
AND THE PULP AND
PAPER INDUSTRY

The manufacture of paper in Canada can be traced back for centuries, although for a long time it was simply a domestic industry. The first paper mill in the country was opened at St. Andrews, Quebec, in 1805, and like all the early mills, it was located on a river because this provided a continuous supply of fresh water plus water power for driving machinery. (Besides that, rivers offered the most convenient means of transport in the days before decent roads or railways.) As population and literacy increased, so did the need for paper, and mills sprang up all around the Great Lakes, the St. Lawrence River and the Maritimes.

FACING PAGE:
Steam alligator Low
Bush, *on Lake Abitibi.*

At first paper was made from rags, but around 1840 it was discovered that it could also be made from wood fibres. In 1864, the first wood pulp mill in North America was established at Windsor Mills, in the Eastern Townships of Quebec. Here, wood chips were boiled under pressure and combined with soda to extract cellulose fibre, which was then washed, bleached, blended and poured over wire screens to produce a fine layer of fibre. This represented the beginnings of the mammoth industry that we know today.

During the 1890s and afterwards, the rapid growth of cities in the United States and Canada led to a voracious demand for newsprint, while at the same time, large stands of spruce were becoming scarce south of the border. As a result, the Americans began looking north, but the governments of Ontario and Quebec both banned the export of pulpwood from any Crown lands. Caving in to the inevitable, the American Congress in 1913 repealed the tariff on imported newsprint. This cleared the way for the investment of huge sums of money for the construction of several giant pulp and paper plants in Canada. Within just five years, the country became the largest exporter of newsprint in the entire world. Millions of tons were shipped abroad, mostly to the United States, every year.

Of necessity, the new plants had to be located near the best sources of supply, and as a result, many were built in remote areas, such as northwestern Ontario, the St. Maurice Valley and the Lac St. Jean region in Quebec, and the upper Ottawa Valley, where spruce was plentiful. The mills also required extensive hydro-electric power, and the result was a surge of dam construction and new generating stations. All this in turn required the creation of whole new towns, at such places as Kenora, Dryden, and Grand-Mère. The ones that will concern us here are Témiscaming, Quebec, and Iroquois Falls. Since Iroquois Falls is the older of the two, we will begin there, in the Abitibi region of Northern Ontario.

STEAMBOATING ON THE BLACK RIVER: (CIRCA 1907–1927)

Steamboating in the Abitibi region falls into two distinct phases: the provision-boat services on the Black and Abitibi Rivers, and the towing operations on the rivers and on Lake Abitibi itself.

Lake Abitibi is one of the largest in the Clay Belt country. Known to the native people as the "middle waters" from its position midway between Lake Temiskaming and the Arctic, it spreads about 42 miles from east to west, and up to 18 miles from north to south, and is divided into two sections linked by a narrow channel. Of the two, the larger, known as Upper Lake Abitibi, extends eastward into Quebec, very close to LaSarre. Both portions contain many

201

ABOVE:

*View of Matheson,
July 13, 1907.*
Courtesy National
Archives of Canada,
PA 92408

BELOW:

*Aerial view of
Iroquois Falls, on
the Abitibi River.*
National Film Board
Photo, courtesy
National Archives of
Canada, PA 111478

Matheson Ont.
July 13 - 1907.

small islands, and to the south hills tower up to 500 feet high. But the lake itself is exceedingly shallow, rarely exceeding a depth of fourteen feet. This, plus its long open expanses, makes it extremely rough and treacherous in windy weather; the waves tend to rebound off the bottom and reach enormous heights during storms. Some boatmen consider it worse than Lake Temiskaming. The turbulence also keeps mud stirred up, and gives the waters a distinctly yellowish colouring.

The same applies to its outlet, the Abitibi River, which drains the southwest corner of the lake in a westerly direction. About five miles downstream was a cataract known as Couchiching Falls, which dropped about 28 feet in two leaps. However, it has been submerged by a dam about nineteen miles farther downstream at Twin Falls. Four miles below Twin Falls the river meets its tributary, the Black River, which has clearer waters and flows in from the southeast. From the junction, the combined stream continues northwest to Iroquois Falls, where there is another drop of about 40 feet. The river then meanders northward, passing beneath the line of the National Transcontinental Railway, now part of the Canadian National, a little east of Cochrane. Eventually it joins the Moose River, very close to James Bay.

Until about 1907, the Abitibi region was exceedingly remote, visited only by small groups of Nishnabis and a few fur traders. In 1686, the Chevalier de Troyes passed through on his expedition to capture the Hudson's Bay Company posts on James Bay. He also built an outpost of his own at the mouth of the Duparquet River. Much later, the Hudson's Bay Company itself opened a depot near the east end of Lake Abitibi, but this was abandoned in favour of LaSarre after the National Transcontinental Railway came through.

The isolation of Abitibi came to an abrupt end early in 1907, when the crews of the Temiskaming and Northern Ontario Railway managed to lay steel as far as McDougall's Chute, which was then a collection of tarpaper shacks beside the Black River, about fourteen miles upstream from its confluence with the Abitibi River. The site took its original name from Bozeal (Billy) McDougall, a Cree trapper who had adopted the name of a Hudson's Bay Company employee and built a post on a hill near the falls (which are now submerged by the dam at Iroquois Falls). Located midway between Englehart and the future site of Cochrane, McDougall's Chute was well situated to become — for a time — the gateway to Abitibi. Prospectors were, as always, fanning out ahead of the railway, and rumours were spreading about gold and iron deposits in the area. Some mines were actually opened up, but the riches of the region were soon to be reckoned in spruce, balsam and poplar rather than in minerals. Hence McDougall's Chute grew rapidly, and by the spring of 1907, it could boast three restaurants and a store. A second store followed, then a hotel and a couple of sawmills, and within a year the population swelled to 500. By the summer of 1908, it became the temporary headquarters of the contractors engaged in building the National Transcontinental Railway, and in April 1908, the village received a post office, called Matheson, after the Provincial Treasurer of Ontario, whose ministry was paying for the Temiskaming and Northern Ontario Railway.

The builders of the National Transcontinental Railway had no intention of waiting for the Temiskaming and Northern Ontario to reach the route of their own line before staring to work — which meant that all their supplies and provisions had to be brought to Matheson and shipped down the Black River. This entailed the use of steam vessels and scows. These were also used to barge commodities down to the Driftwood River, from which point they could be hauled over a short road to Monteith for the Temiskaming and Northern Ontario Railway.

Little is known of these early Black River steamers beyond a few casual comments in some of the local newspapers. On May 3, 1907, the New Liskeard *Speaker* notes that a consortium known as McCrae, Chantler and McNeal was about to launch two steam tugs at McDougall's Chute as soon as the ice broke up. One was to ply to Iroquois Falls and the other from the Falls to "Abitibi" — which probably means from below the falls to the expected crossing point of the National Transcontinental Railway. Presumably, the boats were to assist the railway contractors, although we are told that they would also take prospectors and their supplies. Unfortunately, we are not told anything more, although in August another steamer is mentioned as running down the Frederickhouse River and Lake on a fourteen-mile route to within four miles of Wilson's Lake, where the Temiskaming and Northern Ontario Railway crews were grading a roadbed. In April 1908, we hear that the J.H. Reynolds Construction Company, an American firm engaged in building part of the National Transcontinental, was likewise planning to put a steamer on the Black River to ply to Iroquois Falls, where it had a depot, and a second on the lower part of the river to run to the railway crossing point. Within a matter of months, however, this firm went bankrupt, leaving a great many men unpaid and stranded in Matheson. Perhaps its boats — if it ever had any — went to the Walsh brothers of Matheson, who by August 1908 had three steamers and two motorboats in service, one plying to Iroquois Falls and Twin Falls, the second from Twin Falls to Couchiching Falls, and the third from Couchiching Falls to Lake Abitibi itself. This last boat was evidently intended to deliver provisions to the Low Bush River at the northwest side of the lake, right in the path of the National Transcontinental Railway. By the spring of 1909, the firm of Foley, Welch and Stewart was importing tons of supplies, including logs, both to Lowbush and the Abitibi River crossing. (Tote roads were used in the winter.) A new townsite, to be called Brower, was proposed at the crossing, but instead it was decided that the Temiskaming and Northern Ontario Railway would meet the National Transcontinental about eight miles west, at a fine site situated on a rolling ridge covered with spruce, birch and poplar, with three deep lakes of clean water close by. The new junction was speedily christened Cochrane after the Hon. Frank Cochrane, who was then Minister of Forests and Mines and a staunch backer of the Temiskaming and Northern Ontario Railway. It is tempting to conjecture that the survey party that toured the area travelled on the Black River steamboats.

Despite insects, wet weather, the occasional fire and the tyranny of distance, the rails reached Cochrane late in 1908, and by the summer of 1910, the National Transcontinental had been extended about 60 miles west of the junction and 40 miles east — as far as Lowbush. Cochrane already had a population of nearly 2,000 when the catastrophic Porcupine Fire swept through on July 11, 1911, destroying all but six of its buildings. A like fate befell Matheson on July 29, 1916, when the Matheson Fire, backed by gale-force winds, devastated a swath spreading over 60 miles, destroying several communities and claiming more than 200 lives. Both towns rebounded vigorously.

It may be that some of the Black River steamers were lost in the Matheson Fire, since there is a record of a steam tug called the *Ranger* being imported to the scene from the Great Lakes that same year. The *Ranger* may be identical to a vessel built at Deseronto in 1886 for the Rathbun Lumber Company. If so, she was 46.5 feet in length and registered eight tons. In 1908, she was sold to Thomas Walsh of Kenora — perhaps one of the Walsh brothers who imported three steamers to Matheson that same year. The *Ranger* was presumably a replacement boat; she is listed as late as 1920. In addition, the Stewart Company, which was engaged in scowing supplies to the new dam site at Twin Falls in 1916, built a tram railway to the water's edge at Matheson and (reputedly) imported one or two tugs of its own to assist the process.

The day of the pulp mills had arrived!

≈≈≈≈

It was on February 9, 1914, that the Abitibi Power and Paper Company (now Abitibi-Price Inc.) was officially incorporated by a syndicate headed by Frank H. Anson, although in fact it had actually commenced operations considerably earlier. The company's headquarters were in Montreal, but its operations are centred at Iroquois Falls, on the Abitibi River about nineteen miles downstream from Matheson, where — according to native traditions — an Iroquois war party came to grief while invading the North country during the 17th century.

As early as 1911, the government selected the spot for a townsite, and by that July the Temiskaming and Northern Ontario Railway had opened a station there. (The rails came later.) A rustic squatter town, known as Ansonville, at once sprang up, but the Abitibi Power and Paper Company speedily laid out a proper town, beginning with a large hotel, mainly as a means of attracting the highly qualified professional staff it would need to run the mills. Much later, Ansonville and Iroquois Falls were merged into one. The Abitibi mills were already under construction by 1913, and in November an office was opened at Matheson, along with the first camps.

The man in charge of those camps was O.D. Hennessy, who had earlier been a foreman for the Booth Lumber Company at Fort Coulange, before Mr. Anson — soon to be President of Abitibi — hired him to head the Woods Department of his new firm. It was an excellent choice. Along with a few others, Hennessy headed straight for Matheson, whence they took a gas boat down the river to the Falls. On the way, they stopped at a gravel pit at the mouth of the Shallow River. Suddenly some of the gravel began to slide down on top of a group of workmen. Three were caught in it, and one disappeared from sight. Hennessy and his brother dashed to the spot and started digging with their bare hands, even before the slide had stopped. Soon they cleared the man's head, then proceeded to dig him out. The workman ducked his head in the river to get the sand out of his eyes, ears and mouth, and calmly went back to work. After this little episode Hennessy, with characteristic energy, opened a camp at the Shallow River, and another at the mouth of the Black River. By 1914, the first pulpwood drives were on their way to Iroquois Falls.

By 1913, too, a dam was under construction at Couchiching Falls. Since only a winter road connected the falls with Matheson, all the supplies had to be brought to Lowbush on the National Transcontinental Railway and towed across the lake in scows. A large steam tug was brought in for the purpose. She was probably known as the *Abitibi* (or *Abbitibi*), given that a steamer of that name is reported to have sunk in the region in mid-October of 1913. (A week later she was hauled ashore.) Nothing else is known of her, but she was very likely the first steamboat on Lake Abitibi.

Although the outbreak of war in 1914 led to a chronic shortage of labour, Hennessy soon had several camps set up for extracting logs, around both Lake Abitibi and the Abitibi River system. By 1916, the operations had become more or less routine. Alligator tugs towed booms of pulpwood logs across the lakes to the Abitibi River, where the log drivers took over. Discovering the need for tugs to assist on the river, the company imported two steam vessels for towing and scowing provisions.

One of them was the *Donald Patrick Russell*, a conventional screw tug with an 8.16-hp compound engine. Registered at 4.66 tons, the "Donny Pat" was built at Toronto in 1917 and named for a relative of the owner. She was 40.5 feet in length and had a single deck and a round stern. In December 1917, she was sold to the Abitibi Power and Pulp Company, and presumably entered service the following year, plying mainly between Matheson and Twin Falls, using a scow capable of carrying enough freight to fill six railway cars. Four years afterwards, the firm built a pontoon dry dock at Twin Falls for overhauling its vessels. The *Donald Patrick Russell* was sometimes commanded by Captain Ted Guppy, later of Temagami, who had recently arrived from Haileybury.

Captain Guppy would later recall an incident involving the "Donny Pat" at Twin Falls, perhaps around 1919. He arrived one day to find Hugh Hennessy, the Superintendent of Logging (apparently a son of O.D. Hennessy, who was drowned in 1917), supervising a group of men who were wondering how to clear a huge jam of logs caught in an eddy below the dam. They obtained permission from the hydro authorities to open the sluices. This swept away some of the logs, but a great many still remained. Guppy realized that the "Donny Pat" could remove the rest of the logs more easily than the river drivers, and Hennessy gave him permission to try it. The boat crew attached one end of a boom to an iron bolt drilled into the rocks on shore and the other to the towpost of the tug. As the boom curled around the log jam, the steamer, aided by the current, began pulling forward; the force sometimes caused the water to gush over the stern, but she kept right on. Finally, about six hours later, all the logs were gone. As Captain Guppy remarked afterwards, "It would have taken fifty men a week to do the same!"

Above Twin Falls, the company installed a second steam tug called the *L'Orignal Bay*. Registered at 15.66 tons, this vessel was a sidewheeler, built at L'Orignal, near Hawkesbury, Ontario, in 1912. With a length of 54 feet and a vertical high-pressure engine giving her speeds of ten knots, the *L'Orignal Bay* was considerably larger than the *Donald Patrick Russell*, and was assigned the same kind of duties, plying up to Couchiching Falls. The year of her arrival is not certain, but was probably around 1918. In the winter of 1922–23, the Abitibi Power and Pulp Company spent $3,331.99 overhauling the vessel.

Donald Patrick Russell and the *L'Orignal Bay* served on the Abitibi River for about a decade. The *L'Orignal Bay* last received maintenance in 1927, and the "Donny Pat" in 1928, but in the spring of 1931 they were both listed as "out of service," with the comment that the *Donald Patrick Russell* was now worthless. They must have been dismantled soon afterwards. New tugs, such as the *F.H. Anson*, an 83-foot diesel of 16.14 tons built in 1922, and the *L.R. Wilson*, another diesel of 9.69 tons and named after the vice-president of the company, carried on for many years, but after 1928, steamers disappeared from the Abitibi River.

STEAMBOATING ON LAKE ABITIBI: (CIRCA 1913–1947)

On Lake Abitibi itself there were once several steamboats, but with very few exceptions they were all alligators or warping tugs owned by the Abitibi Power and Pulp Company. This is hardly surprising, given that log towing was the only business on the lake.

There were a few independents. The tug *Abitibi* mentioned in 1913 is not listed among the company's boats, and was evidently imported by the contractors building the Couchiching dam. Around 1917, François Gallichan was using a steam tug to tow logs on the Duparquet and Whitefish Rivers to his sawmill at LaSarre; he may have done the same for some of the other mills in the area. The boat was still operating in 1928.

The Abitibi Power and Paper Company's first alligator was the *Mistango*, which was originally built by Captain John A. Clark of Sturgeon Falls in 1907, to replace an earlier boat of the same name. She spent about seven years on Lake Nipissing before she was shipped north and rebuilt at Lowbush in 1915. With a fir hull 66.8 feet in length and a register tonnage of 39.37, the *Mistango* was an unusually large craft. Her paddlewheels, each fitted with ten buckets, were powered by two Doty high-pressure engines, giving her speeds of nine miles per hour. She was equipped with a 5,000-foot steel galvanized wire cable and a seven-foot cross-arm anchor — to say nothing of axes, lanterns, oars, pike poles, peaveys, a siphon, a generator, oil cans, grease, pails, a life raft, hoses, extinguishers, mattresses and pillows for the crew, dishware, cooking supplies, hammers, nails, tools, wrenches and pointers. Her total value was estimated at $12,750.

The *Mistango* entered service with a double crew of nine hands, working in twelve-hour shifts. Her first master was Captain James Ladouceur, who had just arrived from Haileybury, bringing Ted Guppy with him. The crews, however, were mostly French Canadians, and they teased Captain Ladouceur endlessly for his inability to speak French, despite his name. Ladouceur soon got fed up and left after his first season, while Ted Guppy was groomed to succeed him. By 1916, he had his own tug certificate, and spent the next eight seasons around Lake Abitibi. Objecting to the depressing grey sidewalls of the alligators, Captain Guppy soon got permission to repaint them white.

The pulp and paper industry flourished despite the manpower shortage during the war years, and in 1917 the Abitibi Power and Pulp Company brought in two West and Peachey alligators from Simcoe. One of them, the *Low Bush*, was a very large model, some 69.6 feet in length and listed at 64.99 tons. She had two horizontal Doty engines, and had to be imported in sections and assembled at Lowbush. In 1922, she was rebuilt at La Reine, Quebec, at a cost of $4,094.64. The second tug was a smaller, second-hand model called the *J.J. McCarthy*,

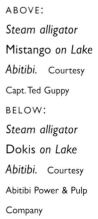

ABOVE:

Steam alligator
Mistango *on Lake
Abitibi.*   Courtesy
Capt. Ted Guppy

BELOW:

Steam alligator
Dokis *on Lake
Abitibi.*   Courtesy
Abitibi Power & Pulp
Company

built in 1911. The *J.J. McCarthy* was 39.1 feet in length, registered 9.73 tons, and had a 20-hp vertical non-condensing engine. She was good for six knots when not under tow and sometimes took loggers out to the camps. Also in 1917, Captain Guppy arranged to buy the little steamer *Scotchman*, which had previously been used as a fishing tug on Lake Temiskaming, and to bring her to Lowbush by rail. After a thorough refit at Macamic, the sturdy little craft, now thirteen years old, became the superintendent's launch and a provision boat for the tugs.

After the First World War, as men began returning home, the Abitibi Power and Pulp Company rapidly geared up for expansion. In the spring of 1920, it announced that it planned to increase its production of newsprint from about 90,000 tons a year to 145,000 tons, valued at about $13, 500,000, of which about 80 percent was destined for American markets. The following year, it added two new giant papermaking machines to its expanded plant at Iroquois Falls, making it one of the largest in the world. In April 1922, it set a new production record of 500.57 tons in a single day, despite two machine shutdowns. In 1925, finding its power supply inadequate, the company arranged to buy the Island Rapids power plant from the Hollinger Consolidated Gold Mines and to add two extra generators. Meanwhile, the camps proliferated around Lake Abitibi, and in October 1923 the firm announced that it would cut 150,000 cords of pulpwood in three camps alone, and purchase 50,000 cords more from the local settlers. Some of this arrived on railway flatcars, but during the navigation season most of it was delivered by tugs.

The towing fleet was also expanding. In 1920, the company obtained four more alligators, some of which were used for assembling booms and bagging logs and others for winching them. One was the *Gooding*, which (like the *Mistango*) was built by the Clarks at Sturgeon Falls, in 1904. The *Gooding* was apparently rebuilt and enlarged from 29 to 38 feet in length, and re-registered at 13.40 tons. She had a fifteen-hp vertical high-pressure engine, good for speeds of four knots, but she was not used very long, and was stricken from the register in 1926.

More successful was the *Dokis*, which was built at Lowbush at a cost of $21,350. Named after a local river (and indirectly after the mixed-ancestry community from the French River area, whose leader acquired the nickname from his attempts to pronounce the word "ducks" in English), the *Dokis* had a 45-hp horizontal high-pressure Doty engine and an Inglis boiler that burned 1.04 cords an hour. Her hull was 75.28 feet in length at the waterline by 16.1 feet in beam and she drew 5.5 feet of water. She had a 7/8-inch 4,000-foot plow steel cable, and was reckoned to cost $3.17 per hour to operate, not counting summer repairs. She was expected to last about 21 years, but in fact was still in existence in 1947. This made her the last surviving Abitibi steam tug. In 1920, the company also bought two more West and Peachey alligators, the *Circle* and the *Teddy Bear*. Both vessels were 41.5 feet in length, registered 12.62 tons, and cost $10,500 apiece. They both had vertical high-pressure 20-hp engines, identical to that of the *J.J. McCarthy*. As it happened, the four new tugs were the last steam vessels acquired by the Abitibi Power and Pulp Company. All of the later boats were diesels.

Work in the camps and on the tugs was monotonously predictable, unless there happened to be an accident. Most of the pulpwood, mainly spruce and balsam, was cut during the winter, and hauled to the lakes and rivers by horse teams. The wood was stored on the ice or in the water, which was cheaper than land storage, and also reduced the risk of fires. The boats would usually leave winter quarters at Couchiching Falls around May 10th, although they might occasionally have to wait at the river source for a few days if the ice hadn't broken up. They would then gather up vast heaps of logs stockpiled sometimes to a height of fifteen feet, and not infrequently they would end up towing large chunks of ice as well, if they remained attached to the logs.

As a rule the smaller tugs were used to boom the logs, while the larger ones winched them across the lake. The boom timbers were made of British Columbia fir logs 36 inches in diameter. (Smaller spool booms were tried, but they didn't work. Being hollow, they floated high and bobbed too much, allowing logs to escape.) Usually, three to five bands were secured across the larger tows to hold them in position, and commonly the big alligators would push on one side of the booms, while the smaller ones pushed on the other, squeezing the tows until the crews could install the bands. Then the big tugs winched the tows over to the Abitibi River (which might take a week or more), while the smaller ones headed for the adjacent lakes to shepherd out additional logs. Very commonly the *Circle* and the *Teddy Bear* would head up to LaSarre or Lake Duparquet on such missions.

The large alligators plied with a double crew, usually consisting of a captain, a mate, two engineers, two deckhands and a cook, operating on double shifts. (In later years, thanks to union pressure, three shifts were instituted.) Much of the towing was done at night, when the winds were low. The standard procedure was to run the alligator ahead of the tow at full speed for a given number of minutes using a stopwatch, then let go the anchor. Every so often, a tug might lose its anchor under roots or rocks on the lake bottom, or the anchor might sink up to sixteen inches into the clay and snap off around the eye. Also, an anchor chain might break if it were twisted. Originally, it cost $2,000 to replace an anchor, until a company employee named Gordon McCharles demonstrated that he could fabricate new ones for only $700 to $800, starting with cardboard cutouts. Several types of chain were tried, but eventually three-quarter plate chain proved the most satisfactory. Care also had to be taken when hoisting the anchors, lest the flukes tear a hole through the hulls.

Winching the booms along was slow but routine work, except when rounding a point or squeezing through the Narrows between Upper and Lower Lake Abitibi, where the current could flow in either direction. If a crosswind was blowing, it might be necessary to anchor and roll the booms with the logs around the headlands, using outboard motorboats and pointers (commonly called "kickers"). Endless problems resulted whenever a tow caught on a rock. As for storms, the captains would judge the weather symptoms, and if a blow set in they would usually anchor in the lee of an island and wait for it to pass. After all, a gale could tow an alligator! In extreme cases, the crews would abandon the tow; better that than risk losing the boats, which could easily be crushed by the logs. As a rule, sweeps were necessary on the lake every two to four years to gather up stray logs, many of which were lost amid the marshes close to shore.

To assure accountability, the company conducted time studies of all its operations. By way of examples, it reckoned that the *Dokis* lost 237½ hours during the 1929 season. Of this, 136 were blamed on the weather, 94 more were spent on repairs, and the last seven resulted from a grounded tow. In 1930, the big alligator lost 191 hours on account of weather and 154¾ on repairs. She did better in 1931, losing only 60¼ hours to the weather and 10¼ more for repairs, plus a delay of four and a half hours when she temporarily lost her anchor. Repairs to the *Dokis* cost $21,811.34 between 1921 and 1938, the record year being 1924, when the bills totalled $4,392.76. On the positive side, to give one example, the big craft was busy for 2,403¾ hours in 1930 between May 16th and October 31st. Her duties included loading and scowing equipment, fuelling, log sweeping, putting a tank on a fuel-oil scow and, of course, towing. One tow involved moving 16,735 cords from the Whitefish reserve to the Abitibi River, a distance of 51.22 miles, accomplished over eleven days in May. Five other assignments that year brought in another 23,286 cords, for a total of 40,021.

Company records provide considerable detail about the *Dokis's* activities in 1931. We find that she conducted eight tows that season, and sometimes collected tows from other tugs. On one tow right across Lake Abitibi, she managed to lose 160 cords out of 8,000. Sometimes she helped to effect repairs to her sister tugs. In July, the diesel alligator *H.D. Hennessy*, which joined the fleet in 1927, had a breakdown and had to abandon tow No. 6 at Gaulthier's Island. The *Dokis* was dispatched to pick it up on July 30th. She arrived on August 4th, assumed the tow at 7:00 P.M., and also collected an additional 1,000 cords (for a total of 6,468) from the Dagenais reserve. By 10:00 A.M. on August 12th, she reached a spot called Cable Crossing. Then the *Dokis* herself broke down, and had to return the tow to the *H.D. Hennessy*. A good 274½ hours were spent on that job.

Of course, the steam alligators burned wood as fuel, which meant that they always had to take along a scow loaded with neatly piled fuel wood. Birch was preferred, because it holds up well in fires. Men were sent to cut the birch into four-foot pieces, usually in the autumn, so that it could dry out over the winter. Entire tug crews — even the cooks — were required to help wood up the scows at the depots; there was always much grumbling, but it took far less time that way. Large wheelbarrows and chutes made of planks and tripod trusses were used to slide the cordwood into the scows. In 1930, it cost $1,829.19 to fuel the *Dokis*. The advent of oil-burning boats of course eliminated these chores and the need for wood scows, which were always a nuisance and were also prone to getting crushed between a tug and her tow.

The alligators were extremely drab and spartan in their fittings and had no heat except for the stoves and boilers. In later years, they were supplied with electric lights and refrigerators, although the *Dokis* never had one. The cooks always left something ready to eat, even when they were off duty, and there was always coffee on the stove, kept hot by the engineers. Toilets (as on the *Dokis*) were outside at first, next to the paddlewheels, with a bar across the inside to serve as a handrail. It is said that a deckhand on the *Dokis* managed to fall past the rail into the wheels one night during the 1930s, and that was the last time he was seen alive.

Work on the tugs was sometimes cold, often arduous, usually monotonous. Captain Ted Guppy was popular with his crews because he would sometimes allow his men to go ashore for a baseball game at LaSarre if conditions allowed. Nonetheless, the captains frequently had trouble with drunken crews, and for that reason the men were never allowed ashore at Twin Falls for more than five or six hours at a time — which gave them little chance to get into mischief at Iroquois Falls, unless they could find a horse. (At one time Ansonville, which was not directly under company control, had five drugstores and as many as twenty bootleggers!) The Abitibi railwaymen were worse than the boat crews, in that most of them were discards from other lines, and on weekends it was the normal thing for the logging locomotives to leave their trains and chug away into town, with the crews clinging to the engines like fleas. One man, a steam crane operator, once returned with 36 pints inside him!

Over the years the marine division of the Abitibi Power and Pulp Company used at least 43 boats, including barges, sailing scows, gas motor launches, winching boats, diesel tugs such as the *F.H. Anson* and the *L.R. Wilson*, and at least seven diesel alligators, including the *John Wolstenholme* (1923), the *H.D. Hennessy* (1927), the *Forks, Driftwood* and *Whitefish* (1937), and the *Duparquet* (1940). Almost all of these vessels had steel hulls, burned oil, and could be crewed by just six men forming double shifts. Predictably, they would be scattered around on many lakes and rivers: thus in 1931, the *Dokis* and the *Kiash* were listed as based at La Reine, the *Circle* at the Whitefish reserve, the *John Wolstenholme* at Macamic Lake, the *Chazel* at Upper Whitefish, Quebec, the *Ghost* at the Dagenais River, and two alligators at Duparquet Lake, along with scows, punts, pointers and canoes.

Very gradually, the steamers in the fleet began to disappear. The *Low Bush* received massive overhauls in 1924 and 1925, then disappears from the record. About that time, the little *Scotchman* received her last maintenance work. In 1927, she was pronounced worthless, and the superintendent transferred to the *Aylen*, a new gas winching boat lately launched at Lowbush. The *Mistango* lasted until 1927, when her winching machinery was installed in the *H.D. Hennessy*. The *J.J. McCarthy* is described as out of service in 1931. The *Circle* ran until 1937, when her hull was condemned. Neither she nor the *Teddy Bear* received any maintenance after 1938. Only the plodding old *Dokis* remained in service into the 1940s, perhaps reprieved by the war, when new boats and machinery were hard to get. She received a massive refit in 1943, when her side planking was rebuilt, and is still mentioned as late as 1947, but after that nothing more is heard of her. She was the last steamboat in the Abitibi region.

The diesels and motorboats carried on for nearly three more decades, but as early as 1965, the last company boats were sold off from the Black River. It had long been realized that logs could be sent down the river without tugs, and even that they could be fed through the dam sluices at Twin Falls en masse without undermining the powerhouse. This discovery was made accidentally one time during the early 1940s, when the boom above Twin Falls broke open, allowing the logs to go off like a gun. They upended in the current and shot over the falls like a great stampede of water buffalo, leaving a boom of sixteen log timbers dangling part way through the sluices. Afterwards, the cook on one of the tugs freed the boom at great risk to his life, using a canoe, tied to the shore by ropes, to approach the boom and cut the link. The company, finding that the logs had not been smashed up as feared, afterwards let them go through the chutes regularly instead of feeding them through one at a time. Downriver, only pointers were required, plus a tail boom to prevent the wind from blowing the logs the wrong way.

By about 1973, new regulations governing the length of trees and logs (intended to reduce waste) made log towing impractical, and besides that, most parts of Lake Abitibi had been made accessible by roads, financed partly by the government. This meant that trucks could now take over the transport of logs, a process known as "hotlogging." By 1975, the Abitibi Power and Pulp Company's entire marine branch had been shut down. Only two tugs still remained: the *Clark B. Davis* (built in 1951) and the *T. Gibbens* (1947), both named after officials in the Woods Division. Both are flat-bottomed steel vessels, about 85 feet in length, and built originally in sections at Owen Sound. They were both laid up in perfect condition at Twin Falls in 1974, and languished there for many years, simply because it seemed impossible to move them to any other waterway.

In 1985, however, a former member of the merchant marine, Eddie O'Donnell, proved the experts wrong. In 1979, he purchased the two tugs, now much vandalized, and (after endless negotiations with the authorities and various contractors) he succeeded — with the help of eight local men and two boats — in hauling the big towboats past the dam and power lines at Twin Falls, relaunching them in the river below, and towing them to Matheson. The "impossible" feat took thirteen days, starting on June 14th. The two tugs have remained on the Black River ever since, and there are hopes of turning them into restaurants — although it would be fitting, one feels, to see at least one of them put back into service as an excursion ship. At least the potential is there. After 60 years, commercial navigation had come to an end on Lake Abitibi.

PULPWOOD TOWING ON LAKE TEMISKAMING: (1903–1979)

Fittingly, the last portion of the steamboat saga brings us back to Lake Temiskaming and the watershed of the Rivière des Quinze, which with its tributaries, extends over 200 miles into the heart of western Quebec.

Pulpwood logs have been towed on Lake Temiskaming since the early 1900s. At first, this was just a side venture for the lumber companies, but by 1914, the New Liskeard *Speaker* noted that, while the Ottawa River was as full of logs as ever, most of them were now pulpwood; the big square timber rafts were a thing of the past. At first, the logs were destined for the mills at Hawkesbury, on the lower Ottawa River, or for the United States, but by 1917, plans were afoot to build another paper mill closer to the supply.

The mill was built by the Riordon Pulp and Paper Company, an English firm which established its offices at Montreal during the war. The company acquired the Hawkesbury mill, and by stages it bought up several existing lumber companies, including the Kipewa Company, W.C. Edwards & Co., and Gilmour & Co., plus a controlling interest in the Ticonderoga Pulp and Paper Company. It also looked at several possible sites for a new sulphite mill. Mattawa was considered, but apparently the company was annoyed by the smug demeanour of the local council and nothing came of it. Haileybury submitted a bid — in vain, because the operation required a limitless supply of fresh clear water. North Temiskaming, or Tête-du-Lac, was also considered, but it had no railway. Finally, in 1917, the company chose South Témiscaming at the foot of the lake, and proceeded to buy the entire site except for the railway lands. Included were all the remaining holdings of the Lumsden Lumber Company, the power dam and Lumsden's Mills itself. The Bellevue Hotel, which Alex Lumsden had established about seventeen years earlier, now became a boarding house for the Riordon staff. The modest homes of the fifteen-odd families living at Témiscaming were acquired and demolished, and soon the company boiler house was erected over the site of the former church. The company viewed the local residents as mere squatters, but eventually it was required to pay them compensation.

The firm decided to wait until the end of the war before building its plant, which would be one of the most modern in the world, but already it was planning a new model town overlooking the lake — the first of its kind in Canada after Iroquois Falls. (This was, of course, a necessity to attract qualified staff and workmen out to a wilderness setting.) The new town was incorporated in February 1920 under the name of Kipawa, but within a year this was changed to Témiscaming. Expert planners were brought in to lay out the streets, making the most of the gently sloping topography, while spaces were allotted for parks, churches and a town square. By 1920, many fine residences were going up, and by 1922 about 1,500 people had moved in, of whom about a third worked for the company. The plant, of course, was built below the town, near the dams at the foot of the lake. As of December 1919, it was in operation, turning out 100, then 175, then 250 tons of pulp daily, mainly for bond paper — unlike Iroquois Falls, which produced newsprint. To supervise construction, the firm engaged Carl B. Thorne, a Scandinavian engineer experienced in paper production. Altogether, the company spent over a million dollars on its new plant. It also acquired some 2,538 square miles of timber limits north and east of Témiscaming.

The Riordon Pulp and Paper Company had good reason to be proud of its achievements, but its rule was despotic. It owned the entire town of Témiscaming, and it never allowed anyone to forget it. No one was permitted to buy his residence, and if an employee died, retired or was fired, his family was given just 30 days to get out, even in wintertime. The company wanted no government interference, no competition and no unions. It had its own police, controlled the local council, and speedily sent dissidents packing. By 1923, some residents were getting fed up and leaving, while others threatened not to pay the three percent rental tax demanded by the company.

But the Riordon Pulp and Paper Company soon had much worse troubles. A brief depression following the war led to a slump in orders, and in October 1921, it had to shut down the mill. Unable to meet its payments, it tried to reorganize, but soon went bankrupt. Some of its creditors formed a new board of management, and within a year the plant was operating again, still under the Riordon name, but in 1925 the Témiscaming and Hawkesbury mills were sold to the Canadian International Paper Company, which was in fact controlled by American interests. (It has even been alleged that Riordon was a mere front for Canadian International Paper all along, and that the bankruptcy was deliberately engineered to allow the American firm to take control.) The Canadian International Paper Company continued to operate the Témiscaming plant until 1972, while the town remained a company town until 1956.

Under the Canadian International Paper Company, production at Témiscaming swelled to 330 tons daily by 1929, and reached 360 tons in 1937, despite the Depression. To sustain all this, the firm bought up limits and opened camps over a vast portion of Quebec, including the Lake Kipawa basin and the Rivière des Quinze watershed, which extended eastward as far as the Parc de la Vérendrye, north of Quebec City. To move the logs, the company used a number of diesel tugs on the des Quinze system, and a steamer on Lake Temiskaming.

This vessel was the *Wilda* (pronounced "Willda"), a fine, steel-hulled screw tug, built at Toronto by the John Inglis Company in 1926. Powered by a second-hand fore-and-aft compound engine and a Scotch marine boiler, the *Wilda* was 71.9 feet in length and registered 44.79 tons. She had a single deck, an elliptical stern and a lapstrake hull. Capable of speeds of twelve miles per hour, the *Wilda* was built to replace the old *Emma Mac*, the last of the Lumsden tugs, which had been sold to the Riordon Pulp and Paper Company around 1918. Initially, it was intended to transfer her name to the new boat, but nobody liked the idea, and company employees were invited to put their suggestions into a hat. The winning proposal came from W.H. Cowper of the Woods Department, who had a daughter named Wilda.

ABOVE:

View of Témiscaming, Quebec, from the Ontario shore. Dominating the scene is the Riordon Pulp & Paper Company mill. The old chapel is still standing.   Courtesy Mr. Gilles Amesse, PH12-4-1

BELOW:

Steam tug Wilda.   Courtesy Mr. Gilles Amesse

Usually commanded by Captain Lornie Gray of Mattawa (previously Master of the *Emma Mac*), the *Wilda* entered service in 1926. Her usual duties were to collect and reboom tows at Opimica Narrows and bring them down to Témiscaming. Sometimes she also swept up stray logs or delivered supplies. The workload proved so heavy that the company ordered a second tug, which was likewise built by the John Inglis Company at Collingwood in 1927. This tug, christened the *T.E. Draper*, after the superintendent of the Kipawa Woods Division, was similar to the *Wilda*, but smaller, with a length of 61 feet and a beam of 19. She, too, was built of steel, and was considered one of the company's most powerful tugs. The *T.E. Draper* was probably the last steam vessel to appear on Lake Temiskaming, but her stay there was brief. After assisting the *Wilda* for two seasons, she was cut into sections and taken to Laverlochère on Canadian Pacific Railway flatcars and thence by horse teams to Riordon Depot at Gillies Bay on Lac des Quinze. There she was riveted back together and relaunched in 1929.

The *T.E. Draper* served on Lac des Quinze for a remarkable 48 years, endlessly running up to the Grassy Narrows bridge and causeway near Moffet to collect log booms and deliver them to Angliers, which served as Canadian International Paper's base of operations in the area. Each tow usually consisted of three or four booms, each containing about 2,700 cords or 100,000 logs. Not surprisingly, a single run took anywhere from 24 to 36 hours, depending on the weather. Below Angliers the logs were fed downstream to North Temiskaming, where another tug took over. Obviously, the company found this cheaper than shipping them down to Témiscaming by rail. In 1954, the *T.E. Draper* was dieselized and became an oil burner; this allowed her crew to be reduced from seven to five. As on Lake Abitibi, the men worked six-hour shifts and lived aboard a large houseboat known as a *chaland*, towed by the tug.

As the Canadian International Paper Company's operations expanded, it ordered yet another tug from the Inglis firm. This was the *J.A.H. Henderson*, a 49-foot diesel that arrived from Collingwood in one piece in 1930. Named after the company's chief engineer, the *J.A.H. Henderson* was put to work on Lac Simard (Lake Expanse), above Lac des Quinze. She did her towing alligator style, using a 700-lb. anchor. Occasionally, if the going became too difficult, the *T.E. Draper* might go to her assistance, passing under the Grassy Narrows bridge by removing her steel mast. The *J.A.H. Henderson* served until about 1950, when she was replaced by a flat-bottomed 53-foot tug called *L'Expense*, which in turn plied until about 1976, when trucks took over the hauling of pulpwood.[5]

On Lake Temiskaming, meanwhile, the Canadian International Paper Company found it convenient to rely on another firm to do most of its towing. This was the Upper Ottawa Improvement Company, which was almost synonymous with log towing on the river for about 90 years.

The Upper Ottawa Improvement Company — commonly called the I.C.O. or Improvement Company of the Ottawa — was chartered under Dominion law on June 4, 1870, for the sole purpose of transporting logs down the river. The "improvements" in question were to consist of dams, piers and timber slides to facilitate the process. The company, in fact, was a conglomerate of almost all the Ottawa River lumber companies, which had discovered that competitive towing was not working well. Again and again, rival gangs of river drivers got in one another's way, and this often led to violence. Consequently, in 1868, most of the lumber barons decided to co-operate by building and maintaining facilities on the river. The Upper Ottawa Improvement Company's charter also allowed it to take over existing structures built by the Department of Public Works. At times, J.F. Booth, J.A. Gillies and C.J. Booth all acted as officers of the company.

At first the Upper Ottawa Improvement Company's operations were confined to those portions of the river between Des Joachims, near Mattawa, and the Chaudière Rapids at Ottawa, but on May 22, 1888, its mandate was extended to include the length of Lake Temiskaming. At the same time, it was given the right to operate its own towboats. The company had already bought out the fleet and assets of the Union Forwarding and Railway

5   On Lake Kipawa, the Canadian International Paper Company also used the alligator *Metabachuan*, which it inherited from the Shepard and Morse Lumber Company.

LEFT:

Steam tug Alexandra, *of the*
Upper Ottawa Improvement
Company.   Courtesy National
Archives of Canada, C 54553
RIGHT:
Steam alligator Matabichouan,
on Lake Kipawa.   Courtesy T.E.
Draper Museum, Angliers

Company in 1886, and within just three more years it also took over all the other independent towing companies on the Ottawa River. We have already noted how it acquired most of the Lumsden tugs in 1903, along with Opemicon Depot. By that time, the Upper Ottawa Improvement Company was operating tugs all the way from North Temiskaming to Ottawa, including such famous vessels as the *Alexander Fraser* (320 tons gross) and the *Albert* (169.76 tons) on Lac Deschênes between Quyon and Aylmer, Quebec; the *G.B. Greene* (255 tons gross) on Chats Lake around Arnprior; the *C.B. Powell* (272 tons) on Lower Lake Allumette below Pembroke; and the steamer *Pembroke* itself (194 tons) on Upper Allumette Lake. All of these tugs were large, mostly double-decked, and sidewheelers, very similar to some of the boats the company was soon to build on Lake Temiskaming.

One of them was the *Alexandra*, long considered the company's "queen ship" in Northern Ontario. Built at Témiscaming in 1903, the "Alex" was a very impressive vessel. With a length of 136 feet and a beam of 26.4, she was actually the largest steamer ever to ply on Lake Temiskaming, although her register tonnage — originally estimated at 198.30 — was somewhat less than that of the two big passenger ships, the *Meteor* and the *Temiskaming*. Nonetheless, when the *Alexandra* was remodelled in 1922, her new tonnage was reckoned at 249.35. She had one full deck, a round stern, and a three-quarter upper deck that left the bow open; three large water tanks were mounted there for the boilers. She was also the first steamer on the lake to have a steel hull, an enormous advantage for a tug. (Her upper works were built of wood.) She was originally a sidewheeler, powered by a fore-and-aft compound Bertram engine and two locomotive-type coal-fired steel boilers, giving her a net horsepower of 84.16 — sufficient to tow up to four booms containing perhaps 250,000 pulpwood logs at a time. Her main handicap was her draft, which came to eight feet and effectively prevented her from operating north of the snyes off Chief Island, near Haileybury. She also required a crew of thirteen, including a captain, a mate, two engineers, two deckhands, two logmen (who were responsible for the booms and the lights), a cook and four firemen, working six-hour shifts. In later years, an extra mate and engineer were added.

The *Alexandra* was provided with a running mate, likewise built at Témiscaming in 1903. This vessel, the *Lady Minto*, was very similar, but a little smaller, with a length of 138 feet and a tonnage reckoned at 254 in 1920. Like the *Alexandra*, the *Lady Minto* was originally a sidewheeler, with a single deck and a steel hull. Unlike that of her sister, her machinery is said to have come from the old Lumsden steamer *Argo*, which had been dismantled the previous fall. It is also reported that the *Lady Minto* could do about fifteen knots when not under tow, and that it was not unusual for her to be bunkered with 90 tons of coal. Even so, she was known to run short. Having a smaller boiler than the *Alexandra*, she required only three firemen, but being less powerful, she could handle just three tows at a time. Nonetheless, that still represents about 200,000 logs.

The *Lady Minto* and the *Alexandra* both entered service in 1903. Their sole duties were to collect tows from the smaller tugs and alligators at Chief Island, take them down to Opimica Narrows, and to bring back the boom timbers for the next tow — along with the occasional scowload of fresh coal. They never ran down to South Témiscaming except to refuel. As for the logs, either the current would convey them the rest of the way, or a small tug would take over.

These other tugs included the *Sampson*, a 41-foot West and Peachey alligator built in 1893, and reputedly used on Lake Temiskaming after 1903, and the *Mink* and *Beaver* (II), both obtained from the Lumsden Company. The *Beaver*, however, lasted only until September of 1906, when she was accidentally destroyed by fire at Témiscaming, while the *Sampson* was stricken from the register in 1912. The *Mink* seems to have left the region for the lower Ottawa River by the 1920s. The Upper Ottawa Improvement Company acquired yet another alligator, called the *Muskrat* (19 tons), which had been built at Simcoe in 1908 to serve on Lake Kipawa. It was probably only in 1919 that the company bought her for service at the lower end of the lake. She was then rebuilt at Témiscaming to a length of 48 feet and her tonnage reduced to a mere 10.09. The *Muskrat* was still running in 1928, and perhaps as late as the 1940s, but finally she was dismantled and left to fall apart at the Depot. She was probably the last wooden alligator to be used on Lake Temiskaming.

The Upper Ottawa Improvement Company showed a strong preference for steel-hulled boats, and in 1912 it engaged Collingwood Shipyards to build such a vessel at Témiscaming. This was the *Wabis*, a double-decked scowlike craft that may have been intended as a replacement for the *Sampson*. The *Wabis* was 68.3 feet in length by 23.1 in beam, and registered 38.07 tons. She started out as a sidewheeler with a brand-new 33.3-hp upright West and Peachey engine. Later she would become a screw steamer. Having a draft of only five feet, she could easily pass the snyes off Chief Island, and was usually used on the north end of Lake Temiskaming. Her first master was a Captain King, probably the same individual who had lately run boats on the des Quinze River during the Rouyn gold rush. Her later skippers included Captain Bourgeois, William Bolsen, Émile Polson, and John ("Jack") Cobb of Haileybury.

As a general rule, the *Wabis* was used to "bag" the logs from the des Quinze River at the boom camp about two miles below North Temiskaming — a spot often called the Gap — and winch them five miles to Chief Island, where each tow, consisting of about 60,000 logs, would be added to the big spool booms at the island. The spool booms consisted of about 100 to 125 "sticks" of square timber, all of which had four flat timbers of British Columbia fir bolted onto them to keep the logs from escaping. By the time three or four such tows had been delivered, one of the two big tugs — the *Alexandra* or the *Lady Minto* — would arrive to take charge, and also to deliver a fresh set of spool booms. The *Wabis* was also used to tow large covered barges or *chalands*, which served as floating homes for the sweep gangs, the men who had the unenviable job of collecting stray logs. The sweep gangs usually consisted of 65 men who lived aboard a pair of big *chalands* known as *dortoirs*, each 55 feet by 12 and housing 32 men apiece, in two-tier double bunks. A stove at the rear was provided to heat up water and (hopefully) to dry the men's clothes, since the work involved a lot of sloshing around in shallow bays full of sawdust and muskeg, and rubber boots were unknown in the early days. (Very often clothes would not be dry by the following morning, and the men would have to wear them wet.) They used pointers and peaveys (pike poles) to gather the logs, which then had to be boomed. If they were lucky, they might have an alligator to help out, but if not, they had to winch their logs along by hand, using a windlass mounted on a raft known as a "kedge crib." (A rowboat was sent ahead with a 150-lb. anchor attached to an 800-foot length of rope. This was dropped and the boat then brought the line back to the tow.) It was hard, rugged work, and often cold and wet as well, but the gangs were well fed. Meals were served aboard another scow, known as a *cuisine*, which served as a floating mess hall.

At Chief Island, one or two alligators would arrange the tows, now containing up to 250,000 logs, for the *Alexandra* or the *Lady Minto*. Both of these used 1,500-foot cables, and the booms might be a mile in length. They also had to be kept fairly narrow, so as to get past Opimica Narrows and allow the passenger ships like the *Meteor* to pass. It usually took anywhere from 80 to 120 hours for the *Alexandra* or the *Lady Minto* to drag the booms down to the Narrows, depending on the winds and the currents. Not infrequently, they might anchor the tows and take shelter at Haileybury or some other spot in the event of bad weather. (After the Riordon mill was established, the booms were usually taken in tow below the Narrows by the *Emma Mac*, and afterwards by the *Wilda*.) The two big tugs also had to take scowloads of coal — up to 70 tons at a time — for delivery to the Upper Ottawa Improvement Company depots at the Gap and the Devil's Snye near the mouth of the Blanche River, where docks were provided. In later years, the "Red Scow" — once the steamer *C.J. Booth* — was used for this purpose.

To supply the boom camps and the sweep gangs with food, mail and provisions, in 1904 the company engaged the Polson Iron Works to build a little workboat called the *Alert*. With a round stern and a steel hull, the *Alert* was 68.3 feet in length and registered 26.37 tons. She had a ten-hp compound Bertram engine that gave her speeds of at least eleven miles per hour,

ABOVE:

Steamer Alexandra *(first version), with boilers on her deck.*

BELOW:

Steam tug Lady Minto *(first version).*

and she was launched at Témiscaming in the spring. Sometimes she scowed coal and other bulk cargoes, at other times she might help the *Wabis* tow the big *chalands* for the sweep gangs. Frequently she would also ferry men to and from the camps and the scows. Only on rare occasions did she assume any tows. In August 1907, she was credited with rescuing two men whose canoe had been swamped off New Liskeard. For many years, she was commanded by Captain Ralph Tait of Mattawa, and sometimes Captain Ernie Gray, brother of Captain Lornie Gray of the *Lady Minto*. The *Alert* plied Lake Temiskaming for 47 seasons, under steam to the last.

Apparently the Upper Ottawa Improvement Company acquired no new boats on the Temiskaming run until the 1920s. In 1923, however, it purchased the steamer *Queen of Temagami*, once part of Daniel O'Connor's fleet on Lake Temagami, and brought her back from Lake Nipissing to serve as a provision boat, along with the *Alert*. The *Queen of Temagami* was much more commodious than the *Alert*, and was probably used to transport large parties of men and supplies without recourse to scows. She apparently remained in gradually diminishing service until the 1940s, but in 1948 — having been beached several years earlier — she was scrapped at Opemicon by order of the new superintendent, Elmer Cotie.

A year after the *Queen of Temagami*'s arrival, the company also purchased a wooden fishing tug called the *Ella* (9.52 tons), which had been built in 1898 and registered at Port Rowan on Lake Erie. She served a long succession of owners on the Great Lakes, until the Upper Ottawa Improvement Company bought her in the spring of 1924. The *Ella*, which was 49.2 feet in length, was used for sweeping logs and towing *chalands* and booms, mainly around Opemicon. She lasted about 20 years, but was reported dismantled by the summer of 1945. Other vessels used by the Upper Ottawa Improvement Company on Lake Temiskaming included the *Lark*, the paymaster's boat, which usually operated from Haileybury where the company had an office, and three warping tugs: the *Seal*, *Alligator* and *Hercules*, all of which were apparently in use until the 1940s or later. According to Captain Jack Cobb (now of Haileybury), who worked for the Upper Ottawa Improvement Company for 40 years, the company once had nine boats on Lake Temiskaming, including diesels.

In 1940, too, the firm built another steel-hulled screw-driven alligator called the *Beaver* — the third vessel of that name on the lake — and used her mainly to prepare booms at Chief Island for the *Alexandra* and the *Lady Minto*. She also assisted the *Wabis* by collecting booms at the des Quinze and Blanche Rivers, or sweeping up stray logs. Sometimes she made trips the length of the lake. Designed by W.N. Zwicker, a German engineer working for the Upper Ottawa Improvement Company, the *Beaver* (III) featured several refinements, including a round bottom and a rounded nose, which allowed her to climb right over the log booms when necessary. A steel basket protected her propeller. Listed at 52 tons, the *Beaver* (III) was a coal-burning steamer, taking a crew of four; later she was dieselized and became an oil burner.

Several of the Upper Ottawa Improvement Company's other tugs were remodelled over the years. During the winter of 1921–22, the *Alexandra* was converted from a sidewheeler to a screw steamer, and fitted out with a third deck and two stacks. This apparently increased her draft — her new propeller had a diameter of twelve feet — but the company was expecting the new control dam at South Témiscaming to deepen the waters of the lake. It did, but even so, the *Alexandra* was still unable to pass the snyes at Chief Island. Around 1929, a new boiler was installed, and later still she was given a new second-hand engine that reputedly came from an American yacht. She continued sailing, usually under the command of Captain Ernie Gray, but during the 1930s, business fell off as a result of the Depression, and the *Alexandra* was left idle for long periods of time.

Also in 1922, the *Wabis* was remodelled and given a new 150-lb. Clyde boiler. Perhaps at the same time, she received a 12.3-hp steeple compound engine made in Sorel; henceforth she was a screw steamer. (She actually had a second steam engine to power the winch for her steel cable, which was one and a quarter miles in length!) Around 1929, the *Lady Minto* was likewise rebuilt and converted into a screw steamer. Very likely it was then that she became an oil burner, but in any case almost the entire fleet was burning oil by 1940, when a refuelling depot was opened at Moore's Cove, a few miles north of Haileybury. By now the fuel could be delivered by truck.

Work on the Upper Ottawa Improvement Company tugs was monotonously routine, except when a storm blew in, and the boats might be forced to abandon their tows — or the winds might shift and blow the booms against the shores, where they would usually break and spill the logs all over the lake. One afternoon during the summer of 1926 or '27, a violent windstorm caught the *Lady Minto* while she was plodding south from Haileybury with three bag booms in tow, and blew both the tug and her tows back up north past Burnt Island. She whistled furiously for help and was presently joined by the *Wabis*, which hooked onto the booms and dropped anchor. But the howling wind still swept everything along in its path, and the two tugs couldn't hold back the logs. Then, around nightfall, the *Alexandra* steamed into view, bringing her (empty) boom timbers with her. Perceiving the situation, she abandoned her booms and came over to assist. All three tugs now anchored and managed to restrain the logs around Chief Island. The storm, however, raged all night, pounding huge waves against the hulls and decks of the tugs. But the anchor chains held, and so did the boom timbers. By noon the next day, the winds abated, and the situation eased back under control.

But the worst storm of all was undoubtedly the notorious Hurricane Hazel, which blew in from the Atlantic and struck Central Ontario on October 15, 1954. Although the great gale had weakened by the time it reached Lake Temiskaming, it still sent waves pounding over the bow and even the wheelhouse of the *Lady Minto*, which was struggling with another tow. The steamer survived, but the boom broke up, scattering several hundred thousand logs all over the central part of the lake. The storm also swamped the *Beaver* at her wharf at the Quinze camp, and the diesel tug *Pembroke*, and did considerable damage to the company's facilities generally. Apparently no lives were lost. The two tugs were, of course, refloated.

The Upper Ottawa Improvement Company was at its height during the 1920s and sometimes employed up to 500 men around Lake Temiskaming, both on the boats and at the boom camps and Opemicon Depot. Some were also engaged to feed logs through the sorting jacks located at Opimica Narrows and South Témiscaming; these were used to separate the Canadian International Paper Company's logs from those destined for the lower Ottawa River. As in Lumsden's time, the boats and booms were serviced and maintained at Opemicon and there they spent the winters, protected from thick ice by the currents rounding the bay. A marine railway allowed them to be drydocked, and sometimes the local alligators would help out, using their cables. Sometimes they would also winch the boom timbers ashore for repairs.

Very gradually, the towing business began to decline on Lake Temiskaming and the Ottawa River as a whole. Paper production decreased during the Depression, and as the roads improved, logging companies gradually resorted more and more to trucks. During the 1930s and '40s the *Alexandra* was frequently laid up for lack of work, until 1951, when, after several years of idleness, she was scrapped at Opemicon and her brass fittings sold. Her sister, the *Lady Minto*, which was cheaper to operate, carried on regularly until 1950, under the command of such men as Captain Bill Riley and Harry Lapensée, both of Mattawa, and Jack Cobb, but after that she was used only sporadically until 1966, when she was dismantled. Her hull, partly cut up with acetylene torches, was scuttled in deep water at Baie du Grand Calumet in 1971, close to the site of the old Latour sawmill. She was, in fact, the last of all the Temiskaming steamboats.

All of the smaller craft were gone by then. The *Lark* was sold to a Pembroke man during the 1940s, then burned on purpose after the purchaser failed to pay the agreed-on price. The *Alert* was scrapped in 1950 by the Zagerman Company, along with the *Alexandra*. The *Wabis* was dieselized during the 1940s and given the additional assignment of delivering aspen logs to the "splint factory" erected at Moore's Cove, between Haileybury and New Liskeard — until the owners, finding that many of their logs were sinking in transit, opted to do their importing by truck instead. Finally, during the summer of 1955, the *Wabis*, now 43 years old, was demoted to a mere scow and used to deliver fuel oil to the Quinze "Gap." Later the hulk became a drilling platform during soil testing on the lake bottom near the Lower Notch dam at the mouth of the Montreal River.

The others followed. In 1952, the Canadian International Paper Company scrapped the *Wilda*, which had lain idle for several years at Opemicon, and apparently replaced her with the diesel tug *J.G. Fleck*, which it imported from Lake Kipawa. (It also used two other diesels called the *W.H. Cowper* and the *F.A. Harrison* on the lake, the latter from 1940 to 1946.) The *Beaver*'s turn came, apparently, in 1960. She had been sunk twice during her career, once during Hurricane Hazel and later by being run up a pier and capsizing, and in her last years she had been converted into an oil burner. In the end, she was stripped and sunk as an anchor near the Porcupine boom camp south of Opemicon. The vanishing steamers were replaced, but the newcomers were all diesels, which required smaller crews.

One of them was the celebrated *P.J. Murer*, an 85-foot steel tug listed at 61 tons. She was assembled and launched at Opemicon in 1948, probably to replace the *Alexandra*, and soon proved capable of towing up to 8,100 cords of wood all the way from Notre-Dame-du-Nord (North Temiskaming) to Opimica Narrows. Captain Jack Cobb, who commanded her from 1949 until 1965, recalls one memorable midsummer night during the early 1950s, when a mounting south wind combined with a back current started producing huge waves. The *P.J. Murer*, which was then towing about 300,000 logs in three booms past Bryson Island, near Haileybury, was driven back into open waters. After struggling with the wheel for over seven hours Cobb gave up, cast off the tow, and made for Martineau Bay. There he phoned the Depot to report what had happened. By the following day, one boom was found at Chief Island, and the other two in a bay on the Quebec side of the lake. Amazingly, they had all held together. The *Wabis* was sent over to retrieve them, and soon had the tow reassembled. Captain Cobb was surprised to have this happen in the summer; fall storms were usually the worst. It was, he said, the only time he ever abandoned a tow.

Besides the *P.J. Murer* the Upper Ottawa Improvement Company built several other small diesel tugs for the Lake Temiskaming division, including the *Bonneville, Deschênes, Quinze* and the aforementioned *Pembroke* and carried on into the 1970s. But the Ontario government finally banned towing as a nuisance and a source of pollution, and in its final years the company could legally use only the Quebec side of the Ottawa River. In Quebec, citizens' groups called for a similar ban, and after a long struggle they had their way. The last tows on Lake Temiskaming were conducted in 1973. Two years later, the Upper Ottawa Improvement Company shut down all its operations on the lake and retired its boats. Some were tied up at Opemicon, others were sold and taken to other waters. The *P.J. Murer* was loaded onto an 80-wheel truck and moved to Georgian Bay in 1979, and was afterwards taken to Kingston to serve as an icebreaker. Around the same time, the Canadian International Paper Company moved the *J.G. Fleck* to the Pembroke area. Only the *T.E. Draper* still survives, in retirement at Angliers, Quebec. After nearly a century, commercial navigation had come to an end on Lake Temiskaming.

ABOVE:
Steam tug Beaver *(III) on Lake Temiskaming.*

BELOW:
Steam tug Wabis.

Steam tug T.E. Draper, on Lake Temiskaming or
Rivière des Quinze.   Courtesy T.E. Draper Museum, Angliers

Diesel tug P.J. Murer, on Lake Temiskaming.
Courtesy Mr. Gilles Amesse

EPILOGUE

The day of the steamboat in Northern Ontario and Quebec had come and gone. It dawned on both Lake Nipissing and Lake Temiskaming during the early 1880s, and on both lakes it lingered fitfully until fairly recent times. On most of the other lakes, steamers did not arrive until the early 1900s, and rarely did they survive the 1920s. It seems rather an anomaly that the old *Belle of Temagami* actually held out until the end of the Second World War.

The boats appeared because they were needed, often desperately, by lumbermen, settlers or mining prospectors. They were discarded, often speedily, as soon as the need for them disappeared. The pathetic end of the *Meteor* went completely unnoticed by the New Liskeard *Speaker*, which had once been carrying regular reports of her activities. In many localities, one feels, steamers in the North were deprived of the chance to make the kind of contributions they might have made. The passenger services on Lake Nipissing and Lake Temiskaming were just moving into "full ahead!" when the railways intruded and pushed them aside. After that, in almost all localities the lake steamers were left with only the crumbs of the trade, and on these they could not long survive. Only with respect to towing were they able to hold their own, until changing technology demanded that steam vessels be converted into diesels or replaced by them. Unlike some regions in the south, such as Muskoka, the boats did not last long enough to be ruined by automobiles.

The decline of the lake steamers was accompanied by the decline of related activities, including picnics and excursions on the lakes and the farmers' market at Haileybury. Before long, the government ceased to maintain the local wharves, which soon fell into ruin. The dock at Guigues, on northern Lake Temiskaming, has been totally washed away, as if it had never been. Scarcely a trace remains of any of the once proud ships that used it. Passenger services have survived on Lake Nipissing to the present day, but it may be that even there they are soon to become history.

Various communities that once were steamboat ports have declined or even disappeared. Latchford, once the "gateway to Gowganda," has never recovered from the collapse of the boat services, although the town is still very much alive. Charlton and the Blanche River villages were all but ruined by the Great Fire of 1922. Some mining towns like Timmins and Rouyn-Noranda are going as strong as ever, but Cobalt, which once touted itself as the "best old town," has been declining slowly since the 1920s, and almost all of its mines have shut down. Its population has dropped from the 20,000 of the glory days to fewer than 1,200, and those who sing the "Cobalt Song" today are very few indeed. New Liskeard, by contrast, is growing steadily. Similarly, South Témiscaming, which was threatened with total extinction when the Canadian International Paper Company shut down its paper mill in 1972, saved itself when the employees banded together, bought the mill, appointed their own board of management, and carried on. Today the plant, once deemed uneconomic, is run by Tembec, a Quebec government corporation, and is doing quite well. It has also saved the railway spur to the town, and may yet save the Canadian Pacific Railway line to

Motor vessel T.E. Draper *on the Rivière des Quinze.*   Courtesy T.E. Draper Museum, Angliers

Mattawa, which connects with it. North of Témiscaming, the tracks to Ville-Marie and Angliers have gradually been lifted.

Of late, boating activity seems to be increasing on Lake Temiskaming, and in response several towns have been upgrading their docking facilities. Haileybury in particular has been building breakwaters, a new marina, a pavilion and a park to develop its waterfront. Boating meets have recently been held at Ville-Marie. And at New Liskeard, where a marina, motel, restaurant and fitness centre have been developed, a diesel cruise boat called the *Island Queen* has recently entered service, offering sightseeing trips down to the Devil's Rock and beyond, reviving a tradition that goes back to the *Meteor*.

There are even new signs that the old steamboats have not been totally forgotten. One indeed, still survives. The old tug, *T.E. Draper*, her long years of service ended, has been beached at Angliers and converted into a museum piece, serving as a memorial to the days of pulpwood towing on the Rivière des Quinze. In addition, many are the families who secretly cherish the mystique that their forebears arrived on the *Meteor*. When the town of Haileybury celebrated the 60th year of its existence, many citizens dressed up in old-time style and boarded the *P.J. Murer*, which had been chartered for the occasion, for a short cruise, honouring the fact that their ancestors had often done the same on a steamboat. Television crews were on hand to catch them disembarking into pointers — as the early settlers had had to do. And at Ville-Marie, when a granite monument was unveiled in 1986, commemorating the foundation of the town a century earlier, everyone agreed that it should carry a likeness of the *Meteor*. What better symbol of the birth of their community could be imagined?

The Timiskaming steamboats are gone. But they served the North well in their time, with results that may still be seen today.

225

BIBLIOGRAPHY

Primary Sources
Government Reports
Canada:
Department of Marine and Fisheries:
Annual Report, 1903–1904
Steamship Inspection Reports, 1891, 1892,
　　1896, 1904, 1906, 1910, 1914, 1920,
　　1935
List of Vessels on the Registry Books of the
　　Dominion of Canada, Volumes for 1886,
　　1902–1909, 1916–1918, 1920

Department of Public Works:
Annual Report, 1909

Department of Railways and Canals:
Shipping Registers (Hamilton, Kitchener,
　　Montreal, Ottawa, Owen Sound, Port
　　Burwell, Port Dover, Port Rowan,
　　Quebec City, Toronto)

Quebec:
Statutes, 15th Legislature, 1920

Albums, Files and Manuscripts:
Abitibi Power and Paper Company: *Files*
　　(Marine Division)
Dumulon Family Album, Joseph Dumulon
　　House, Rouyn
Dunn, Gary: *Shipping on Lake Temiskaming*
　　(no date)
Lafleur, Hank: Document, Haileybury Fire
　　Museum (no date)
Lumsden, Alexander: Last Will and
　　Testament
Lumsden, Margaret: Last Will and
　　Testament
Mason, John: Memo (no date)
Mills, John M.: *World Ship Society*
　　Compilation

Newspapers
Bracebridge *Herald*
Haileyburian & Temiskaming Mining Journal
　　(Haileybury)
Lindsay *Weekly Post*
La Sentinelle (Mattawa)
La Patrie (Montreal)
Temiskaming Herald (New Liskeard)
Témiscamingue Gazette
Temiskaming Speaker (New Liskeard)
North Bay Nugget
Ottawa Citizen
Ottawa Evening Journal
Ottawa Free Press
Porcupine Advance
Sudbury Star
Toronto *Globe*

Periodicals and Brochures
Agriculture Temiskaming (1910)
Collingwood Bulletin
Farr, Charles Cobbald: Pamphlet
The Quarterly (Ontario Northland
　　Transportation Commission) 1969
The Railway and Shipping World (1903)

Secondary Sources
Barnes, Michael: *Gateway City: The North*
　　Bay Story, North Bay, 1982
Barnes, Michael: *Link With a Lonely Land:*
　　The Temiskaming and Northern Ontario
　　Railway, Erin, 1985
Campbell, William A.: *The French and*
　　Pickerel Rivers, Their History and Their
　　People, Sudbury, 1991
Caron, L'Abbé Ivanhoé: *Un nouveau centre*
　　de colonisation, Quebec City, 1915
Directory of Ontario, 1899 Edition
Dobrich, Captain Louis: *Guide to Lake*
　　Nipissing, Surgeon Falls, 1983

Dorion, Charles: *The First 75 Years: A Headline History of Sudbury,* Canada, Devon, 1958

Fancy, Peter: *Silver Centre: The Story of an Ontario Mining Camp,* Cobalt, 1985

Fancy, Peter: *Temiskaming Treasure Trails, The Earliest Years,* Cobalt, 1992

Farmiloe, Dorothy: *Elk Lake: Lore and Legend,* Little Current, 1984

Gard, Anson A: *Gateway to Silverland* (3 books) Toronto, 1909

Gaudet-Brault, Jeannine: *Temi-Kami: eaux profondes,* Béarn, 1981

Gourd, Benoit-Beaudrey: *Abitibi-Témiscamingue: Quatre études sur le Nord-ouest Québecois,* Montreal, 1974

Groom, Maude: *The Melted Years,* New Liskeard, 1971

Hodgins and Benidickson: *The Temagami Experience*

Hunt, Joyce: *Latchford: Heritage Logging Days,* Latchford, 1992

Laflamme, Jean M.: *L'Abitibi-Ouest à l'époque de ses pionniers,* LaSarre, 1966

Lamirande, André E. & Gilles L. Séguin: *A Foregone Fleet: A Pictorial History of the Steam-driven Paddleboats on the Ottawa River,* Cobalt, 1982

Lavallée, Omer: *Narrow Gauge Railways of Canada,* Montreal, 1972

Macdougall, J.B.: *Two Thousand Miles of Gold,* Toronto, 1946

Mitchell, Elaine Alla: *Fort Timiskaming and the Fur Trade,* Toronto, 1977

Moore, Kermot A.: *Kipawa: Portrait of a People,* Cobalt, 1982

Pioneer Days in the Township of Nipissing, Nipissing Township Council, 1974

O'Dwyer, Rev. William C.: *Highways of Destiny: A History of the Diocese of Pembroke, Ottawa Valley, Canada,* 1964

Pain, S.A.: *Three Miles of Gold*

Paquin, Normand: *Histoire de l'Abitibi-Témiscamingue,* Rouyn, 1981

Riopel, Marc: *De la Baie des Pères à Ville-Marie, 1886–1986,* Ville-Marie, 1986

Riopel, Marc: *Opemicain, au cœur de la forêt de flottage du bois au Témiscamingue, 1866-1987*

Steer, Wilston: *Highlights of the Near North's History,* North Bay, 1990

Surtees, Robert J.: *The Northern Connection: Ontario Northland Since 1902,* North York, 1992

Taylor, Bruce W.: *The Age of Steam on Lake Temiskaming,* Cobalt, 1993

Trainor, Patricia Ann: *Biographies of the Sudbury Region,* Sudbury, 1979

Tucker, Albert: *Steam Into Wilderness: Ontario Northland Railway 1902-1962,* Don Mills, 1978

VandenHazel, Bessel: *From Dugout to Diesel: Transportation on Lake Nipissing,* Cobalt, 1982

Whitton, Charlotte: *A Hundred Years A'Fellin': A History of the Gillies Brothers Lumber Company,* 1943

The author is also indebted enormously to the staffs of most of the libraries of Northeastern Ontario and Northwestern Quebec, and to a great many museum and historical societies, including the Cobalt Mining Museum, the Englehart and Area Museum, the Haileybury Fire Museum, the House of Memories Museum at Latchford, the Elk Lake Museum, the Gowganda and Area Museum, the Matheson Museum, the New Liskeard Museum, the North Bay Museum, the North Himsworth Museum at Callander, the Nipissing Pioneer Museum, the Joseph Dumulon House at Rouyn, the T.E. Draper Museum at Angliers, and the Société d'histoire d'Amos for all their splendid co-operation.

ACKNOWLEDGMENTS

The author wishes to thank the many private citizens who have freely provided pictures and information, without which this book would not be what it is. Among them are:

Mr. William Armstrong of South Himsworth

M. Gilles Amesse of Ville-Marie

Mr. George Alvin Bateson of New Liskeard

Mme Yvette Beauchemin of Ville-Marie

Mr. Clem Bolan of Haileybury

M. Émile Boucher of Témiscaming

Mrs. Margaret Brown of Temiskaming

Mr. Ronald Brown of New Liskeard

Mr. Arthur Burns of Latchford

M. Jacques Chartier of Ville-Marie

Captain John Thomas Cobb of Haileybury

Mr. Brian Cockburn of North Bay

Mr. Leonard Cunningham of Kipawa

Mrs. Margaret E. Douglas of White Rock, B.C.

Mr. Lester Durham of Matheson

Mrs. W.H. Durrell of New Liskeard

M. Albert Fleury of Ville-Marie

Mr. David E. Ford of Gowganda

Captain Donald Green of Callander

Mr. Tom Gregory of Englehart

Captain Edwy T. (Ted) Guppy of Temagami

Mr. George Herbert of Haileybury

Mr. Frank Herron of New Liskeard

Mr. Charles Humphrey of Temagami

Mr. Patrick Hurley of Latchford

Mr. William Johnston of Callander

M. Gilles Labranche of Ville-Marie

Mr. Hugh Lynn of Témiscaming

Mr. Alex MacLaurin of Westmount

Captain Michael J. Masson of Callander

Mr. Gordon McCharles of Iroquois Falls

Mr. William McDonald of Larder Lake

Mr. Donald McKelvie of New Liskeard

Mr. David McLaren of South Lorrain

Mrs. Rita Moon of Sturgeon Falls

Mr. Duncan Mowat of Mowat's Landing

Mr. Gordon Page of Temagami

Mme Lucienne Paré of Ville-Marie

Mr. Bruce Pringle of North Bay

Mr. Melvin Robb of Haileybury

Mrs. Barbara Robertson of Rosedale (Toronto)

M. Jean Robitaille of Val d'Or

Mr. James Sheldon of Larder Lake

Mrs. A.B. Short of Haileybury

Mr. Douglas Stuart of Zeta

Mr. Ralph Switzer of Latchford

Mr. Walter Sylvester of Charlton

Mrs. Charles Tucker of New Liskeard

Also, a special word of thanks is due to Mr. Alldyn Clark of Bracebridge for diligently copying most of the pictures used in this book.

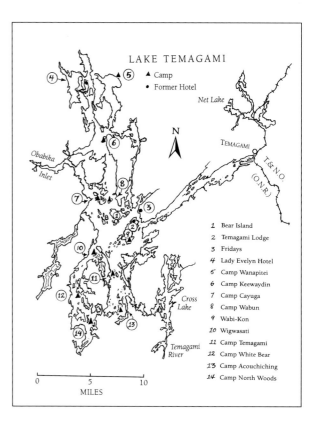

LAKE TEMAGAMI

▲ Camp
● Former Hotel

Net Lake

TEMAGAMI

T & N.O.
(O.N.R.)

Obabika
Inlet

Cross
Lake

Temagami
River

N

1   Bear Island
2   Temagami Lodge
3   Fridays
4   Lady Evelyn Hotel
5   Camp Wanapitei
6   Camp Keewaydin
7   Camp Cayuga
8   Camp Wabun
9   Wabi-Kon
10 Wigwasati
11 Camp Temagami
12 Camp White Bear
13 Camp Acouchiching
14 Camp North Woods

0   5   10
MILES

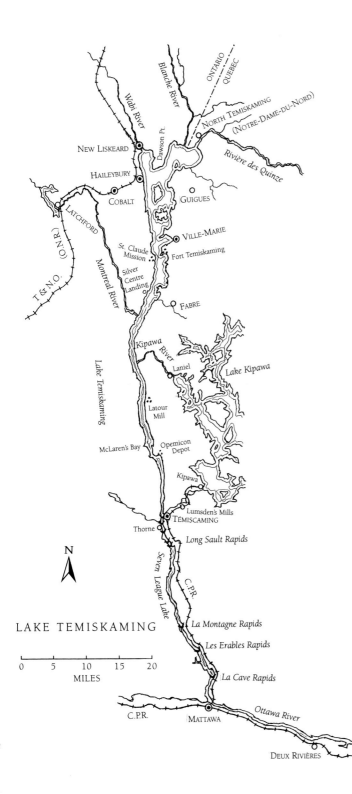

Wabi River

Blanche River

ONTARIO
QUEBEC

NORTH TEMISKAMING
(NOTRE-DAME-DU-NORD)

Rivière des Quinze

NEW LISKEARD

HAILEYBURY

COBALT   GUIGUES

LATCHFORD

Dawson Pt.

VILLE-MARIE

St. Claude
Mission   *Fort Temiskaming*

Silver
Centre
Landing

FABRE

Montreal River

Lake Temiskaming

Kipawa River

Laniel   *Lake Kipawa*

Latour
Mill

McLaren's Bay   *Opemicon*
Depot

Kipawa

Lumsden's Mills
TÉMISCAMING

Thorne   *Long Sault Rapids*

Seven League Lake

C.P.R.

N

LAKE TEMISKAMING

0   5   10   15   20
MILES

La Montagne Rapids

Les Erables Rapids

La Cave Rapids

C.P.R.   *Ottawa River*
MATTAWA

DEUX RIVIÈRES

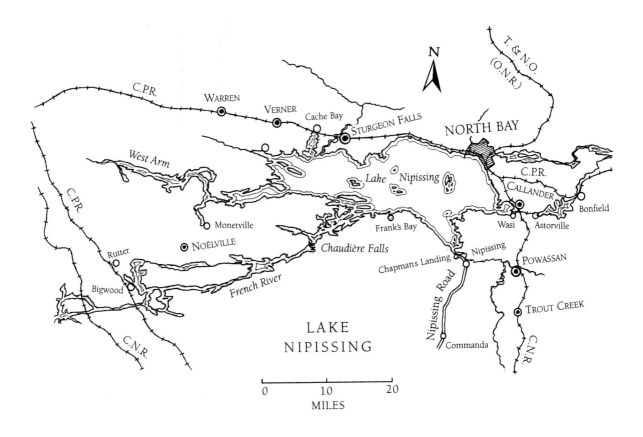

N

LAKE
NIPISSING

C.P.R.

WARREN

VERNER

Cache Bay

STURGEON FALLS

NORTH BAY

T. & N.O.
(O.N.R.)

West Arm

Lake   Nipissing

C.P.R.

CALLANDER

C.P.R.

Monetville

NOËLVILLE

Frank's Bay

Bonfield

Wasi

Astorville

Rutter

Chaudière Falls

Chapmans Landing

Nipissing

POWASSAN

Bigwood

French River

Nipissing Road

TROUT CREEK

C.N.R.

Commanda

C.N.R.

0   10   20
MILES

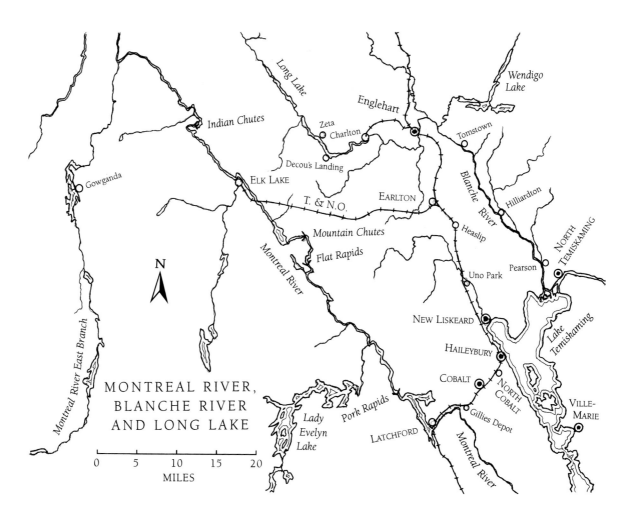

Indian Chutes

Long Lake

Englehart

Wendigo
Lake

Zeta

Charlton

Tomstown

Gowganda

Decou's Landing

ELK LAKE

EARLTON

Blanche River

Hilliardton

T. & N.O.

Mountain Chutes

Heaslip

Pearson

NORTH
TEMISKAMING

Montreal River

Flat Rapids

Uno Park

NEW LISKEARD

Lake
Temiskaming

Montreal River East Branch

HAILEYBURY

MONTREAL RIVER,
BLANCHE RIVER
AND LONG LAKE

COBALT

NORTH
COBALT

VILLE-
MARIE

Lady
Evelyn
Lake

Pork Rapids

LATCHFORD

Gillies Depot

N

Montreal River

0   5   10   15   20
MILES

INDEX

Note: Asterisks (*) = picture(s)